EM2N
City Factory

Mathias Müller
Daniel Niggli
Caspar Schärer
Medine Altiok

Park Books

Table of Contents

Essays

21	City Factory
22	Phantom Pain
25	*Degré Zéro* versus Context
47	A Park Named "Bäcki" Max Küng
339	Toni Campus: Cum Grano Salis II Marcel Meili
373	The Architect as Policy Whisperer (in Comes the Space Producer) Peter Swinnen
463	The Beauty of Chaos
475	Plea for a City of Tolerant Coexistence
479	Emptied Typologies: Frameworks for Something Else to Happen Marc Angélil

Love Letters

31	Four-City Corner
181	SESC Pompéia
219	Decorated Shed
239	Engineering Building, University of Leicester
284	Long-Span Roofs
301	Nemausus
304	Rampenhaus Schwerzenbach
365	Ron Davis House, Winton Guest House
423	Rampenhaus Schwerzenbach Revisited
451	Maag Campus

Meta Texts

55	Archipelagos and Islands
74	Accumulation
85	Appropriability
116	Infrastructural Buildings
125	Prototypology and Learning from What's There
259	Intelligent Carcasses
313	Parking Garage as Prototypology
397	Everything is Transformation

Photo Spreads

1	Into the City Joël Tettamanti, Damian Poffet
46	Bäckeranlage GRRRR
77	Backyard Scenes Simon Menges
117	Viaduct Impressions GRRRR
205	Transitional Spaces Simon Menges
261	Industrial Spaces Simon Menges
305	Ramps Simon Menges, Damian Poffet
377	Toni Campus Interiors
389	Toni GRRRR
444	KANAL Brut
481	Leaving the City Damian Poffet

Table of Contents

Projects

35	Bäckeranlage Community Center
66	Glattpark
73	Leutschenbach Schools
96	Viaduct Arches
127	Hürlimann Brewery
129	Alpine Bath Montafon
134	Zellweger Luwa Site
182	Mongolian School Project
188	Cinémathèque suisse
202	Rosenberg
213	School Complex Blumenfeld
217	Hardbrücke Station
220	Herdern Railway Service Facility
231	Viscosistadt
240	Headquarters Roshen
249	Headquarters Sedorama
269	Lucerne School of Art and Design
279	Stapferhaus
286	Heuried Sports Center
302	Zugerland Verkehrsbetriebe
342	RTS Campus
344	HSG Learning Center St. Gallen
349	Museum of Natural History and State Archives
366	WIN4 Sports Center
375	*Together!* Exhibition
399	KANAL, Brussels
415	Office and Commercial Building Binzstrasse
424	New Housing on Briesestrasse
441	Koch-Areal
448	Uster Culture Center
453	Hammerbrooklyn
465	Oerlikon Sports Center

Toni Campus

26	Back Story
87	Interim Use
154	Design Competition
162	Redevelopment
244	Tower Stairs
256	Demolition
315	In Use
377	Interiors

Miscellaneous

54	The Great Feast
58	Zurich as Archipelago
92	The City in Parcels
180	EM2N Dreamland
341	*Wir kennen uns doch kaum*
431	Office Block as Typology

End Matter

487	EM2N Staff Former Staff
488	List of Works
493	Image Credits
494	Imprint

Advocating for a City of Tolerant Coexistence

Andrew Alberts
Filip Dujardin
Roger Frei
GRRRR
Simon Menges   Marc Angélil
Damian Poffet   Max Küng
Joël Tettamanti   Marcel Meili
                Peter Swinnen

← 1–8   ↑ 9   10 ↓   11 →   12 →

City Factory

Mathias Müller
Daniel Niggli

When architects talk about their projects and built works, the terms "place" and "city" tend to come up a great deal. Architecture is often said to be informed by a "sense of place," to be "place-specific," and "in harmony with the city."

But when you actually visit architect-designed "places" such as Affoltern or Neu-Oerlikon in Zurich, you can't help but ask yourself: "Is this a real 'place'? Is it a kind of 'city'? And if so what kind?"

The driving force behind this book is our dissatisfaction with many of the places architects, ourselves included, have helped to create. To us, they often seem lifeless, overdesigned, and unduly regimented—perfected to the point of ossification. What has been lost along the way is the potential for appropriation, the courage to allow spaces to not only permit but deliberately provoke genuine participation and interaction, with all the conflicts that may entail.

Evidently, a city is more than just the sum of its good buildings, however carefully planned and designed they may be. It is also about living, about the public realm, perhaps even about variety or, that great enemy of planning, unpredictability. A city is collaborative and cultural, the collectively built expression of a society with all its contradictions and conflicts.

Architecture and the city have long been treated as an indivisible pair, and not just since Aldo Rossi's *L'architettura della città*[A] but going right back to Leon Battista Alberti's *De re aedificatoria*,[B] in which the great Renaissance architect opined that a house is "in its turn a small city," thereby suggesting organizational and typological parallels. But are the two really mutually dependent? After all, it's not hard to think of outstanding houses that are anything but urban; Palladio's villas in Veneto, for instance, only make sense as islands in the expansive landscape of that region. Conversely, there are fantastic cities that get by almost entirely without great architecture, or at least don't owe their greatness to architecture. Take destroyed and generically rebuilt places such as Izmir, or sprawling megacities such as Mumbai that fascinate us with their endless contrasts and bustling life.

In our view, the idea of the city is stronger than any architecture. Cities are more exciting, varied, lively, forgiving, and surprising than any one piece of architecture, however good it might be. They are inevitably more complex and interesting than individual buildings; after all, they are composed of countless layers of history and built upon the collective intelligence of their inhabitants.

Never before has so much been built in Switzerland and at such cost. But where is the common idea underpinning all this construction? Is it merely about responding to specific conflicts and narrow interests and planning each case in isolation? Or is there a vision of a shared environment we are all helping to build? Our vision of an ideal city bears the working title "city-factory." Its starting point is not a particular aesthetic form or structure, but urban life itself; to us, it should be a place where people's lives and work intermingle and where gentry and precariat can intermix. It should be vibrant and bustling, a far cry from the sterility of manufactured cityscapes.

[A] Aldo Rossi, *L'architettura della città*, Padua, 1966; English translation: *The Architecture of the City*, MIT Press, Cambridge, Massachusetts, 1982.

[B] Leon Battista Alberti, *De re aedificatoria*, Rome, 1485; English translation: *On the Art of Building in Ten Books*, MIT Press, Cambridge, Massachusetts, 1988.

Phantom Pain

Mathias Müller
Daniel Niggli

1

It seems kind of familiar, this place. Have we been here before? Wilhelminian façades, French windows, ground floor colonnades with shop windows behind stone pillars. Have we somehow ended up in downtown Berlin, Friedrichstrasse maybe? But then why is the street so deserted? Overhead a plane is coming in to land, its rumble getting gradually louder. Around us, the stone slabs' yawning gaps lend the facings a strangely fake air. The constantly repeating windows look similarly synthetic, the ground floor frontages like theatrical backdrops. It feels less like a city and more like a simulation of urban realm.

Then suddenly it dawns on us: we've been taken in by a simulacrum. This distinctly neo-Wilhelminian streetscape belongs to a new-build development on the outskirts. We walk down the road. After a few paces, the perimeter blocks suddenly stop, giving way to woodland fringes, railroad tracks, a gas station, low metal-shed warehouses, and big empty parking lots.

What is the meaning of this peripheral facsimile? Is it a proper town or just a surrogate? What makes a town a town, a city a city? Is simulating the look of a city enough to create urban realms? Or is urban life equally necessary? To what extent is the urban realm defined by its buildings and to what extent by their programming, by the activities that take place there?

At the heart of this simulated urban realm is a small pedestrianized square overlooked by a modest tower block. With its printed glass façade, the latter looks strangely modern and cosmopolitan, as if it were in Tokyo, Singapore, or New York, and not out here in the sticks. It's like a simulation of the future within a simulation of the past—a place where layers of time and levels of reality start to slip, a fever dream of optimism, master plans, underground garages, planted courtyards, façade systems, CCTV cameras, and landscaping. Of urban longing. Of phantom pain.

1
Alexa Wright, *After Image – RD2*, art project, 1997. Excerpt from the project description: "Date of amputation: October 1995. Time post amputation: 21 months. Age 71: Male. Road accident in which arm was crushed [. . .]. The phantom is continuous; it takes the form of my hand. It is sometimes painful and sometimes just sensation. I feel I can control the movements of the hand until I suddenly realize that it isn't there. The hand is [a] slightly clenched fist, and that doesn't really change; it can only go about three quarters unclenched. [. . .] The hand is the same size as my real hand, but much heavier. It itches a lot of the time and I want to scratch it. I can kid myself that I can make the phantom limb move. [. . .] I can't imagine being without the phantom because it is there all the time and it is very much like eating or breathing: I can put up with it quite adequately and would probably miss it if it went away. I might wish it wasn't so irritating, but I think I would rather keep it as it is than risk losing it."

Phantom Pain

Mathias Müller
Daniel Niggli

The Modern City: Functional Zoning

Given the dreadful living conditions that prevailed in parts of Europe's industrial cities in the 19th and early 20th centuries, the *Athens Charter*,[A] published in 1933 by leading modernists, demanded that cities be divided strictly into separate functional zones—for dwelling, for work, for recreation, and for transport. Following the devastation of World War Two, the requisite postwar reconstruction gave the functionalists their big opportunity. Although Team Ten and others were quick to criticize their technocratically oriented urban planning concepts, the dogma of spacious, car-friendly cities would go on to shape urban planning around the world for decades to come.[B] That this had destructive consequences for the spatial and socioeconomic fabric of traditional cities, leading to the suburbanization of their outskirts, is well established and has been a key aspect of critical postmodern discourse from the 1960s to the present day.

The Postmodern City: Urban Investment Vehicles

Since the 1960s, the economy has seen increasing tertiarization—a trend further accelerated in the 1990s by the globalization-driven structural shift. As a result, dirty industry, the initial reason for such functional zoning, has disappeared from our cities, indeed from central Europe as a whole, leaving behind vacant industrial premises in prime locations. Many of these erstwhile production facilities were reborn as affordable spaces for artists and other creatives, as well as for leisure activities, all manner of subcultures, and local craft businesses and traders. In the process, they became key "enabling platforms": as the attractions of urban living were rediscovered after the late 1990s, these temporarily repurposed industrial sites were soon transformed into drivers of urban development, mostly via conversion into apartments and offices.

Around the turn of the millennium, it also became apparent that the globalization of finance was increasingly drawing real estate into the orbit of global capital. Urban land was no longer just something used to provide living space or office space, it was also becoming an ever more attractive target for anonymous investment vehicles. All too often, the architecture that results from such financial speculation is characterless and generic; after all, instead of being designed for a particular client or purpose, it is primarily built with returns or a particular social milieu in mind, i.e. for global investment funds or for some notional average consumer. Many cities that, on the surface, seem commercially successful are increasingly gentrified, segregated, and poor in sensory experience, being no longer sites of production but merely places of habitation and consumption.

[A] Congrès Internationaux d'Architecture Moderne (CIAM), *The Charter of Athens*, edited by Le Corbusier, Paris, 1943.

[B] See: http://www.team10online.org; under "Meetings" in the section "Team Ten" is a discussion of Team Ten's contribution to CIAM IX, Aix-en-Provence (France), July 19–26, 1953: "The Smithsons presented their sociologically informed 'Hierarchy of Association' diagram which they prepared with their MARS colleagues Bill and Gill Howell and their 'Urban Re-Identification Grid'. These contributions proposed replacing the 'functional' hierarchy of dwelling, work, transportation, and recreation of the Athens Charter with what they referred to as the scaled unities of house, street, district and city [...]" Annie Pedret.

Phantom Pain

2

3

2 + 3
Müller-Martini-Areal, Zurich, by Marc Kocher Architekten and Arassociati (successor to Studio Aldo Rossi), 2006. Excerpt from the project description on the architects' website: "Street—square—courtyard: Large gates in the residential building and passages in the office building lead to the quiet courtyards and a square that connects both buildings. Thus, important urban features and elements that were lost in the architectural landscape of the postwar period, [the] street, square, courtyard, and passages, have been reinterpreted and merged to create a new whole."

Degré Zéro Versus Context

Architecture can, of course, be developed as an ideal, as an abstract intellectual construct or prototypical concept that is detached from real places and their manifold influences. Ideally, such an ideal would never be built, thus preventing actual physical objects with all the compromises they bring from diluting the purity of the vision.

We take a different view of architecture. Architecture neither exists in a vacuum nor develops solely from within. It is always a reaction to something external, be it noteworthy buildings created by previous generations and still inspiring us today, or personal experiences that we carry with us like a metaphorical backpack. Our designs can also be limited or guided by the specific site and its physical and virtual characteristics, such as the layout of a lot, its topography, the relevant building codes, the client's intentions, and the budgetary constraints—in short, all those things that make up the political, social, economic, and cultural context.

Wherever we work, we're never starting from scratch; there are always traces of previous human activity. Every project can thus be seen as a further modification of humankind's creations. For this environment in which everything has, in one way or another, already been influenced or shaped by human hands—from vegetation to topography to the global climate—scientists coined the term "Anthropocene."

For us as architects, that context means two things. Firstly, it raises important questions of authorship: If our architecture is always developed within settings created by others, then we're never the sole authors of it. Just as there were architects before us who shaped the setting in which we work, so there will be people after us who react to or modify our work. Secondly, it also raises questions about the formal and temporal discreteness of our interventions. If architecture is inevitably shaped by the context and the traces of what came before, it can never develop in isolation and will always bear within it the traces of multiple eras.

Toni Campus: Back Story 26 1924–1999

Toni Campus: Back Story

← 1   ↑ 2

1 + 2
Opened in 1977, the Toni dairy was designed to receive, store, and process one million liters of unpasteurized milk. The processed milk and other dairy products (such as yoghurt, butter, cream, cheese, ice cream, and powdered milk) were packaged up and shipped out from here.

Toni Campus: Back Story 1924–1999

3 ↑   ↓ 4

Toni Campus: Back Story   29   1924–1999

3
Zurich, soccer game at Förrlibuck stadium, aerial photo from 100-meters, altitude, Walter Mittelholzer, 1925. In 1924, a stadium with 4,000 seats and a standing capacity of 14,000 was built for the Young Fellows soccer club on agricultural land at Förrlibuck. On May 18, it hosted its first international match, a friendly between Switzerland and Hungary, in front of a crowd of 20,000. The game ended 4–2 to the Swiss. The presence of infrastructure such as road and rail routes is already clearly visible in the surrounding area.

4
In 1972, work began on the construction of a processing plant for the Toni dairy, leading to more intensive usage of the site and the laying of infrastructure such as access roads and ramps. Stacked vertically above a basement area dedicated to logistics, the dairy's four production levels were accessed via external delivery ramps joined together in a rising spiral. The dairy complex became an integral part of the infrastructural landscape, lending it a more monumental dimension.

5
Section of the Zurich street plan, from around 1920. As a large-scale 20th-century facility, the new stadium couldn't be accommodated within the fine-grain fabric of the traditional urban core and had to therefore be built on the outskirts. Numerous other substantial construction projects, such as stations, docks, warehouses and other logistics buildings, administrative and college buildings, barracks and their parade grounds, industrial premises, and slaughterhouses were also forced to seek suitable sites outside the old city boundaries. These structures introduced a new scale to their respective locations that guided the proportions of subsequent developments. Thanks to their dispersed arrangement alongside infrastructure such as road or rail routes, they also resulted in the creation of archipelagos on the hitherto undeveloped urban fringes.

6
The arrival of large logistics facilities brings significant further densification of the infrastructure. Construction of the new Migros headquarters in Herdern in 1964, for instance, added a huge distribution center. By the late 1950s, Young Fellows' Förrlibuck stadium had already been appropriated—with the city council paying a knockdown price as compensation—and demolished in order to make way for redevelopment.

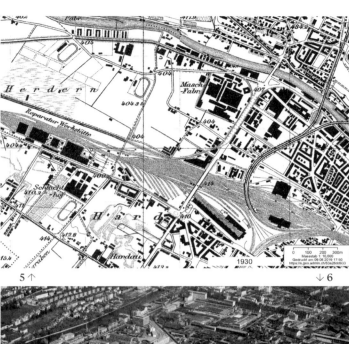

5 ↑   ↓ 6

7

7
New rail and road bridges such as Hardbrücke and Duttweilerbrücke are built across the tracks that cut a broad swathe through the urban landscape. Construction of the former as well as the road to the Hardturm stadium sees the freeway network spreading into the increasingly built-up valley floor.

Toni Campus: Back Story

1924–1999

8

9

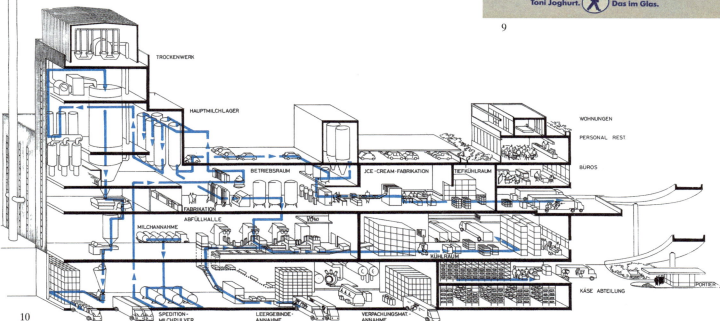

10

11 ↑

↓ 12

8 + 10
The building's volumetry resulted directly from the spatialization of the production process, essentially unmediated by urban design considerations or architectural ambitions. In the vertically organized high-rise section, milk and milk powder were stored in stacked tanks. From there, these raw materials cascaded with the aid of gravity down to the production levels below, where they were turned into various dairy products. The broad, low-rise section featured efficient, horizontally organized production and logistics processes spread across vast, stacked levels.

9
The Toni dairy's best-known product was a yoghurt sold in returnable jars. This cult classic is still made today by the dairy's successor company, Swiss Dairy Food AG, though these days it comes in non-returnable jars.

11 + 12
At peak times, the dairy was processing more than one million liters of milk per day, which equated to roughly a third of all the milk produced in Switzerland. In the mid-1990s, severe overcapacity in milk production sent the dairy into the red; by 1999, the Toni group was no more.

Four-City Corner

There is a place we're very fond of because, within one small area, it presents more urban life, or rather, more interpretations of urban life, than anywhere else in Zurich. We call it "Four-City Corner." There, on the bridge over the Limmat and Sihl rivers next to the Dynamo youth center, you can see everything at once while never quite making out the whole picture.

Looking upstream along the Limmat, we see the "official" face of 19th- and early 20th-century Zurich up ahead. Proud administrative buildings line the waterfront. Platzspitz, once Zurich's first park and now a popular lunch spot, nestles between the two rivers, while the framed view of the old town and its church towers conveys history and heritage. The view through trees of the Swiss National Museum summons up the young nation's carefully cultivated self-image. A city of projection and promenading, of education, edification, and outward representation.

Turn 90 degrees to the right, i.e. southwest, and you again see views of a 19th-century city, but here they tell a very different story. Arrayed behind the Sihlquai, where the embankment has been transformed into an arterial road, is a diverse mix of building types and architectural forms. Standalone buildings, fragments of perimeter development, and more recent infrastructural architecture testify that this is not just a place of official representation, but also one where people live and things are made. The rather grand late 19th-century apartment buildings, built shortly after the city's railroad station had provided new connections to the world, feature large display windows at street level. Here, we find premises for retail or quieter forms of commerce, while adjacent properties house workshops, warehouses, and garages—spaces for making, storing, or parking. Most of the buildings in this area have seen multiple changes of use over time. The most enduring usage type is residential accommodation—everything else seems to adapt readily to the needs of the day.

Turn another 90 degrees to the right and you gain a panoramic view of a vibrant and verdant inner-urban infrastructural landscape. Here, the turbulent brown Sihl and the calm green Limmat are separated by a high channel wall, allowing them to flow alongside each other at different levels. A weir across the Limmat feeds water to a hydroelectric power station. In summer, the channel is dotted with the heads of swimmers, while further down at the Oberer Letten lido, the many bodies coalesce into a single swimming mass. Below the Nordsteig bridge, traffic thunders along the four-lane Wasserwerkstrasse leading to the Milchbuck Tunnel freeway feeder. Right by the former is the Dynamo youth center, a strangely awkward-looking building from the 1980s whose previously pink exterior has now been repainted anthracite. In the distance, the river is spanned by rail bridges, one that once carried the Letten line and another for the still operational Oerliker line. Beyond them, the latest addition to the skyline, a grain silo the size of a tower block, marks the transition from urban core to Limmat valley area.

Make a third 90-degree turn to the right and you're faced with an imposing conglomerate of buildings that cluster and clamber randomly up the slope, a jumble of varying volumes, diverse materials, anonymous architecture, and stock infrastructure. Two centuries ago, this was a steep valley

Four-City Corner 32 Love Letter

West ↑ ↓ East

Four-City Corner

Love Letter

South ↑   ↓ North

in which the Waltersbach stream plunged into the Limmat. Since then, the topography has been recast, the stream diverted underground, and the slope fully exploited for urban development. Densified to the max but lacking any clear design concept, this grotesque agglomeration is a monument to the concrete-heavy, speculation-fueled Zurich of the 1980s. Only the differences in elevation have survived—these can be negotiated via a set of steps named Waltersteig, which serves as a weekend parkour course for local youths but is otherwise mostly deserted. Overlooking this unsightly scene is the Marriott Hotel, a boxy, anonymous tower that is both part of the neighborhood and detached from it.

At Four-City Corner, different layers of topography, infrastructure, architecture, and usage are overlaid to create a dense fabric of structures, atmospheres, and ideas. Little of it truly goes together, and yet it adds up to an incomparably urban atmosphere, a culture clash in which Arab tourists from the Marriott Hotel sit sipping tea at Chuchi am Wasser, young metalworkers wield blowtorches outside the workshop next door, overheated urbanites dive in the river, joggers weave their way through the crowds, and, later in the evenings, black-clad figures assemble outside the Dynamo center's basement concert venue as traffic of all kinds rushes around them.

We love this spot because nowhere else in Zurich is as intense, lively, and contradictory—as full of urban life. Let us create more of it, starting now.

Bäckeranlage Community Center

1

1 + 3 →
In 1901, the Bäckeranlage park, one of Zurich's first planned green spaces, was established in the fast-growing working-class district of Aussersihl, which had recently been incorporated into the city (1893). Devised by landscape designer Evariste Mertens, it followed in the tradition of dignified green spaces for the well-to-do. A place of control and outward representation, the park lent itself less to sports and games and more to the taking of civilized strolls. Broad paths between fenced-in flower beds and benches dictated the routes of such strolls.

2
In the center of the park was a bandstand, a symbol of how the well-to-do viewed culture as a "civilizing" influence on the proletariat.

2

Bäckeranlage Community Center 1999–2004

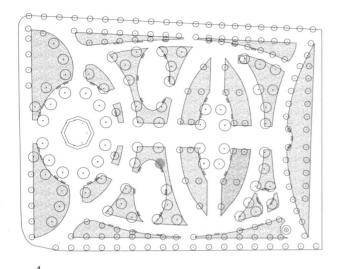

4

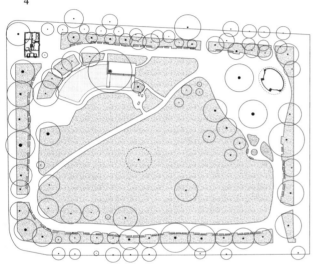

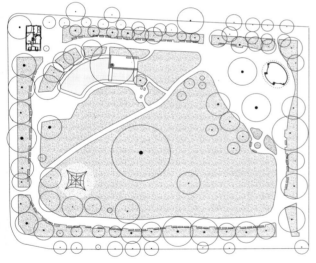

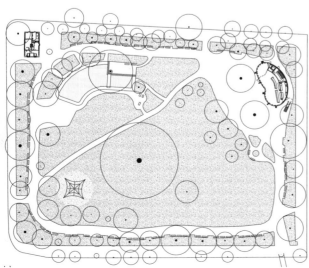

5

4
The history of the Bäckeranlage park is one of successive transformations; here, plans from 1901, 1938, 1979, and 2004 show the park at different points in time.

5
It soon became evident that locals had not embraced their new park. In the late 1930s, Evariste Mertens's sons thus redesigned it to create a "garden as living space." Little was retained of the original pathways, new grass areas were laid out, and a less centrally located bandstand was built. The surrounding ring of street trees remained the key defining element. There were far fewer rules to follow, with visitors even permitted to walk on the grass and go paddling in the pond.

6+7
In the 1990s, the park increasingly became the preserve of homeless people and drug addicts, with some of the homeless taking up residence in the new bandstand and locals largely shunning the park. Listed as a heritage monument in 1989, the bandstand had a highly unusual structural design, with the two acentric toadstool pillars on which the concrete roof rests delicately balanced by thin tension rods at the rear. When workmen severed the rods in 1997 during a botched renovation, the roof tipped forward and collapsed. Having become more and more neglected in the 1980s and '90s due to its monopolization by marginalized people and addicts, the park was temporarily closed in 2001.

Bäckeranlage Community Center

1999–2004

6 ↑ ↓ 7

8

By erecting a kiosk container, the authorities hoped to bring new life and activity to the space, providing a counterweight to the alcoholics and drug addicts. This first step in the "normalization" of the park in the early 2000s proved successful, thanks in part to a significant police presence. Local residents increasingly returned to the park, and children again used it for relaxation and play.

9

Newspaper article about the situation in District 4.
Tages Anzeiger, June 30 2011

8 ↓ 9 →

Spielen zwischen Spritzen und Dealern

Während das Projekt Langstrasse Plus die Bäckeranlage erfolgreich für die Familien zurückerobern konnte, bleibt der Zeughaushof Brachland. Schuld daran sind die Machenschaften in einigen angrenzenden Häusern.

von **Tina Fassbind**

Es ist ein sonniger Dienstagnachmittag auf der Bäckeranlage. Dutzende Kinder spielen in einem der drei Sandkästen auf dem Areal, lassen sich auf der Schaukel hin und her schwingen oder toben im Wasserbecken. Auf der Wiese machen es sich die Leute auf Decken gemütlich, sind in Gespräche vertieft oder bräunen sich an der Sonne. «Die Bäckeranlage ist wie eine grüne Oase im Langstrassenquartier und für die Bevölkerung und die Familien ein Ort zum Entspannen und Sichtreffen», lobt André Bleiker vom Quartierverein Aussersihl-Hard die Grünanlage im Kreis 4.

Noch in den 90er-Jahre wären solche Szenen undenkbar gewesen. «Damals waren hier vor allem Alkoholiker und andere Randständige», erinnert sich Rolf Vieli, Projektleiter von Langstrasse Plus (siehe Box). «Richtig schlimm wurde es, als die offene Drogenszene am Letten verschwunden ist. Die Bäckeranlage wurde danach zum Hauptumschlagplatz für Drogen in Zürich. Die Zustände waren unhaltbar.»

Als der Driving-Deal noch stattfand

Zu diesen schlimmen Zuständen haben auch die Machenschaften in einer Problemliegenschaft an der Helmutstrasse gleich neben der Bäckeranlage beigetragen. In dem Haus wurde mit Drogen gehandelt. «Vor dem Haus fand der Driving-Deal statt», so Vieli. «Die Leute kamen mit Autos aus der restlichen Schweiz und dem Ausland hierher und brachten die Drogen oder holten sie ab.»

Die Auswirkungen auf den öffentlichen Raum seien katastrophal gewesen, so Vieli. «Was in dem Haus geschah, hat der Bevölkerung Angst gemacht. Und die Leute, die hier ihre Drogen holten, gingen danach in die Bäcki, wo sie den Stoff verkauften, bunkerten oder konsumierten.»

Im Laufe der Zeit konnte die Situation an der Helmutstrasse entschärft werden. «Es hat ein Besitzerwechsel stattgefunden. Mit dem neuen Eigentümer haben wir im Gespräch nach Verbesserungen der Situation gesucht und Lösungen gefunden», so Vieli. Handlungsbedarf gäbe es daher heute keinen mehr. «Im Moment lebt es sich gut hier.»

Die Angst vor Randständigen

Ganz anders sieht die Situation rund um den Zeughaushof aus, dem anderen grossen, begrünten Freiraum im Kreis 4. Dort halten sich nach wie vor Randständige und Drogensüchtige auf, die Flaschen und Spritzen liegen lassen. Und auch dort haben die Probleme ihren Ursprung in den Liegenschaften der angrenzenden Kanonengasse. «Früher waren dort Bordelle. Heute sind es Drogenumschlagplätze. In den Wohnungen leben Drogenabhängige und es gibt auch Menschenhandel», weiss Vieli. Auch hier habe das einen negativen Einfluss auf den Freiraum im Zeughausareal. «Wenn es in einem Gebiet zu viele Randständige hat, haben andere Angst – vor allem Familien mit Kindern.»

Anders als auf der Bäckeranlage zeigen die Aufwertungsbemühungen der Stadt auf dem Zeughausareal noch kaum Wirkung. «Es läuft kulturell noch zu wenig hier. Unsere Hoffnung ist, dass wir den Platz mit mehr Aktivitäten besser beleben können.» Vieli sieht beim Zeughausareal aber noch ein weiteres Problem: «Man weiss nicht, was mit dem Areal in Zukunft passieren wird. Wenn ein Gebiet keine klare Bestimmung hat, bleibt es ein Unort.»

«Günstiger Wohnraum darf nicht Luxusprojekten zum Opfer fallen»

Rolf Vieli ortet bei den Anwohnern zudem die Befürchtung, dass der Park gentrifiziert werden könnte: «Die Leute haben Angst, dass es keinen Platz mehr hat für die normale Bevölkerung, weil alles viel teurer wird.» Für André Bleiker bedeutet der Erhalt von tiefen Mieten sogar «das A und O» fürs Quartier. «Günstiger Wohnraum darf nicht Luxusprojekten zum Opfer fallen, in denen Familien mit einem tieferen Einkommen keinen Platz mehr haben.»

Vorerst seien diese Befürchtungen allerdings unbegründet, meint Vieli. «Die Durchmischung im Quartier ist noch relativ gut. Jetzt kommt es darauf an, wie sich die Stadt in Zukunft positionieren wird und ob sie den Wohnraum für den normalen Mittelstand behalten kann oder nicht.»

Bäckeranlage Community Center

1999–2004

10

10
Following the park's successful "normalization," the city council wanted to further improve it by adding a new community center. In 1999, the design competition was won by EM2N's "Mogli" proposal, which sought to make not just the new center but the whole park a neighborhood hub. Designed to bring activity to the park, the proposed building aimed first and foremost to serve its surroundings and exhibited a restraint that would allow the park to still play the lead role. Thanks to careful positioning, it would allow all the existing trees to be retained, its modest footprint would eat up as little green space as possible, and its form and façade design would harmonize with the arboreal backdrop.

11
In political debates, however, the proposal came in for strong criticism, primarily due to the projected 5.5-million-franc cost. Each party had its own ideas regarding how much a new community center is worth. The right-wing opposition party, the SVP, advocated spending nothing on it at all.

11

12
Eventually, the council assembly agreed on a compromise in which the budget for the project was halved. A new proposal was thus required. Our ambition was to retain as much floor space as possible, despite the dramatically reduced budget. In order to do so, we opted to cut costs by radically rationalizing the fit-out. At the same time, we were determined that the new building should not look like the result of a cost-cutting exercise, meaning we needed to rethink the design. We thus changed the overall form from a prism to a cute kidney shape and abandoned the printed-glass façade in favor of painted timber facings.

13
It's not just the new building that acts as a neighborhood hub but the whole park and its surroundings. The park and community center, the yards of the nearby Feld, Aussersihl, and Kernstrasse schools, and the pedestrianized Hohlstrasse all come together to form a larger whole, a genuine neighborhood hub.

Bäckeranlage Community Center

Bäckeranlage Community Center 43

Bäckeranlage Community Center 44 1999–2004

← 14 + 15
In urban design terms, the completed project retains the key characteristics of the original proposal. The building opens out towards the park as much as possible, the vertical spatial arrangement and relatively small footprint ensure existing trees can remain, and the architecture harmonizes with the arboreal backdrop. Thanks to its dark "British racing green" hue, its clustered perforations around the large windows, and its decorative lettering, the building echoes both the color of the surrounding trees and the scale of their foliage.

16
The concave building nestles beneath one of the large trees that characterize the park. The ground floor opens out onto the gravel area in front and overlooks the large playground.

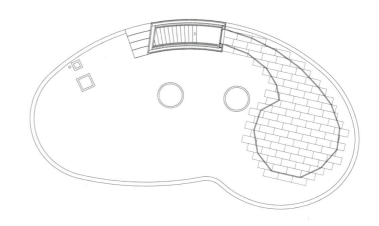

16

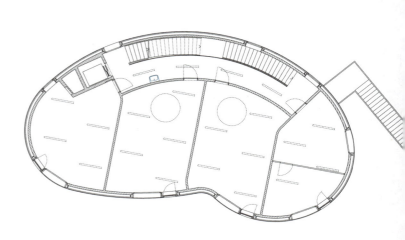

17
The new design's curvilinear form needed to be built cost-effectively. We therefore used a simple strategy of combining multiple overlapping circles. To stay within budget, the project followed the principle of "space before surface." A lower standard was applied throughout the build, while structural elements and design details were simplified. The curving walls of the envelope were made from calcium-silicate brick, elevated by different internal color schemes on each floor.

18
Plans for the ground floor, two upper floors, and roof terrace.

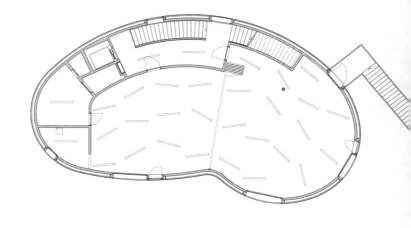

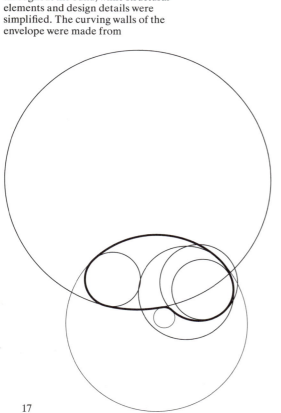

17

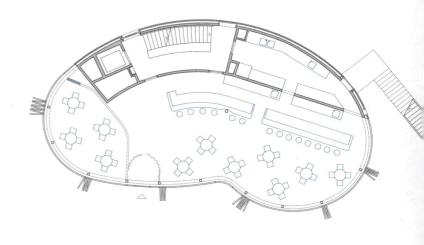

18

Bäckeranlage Community Center 45 1999–2004

19

20

21

19
The accessible roof terrace offers treetop views.

20
The upstairs function room is available for anyone to hire. A flexible partition allows it to be split into two spaces.

21
The top floor contains various spaces for use by local groups, along with the center management's own offices.

22
A large restaurant brings life to the ground floor. The glass frontage can be completely opened up, extending the restaurant out into the park in good weather and blurring the boundary between outside and in.

23
A cascading staircase provides a physical and visual link between the different floors, while the use of bold color makes for a playful and distinctive circulation space.

23

22

A Park Named "Bäcki"

Max Küng

001 It's Tuesday morning, March 8, 2016, and so far snow is the only thing to be seen; there was a surprisingly heavy fall and it has settled. The time is eight o'clock. At the community center in the Bäckeranlage park, the glass-walled ground-floor restaurant—which bears the name "B"—is just opening up; Fela Kuti blares from its speakers, filling the still empty space with sound. The park is cloaked in a blanket of white. The climbing frame at the space's western edge seems to rise from the ground like a giant snow-laden spider's web, and the swings, too, are topped with a layer of thick, wet snow. To see the park so lifeless and unpeopled is a rare sight indeed. No dog owners letting their pooch poop on the grass. No girls dragging their plastic sled up to the hill by the pavilion. No boys trying to clamber onto one of the bronze, frozen-in-motion horses. No vagrants sharing a bottle of wine. No street workers from the SIP, the municipal safety and prevention department, and no VW police van slowly patrolling the gravel paths, eyes peering out from within. No one but Mr. Blackbird, elegant as ever in his inky dress, stalking his way through the snow then hop-flitting away into a border. Before long, though, the park is awash with young children decked out in hats, gloves, and colorful clothing, whooping and hollering as they arrive. Soon, the first snowman is standing, snowballs are flying in all directions, and parents are shoving buggies through the slush. The day has begun.

002 We just call it "Bäcki." Officially, the park is called "Bäckeranlage," which is a little odd given that at no point is Bäckerstrasse even tangential to it. In fact, Bäckerstrasse, coming from the Stauffacherstrasse end, terminates at Helvetiaplatz. Although, to be precise, were you to come tearing out of Bäckerstrasse—in a getaway car after a casino heist, let's say—you wouldn't make it across Helvetiaplatz but would instead ram a wall, and perhaps smash into Karl Geiser's sculpture Denkmal der Arbeit. Road names, though, tend to look back to the past rather than ahead to the future. And up until the 1950s, that past was still present. Back then, the corner where Bäckerstrasse meets Stauffacher and where red "OCHSNER SHOES" lettering now blazes brightly from the roof and shop windows, bore signs for "Cailler" and "Bäckerei-Conditorei zu Pfistern J. Jäger"—the latter a ground floor bakery and patisserie. Moreover, Bäckerstrasse was longer in those days; until a change of course in the 1950s, it ran all the way to the edge of Altstetten and hence alongside Bäckeranlage. Interestingly, a new *bäckerei* opened up recently on Helvetiaplatz bearing the name John Baker (were I to open a *metzgerei* in Zurich, I'd surely call it James Butcher...), thus filling the previously bakery-free space between Bäckeranlage and Bäckerstrasse. But all this is by the by. We just call it "Bäcki"—period.

003 Today, the kidney-shaped community center and restaurant nestles peacefully in the park, but its construction was the subject of fiercely contested debates on the city council. Dubbed "Mogli," the original proposal was for a six-story glass building, a design that emerged victorious from the competitive tender process. But residents resisted, railing against the 5.45-million-franc scheme. They wanted to spend just 1.9 million on a café plus a kiosk and toilets. "Mogli" was eventually abandoned, but a 3-million-franc compromise was agreed and the new building opened on August 16, 2004. The *Tages-Anzeiger* newspaper wrote at the time of its inauguration: "According to a council decision, the new community center should cost no more than three million francs. To avoid having to make significant cuts to the floor space, the architects went for a barebones fit-out. The floor slabs are made of unfinished concrete, the walls of industrial calcium-silicate brick, and the plumbing and wiring were left exposed. The only luxury is color, which was liberally splashed across the interior so that bright yellow, orange, and frog green hues radiate out into park, echoing its grassy expanses and blooms."

004 Mogli (or Mowgli in the original English text) is the name of the boy in Rudyard Kipling's *Jungle Book*, a foundling who grows up amidst the animals of the Indian jungle and whose adventures, as he goes from playful child to young man and finally to king of the animals, form an archetypal coming-of-age story. The law of the jungle is tough, even in the urban jungle of Zurich's District 4.

005 In an as yet unnamed novel, set to be published by Kein & Aber in fall 2016 or spring 2017, there is a scene that's set in the Bäckeranlage park.[A] A real estate dealer named Fabio is sitting on a bench, waiting for Aschi, a squatter who occasionally gives Fabio inside information from the local scene. For some time, Fabio has been observing a ladybug crawling along his arm.

"He stared at the spotted creature until it became a dot, a small dot that got smaller and ever smaller and finally disappeared and Fabio lost himself in a nothingness that is not nothing, but rather the teeming grass expanse of the park, which, as always in summer, was thronged with people at leisure while, around the edges, people for whom leisure had at some point become an occupation, doubtless for valid reasons, were standing near the paddling pool, drinking cartons of wine. Suddenly two guys appeared carrying rolled-up rugs that they proceeded to lay out on the grass. The pair then disappeared again before returning to the grass, this time carrying a table tennis table between them, which they placed on the old worn rugs and on which, with much excitement and hollering, they promptly began playing. Each smash produced a bright smack as the ball landed, pinging off the table edge and away into the grass before being sluggishly retrieved by one of the players. Soon a third joined the party and the hollering crescendoed: he'd brought with him a twelve-pack of beer.

"Fabio hated all this; the park made him uneasy. Doubtless the bushes behind the bench he was sitting on were full of used, blood-smeared, bacteria- and virus-ridden needles and human feces and condoms and sick and bits of glass from smashed vodka bottles. It was Aschi's idea to meet here and, at the time, Fabio had thought nothing of it, which was a source of annoyance to him now. Where was the guy anyway? Fabio looked at his watch. The smell of burnt flesh wafted over from a disposable barbecue, around which a large clan was crouching as if they were Neanderthals gathered around a campfire. Inevitably, one of their number was clutching a guitar. A female laugh rang out across the grass, a light sound that briefly rose above all the others: the noise of the street behind him, the distant buzz of a saw on an unseen building site, the pounding of paws on grass as a dog

[A] Max Küng, *Wenn du dein Haus verlässt, beginnt das Unglück*, Zurich, 2016 [Editorial Note].

A Park Named "Bäcki"

Max Küng

chased a frisbee, catching it in mid-air and returning it to where the vagrants were gathered.

"Eventually, Aschi showed up and sat next to Fabio on the bench. 'I hate this place,' said Fabio. 'Me too,' replied Aschi, 'although probably for different reasons. Used to be that you could feel free here. You could just BE. Now you have police patrolling all the time and harassing marginalized people, and moms from expensive new-build apartments sipping latte macchiatos, droning on at each other about postnatal depression and their kids' problems at school.'—'It could be a nice park,' says Fabio without much conviction, 'if they would ban juggling. Or barbecuing at least. The stench of it is disgusting.'—'Don't worry,' says Aschi, 'it'll happen soon enough. I guarantee it. This place is gentrifying fast. Soon you'll have a nice, high-tone park with neatly cut grass, sealed trash cans, and CCTV. And maybe private security guards doing patrols.' Fabio looks across at Aschi and is struck dumb. 'You're not rolling a joint there, are you?'—'It's just tobacco, man. Chill. Just healthy, additive-free tobacco. Do you want one?' Fabio looks at Aschi with annoyance. 'I don't smoke.'—'I know that. Chill, man, was just a joke.'"

006 On August 4, 2007, the *Neue Zürcher Zeitung* newspaper published an article about the park with the headline "Die Bäckeranlage als grüne Oase im Kreis 4" ["Bäckeranlage, a Green Oasis in District 4"]. Reading it, I wondered to myself if anyone had ever seen a gray oasis. Or a black one. Or a raspberry-red one. Isn't "green oasis" as tautological as "dry desert"? At any rate, it went on: "Long-time residents, meanwhile, warn that this one-time problem area is 'becoming a chichi hangout'. We're seeing more and more big flash cars pulling up in District 4, presumably from other, more upscale neighborhoods. It seems to be trendy to take the whole family to the 'Bäcki' for a few hours." Big flash cars: the new bogeymen.

007 I know people who love their "Bäcki," I know others who can't stand the place—for reasons as varied as people are themselves. Personally I rather like it. For one thing, it has trees. Trees are always good. Anyone who's anti-tree should own up; they can have a punch in the face from me. Secondly, the park allows your gaze to roam, and roam quite far before it finally hits a façade. Thirdly, it's a genuinely good place to spontaneously meet or bump into friends and acquaintances and have a beer, and then another, and then another. Also, the landlord at "B" gets his wine from Heuberger am Hallwylplatz, which means it's good stuff.

008 In Kurt Früh's movie *Bäckerei Zürrer*, there's a scene set during a concert at the old Bäckeranlage's bandstand. In it, we see Marcel sitting on a park bench and saying to Frollein Zürrer in his French Swiss dialect: "No, I don't like Zurich so much. I live with my parents in Yverdon. Vous savez: Yverdon, it is French. Il y en a un petit peu de parfum de Paris."

009 At the children's flea market, taking place at the park's northernmost edge where kiddies race through the shallow water in summer and vagrants sit or stand around near the toilets and bottle bank, I bought a Matchbox car, a Lotus Esprit from the Bond movie *The Spy Who Loved Me*—the one that could swim and dive, and fire missiles at airborne helicopters from its back. My neighbor was selling it for one franc. I bought it for my kids, though really I mainly bought it for myself; I had the very same model when I was little. Then I went back to the stall where we were hoping to sell our things to other kids. Suddenly I felt something underfoot, so I looked down at the ground and realized I'd stood on something. I stepped to one side and saw it was a used condom. I was standing on a used condom at a children's flea market. A very Bäcki sort of experience.

010 My younger son is six. What he likes best about the park is the big round swing. He's genuinely spent hours on that thing, swinging back and forth, back and forth, and yelling "Faster, Daddy, faster!" My older son (the family member most familiar with the park because his school is there), he's ten and what he likes best about the park is the café's apple and poppyseed cake. The ten-year-old asked me right back what I liked best about the park. I said, "Let me think." Then he quickly added, "And what do you like least?" That was an easier one. "The shabby blue Ron Arad Vitra chairs in the restaurant, in particular their legs—because the rubber feet have come off and not been replaced so that they squeal and scratch on the concrete floor when you drag them around. That makes my blood twist and the hair on the back of my neck stand up; it sounds like contemporary classical music or the noises you might hear as you're dying."

011 In the park, there's a box by a border near the slide. It's plastered with graffiti; someone has sprayed HYPE on it in big red letters with black shadows. This maybe hip-height box has a sloping lid. If you put your beer down on it, you have to be careful your tumbler isn't claimed by the Earth's pull. Children like to clamber onto the box, then jump down to the gravel. I seem to remember there once being another box next to this one but, then again, I'm not sure. It's like a lot of things you remember: you're not certain whether that's really how it was. At any rate, there's this box in the park, which has a lock on it. Somebody once told me the story of what it once contained, namely a mobile fence. Apparently this fence was specially designed for the park—by an actual designer—for the park nannies to use. On Fridays between 9 and 1 o'clock, you could leave your kids with the nannies for five francs per hour or part thereof. The fence, I was told, cost 30,000 francs and was used three times. Whether the story is true or not, I don't know. I can believe it though—in Zurich, stories like this are often true. There are no park nannies here anymore. Just meter maids who converge on the park from all directions at 10:15 on the dot, sporting dark-blue uniforms and taking last drags on cigarettes before entering the café for their morning coffee-and-cookie ritual, then coming out half an hour later and slipping tickets under the windscreen wipers of nearby cars, tickets that today come in little plastic wallets on account of the weather.

012 The lunch menu is being chalked up on the wall-hung blackboard: celeriac piccata with spaghetti and tomato (19 fr.), panciotti al brasato with pesto and asparagus (21 fr.), pasta napoletana (15 fr.). Ten years ago, a plate of spaghetti napoletana was 14 francs.

A Park Named "Bäcki"

013   It was a summer's day. We were sitting in the shade of a tree at one of the community center's round metal tables, drinking Grüner Veltliner wine. The metal tables have one major advantage over the beer garden benches: their chairs come with backrests. At a certain age, you start to appreciate backrests. The kids were scattered across the park, off on little adventures. Some were hanging from the climbing frame like sloths. Others were buying ice cream and purple-hued pop made in Valle Mesolcina. Others still were playing hide-and-seek. One of the hiders came over to our table and said, "There's a man in the bushes."—"What?" replied the dads, while the moms jumped up, yelling "Where?"—"Over there," the child said, pointing in a fairly vague direction. "There's a man crouching in the bushes and I wanted to hide next to him and he sent me away and when I asked him what he was doing, he said he's a policeman and he's watching gangsters. He had binoculars and a uniform and a gun, too, I think." The moms soon returned and confirmed the story. There really were cops in the bushes, squatting as if they were taking a dump. No sign of any gangsters though.

014   Still Tuesday, March 8. By the afternoon, it's getting warmer and the snow is turning to rain. Just a few hours until the day is over.

The Great Feast 54

1
People attending the traditional Feast of 10,000 Families during Chinese New Year in Wuhan.

Archipelagos and Islands

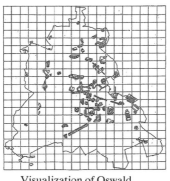
Visualization of Oswald Mathias Ungers's "city in the city."

At a talk at London's Architectural Association School of Architecture, the Dutch architecture critic Roemer van Toorn[A] spoke about the transition from an "either/or" to an "and" society; that is, a society in which either/or concepts such as specialization, transparency, and polarity are superseded by concepts such as networks, chaos, and ambivalence. Similar developments have taken place in the urban realm. The clear spatial, functional, and social structures of concentrically organized urban cores have, in more suburban areas, largely disappeared. Instead, they are defined by what we might call archipelagos. It's a term that dates back to 1970s Germany, when the Wall still stood and West Berlin was shrinking. That situation inspired a group of architects around Oswald Mathias Ungers at Cornell University—among them Rem Koolhaas—to develop a conceptual model for the future of this enclave city. In Ungers's vision of the urban archipelago, bold and radically divergent structures would rise like "islands" from an "ocean" of verdant landscapes.

Parc Monceau.

At roughly the same time as Ungers, Englishman Colin Rowe and his French coauthor Fred Koetter propounded similar theoretical ideas in *Collage City*,[B] using landscape gardens such as Parc Monceau as a critical tool and a model for the modern city.

In his project "The City of the Captive Globe," Rem Koolhaas then exported the archipelago to New York, transposing it onto the rigid grid of Manhattan. Here, the island concept is taken to the extreme, with the street grid transformed into an ocean from which individual blocks, as illustrated by Madeleine Vriesendorp, rise like islands that are as programmatically diverse as possible.

This transposition of Ungers's archipelago to a "prospering" metropolis opened up new opportunities for the use of the archipelago as a conceptual blueprint. After all, in contrast to traditional urban design theories, which often revolve around uniformity and continuity, the archipelago can accommodate difference and discontinuity.

"The City of the Captive Globe." Rem Koolhaas, Madeleine Vriesendorp.

In the early 1980s, Zurich-based author Hans Widmer, writing under the pseudonym P. M., borrowed this island idea for his anarchic utopia *bolo'bolo*.[C] Bolos are "friendly" islands of self-governing communes surrounded by the "hostile" ocean of capitalist normality. Rather than being isolated phenomena, these islands gradually spread across the entire city. Although the "bolos" develop a high degree of differentiation from their

bolo'bolo
Hans Widmer, alias P.M.

surroundings, they are not remote, inward-looking entities, seeking instead to maintain relations with the outside world, while the bolos themselves are economically and ideologically interconnected. Here, the archipelago becomes a sociopolitical instrument of urban development.

Disneyland could perhaps be read as a capitalist counterpart—as a menagerie of attractions recreating architectural, environmental, and cultural themes from around the world, an archipelago of entertainment and maximum capitalistic exploitation.

As an urban design model, the archipelago has lost none of its relevance. After all, a city—and urban life in general—cannot thrive on homogeneity alone; it also needs to have variety, to feature contrasting parts. Medieval monastery complexes offer early examples of urban islands in the landscape or "cities within cities." They were places to live, work, make, and acquire knowledge, with sacred spaces existing alongside functional infrastructure.

Disneyland as archipelago.

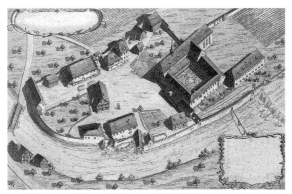

The monastery of Töss near Winterthur.

The new industries of the 18th and early 19th centuries, on the other hand, created places, both in the countryside and on urban peripheries, that followed the logic of their production processes, resulting in hitherto unknown densities, scales, and atmospheres. It's surely no coincidence that Johann Rieter set up his textile machinery plant in the former monastery of Töss to the south of Winterthur's urban core.

Often, industrialists built veritable "cathedrals of production" outside city boundaries; the Menier chocolate factory at Noisiel, designed by Eiffel Tower architect Charles Léon Stephen Sauvestre, was even nicknamed "La Cathédrale."

In village settings, monumental silos for the industrial-scale storage of agricultural products broke radically with the scale of existing structures, prefiguring in a sense the impact of rural tower blocks.

The basic principle of archipelagos and islands can still help us to find appropriate solutions to urbanistic challenges today. From a 20th-century perspective, discontinuities in the urban fabric, existing

Maggi factory, Kemptthal:
an urban island in a rural setting.

Archipelagos and Islands

Menier chocolate factory, Noisiel, by Charles Léon Stephen Sauvestre.

contrasts in density, and clashes of usage were often viewed solely as problems. If, however, we consider such a cityscape as a complex arrangement of diversified islands, then its atmospheric and programmatic contrasts and schisms become a logical part of the whole. Selected locations can then be boosted and densified, while differences (even period-related ones) can be deliberately enhanced. Rather than having to blend with some holistic whole, these islands are allowed to be divergent. They can be low- or high-density and their urban realm can differ significantly from those of nearby islands. Critical to their success is their inherent spatial and programmatic richness and the connectivity of their margins. A city conceived along these lines consists of independent and often disparate parts that connect with each other across the spaces between them. These "unbuilt" intermediate spaces—the white in a black-and-white plan—play an extremely important role, providing the overarching infrastructure that links the individual islands. Seen in this light, public space and transport infrastructure of all kinds are the glue that holds everything together and hence deserve appropriate architectural care. Fundamentally, the archipelago concept thus represents the idea of a synchronous city that no longer revolves around the homogeneous, rational (and now obsolete) image of traditional society, instead allowing the fragmentary and heterogeneous nature of today's world to be expressed.

Silos against a rural backdrop—like tower blocks in the countryside.

Study for Olten-Süd, EM2N/Urs Primas: dense islands within a park-like landscape.

A
Roemer van Toorn, "The Society of the And," talk at the AA School of Architecture, London, March 16, 1999, https://www.youtube.com/watch?v=3wD628ruX1U (last accessed March 7, 2022).

B
Colin Rowe, Fred Koetter, *Collage City*, Cambridge, Massachusetts/London, 1978.

C
Hans Widmer, *bolo'bolo*, Zurich, 1983.

Zurich as Archipelago 58

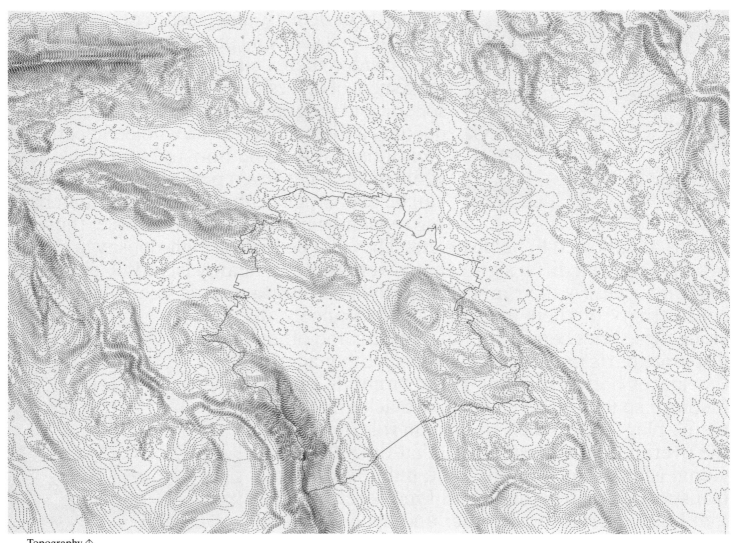

Topography ↑

Zurich as Archipelago

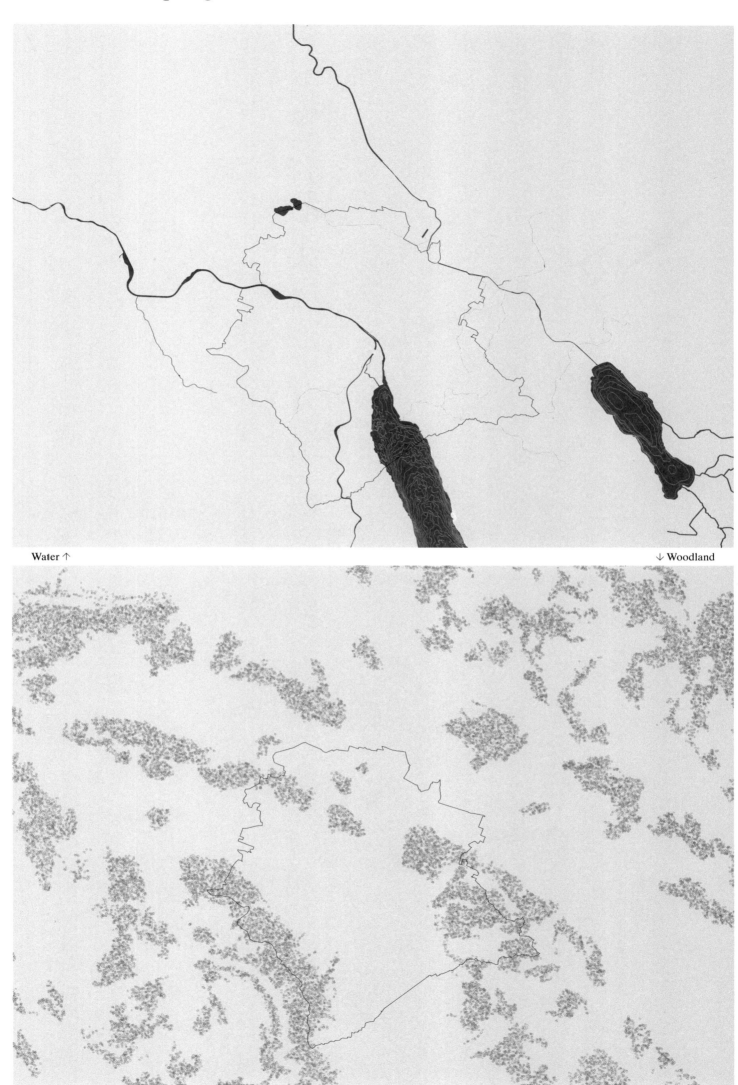

Water ↑   ↓ Woodland

Zurich as Archipelago 60

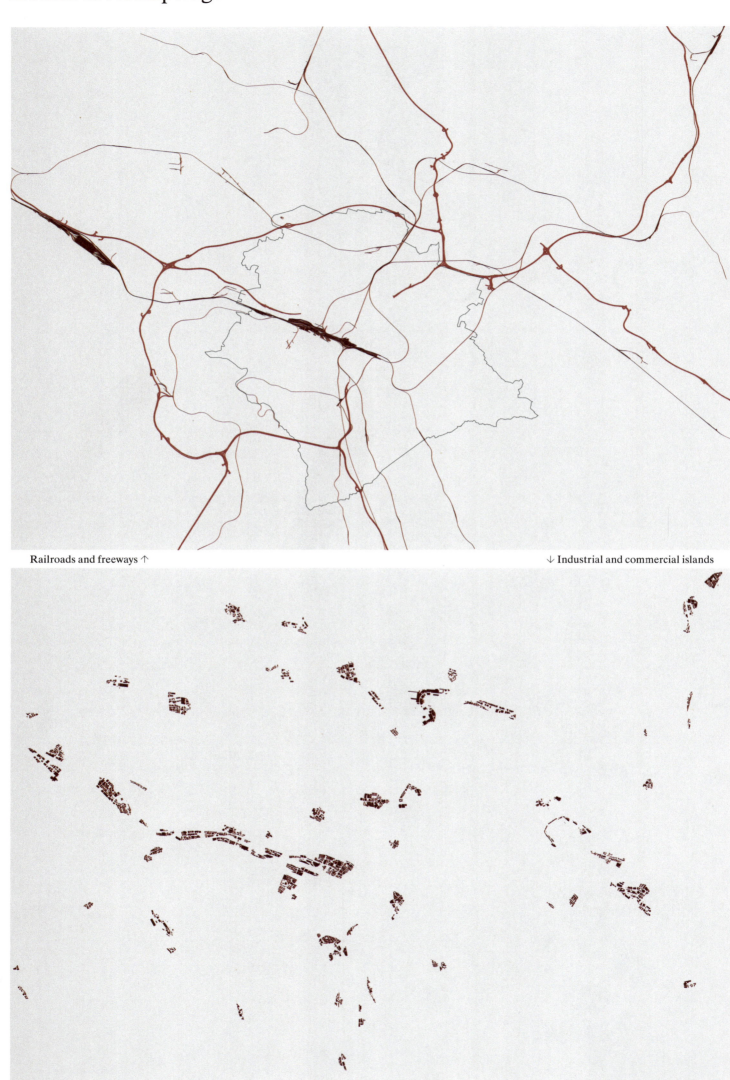

Railroads and freeways ↑

↓ Industrial and commercial islands

Zurich as Archipelago 61

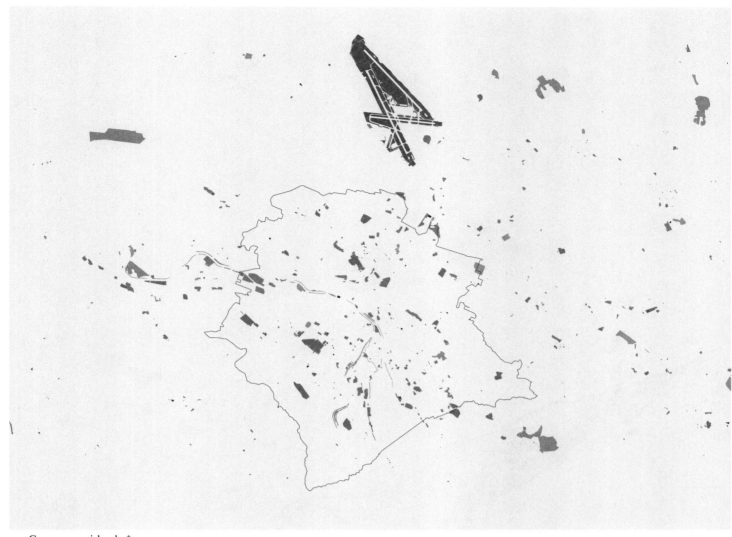

Green-space islands ↑

When the various different elements are overlaid,
the city's archipelago aspect is revealed
↓

Zurich as Archipelago

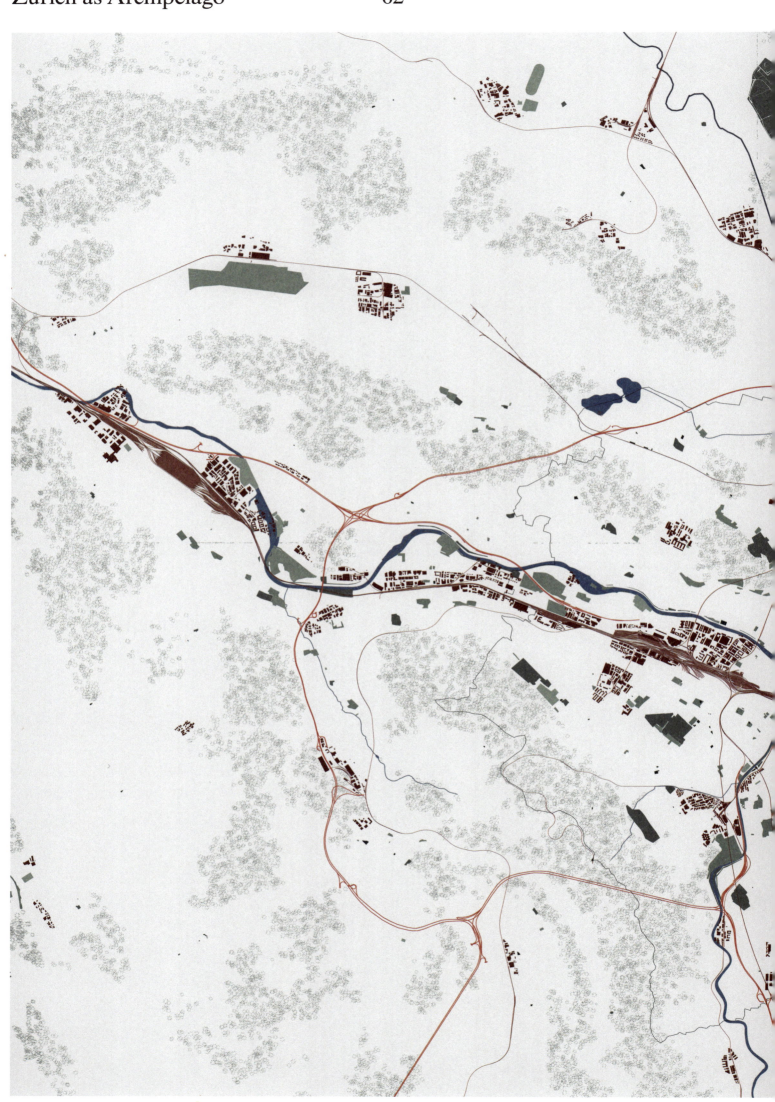

Zurich as Archipelago

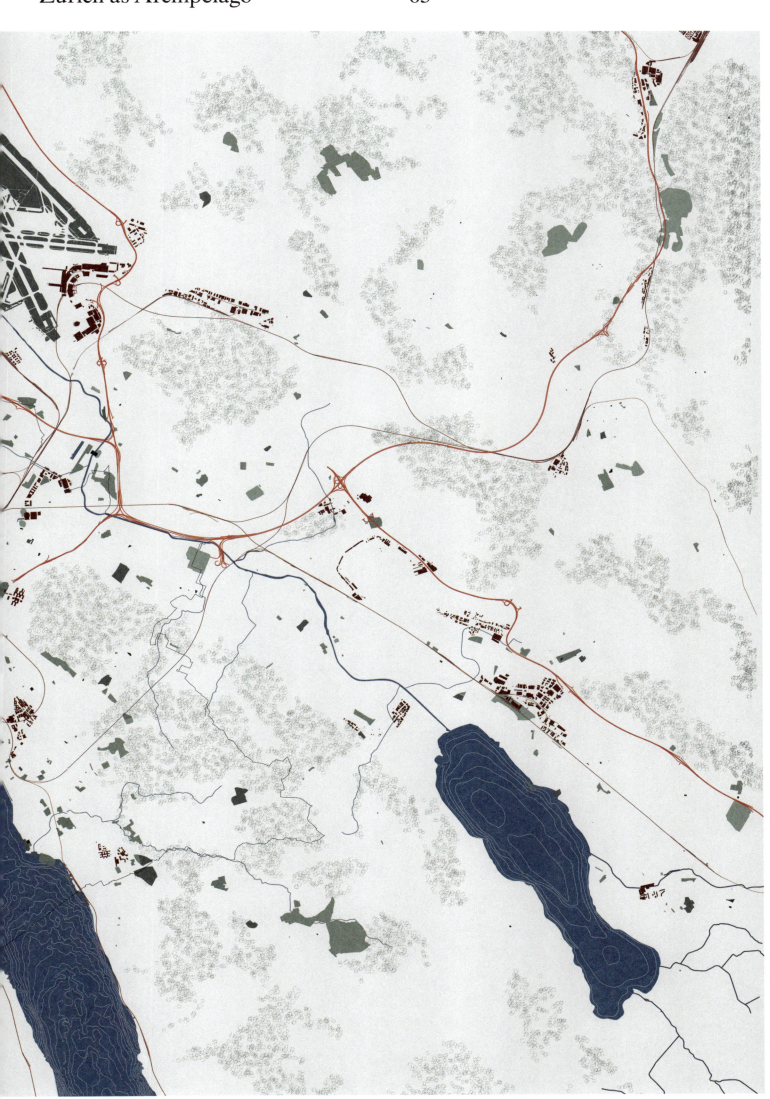

Zurich as Archipelago

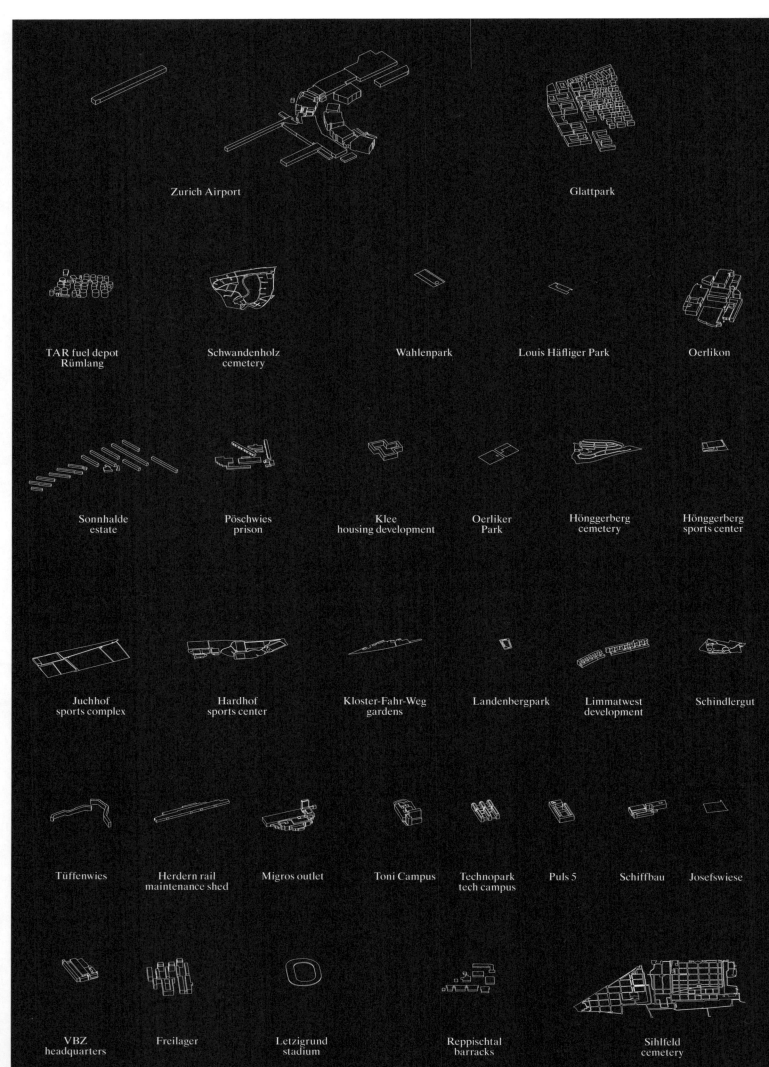

Zurich as Archipelago

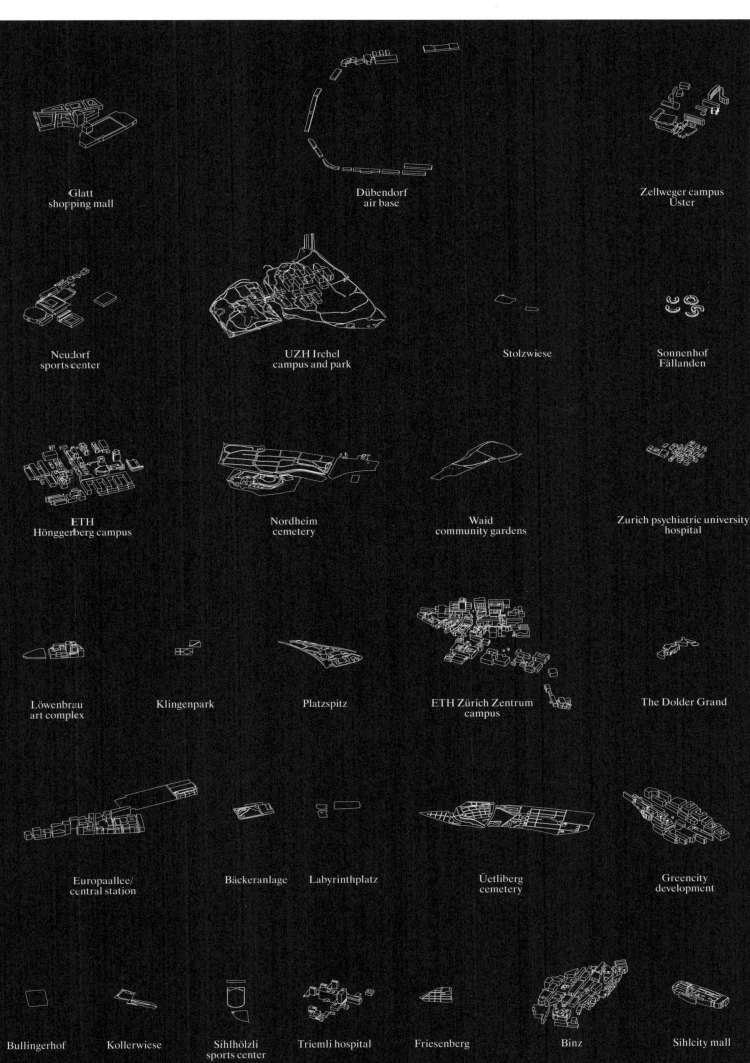

Glattpark

Glattpark

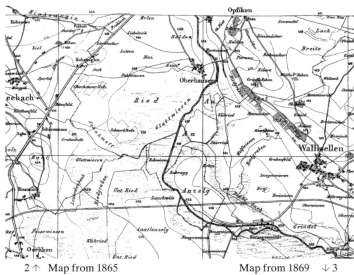

2 ↑ Map from 1865

← 1
Following the logic of the urban periphery, the Glattpark green space slots into the established fabric of infrastructure, heavily densified islands, and greenery, a fabric that is itself overlaid on a backdrop of low-density development or sprawl. The Glattpark development is an exception to the urban sprawl, though it follows the same rules in terms of infrastructural access and island diversity.

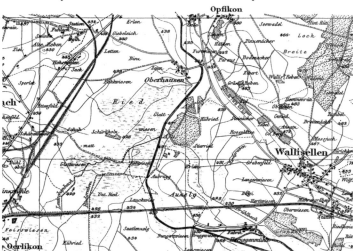

Map from 1869 ↓ 3

Map from 1940 ↓ 4

2–6
This story of the Glatt valley is one of an intermediate space that gradually filled up with infrastructure and buildings. Over the years, irrigation channels, roads, tram tracks, and freeways carved up the flat and originally marshy plain between the villages of Seebach, Wallisellen, Opfikon, and Schwamendingen, transforming this natural space with the Glatt river at its heart into an infrastructure-dominated realm. Often, anything that was too big for the city proper or too unsightly for "civilized" residential areas was instead located in this faceless in-between space, including a velodrome, an indoor stadium, a sewage treatment plant, a civil defense shelter, a cement factory, a waste incinerator, the campus of a Swiss television network, and much more besides.

7
Newspaper article about "Europe's most expensive field." Aided by its high infrastructural density, the Glatt valley goes from peripheral intermediate space to extremely well-connected, centrally located development zone. For all its locational advantages, however, the area remains crisscrossed by boundaries between municipalities and lots and by large-scale infrastructure. Lying between the municipality of Opfikon and the city of Zurich, the Oberhausserriet area was long dubbed "Europe's most expensive field" by the media. For decades, however, a complicated patchwork of ownerships and responsibilities foiled any development, until a zoning plan finally undid the Gordian knot. That plan aimed to create a new mixed district that would straddle municipal boundaries and feature its own recreation area, to be known as Glattpark. The incorporation of the park as a key magnet and central public space has led to a structural inversion of the settlement pattern, with what was once the periphery becoming a new core.

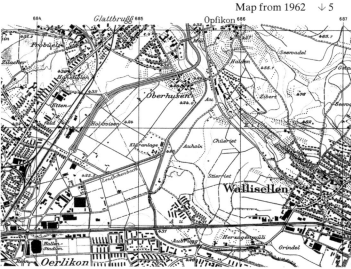

Map from 1962 ↓ 5

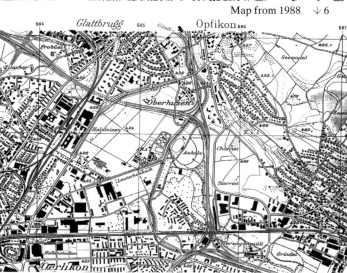

Map from 1988 ↓ 6

Glattpark

ZÜRICH UND REGION

Donnerstag, 2. November 2000 · Nr. 256

Im heute landwirtschaftlich genutzten Oberhauserriet soll ein neuer Opfiker Stadtteil entstehen. Das Areal umfasst gut 67 Hektaren zwischen Thurgauerstrasse (im Hintergrund) und Glatt. (Bild Bally)

Der grosse Wurf auf der «teuersten Wiese»
Im Oberhauserriet wird ein neues Quartier geplant

Im Opfiker Oberhauserriet entsteht auf dem Reissbrett ein neuer Stadtteil. Geplant sind Wohnungen für 6600 Personen, Büros für 7300 neue Arbeitsplätze und ein Park mit See. In einer ersten Etappe soll der nordwestliche Teil des Areals bebaut werden. Die Stadt Zürich als grösste Grundeigentümerin will ihren Landanteil verkaufen.

ark. Vom Hängebauchschwein über das Schaf bis zum Braunvieh gibt es kaum eine Nutztiergattung, die man im Opfiker Oberhauserriet nicht beim Weiden besichtigen könnte. Das 674 000 Quadratmeter grosse Gelände zwischen Zürich und dem Flughafen – wegen seiner verkehrstechnisch günstigen Lage oft als «teuerste Wiese Europas» bezeichnet – wird heute vorwiegend landwirtschaftlich genutzt. Mit der Gutheissung des Quartierplans Oberhauserriet durch die kantonale Baudirektion findet die extensive Nutzung des Gebiets nun wohl ein schnelles Ende (NZZ 18. 10. 00). Die gut dreissig Landbesitzer haben sich im Quartierplan auf ein Nutzungskonzept geeinigt. Entlang der stark befahrenen Thurgauerstrasse wird gegenüber von bestehenden Geschäftshäusern und Hotels («Renaissance», Textil- und Modecenter TMC, Galleria und weitere) eine dichte Dienstleistungszone erstellt. Östlich anschliessend folgen zum geplanten See hin eine Zone mit Mischnutzung und eine reine Wohnzone. So sollen Raum für 7300 Arbeitsplätze und Wohnungen für 6600 Menschen entstehen.

Bevölkerung wächst um 50 Prozent

Damit wächst die Einwohnerzahl der Stadt Opfikon um gut 50 Prozent auf fast 20 000. Stadtpräsident Jürg Leuenberger ist überzeugt, dass dieses Wachstum zu verkraften ist. Um zu verhindern, dass eine Satellitenstadt entsteht, soll die trennende «Schlucht» Thurgauerstrasse über- und unterquert werden. Geplant ist weiter eine schulische Einbindung. Die Oberstufe soll zentral geführt werden, im neuen Stadtteil will Opfikon nur einen Kindergarten und möglicherweise ein Unter- und Mittelstufenschulhaus errichten. Leuenberger hofft, dass auch ein Teil des Opfiker Gewerbes im neuen Quartier heimisch wird und so eine Klammer zur bestehenden Stadt schafft.

Als Zielpublikum für die Wohnnutzung sieht Leuenberger «eher jüngere Leute, die ein gutes Freizeitangebot schätzen und im Business tätig sind». Damit seien durchaus auch Familien gemeint. Da es sich beim Oberhauserriet um die fluglärm ärmste Gegend der Stadt handelt, sieht Leuenberger keinen Konflikt mit der Nutzung als Wohngebiet. Die neuen Wohnungen seien sogar eine mögliche Alternative für Opfiker, die in stärker lärmbelasteten Quartieren der Stadt wohnen.

Teilweiser Rückbau der Kläranlage

Der Park, eine der Hauptattraktionen im Freizeitangebot des Projekts, soll 124 000 Quadratmeter einnehmen und umfasst das Gebiet zwischen der bebauten Zone und der Glatt. Die am Fluss gelegene Stadtzürcher Kläranlage wird im Bereich der Klärbecken teilweise verkleinert und die frei werdende Fläche dem Park zugeschlagen. Eine zusätzliche Aufwertung des Erholungsgebiets erhoffen sich die Verantwortlichen durch die Renaturierung der Glatt nördlich der Kläranlage. Im Park wird gleichzeitig mit dessen Eröffnung im Jahr 2006 die Grünausstellung «Terra» stattfinden. Diese solle sich schwergewichtig der Frage widmen, wie Städte heute sinnvoll begrünt werden könnten, erklärt Jürg Leuenberger. 2006 dürfte gemäss dem Opfiker Stadtpräsidenten für das ganze Oberhauserriet zu einem Schlüsseljahr werden. Bis dann sollten nicht nur die ersten Büros und Häuser bezogen, sondern auch der erste Ast der Glatttalbahn betriebsbereit sein. Die geplante Strecke führt vom Bahnhof Oerlikon zum Flughafen mit zwei Stationen im Bereich Oberhauserriet.

Befürchtungen, dass sich der grosse Wurf auf der grünen Wiese nicht realisieren lässt, hegt Leuenberger keine: «Auch wenn sich die Konjunktur wieder abschwächen sollte, wird sich dies nicht zuerst bei uns auswirken.» Gegenwärtig sei die Lage eher so, dass er fast täglich mehrere 10 000 Quadratmeter Opfiker Boden an interessierte Investoren verkaufen könnte. Deshalb werde es nicht lange dauern, bis die Baupläne im Oberhauserriet zur Umsetzung gelangten.

«So schnell wie möglich loslegen»

Bei der Allreal AG, einer der grossen Landbesitzerinnen, bestätigt man diese Aussage. «Wir wollen so schnell wie möglich loslegen», sagt Jürg Issler, Mediensprecher des Generalunternehmers. In der ersten Bauetappe – sie umfasst den nordwestlichen Viertel des Areals – plant Allreal die Erstellung eines Dienstleistungsgebäudes und einer Wohnüberbauung. Investieren werde man voraussichtlich selber, so Issler. Er hebt die hohe Standortgunst der künftigen Arbeitsplätze hervor, das Allreal-Gebäude soll direkt gegenüber der Station Stelzen der Glatttalbahn zu stehen kommen. – Die Stadt Zürich, die als grösste Eigentümerin knapp die Hälfte des ganzen Areals besitzt, will ihren Anteil verkaufen. «Wir bauen grundsätzlich nicht ausserhalb der Stadtgrenze», sagt Arno Roggo, Leiter der städtischen Liegenschaftsverwaltung. Der Stadt ist es aber nicht gleichgültig, was im Oberhauserriet passiert. Eine gute Durchmischung habe Priorität, erklärt Roggo. Die Rahmenbedingungen seien zwar geschaffen, diese gelte es aber noch mit Inhalt zu füllen.

Roggo lässt durchblicken, dass man das Land gerne an die Stadt Opfikon verkaufen würde, falls Interesse und «gestalterischer Wille» vorhanden seien. Der Opfiker Stadtpräsident gibt sich zurückhaltend. Wenn eine solche Anfrage eintreffe, werde man sie sicher prüfen, so Jürg Leuenberger. Ausgeschlossen sei aber, dass seine Stadt Landhandel betreiben werde.

Bevor die Bagger zum Hochbau auffahren, investieren die Grundeigentümer rund 20 Millionen Franken in die Erschliessung des Geländes mit Strassen und Werkleitungen. Laut dem Opfiker Bauvorstand Roland Stadler soll der Bau bis Mai 2002 abgeschlossen sein. Als Hauptverkehrsader ist ein Boulevard parallel zur Thurgauerstrasse vorgesehen. Rechtwinklig zum Boulevard werden drei Stichstrassen gebaut, die die Wohnzone mit der Thurgauerstrasse verbinden. Der Verkehr soll möglichst spärlich durchs Quartier fliessen. Stadler hofft, dass motorisierte Pendler und Besucher die zwei Parkhäuser im Norden und im Süden benützen werden, während die Bewohner am Ende der Stichstrassen eine beschränkte Zahl von Parkplätzen erhalten. Der Boulevard soll eine veritable Flaniermeile mit Strassenrestaurants und Geschäften werden. Dort, wo heute noch die Kühe weiden, wird man wohl schon bald deren Milch kaufen können.

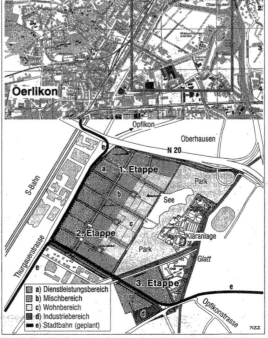

Das Opfiker Oberhauserriet, dessen geplante Nutzung und die Etappierung der Bauarbeiten im Detail; oben der Ausschnitt aus dem Zürcher Stadtplan.

Glattpark

8

9

8
The design competition for the Glattpark project was about giving shape to this new peri-urban center. We imagined the park not as a romantic counterweight to the urban periphery, but as a continuation of it. Our design worked with what was already there: a robust infrastructural framework, complemented by urban islands accommodating disparate usages. We viewed this peri-urban setting as an archipelago, an agglomeration of islands set against an infrastructural backdrop.

9
The surrounding infrastructure—roads and paths plus bodies of water—was a defining factor in the design of the park. We ensured all pathways were routed into and across the space, creating an infrastructural network that ensures optimum connections between the park and its environs.

10
The look of the park is dictated not by a carefully composed, harmonious representation of landscaped nature but via the heterogeneity of its diverse parts, its various islands establishing contrasts across the infrastructure elements that pass between them.

11–21
In the run-up to the competition, various interest groups expressed their specific concerns regarding the new park: from environmentalists, aquatic biologists, noise mitigation experts, and neighborhood developers to those seeking to use the park for sports or leisure. Instead of attempting to amalgamate their wants and needs within one overarching solution, we created disparate islands for different usages. The result is a stimulating ensemble in which contrasting worlds coexist yet also add up to a heterogeneous whole.

10

Glattpark

11
Noise control berm
made of excavated material

16
Reedbed for initial
water treatment

12
Secondary
water treatment

17
Playing field island

13
Former sewage works
repurposed as an island
for high-noise leisure uses

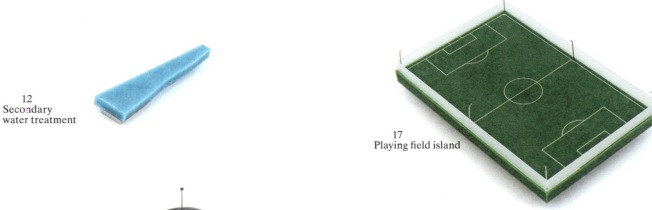

18
Swimming pond

14
Lily pond for initial
water treatment

19
Woodland area
as environmental mitigation

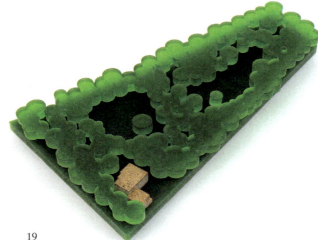

15
The existing civil defense shelter is integrated
into the park's system of islands

20
Traditional city park transplanted
from the city to the periphery

Glattpark

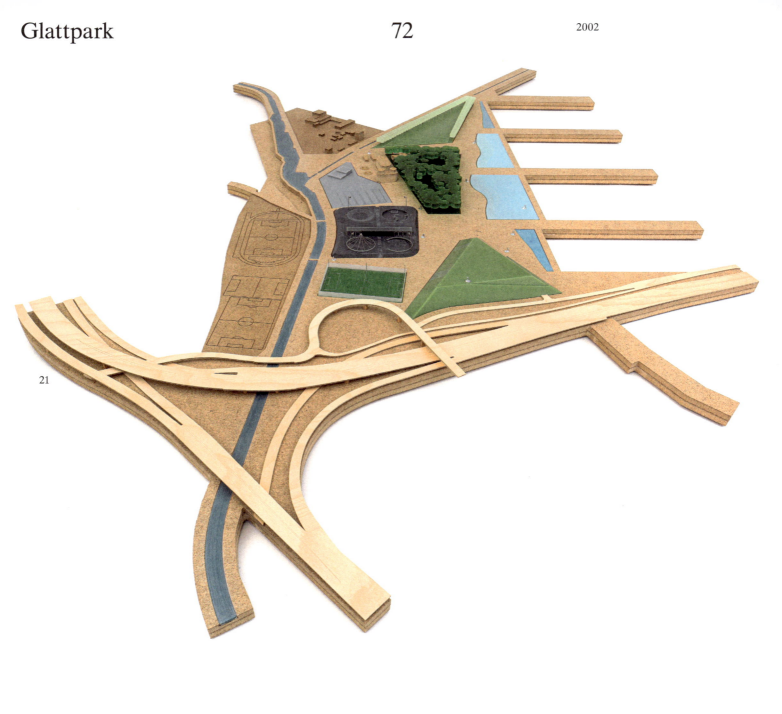

Leutschenbach Schools

2002–2003

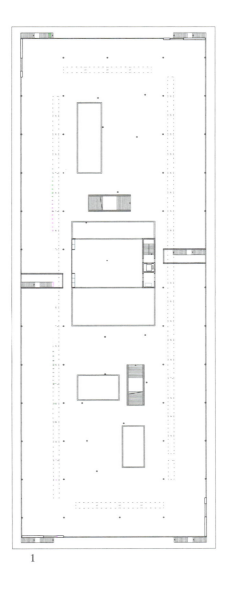

1

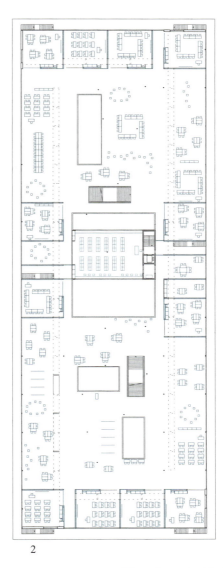

2

3

The only constant in life is change. Technological innovation, social upheaval, demographic shifts, new forms of transportation and new ways of producing goods and knowledge: all this poses an ongoing challenge for architecture and urban design, two disciplines in which, at least in a European context, notions of longevity and permanence are ingrained. How can something as fixed as a built structure respond to new and different spatial requirements? How can buildings or developments retain relevance when the environment around them is constantly evolving?

1
A generic floor plan provides scope for a (theoretically) limitless variety of usage types. The building-as-shelf-stack concept allows the space of the empty lot to be multiplied vertically, allowing for genuine density of usage.

2
When it comes to schools, one set of reforms follows another, in which new teaching methods, new school and class structures, and even site mergers may have to be accommodated. Moreover, demands for greater digitization, more personalized teaching, and more lifelong learning are calling into question the very role of schools as centers of learning. These ongoing dynamics mean that school premises, not unlike airports and railroad stations, are constantly being remodeled.

3
A school as a kind of shelf-stack system that allows for flexible usage. Each classroom has a balcony, while the interior is illuminated via large courtyards. This stack system doesn't assume any particular form of teaching; instead, its open structure alloes the school to adapt to whatever new educational structures arise over time.

4
Internal landscape from *No-Stop City*, Andrea Branzi, Archizoom Associati, 1969.

4

Accumulation

1968   until 2012

Accumulation

Switzerland's 20th-century history could, in a nutshell, be described as an era of expansion—of population growth, economic development, and globalization, of a growing knowledge economy, of all-embracing digital connectivity, and of increasing personal prosperity and social stability. In this context, it's not surprising that the size of each individual's environmental footprint has continually increased. The story of the city and of its architecture has been one of an ongoing accumulation of artifacts, of permanent accretion. As places for producing goods—be they material or immaterial—cities have been particularly shaped by such accumulation. Together with the prevailing economic mechanisms, the spatial and atmospheric consequences of such growth and transformation processes have become increasingly detached from ideological and formal concepts of the city.

Architecture, wrote Aldo Rossi in his 1966 book *L'architettura della città*,[A] has always been "inseparable from civilized life and the society in which it is manifested." Seen in that light, the physical manifestations of architecture and planning across the past century in Switzerland give a decidedly unfavorable impression of the state of Swiss society. The built reality is, in no small way, a material translation of social and economic policies. The effects of accumulation on urban areas over time are even more immediately apparent in transitional zones and urban agglomerations, where, thanks to a culture of distance and delineation, the rational mechanisms of spatial development have, despite a phalanx of rules, regulations, and planning instruments aimed at imposing order, resulted in something entirely devoid of order, a random juxtaposition of different buildings and schemes that comes across as an ideology-free matter of fact. As Marc Angélil aptly puts it, there seems to be a connection between this pervasive desire to impose order and the amorphousness of what actually takes shape on the ground, the logic of rationality thus leading to irrational outcomes. The combination of ever-increasing complexity and loss of political control results in cities, or rather urbanization processes, that express disorder rather than order and dissimilarity rather than homogeneity. Thanks to what Colin Rowe and Fred Koetter call the "crisis of the object,"[B] the good and bad qualities of individual, self-contained buildings are further exaggerated and emphasized. We're all familiar with the periphery's chaotic miscellany of fragmented natural and agricultural landscapes, of old farmsteads, sewage works, and infrastructure facilities (shifted to the outskirts only to be reeled in again by urban sprawl), of sports complexes, used car dealers, and parking lots, of housing projects, industrial islands, shopping malls, and gas stations, of business parks, community garden plots, and more. Despite the indeterminate and seemingly random nature of this development, each site is governed by an invisible framework of rules and regulations. Genuine no-man's-land has long since ceased to exist. Nonetheless, it's these edgelands that offer scope for usages that can no longer be accommodated within the narrow confines of the "traditional" city. Ultimately, core and periphery are mutually dependent—because the one wouldn't be able to function properly without the other.

[A] Aldo Rossi *L'architettura della città*, Padua, 1966; English translation: *The Architecture of the City*, MIT Press, Cambridge, Massachusetts, 1982.

[B] Colin Rowe, Fred Koetter, *Collage City*, Cambridge, Massachusetts/London, 1978.

Accumulation

Mathias Müller / Daniel Niggli

How, where, why, and to what extent different forces influence the generation of urban realm is not something that's easily disentangled, but one thing is at least fairly certain: new urban architecture is rarely developed on a blank canvas. Every built intervention has to be measured against what is already there. With their attempts to set themselves apart from what had gone before, and their demands for societal reform, the pioneers of early 20th-century modernism aimed to achieve a radical break from the past and a complete reprogramming of society via a new "grand narrative." That their vision failed was due in part to its inability to embrace simultaneity, to allow things to exist side by side or on top of each other. Instead, the new had to replace the old; in other words, it was either/or. In Andre Corboz's *The Land as Palimpsest*, the city is defined as a place of collective memory where events and artifacts accumulate in layers. In this interpretation, past and present always exist in parallel. A palimpsest is inherently accretive; in other words, it is multi-layered, allowing things to exist on top of each other at the same time.

The inescapable reality of our ever-expanding accumulations of physical things, especially in urban agglomerations, can hardly be addressed via a tabula rasa approach, via an attempt to superimpose a new (or rather an old) holistic vision of an ideal city. Instead, there needs to be a change in culture, a shift away from distance towards proximity, from homogenization towards differentiation, and from separateness towards togetherness. Instead of implanting concepts imported from elsewhere, we need to focus on solutions that utilize and emphasize the undervalued or hidden qualities these places already possess. The existing fabric itself would then form the starting point for transformations. In a city of parallel realities, we need to ensure morphological and typological structures (be they built or unbuilt) are flexible, robust, and resilient in concept so that they will be able to cope with future changes of use. Alternatively they could, contrarily, be made temporary, transient, agile, and almost entirely usage-orientated. Both approaches can act as catalysts, opening up space for appropriation—especially when it comes to the kinds of usages which the urban core can no longer accommodate. The issue of flexible versus specific, or of how much control one is willing to cede, would thus need to be considered at every level—from urban design plans to architectural details.

1 ↑   2 ↓ 3 →

4 ↑

5 ↓

↑ 6

7 ↑   ↑ 8

9 ↑ 10 ↓   11 ↓   12 →

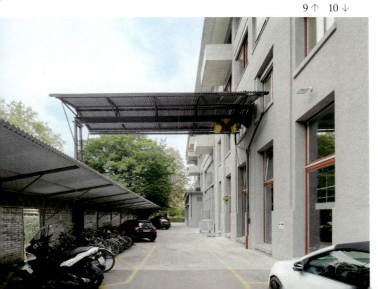

13 ↑   ↓ 14

Appropriability

Mathias Müller, Daniel Niggli

Here, at last, were the premises they'd been seeking for so long. The spaces were nicely aged but in full working order. One and a half stories high, the main hall is vast in depth yet bright throughout, thanks to glass rooflights overhead. The last bits of machinery had already been dismantled and removed by a team of mechanics, the linden-green metal lockers sold off for bargain prices. Only the large hand-wash fountains remained unsold, standing like reverential relics in the high, light-filled space, which smelled vaguely of metal and lubricating oil. The patchwork of floor coverings, the trolley hoist hanging uselessly from an overhead beam, and the Playmate calendar affixed to a riveted steel pillar are the sole clues to the space's previous usage as a mechanical engineering workshop.

Large folding doors in the façade promise easy entry and good access for deliveries. The insertion of a few plasterboard walls would enable the huge space to be divided up into smaller studio spaces to allow each tenant to fit out their own area as they wish.

The hard concrete floor retains traces of the premises' previous usage, such as the odd protruding screw where the large milling machines and lathes once stood. Once these have been cut away, the floor could be either left as it is or coated with two-component paint to help it stay dust-free. Large bundles of cables hanging from the cable trays between the pillars suggest electricity is already connected, likewise the still serviceable fluorescent lamps. The space itself has no running water, but there are lavatories from where water could be fed to the individual units, while wastewater could be fed away via the channel running down the center of the floor. The latter's asphalt is still in good condition, so opening it up to plant greenery would make little sense. Instead, the large metal canisters rusting away in the glass-roofed porch could be filled with soil and planted with shrubs, climbing plants, and vegetables. Perhaps within a few months, the once rather dreary courtyard will have been transformed into an attractive oasis; maybe the new tenants' logos and names will have been painted straight onto the whitewashed brick façade and a large lettered logo sprayed at the most prominent corner by a graffiti artist friend. In short: this place is ripe for appropriation, for sparing interventions to blend with the existing fabric and create a wonderful mix of old and new.

Three years on, the place has indeed been filled with new life. Long ropes hang from the metal girders, the floor is laid with thick mats—a children's circus is rehearsing its latest number in the main hall. In the adjacent building, discarded cable drums are being transformed into all manner of furniture, while students have rented the upstairs space and made it into a shared studio. Some of the halls serve as storage space, others are still empty. There are plans to turn the largest of them into an event venue; a free church intends to use it for mass worship on weekends. The easiest to convert are, of course, the vertically stacked, well-lit, heated offices where the engineering and admin departments were once housed. Now they provide workspaces for filmmakers, building services planners, designers, engineers, and freelance journalists. A design school, too, has rented studio spaces for its students. In the midst of this lively mix of new usages is the old canteen, where a group is trialing a new restaurant concept. The interior is almost unchanged, calling to mind the time when hundreds of overalled workers would sit down to eat the same set menu. Now there's a selection of soups and salads on offer, as well as coffee and cakes. In summer, barbecues and parties are held outside amidst improvised planters made from old oil drums.

Toni Campus: Interim Use

1 ↑

↓ 2

3 ↑

4 ↑   ↓ 5

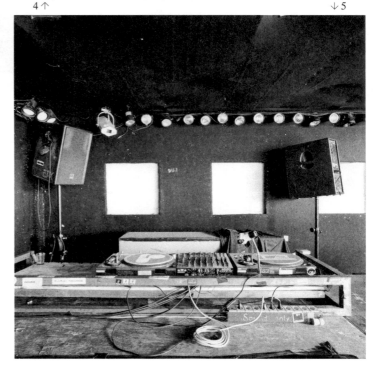

1–26
For decades, the vast chromium-steel-clad colossus of the Toni dairy was a Zurich landmark, an unmissable feature of what was then the urban periphery on the edges of District 5. With its expressive high-rise and low-rise volumes, its chimney, delivery ramp, and Toni logo, it was an everyday icon that the city's youth soon took to its heart. After the dairy group's bankruptcy, the site saw a number of years of interim use. These different usages showcased the potential of its spectacular spaces, with techno parties and other leisure activities introducing new generations of Zurichers to the site. The roof was transformed into the techno club's garden, the high-rise section played host to pursuits such as beach volleyball and indoor climbing, and the large spaces of the low-rise section were regularly reimagined to accommodate exhibitions and other events.

1–5
The site's three nightclubs—Toni-Molkerei, Dachkantine, and Rohstofflager—were fixtures of Zurich's nightlife scene for many years.

Toni Campus: Interim Use

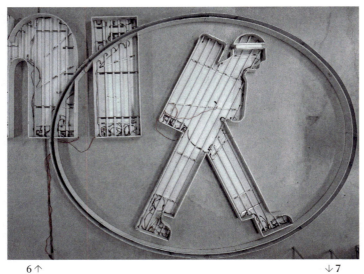

6 ↑

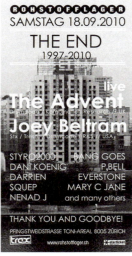

↓ 7

8 ↑

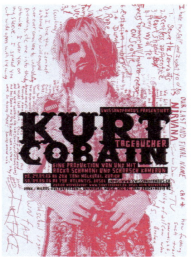

↓ 9

10 ↑ ↓ 11

6–11
New usages co-opted the dairy's history and its charming dairyman logo.

Toni Campus: Interim Use

12

12, 14 + 15
Nightclub Toni-Molkerei, in what was the truck repair shop.

13
Dachkantine nightclub. Music festival m4music.

14 ↑

13

↓ 15

Toni Campus: Interim Use

16

17 ↑   ↓ 18

19   ↓ 20

21

Toni Campus: Interim Use

22

23

16
Tutanchamun exhibition.

17
Premises of the beach volleyball club, beachers.ch.

18 + 19
Exhibition of work by Zurich University of the Arts students.

20
Nightclub Toni-Molkerei.

21 + 23
Stella Fashion Night.

22
Filming of *Pepperminta* by Pipilotti Rist.

24
Performance of *Medeamalika*, adapted from Euripides.

24

The City in Parcels

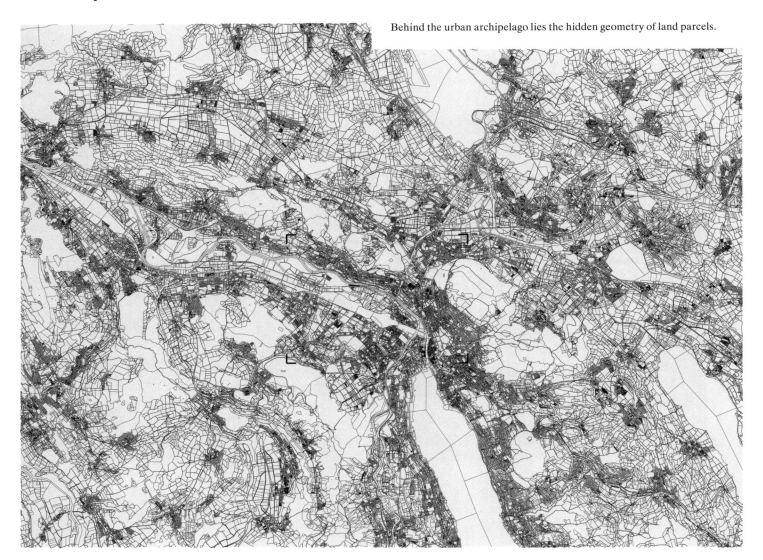

Behind the urban archipelago lies the hidden geometry of land parcels.

Political boundaries and ownership patterns have a formative influence on the city.

The City in Parcels

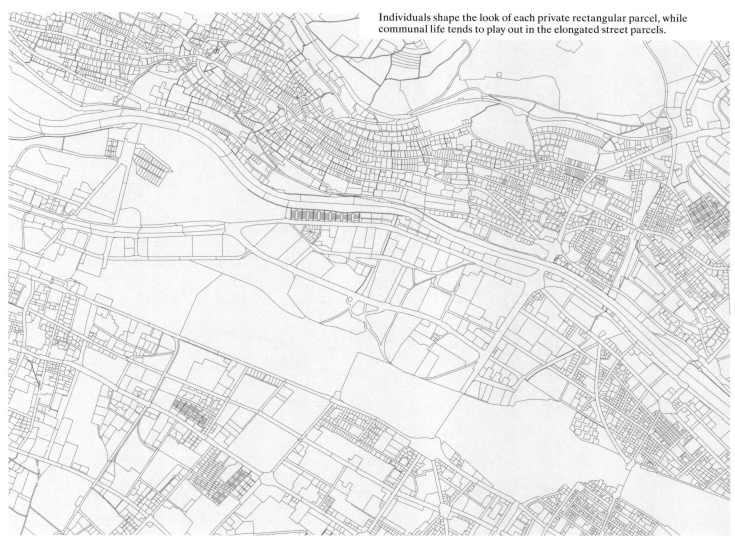

Individuals shape the look of each private rectangular parcel, while communal life tends to play out in the elongated street parcels.

The parcels' unseen dividing lines influence the scale, grain, and form of their buildings.

The City in Parcels

94

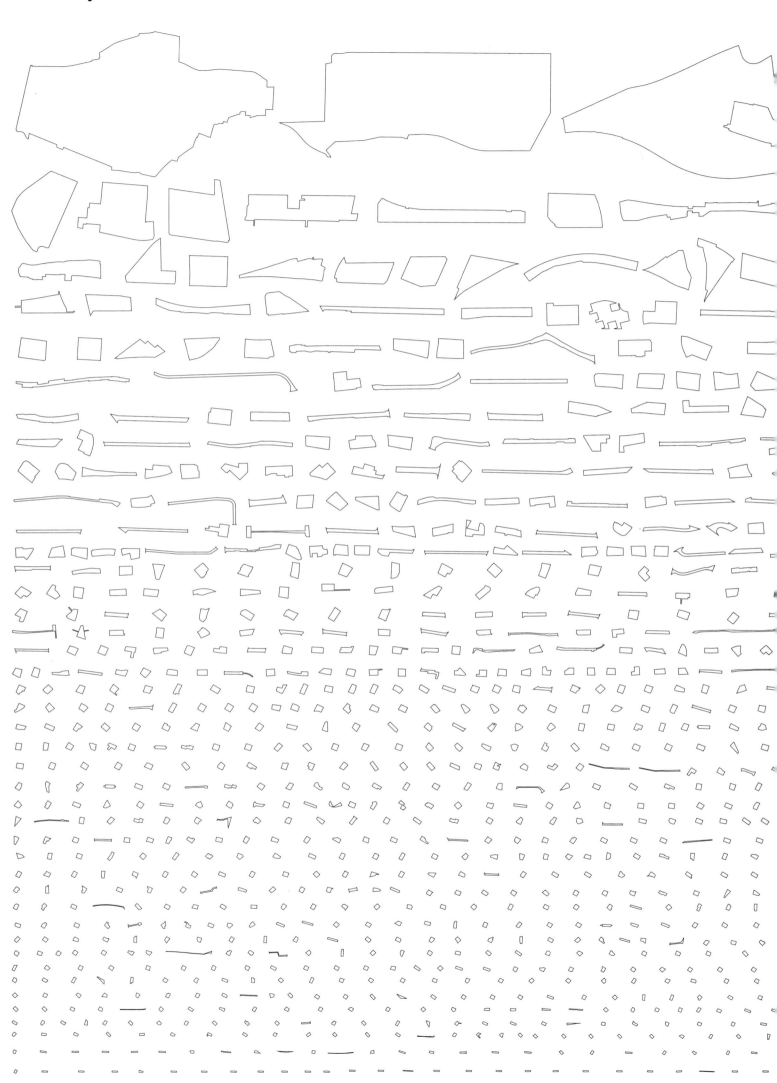

The City in Parcels

↓ Parcels by shape

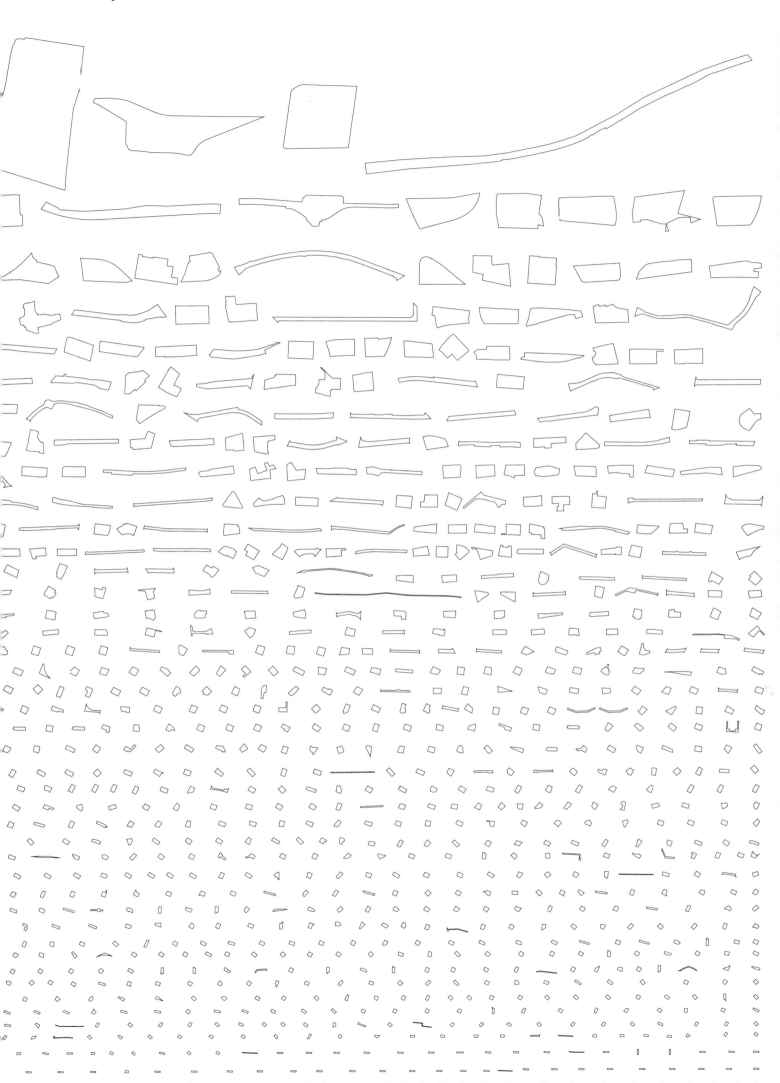

Viaduct Arches

← 1   ↑ 2

3

4

1–4
When the viaduct brought railroad infrastructure to the city's outskirts, the city had yet to catch up. But its designers, unlike those behind many of today's infrastructural works, took their role as urban trailblazers seriously. The carefully chosen materiality—blocks of cut stone for areas where perimeter developments were planned and openwork steel bridges for where roads would go—anticipated the urban growth that was still to come and helped to predetermine the cityscape.

5
Completed around the turn of the century, the new structure greatly impressed the citizenry, stacking lines at different heights and thereby creating its own kind of urban poetry. Up on the viaduct, passengers could look down on the streets as the trains seemingly traveled through and over the city, offering up new urbanistic perspectives. Color lithograph by Otto Baumberger, 1918.

6
In the Middle Ages, the amphitheater at Arles was completely built over and repurposed. The town shrank and retreated to within the boundaries of the ancient edifice, reinterpreting it as a novel urban form. A Roman ruin thus provided the skeleton for a new organism. The amphitheater in the 18th century, engraving by Jean Baptiste Guibert.

5

Viaduct Arches

6

7

8

Over time, the voids of the viaduct became home to enterprises such as construction industry, storage facilities, auto repair shops, and other operations that didn't fit into or had been pushed out of areas with traditional perimeter development.

7–9

As District 5 metamorphosed from a working-class neighborhood to a nightlife hotspot, a restaurant, shops, and clubs also moved into the arches. Traces of these interim usages, such as paint, fragments of fascia board, and graffitied pillars, accumulated around the arches.

10 →

The Letten viaduct's combined foot and bike path provides a new kind of elevated public space, offering a different perspective on the neighborhoods it passes through. This novel active-travel route links up previously unconnected places, leading from the Oberer Letten lido across the Limmat river to the Josefwiese park, and could, in future, perhaps be extended across the swathe of railroad tracks and on into District 4. Numerous access points connect the path with the street level below.

8

9

Viaduct Arches 100 ↓10

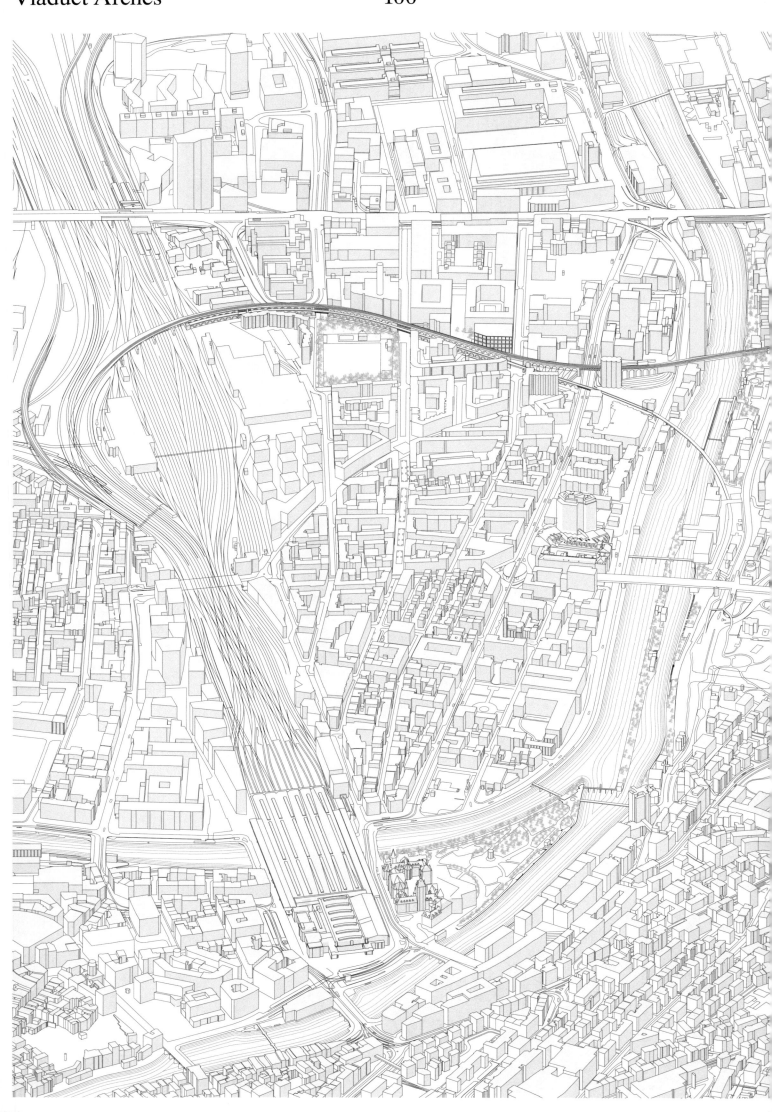

Viaduct Arches

Viaduct Arches

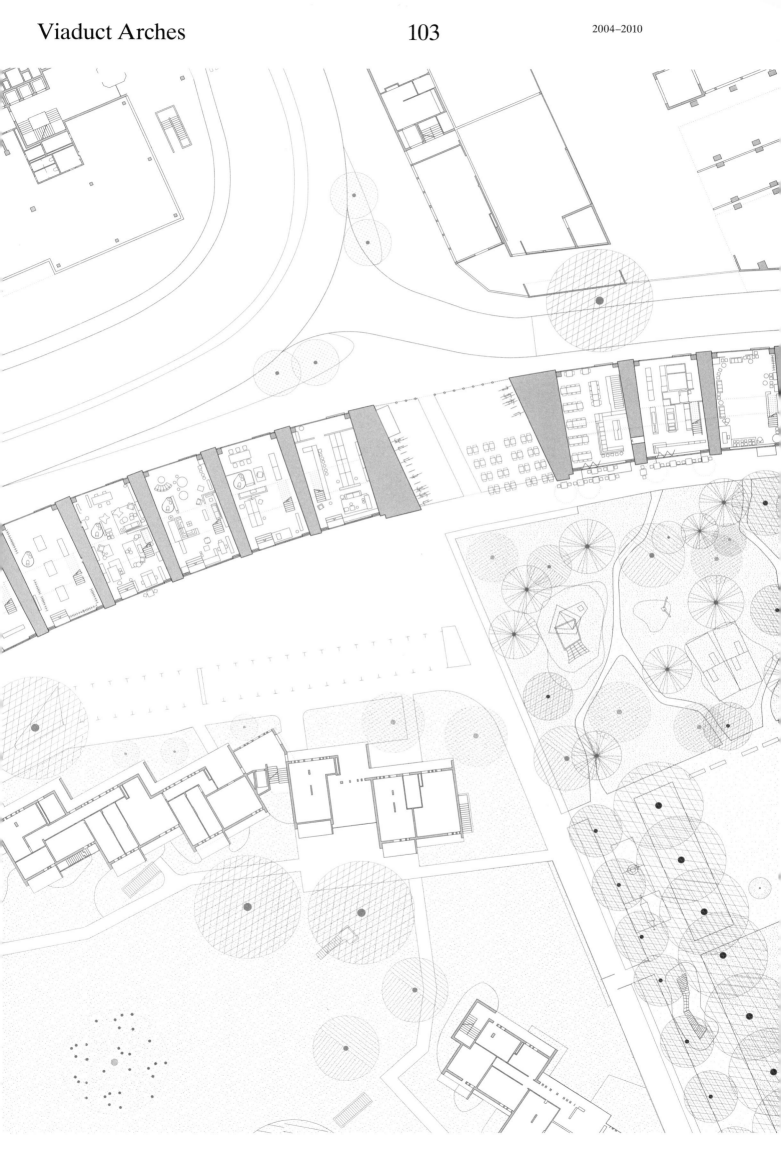

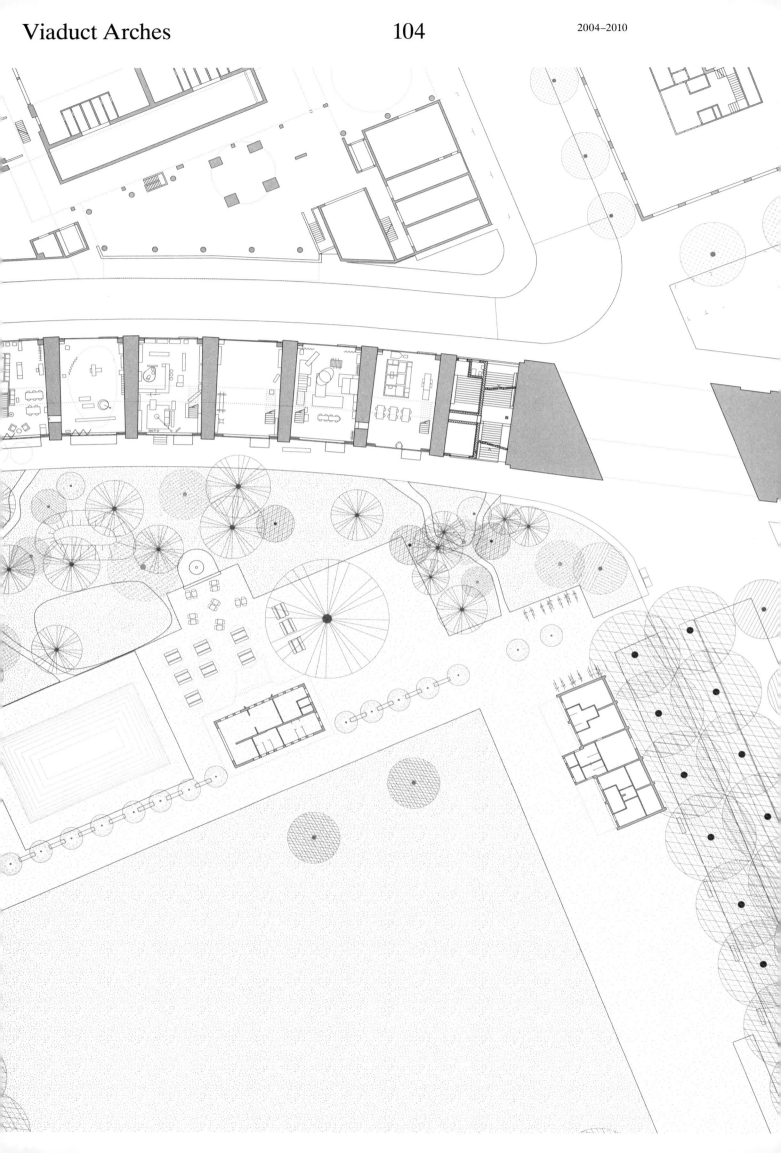

Viaduct Arches

Viaduct Arches

Viaduct Arches

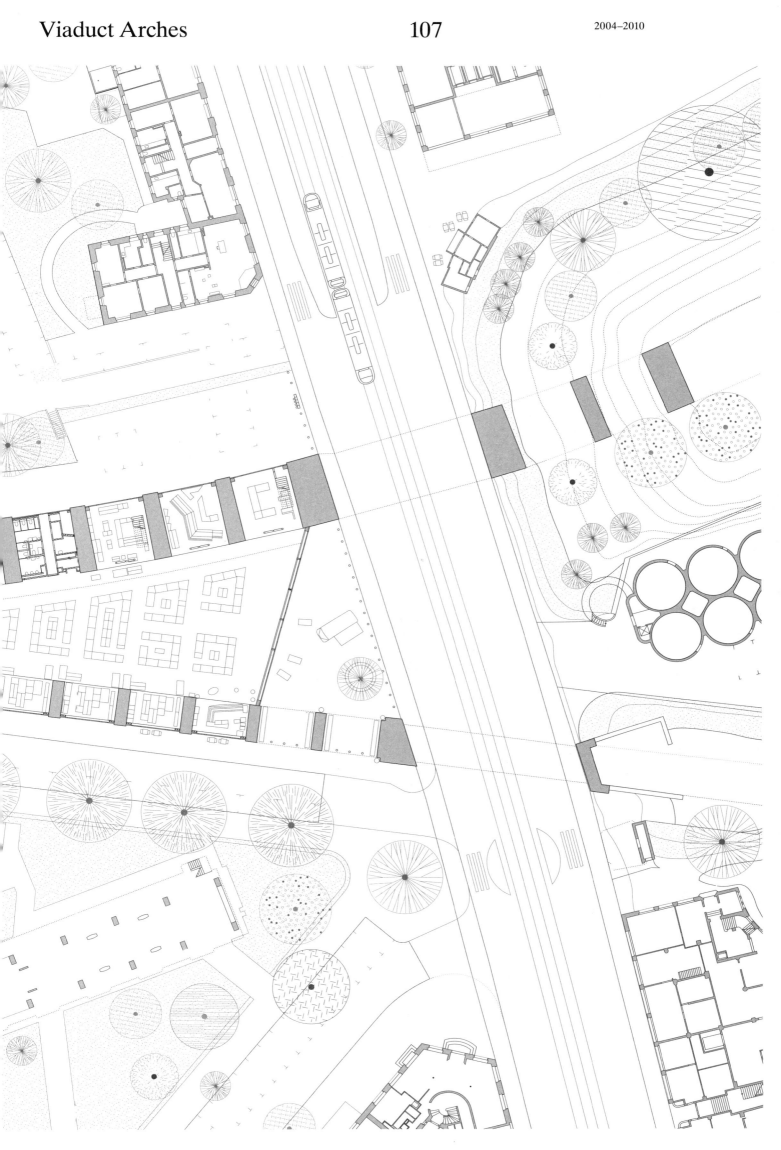

Viaduct Arches

12 ↑   ↓ 13

Viaduct Arches

Viaduct Arches

Viaduct Arches

11, 15 + 16
At Limmatstrasse, the routes of the Wipkingen and Letten viaducts diverge, forming a triangular urban space previously used by a building firm. The competition brief left it to participating practices to decide what kind of activity should take place on the site. We proposed building a market hall, devising a complex, wide-span, folded-plate roof structure that follows the logic and geometry of the two viaducts' arcs.

← 12 + 13
Adjacent to Josefwiese, a park-like buffer zone was added. Based on a design by landscape architects Schweingruber Zulauf, it features a children's playground, a barbecue area, and a public lawn.

14
The line across the Letten viaduct is no longer in use, allowing it to be sealed and insulated from above. The Wipkingen viaduct remains operational, however, so the same couldn't be done here. As a result, some of the rainwater that filters through the trackbed's gravel could potentially still run down the pillars. In each arch unit, the pillars were thus equipped with twin rain channels, allowing rainwater escaping from the stonework to drain away.

17
New elements feature restrained colors and leave the stone walls intact.

18 + 19
The understated backdrop of old arches and new elements allows the shop designs and window displays to stand out.

Viaduct Arches

20 ↑

↓ 21

22 ↑

↓ 23

Viaduct Arches

24

20
Even the nooks beneath the new path's access points provide interesting spaces that can be meaningfully used.

22
The surfaces' simple and honest materiality can handle their sometimes rather unceremonious appropriation by taggers and sprayers.

21 + 23
The new path is connected to the street level via numerous access points

24
The roof of the market hall echoes the rhythms of the two viaducts and translates them into a series of folded plates that perform structural functions, regulate runoff, and illuminate the hall via large skylights.

25 →
The varied usages create a vibrant, multifaceted vibe and ensure life spills out into the neighborhood at different times of day.

Viaduct Arches

Infrastructural Buildings

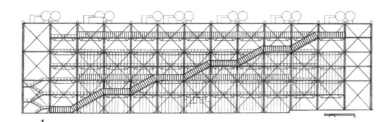

According to conventional readings of urban design, infrastructure is the framework around which buildings can be built—in other words, it's an autonomous domain, one comprising roads and other transport infrastructure, utilities of all kinds, and open spaces such as parks. Without this basic framework, no city would be able to function and no architecture could be produced. On industrial sites, however, this traditional distinction between infrastructure and buildings is often blurred—indeed, it can be hard to precisely distinguish between infrastructure and buildings. The boundaries between buildings and delivery ramps, bridge structures, covered outdoor facilities, circulation areas, and so on are fluid; buildings and infrastructure merge into one. Conversely, buildings are also often infrastructural in concept. They feature both actively operative elements and areas as well as passively used spaces. The facilities' spatial and structural design allows usages to be relocated and buildings to be subdivided or vertically and horizontally extended, while the utility infrastructure can grow or shrink without rendering buildings obsolete. The underlying systems, in other words, are exceptionally efficient and adaptable. If, meanwhile, new production methods and technologies lead, as is hoped, to a reindustrialization of the economy ("Industry 4.0"), then the city could conceivably be viewed as a locus of production once more. This would, however, require new structures and urban spaces with a similar potential for appropriation and identification as those created in the industrial age—what Aldo Rossi might have called infrastructural monuments. Such typologies would oscillate between building and infrastructure, evolving from the DNA of existing typologies in a kind of genetic recombination process. The resulting self-confident architecture would boast a high degree of elasticity, offering scope for diverse usages, be it for work, production, or even homes. As incubators of hybrid usages, these prototypologies would in turn influence the wider urban context.

1
Piano and Rogers's 1977 design for the Centre Pompidou interpreted the museum as an industrial shelf stack with lofty 7-meter-high ceilings. Circulation elements and mechanical services were left exposed on the outside to allow for freely configurable spaces inside.

2
Tattersall in Charlottenburg, Berlin: multistory building for the stabling of riding and driving horses. Photo: Willy Römer, 1910.

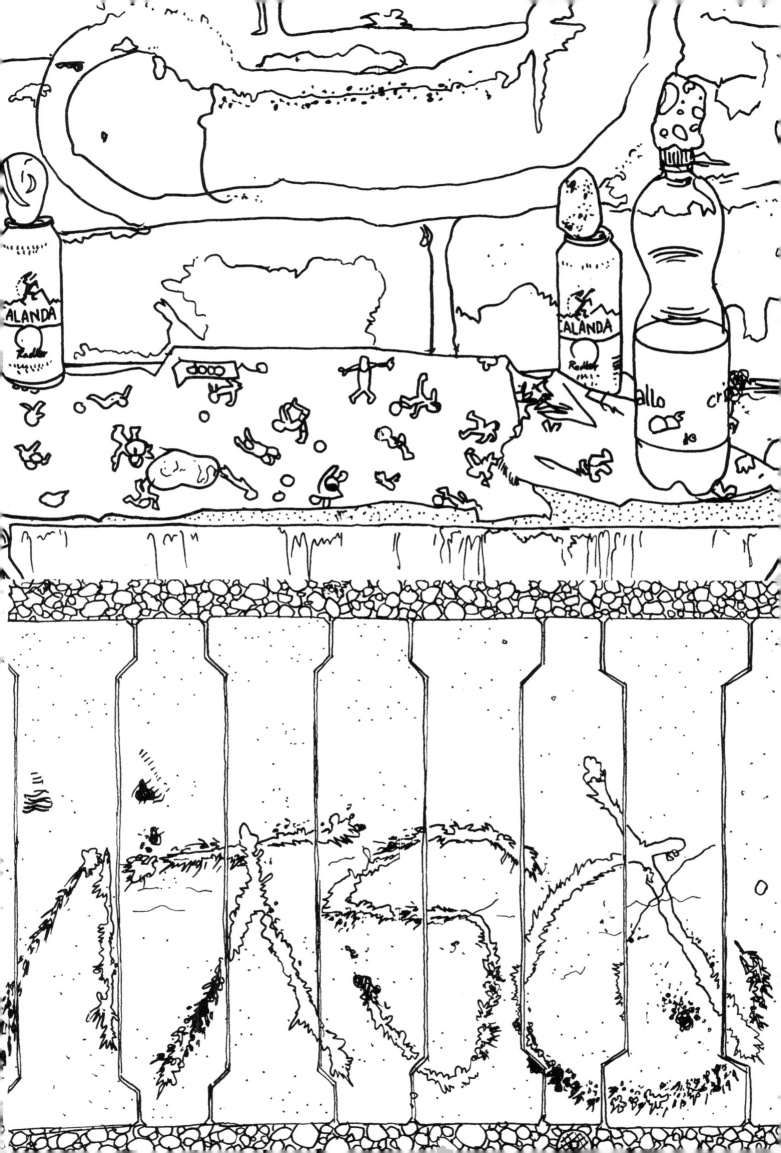

Prototypology and Learning from What's There

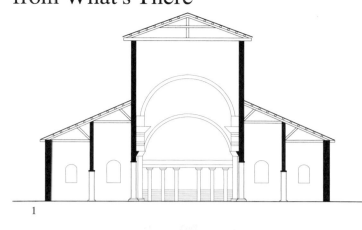

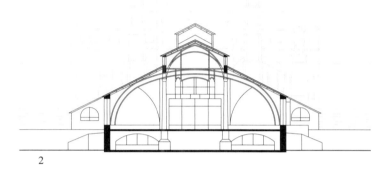

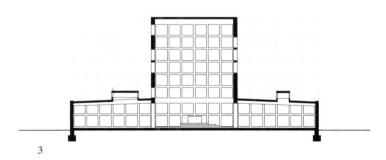

1
Built during the Constantinian shift, St. Peter's Basilica took the typology of Roman basilicas and translated it into a church. Recreated section of the old St. Peter's Basilica, Rome.

2
Later the basilica served as a typological template for the industrial age's factory halls, allowing for spaces with large spans. Section of the Sayner Hütte foundry, Heinrich Daniel Jacobi, 1830.

3
The basilica typology—complete with the design language acquired via its industrial appropriation—is then retranslated into contemporary religious architecture. Church of St. Antonius, Essen, Rudolf Schwarz, 1959.

How do new typologies arise? It's generally accepted that new functional requirements, innovations in building technology, and specific building regulations can all lead to the development of novel typologies. But we far less frequently consider that typological innovation can also result from the staying power and limitations of the built fabric. When an awkward existing building thwarts a particular usage, it can lead to a loosening or reassessment of the straitjacket of established functional, spatial, and typological definitions. The result is a scenario in which it's no longer just about imposing a predefined solution, but about finding out what usages can actually be realized within the existing fabric. Such situations can give rise not only to previously unknown forms of usage but also to new typologies. A prime example is the way vacant factory buildings in New York's Gridiron District were turned into artists' studios in the 1960s, and then later converted into loft apartments. The wide expanses of these factory floors prompted an open-plan live/work interior style that quickly gained popularity as an expression of hip urban living. Before long, this new typology of loft apartments, of vertically stacked, high-ceilinged open spaces furnished with standalone pieces, was establishing itself as a design principle in its own right, influencing not just industrial conversions but new-build developments too. The original concept of open-plan loft living, which arose as a response to the specific circumstances of the Gridiron's factory spaces, the dimensions of which were not conducive to conventional floor plans, ultimately mutated into a globally applicable new-build typology associated with a particular lifestyle. This practice of learning from what's there is not uncommon in architecture—think of how the basilica typology of Roman market halls was applied to early Christian hall churches, or how the Hagia Sophia was converted from a Christian to a Muslim place of worship, the addition of minarets to a central dome creating a new and hitherto unknown style of mosque that then spread around the globe. With their broad spans and generous floor plans, basilicas also inspired some of the early 19th century's first industrial buildings, such as the Sayner Hütte foundry in Bensdorf, establishing a spatial and structural template that was adopted almost unchanged for subsequent new forms of industrial production. In the 20th century, Rudolf Schwarz's industrial-look basilica—the church of St. Antonius in Essen—then brought this process of structural transformation and atmospheric translation full circle. If we want to cultivate new typologies in order to find solutions to today's spatial requirements, it might therefore sometimes be worthwhile experimenting with the insertion of conventional usages into ill-suited spatial containers. Ideally, this kind of experimental conversion would allow us to learn from what's there, a process you might call anti-functionalist design.

1
The transfer of typologies and architectural elements played a key role in the design of industrial breweries too. For the new Brauerei Feldschlösschen building (1882–1902), a sober-looking former aniline works was transformed via castle-style additions and alterations into a factory-cum-fortress.

Hürlimann Brewery

2

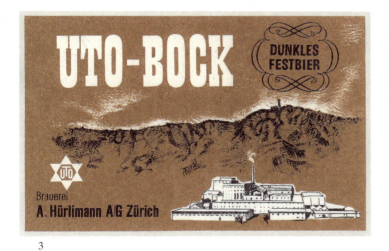

3

2 + 3
Brewery buildings have often been used for branding purposes, sometimes even appearing on labels. In the case of Brauerei Hürlimann, a functional brewery complex was represented as a medieval fortress perched on a hill.

4
As in many breweries, the production process was vertically organized. Spring water and raw materials were stored in upright tanks high above the ground, and the malting and brewing processes were gravity-assisted. Extensive cellar vaults within the hillside were used to store the finished product. The filled beer barrels were rolled down a tunnel leading from the vaults to the brewery's own loading station, then distributed by rail and horse-drawn cart. The Hürlimann complex is thus a reflection of the production processes it housed: vertical storage and brewing, underground storage, and ground-level logistics. External form followed internal function, though the prominent hilltop location meant the brewery was also a highly visible urban landmark.

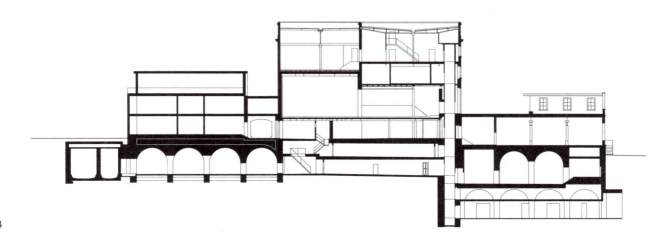

4

Hürlimann Brewery

2004

For the planned conversion of the old Hürlimann brewery into a thermal spa, we took our cue from the existing building's imposing, contrasting, and highly atmospheric spaces, which still had a great story to tell. What if you filled these spaces with water, thus creating a new kind of vertical spa? Our proposal echoed the vertical brewing process, but reversed the order so that the journey would go from bottom to top. Compared with conventional spas, a vertical thermal spa offers a completely different spatial experience; here, water is an omnipresent element, cascading, flowing, and tumbling throughout the building.

5 + 6
The existing spaces formed the starting point for the design of the spa experience, with the brewery's vertical arrangement inspiring the typological innovation of a vertical spa.

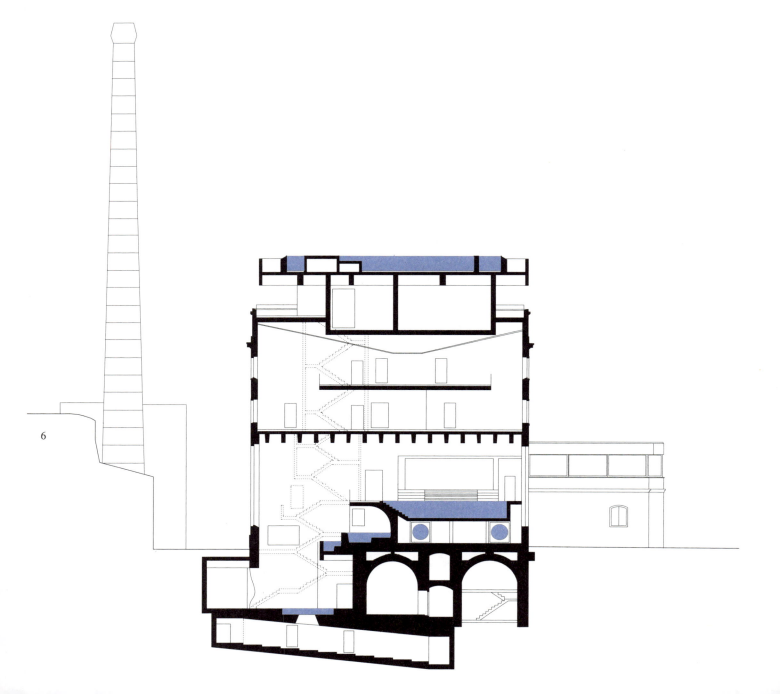

Alpine Bath Montafon

7 + 8
The vertical spa experience was also the typological principle behind the Alpenbad Montafon proposal, which envisioned a wellness spa that would rise upwards and thus communicate directly with the surrounding mountains.

This vertically organized spa concept inspired by the historic fabric later came into its own in our design for the Alpine Bath Montafon. Although there would have been sufficient space to develop the scheme horizontally, we opted to stack the various spa areas in a compact tower arrangement. Our proposal juxtaposed the mountainous Montafon backdrop with a kind of hollowed-out rock that, rather like an old castle keep, would offer up new secrets at every turn. The design comprises a large open-plan space above which the various baths and saunas are hewn into a solidly built volume like caves into rock. The diversity of the different spa areas results in highly divergent spatial figures that join together to create a *promenade architecturale*.

This recasting of a prototypology demonstrates how the superimposition of a functionally defined assignment on a spatially specific existing building can result in a new spatial concept, a new typological pattern that can subsequently be applied to a completely different site. Such a prototypological practice thus takes spatial and organizational innovations from particular conversion projects and applies them in the design of new-build projects.

Hürlimann Brewery

130

2004

9
The axonometries for each project show how the vertical arrangement produced similar yet distinctly different results in each case. With the Hürlimann brewery project, half of the spa area was to be housed in the underground vaults. Guests would be guided upwards through a massy volume, from which they could access the landings of the cascading staircase. The spa experience would then end at a rooftop pool offering panoramic views of Zurich.

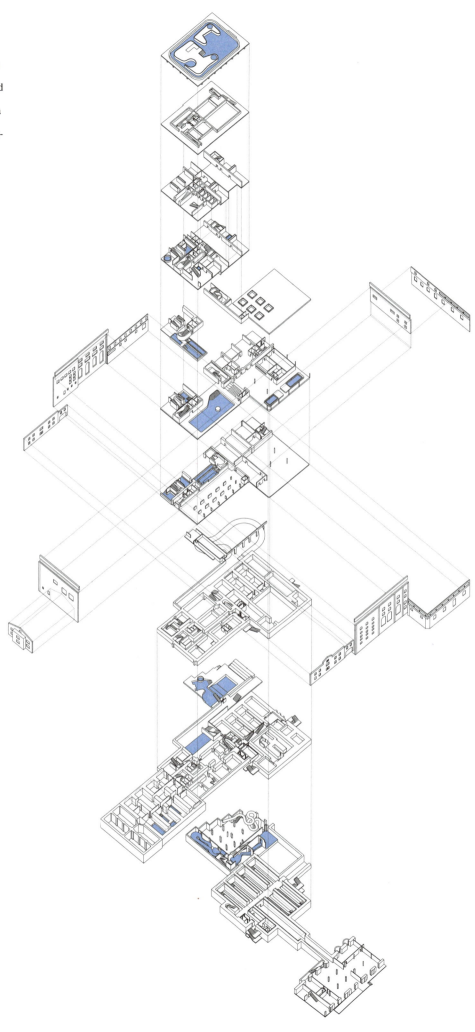

Alpine Bath Montafon

131

2006

10
Unlike the Hürlimann brewery project from which it took its cue, the spa in Schruns was, with the exception of the locker rooms, to be entirely above ground. Here, our proposal contrasted a vertically stacked wellness spa with a horizontally arranged entrance area and family spa, the latter opening up to the outdoor area. With its cave-like spaces and sprinkling of carefully placed openings, the vertical wellness spa was designed to converse with the surrounding mountains.

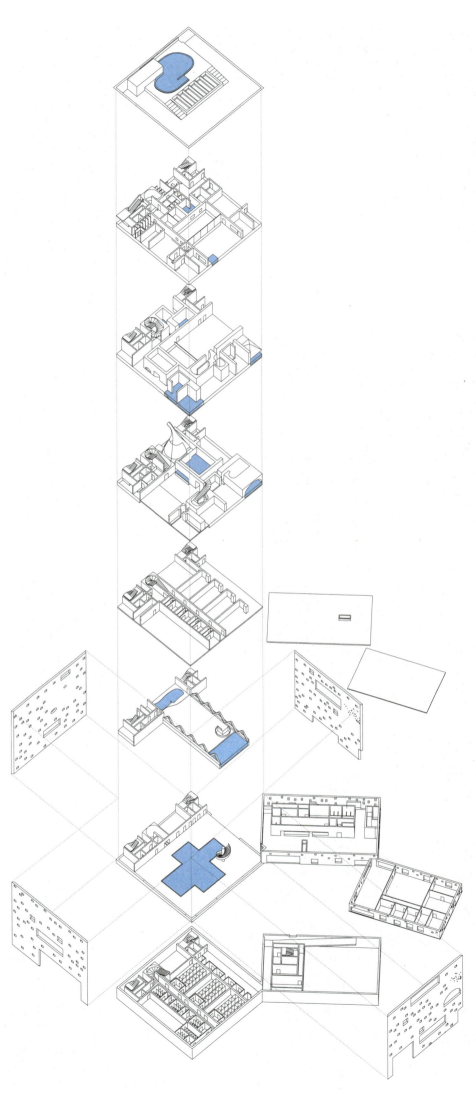

Hürlimann Brewery 132 2004

11 ↑   ↓ 12

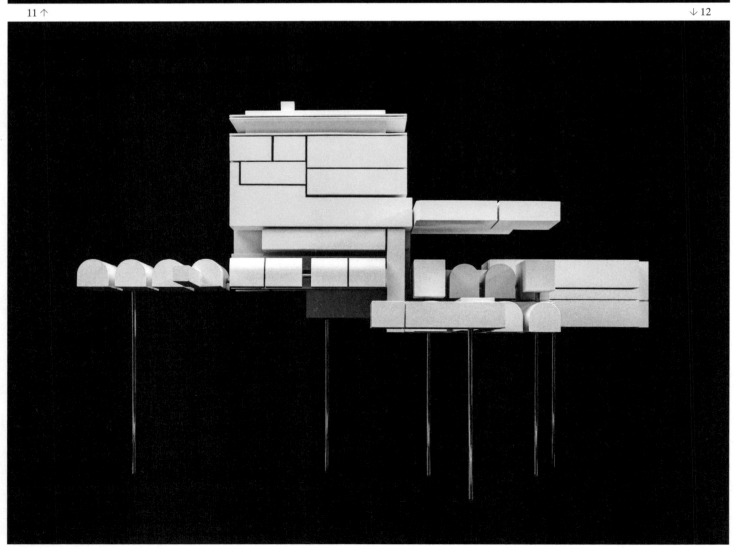

Alpine Bath Montafon

2006

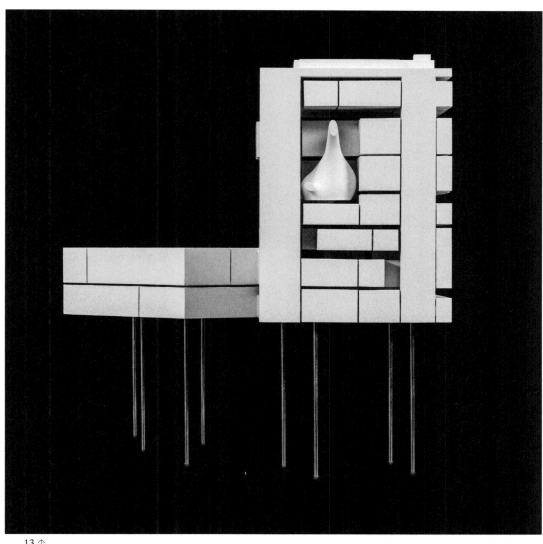

11–14
The prototypological evolution outlined here shows how the combination of a spatially defined existing building with a functionally specific assignment can produce a whole new typology. This can then be applied in a different context or at a different site. Such a prototypological practice results in typological innovations that can also prove effective in completely different and even generic contexts.

13 ↑   ↓ 14

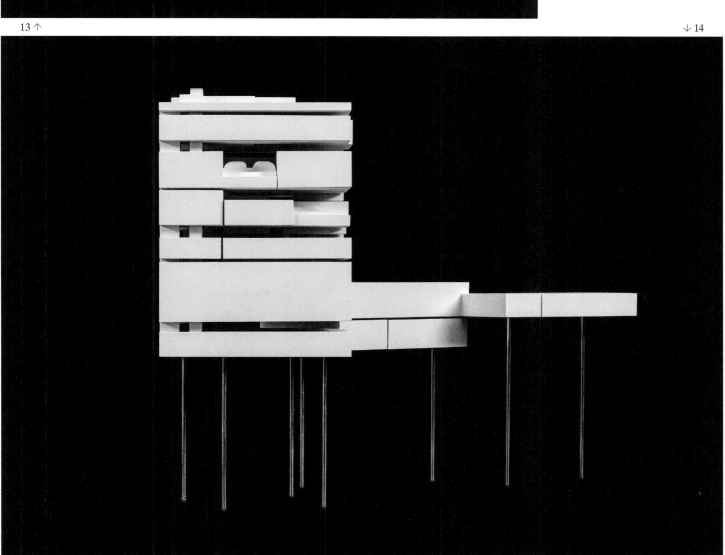

Zellweger Luwa Site

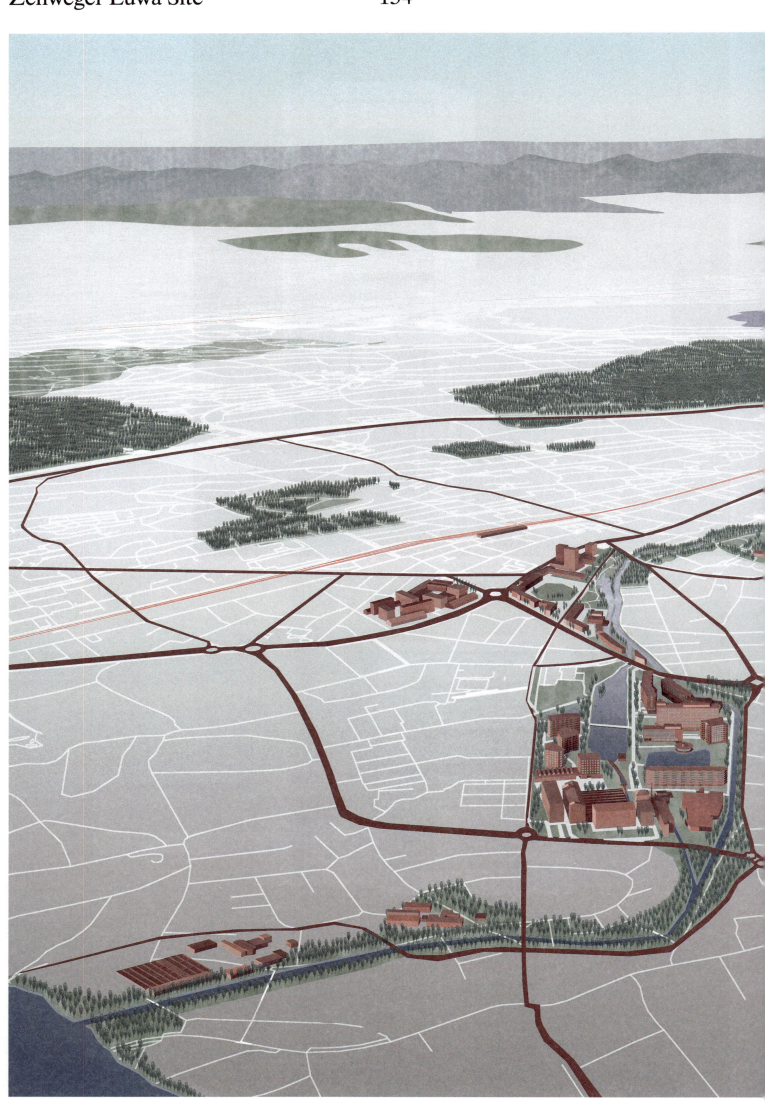

2 ↑   ↓ 3

Zellweger Luwa Site

2005–2021

1–3
The Zellweger Luwa Site runs alongside the Aabach river in Uster in the canton of Zurich. From 1820 on, the harnessing of water power on this 11-kilometer-long waterway transformed it into a center of Swiss cotton manufacturing within just a few years. Today, the place is a verdant idyll, thanks to the surviving millponds and an impressive array of mature trees.

4
By the late 18th century, the energy of the Aabach was already being used to power the Niederuster mill.

5
Development of the Zellweger Luwa Site was then kick-started in 1842, when industrialist Heinrich Kunz built his first large-scale spinning mill.

6
Kunz started off with one artificial pond and a network of channels, but gradually expanded these until eventually a trio of ponds and an extensive system of channels defined the site.

7
In 1925, Zellweger Uster AG—which would go on to become a world-leading manufacturer of textile machinery and industrial electrical engineering solutions—moved its operations to what had been Kunz's spinning mill. In 1961, it had a new headquarters built by Zurich-based architect Roland Rohn, along with an exhibition pavilion in the middle of the Herterweiher pond. In 1993, the company merged with Luwa AG to form Zellweger Luwa AG, the control and measurement systems division of which was spun off in 2003 and renamed Uster Technologies AG. A world leader in textile quality control systems, the latter is still based on the campus, though the wider site has been redeveloped by Zellweger Park AG. Following that redevelopment, which began in 2005, the site now features a mix of residential and commercial usages.

8
An aerial view shows the extent to which the Zellweger campus, with its strong identity and prominent appearance, differs from the fine-grain settlement pattern of its surroundings. Its expanses of water and numerous trees create a dreamy, park-like atmosphere, while the diverse structures make for a distinctive place that is characterized by large-scale forms. The juxtaposition of pavilions, industrial sheds, slab blocks, towers, and other striking typologies adds interest and variety.

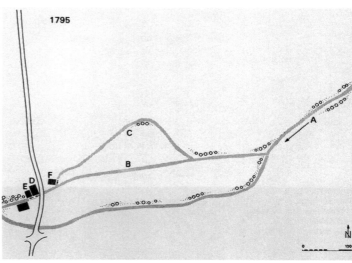

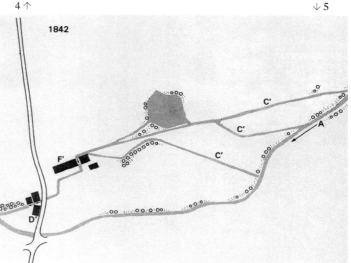

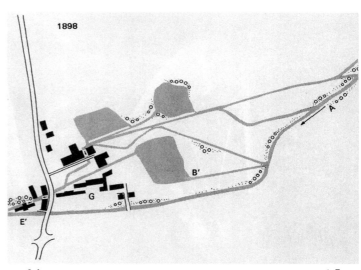

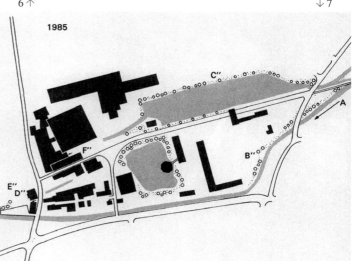

Zellweger Luwa Site

9

10

11

9
Roland Rohn's striking designs emphasized the global aspirations of Zellweger Luwa AG. Rohn translated the watery landscape, originally developed solely for the purposes of energy generation, into a picturesque backdrop, siting his buildings so as to produce deliberate reflections in the Herterweiher pond.

10
Water power is still a feature of the site, thanks to a small hydroelectric power plant.

11
The muscular typologies of former factory buildings shape the face of the campus, where manufacturing and service industries retain a strong presence.

12
The arrangement of island lots within verdant surroundings echoes the island-in-an-island character of existing industrial sites along the Aabach river. The various lots each have their own distinct feel and morphology, while specific frameworks and site parameters define their respective developments. In contrast to conventional planning processes, there is stricter regulation of the lots' external relationships than of their internal relationships.

Zellweger Luwa Site

2005–2021

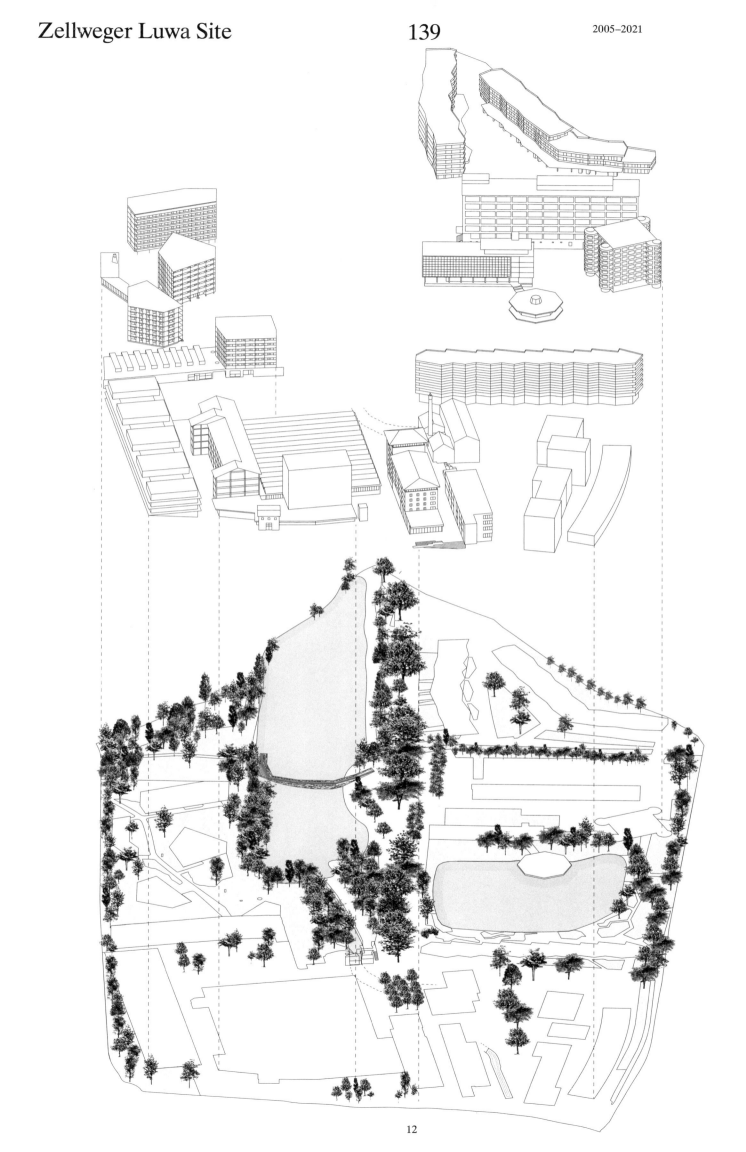

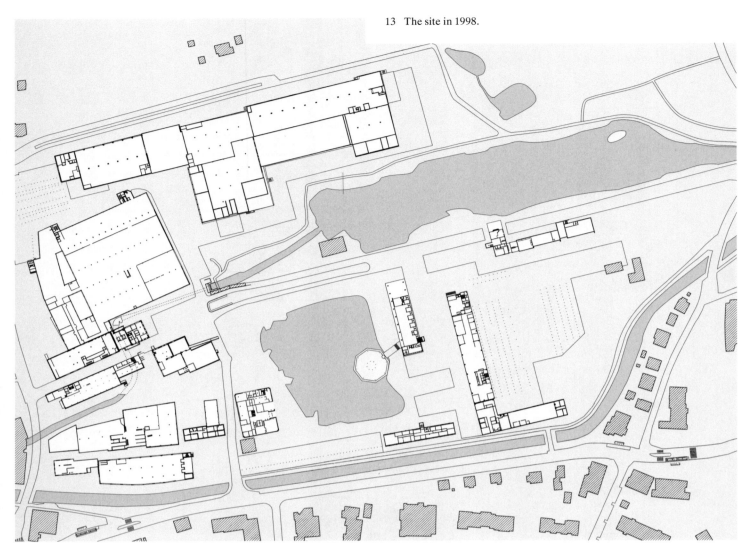

13   The site in 1998.

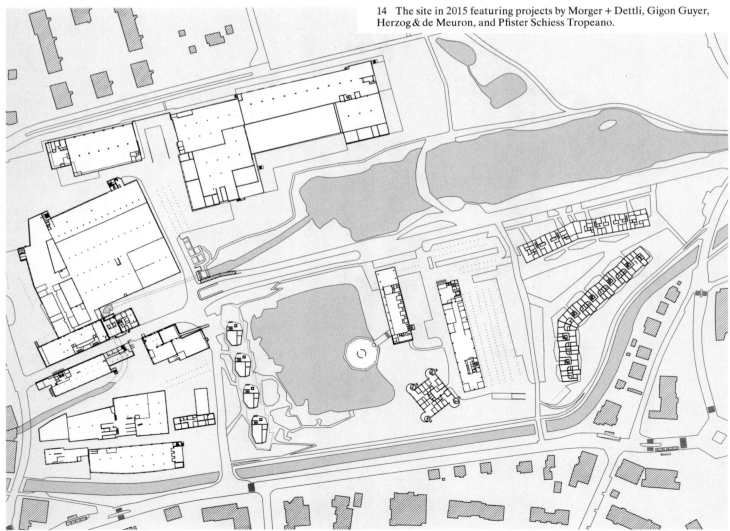

14   The site in 2015 featuring projects by Morger + Dettli, Gigon Guyer, Herzog & de Meuron, and Pfister Schiess Tropeano.

Zellweger Luwa Site

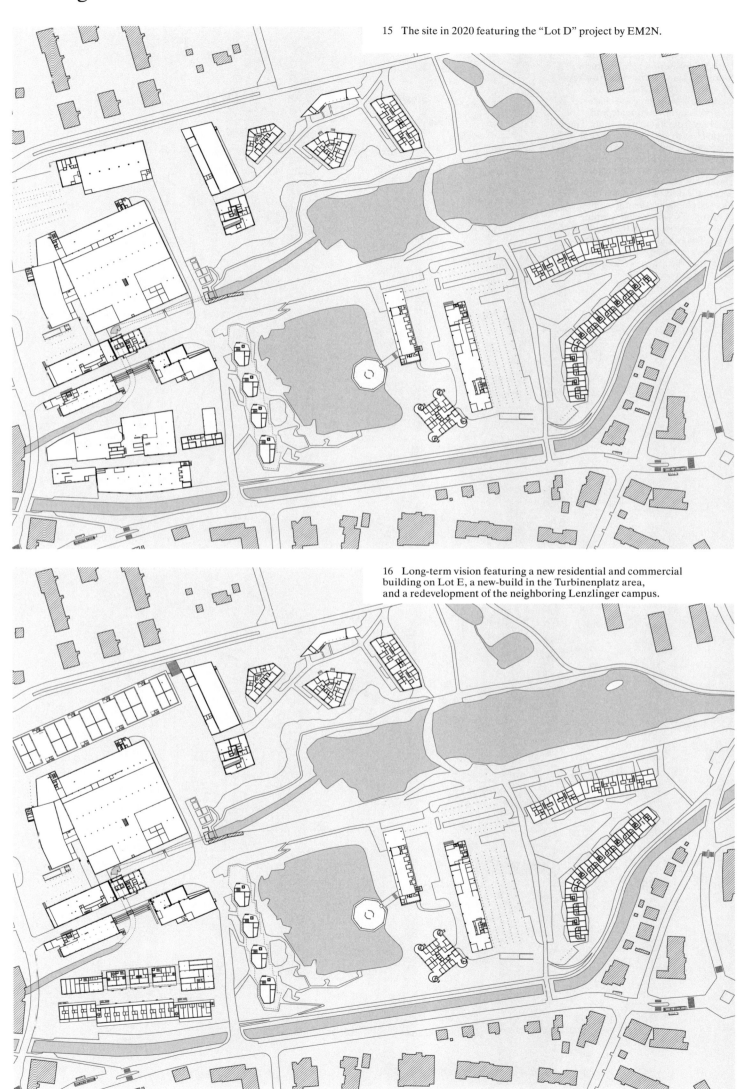

15 The site in 2020 featuring the "Lot D" project by EM2N.

16 Long-term vision featuring a new residential and commercial building on Lot E, a new-build in the Turbinenplatz area, and a redevelopment of the neighboring Lenzlinger campus.

Zellweger Luwa Site

17
For the master plan, developed in conjunction with landscape architects Schweingruber Zulauf (now Studio Vulkan), we followed two key objectives. The first was for the campus to retain its island character, its differentiation in scale and typology from its surroundings. The second was to guarantee optimum interconnection with the surroundings, ensuring the campus would no longer be seen as a no-go area and instead be treated as a publicly accessible part of Uster. We thus focused chiefly on honing the figure of the open spaces and developing their connections with the neighborhood. Today, the new figure of the campus's green space blends seamlessly with the green corridor of the Aabach river.

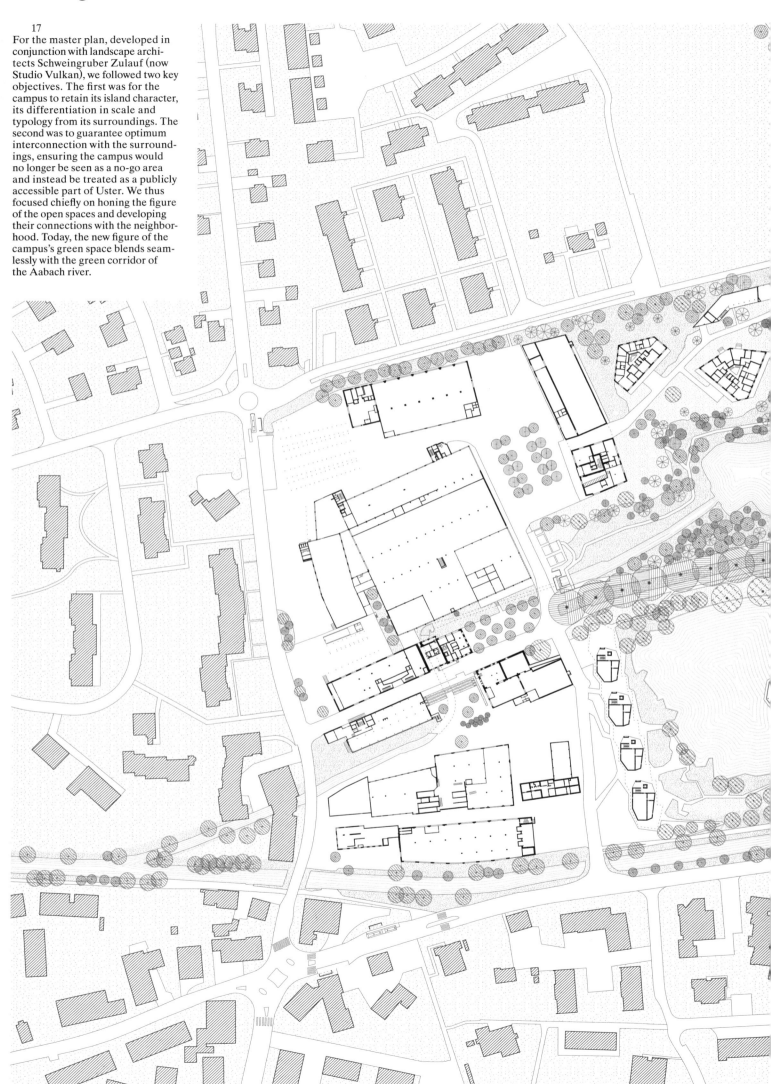

Zellweger Luwa Site

Zellweger Luwa Site

18 ↑

18
Thanks to the involvement of the Walter A. Bechtler Foundation in its redevelopment, the campus has been able to welcome works by important contemporary artists. Created in 2010, Tadashi Kawamata's *Drift Structure* spans the Zellweger Weiher pond.

19
Lutz & Guggisberg's *Werkhof* installation also serves as play equipment for the children who live in the Gigon Guyer-designed blocks.

20
In 1971, Victor Vasarely's wall works *Gestalt Rot*, *Gestalt Grün*, and *Gestalt Gelb* were installed in the foyer of Roland Rohn's office building. They were later joined by Guyton/Walker's sculpture *Untitled* (2012) and a quartet of pieces by Oscar Tuazon: *Erector* (2011), *I Put Food on the Table* (2012), *The Carnal Plane* (2013), and *Walk through Walls* (2017).

21
In 1991, Richard Kissling's 1899 sculpture *Helvetia und Merkur*, which originally graced the Bankverein building on Zurich's Paradeplatz, gained a new long-term home in front of Rohn's office building.

↙ 20

↓ 21

22 ↑   ↓ 23

Zellweger Luwa Site

← 22
After a 25-year search, a fitting location was finally found for Sol Lewitt's 1984 sculpture *Cube*, which was installed next to Lot D in 2011.

← 23
In 2010, Peter Fischli and David Weiss created the *Moosfelsen* sculpture next to the Zellweger Weiher pond.

24
The old spinning mill was converted into apartments by Pfister Schiess Tropeano in 2018.

25
Together with the exhibition pavilion in the Herterweiher pond, Roland Rohn's impressive office building was completed in 1961.

26
In 2013, Morger + Dettli realized a residential development by the Herterweiher pond.

27
Also completed in 2013, Gigon Guyer's apartment building contains 74 apartments, a nursery, and a café.

28
Overlooking the Herterweiher pond is Herzog & de Meuron's 32-apartment tower from 2015.

25

26

27 ↑   ↓ 28

29
Comprising five apartment buildings and an art gallery, EM2N's own project from 2020 brought the campus's initial redevelopment to a close.

30–36 →
As part of this last phase, gallery premises were created for the exhibition of artworks from the Bechtler Collection. Lit by a series of rooflights, the large main space was envisioned as a new home for Walter de Maria's *The 2000 Sculpture*.

30 ↑

↓ 31

Zellweger Luwa Site

32 ↑

↓ 33

Zellweger Luwa Site

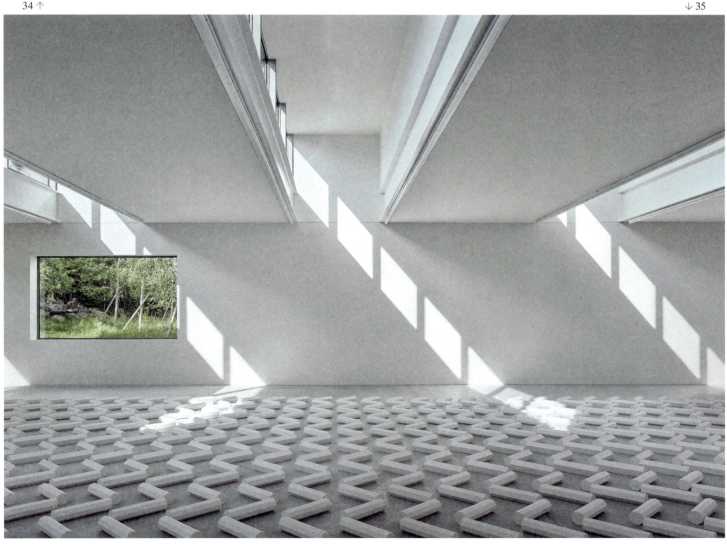

Toni Campus: Design Competition

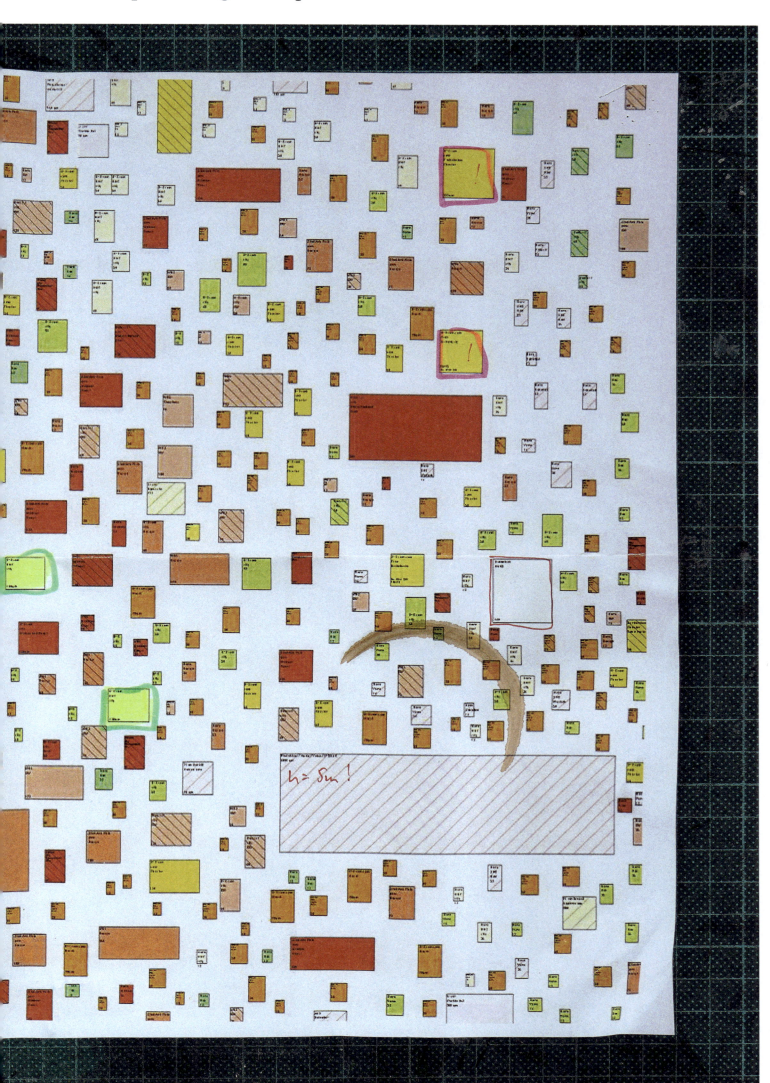

Toni Campus: Design Competition

Toni Campus: Design Competition

In 1999, Swiss Dairy Food AG closed its Toni-Molkerei processing plant and asked Herczog Hubeli Comalini Architekten to draw up a private master plan for the site, which offered between 65,000 and 80,000 square meters of mixed-use floor space. Following Swiss Dairy Food's bankruptcy, the site passed to Zurich's cantonal bank, which, having no firm ideas about its future use at this point, gave permission for interim cultural usages. The canton then proposed using the site as a college campus, launching a feasibility study to look at whether the new Zurich University of the Arts, which had resulted from the amalgamation of Zurich University of Music and Theater and Zurich University of Design and Art, could be accommodated on the site, together with two departments of Zurich University of Applied Sciences. In 2005, the canton invited tenders for a study contract for the site.

← 1
Encompassing 2,369 spaces and an internal volume of 491,000 cubic meters, the project's programming requirements were vast in scale and complexity. At first, the sheer number of different spaces and usages felt overwhelming, and we initially struggled to come up with architectural criteria for their meaningful and logical organization.

← 2
We were, however, impressed with the muscularity of the existing structures, which offered spaces reminiscent of Piranesi's *Carceri*.

Toni Campus: Design Competition

2005–2006

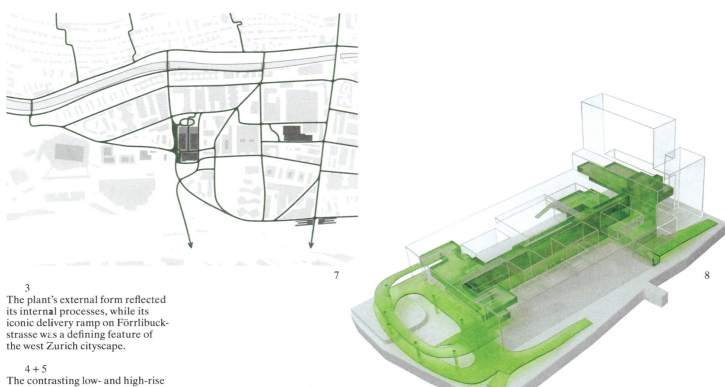

3
The plant's external form reflected its internal processes, while its iconic delivery ramp on Förrlibuckstrasse was a defining feature of the west Zurich cityscape.

4 + 5
The contrasting low- and high-rise volumes presented very different spatial possibilities.

6
A comparison with Gottfried Semper's ETH polytechnic building underlines the immensity of the existing building.

7
How could we prevent this huge mass in the middle of the city from coming across as a closed and unapproachable form? How could we integrate the campus into the city and make it accessible to the general public? The answer lay firstly in west Zurich's new active-travel and green-space axes, and secondly in the existing delivery ramp. We decided to route pedestrian pathways right through the building and to use the ramp for access.

8 + 9
The idea of routing pathways through the building was the starting point for our "internal urbanism" approach. To connect the main hall and the ramp, we developed a system of streets, squares, and cascading staircases; this provided a three-dimensional plan within which "addresses" and "parcels" for the various usages could be arranged.

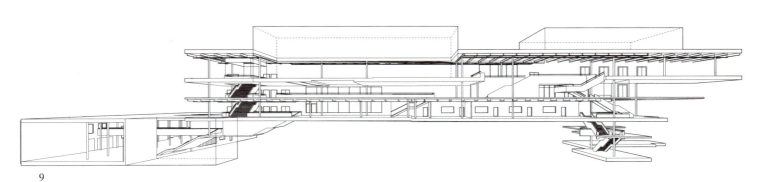

10
The external delivery ramp was reinvented as a vertical culture boulevard, an urban interface between the university and the city, allowing this iconic feature to play a key role in the new Toni campus.

Toni Campus: Design Competition

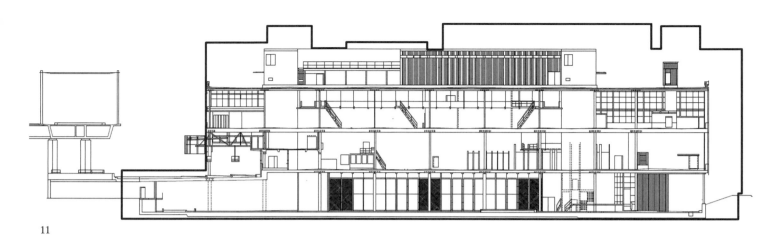

11

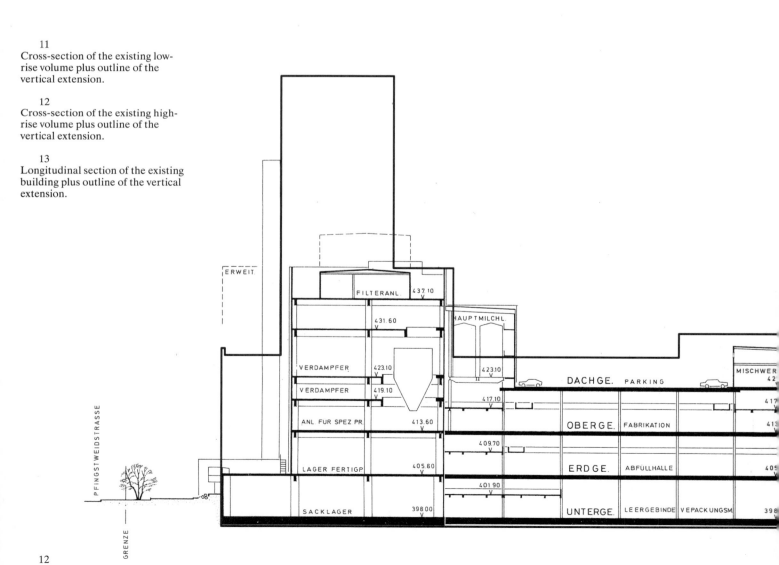

12

11
Cross-section of the existing low-rise volume plus outline of the vertical extension.

12
Cross-section of the existing high-rise volume plus outline of the vertical extension.

13
Longitudinal section of the existing building plus outline of the vertical extension.

Toni Campus: Design Competition

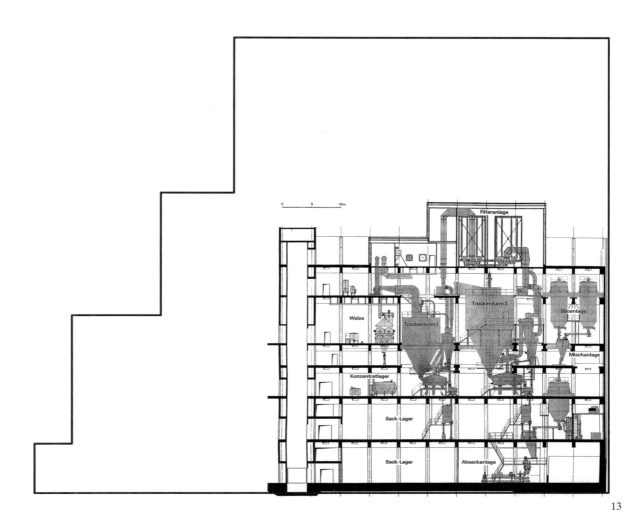

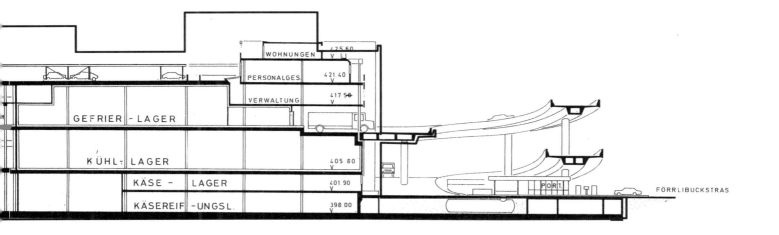

Toni Campus: Redevelopment

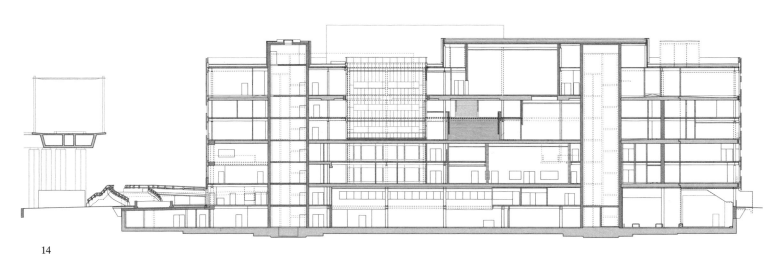

14

14
Cross-section of the low-rise volume.

15
Longitudinal section.

16
Cross-section of the high-rise volume.

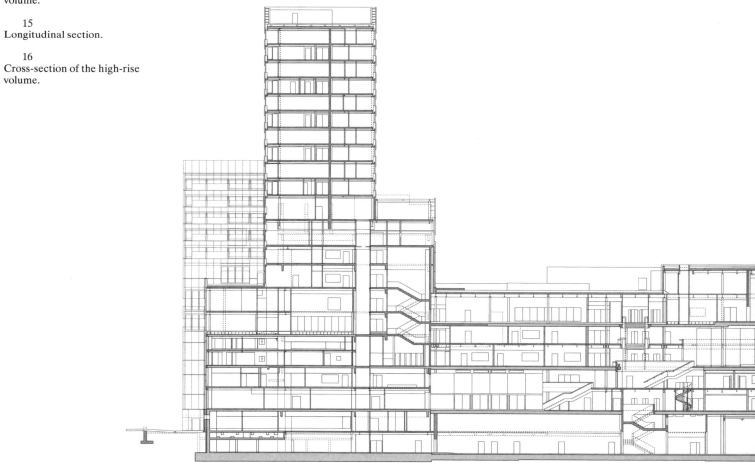

15

Toni Campus: Redevelopment

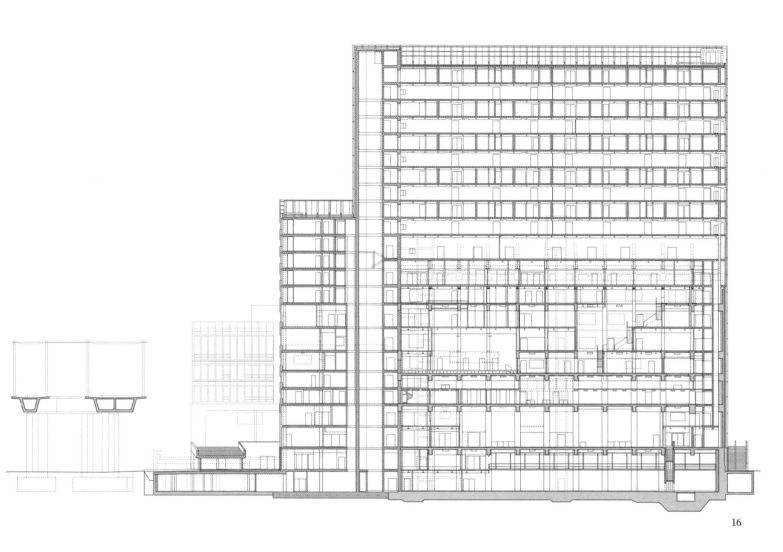

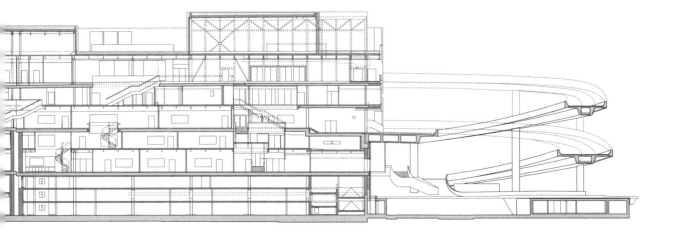

Toni Campus: Redevelopment

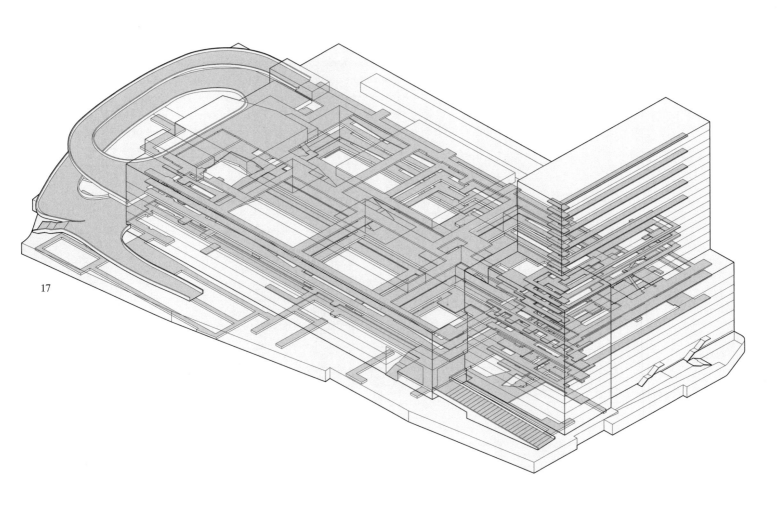

17
The internal circulation system reaches into every corner of the vast building, transitioning gradually from publicly accessible to restricted areas.

18
As in a city, the most public usages are at the most important intersections of the internal "street" system, while more restricted usages take place in outlying areas. Usages that require less depth, such as the apartments, are located in the tower. High-ceilinged spaces which can't be accommodated within the 10 × 10-meter grid of supports, such as the concert and ballet venues, are moved to the roof of the low-rise section. The varying grain of dimensions and usages results in a diverse and complex conglomeration of spaces.

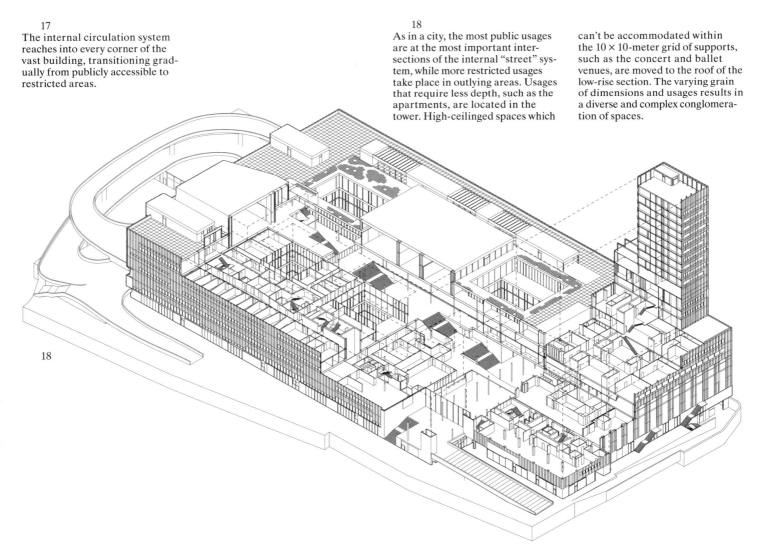

Toni Campus: Redevelopment

2005–2006

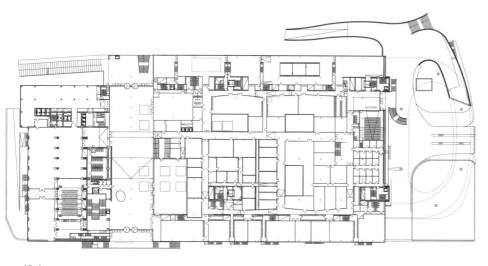

19 ↑

↓ 20

19 + 20
Following the sale of the project by Zurich's cantonal bank to Allreal in 2008, it became apparent that the spatial requirements would be subject to further modification, even though demolition work was, in part, already ongoing. The early plans envisioned a main lecture hall and third-party usages such as a large refectory, an art gallery, and a cabaret theater for Level E03, but these were abandoned in 2010 to create space for a provisional home for the Museum of Design. The size of the refectory was thus reduced, while a cinema sound studio was added next to the movie theater.

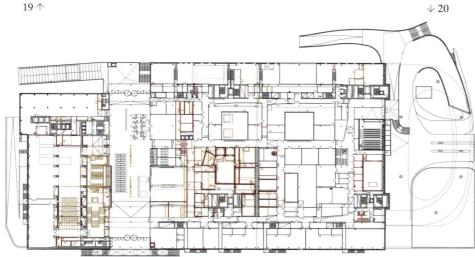

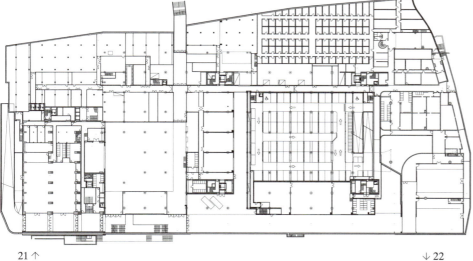

21 ↑

↓ 22

21 + 22
The basement level, E01, saw even greater change. Originally, a 3,000-capacity exhibition and event venue with a large stage had been planned, but this was subsequently ditched in favor of additional rehearsal stages, an enlarged workshop, and archive spaces for the Museum of Design.

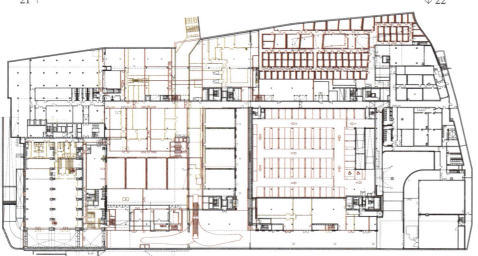

Toni Campus: Redevelopment

2005–2006

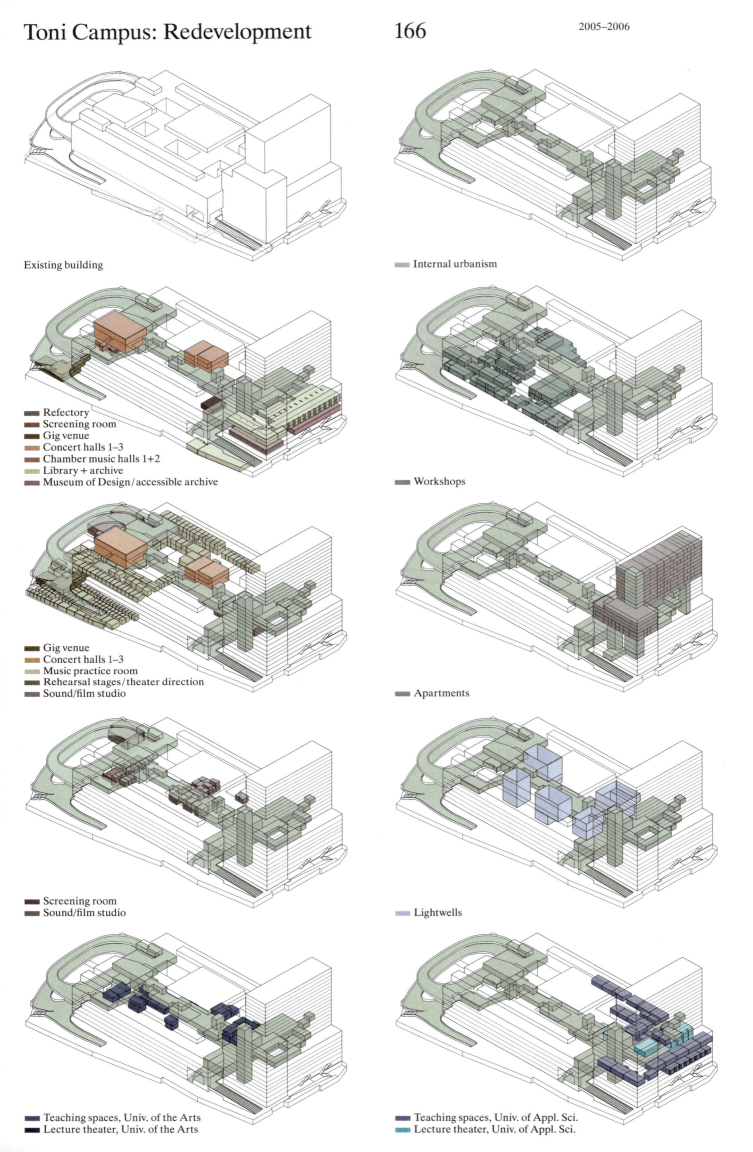

Toni Campus: Redevelopment

2005–2006

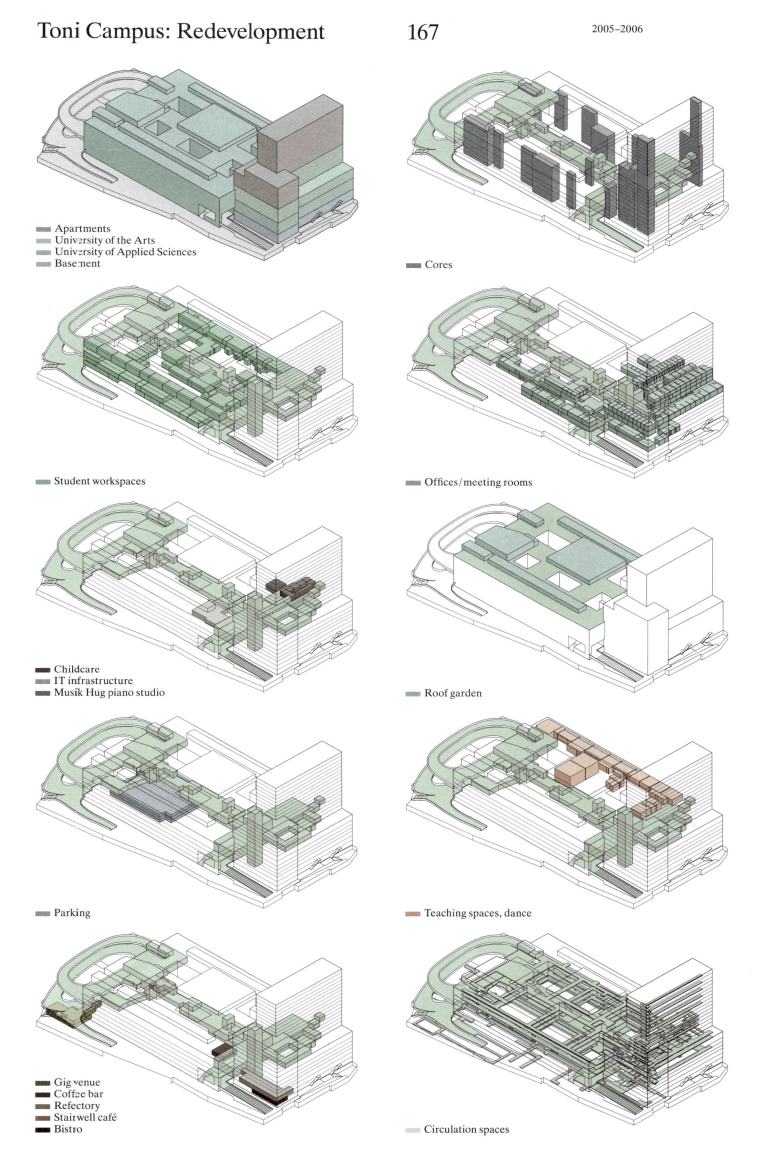

Toni Campus: Redevelopment

23
Situated one story below ground, Level E01 housed the dairy's main delivery bays. Trucks would drive up along the one-way delivery road and pull up outside Hall 5000.

1. Finished goods store
2. Bagging machine
3. Heating oil store
4. Milk reception
5. Hall 5000
6. Delivery area
7. Substation
8. Refrigeration/compressed air
9. Ice-water tank
10. Raclette cellar
11. Electrical switchboard
12. Parts store
13. Workshops
14. Shelters
15. Auto repair shop

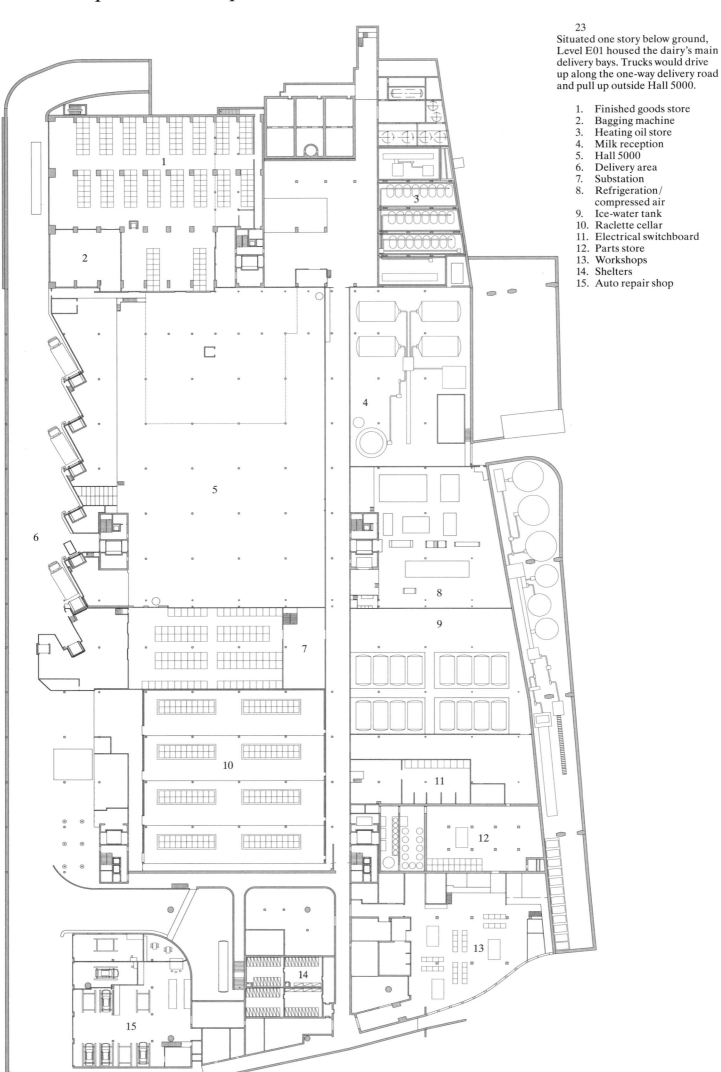

Toni Campus: Redevelopment

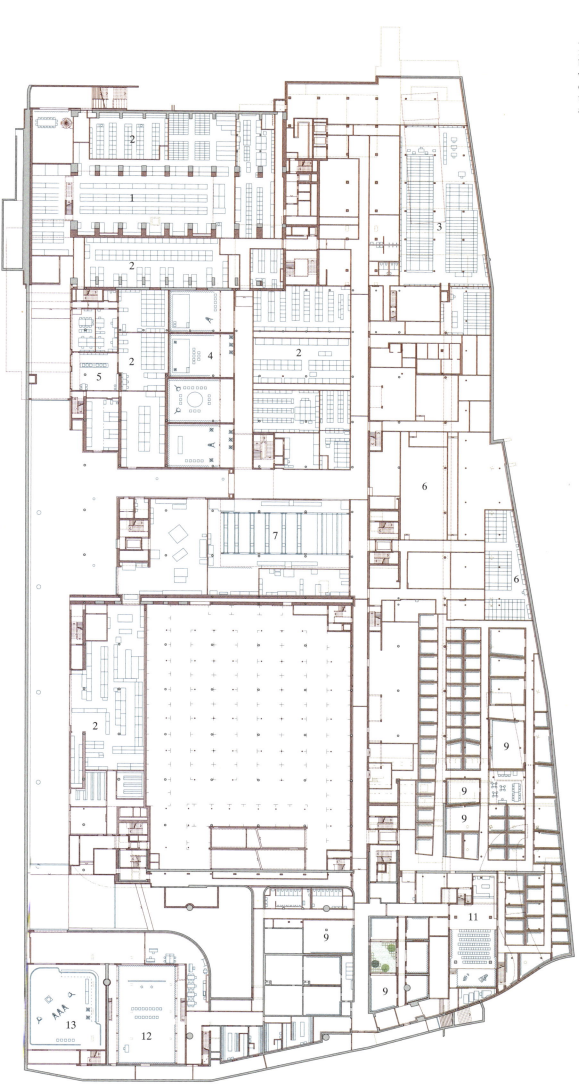

24
After redevelopment, Level E01 remained the main delivery area but also gained new functions, with particularly space-intensive or logistics-based usages, or those that don't require daylight, being accommodated here.

1. Accessible archive (museum)
2. Public displays (museum)
3. Archive (library)
4. Rehearsal stage (theater)
5. Lighting and stage equipment hire
6. FM/infrastructure
7. Workshop
8. Parking
9. Music teaching room
10. Music practice room
11. Gig venue
12. Rehearsal stage
13. Sound/film studio

Toni Campus: Redevelopment

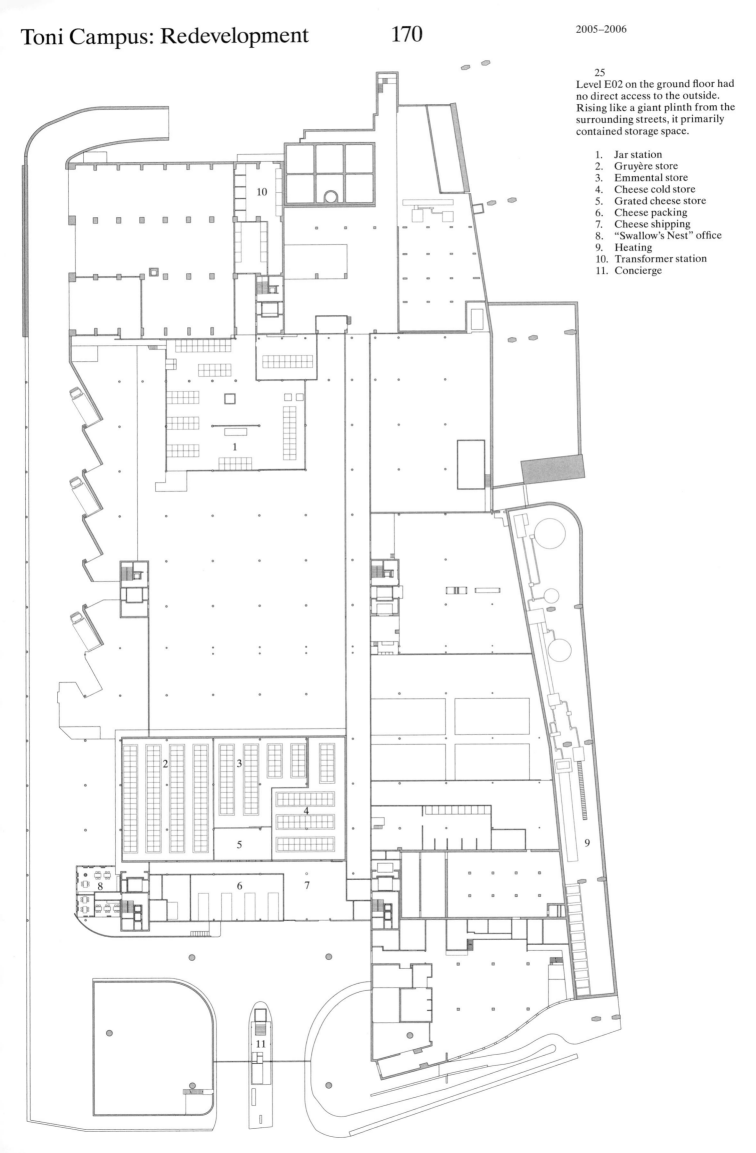

25
Level E02 on the ground floor had no direct access to the outside. Rising like a giant plinth from the surrounding streets, it primarily contained storage space.

1. Jar station
2. Gruyère store
3. Emmental store
4. Cheese cold store
5. Grated cheese store
6. Cheese packing
7. Cheese shipping
8. "Swallow's Nest" office
9. Heating
10. Transformer station
11. Concierge

Toni Campus: Redevelopment

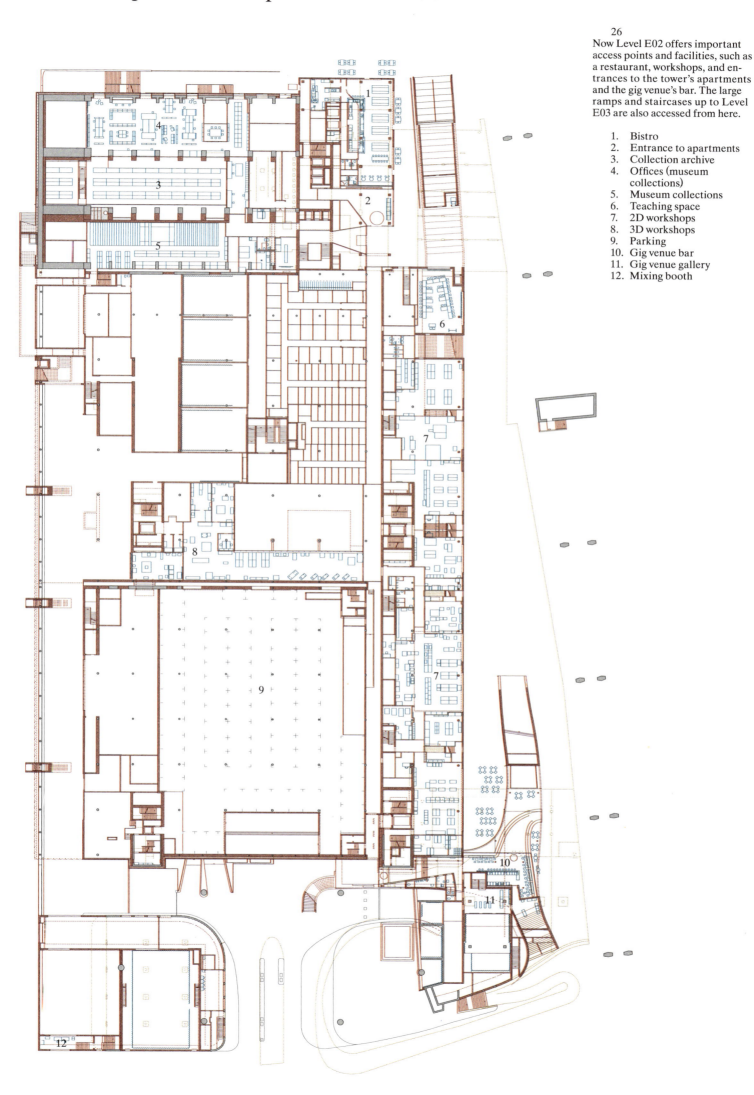

26
Now Level E02 offers important access points and facilities, such as a restaurant, workshops, and entrances to the tower's apartments and the gig venue's bar. The large ramps and staircases up to Level E03 are also accessed from here.

1. Bistro
2. Entrance to apartments
3. Collection archive
4. Offices (museum collections)
5. Museum collections
6. Teaching space
7. 2D workshops
8. 3D workshops
9. Parking
10. Gig venue bar
11. Gig venue gallery
12. Mixing booth

Toni Campus: Redevelopment

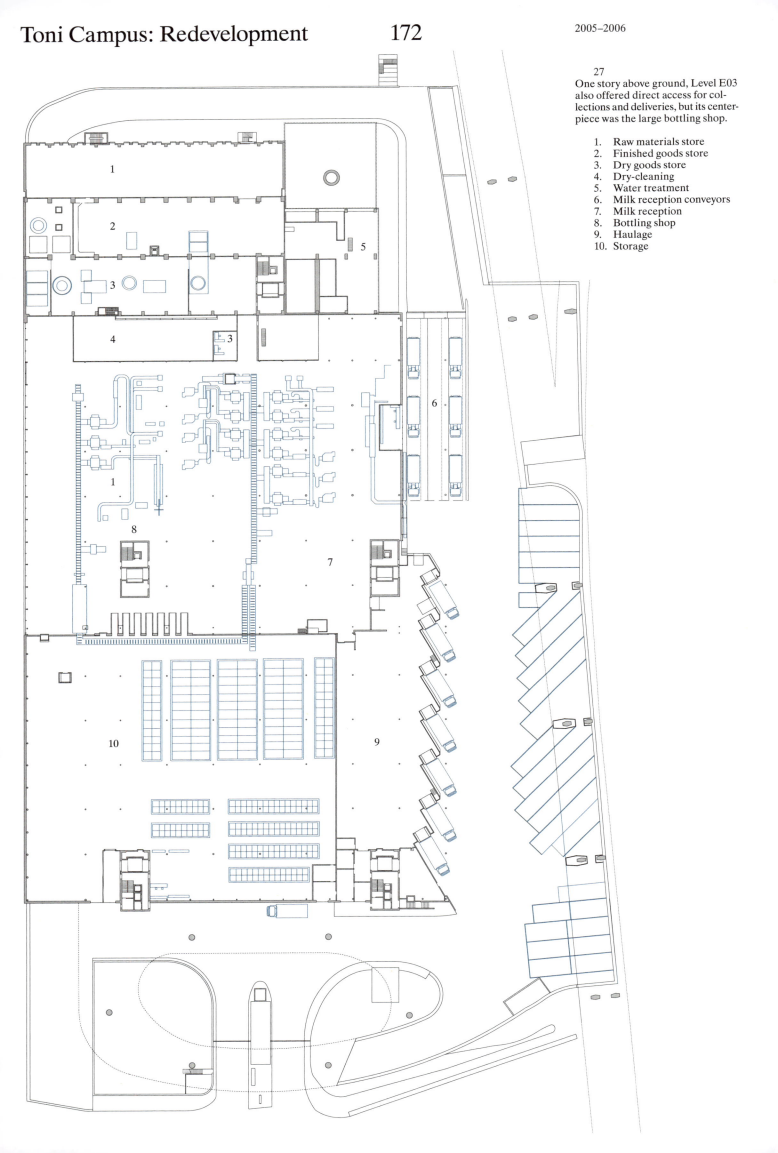

27
One story above ground, Level E03 also offered direct access for collections and deliveries, but its centerpiece was the large bottling shop.

1. Raw materials store
2. Finished goods store
3. Dry goods store
4. Dry-cleaning
5. Water treatment
6. Milk reception conveyors
7. Milk reception
8. Bottling shop
9. Haulage
10. Storage

Toni Campus: Redevelopment

28
Today, Level E03 forms the main story of the university campus. Here, a large entrance hall welcomes students and visitors, while other usages involving a high degree of public access—such as the Museum of Design, the refectory, a café, a shop, and lecture theaters—are found on this level as well. Also accessed from here is the x-shaped internal circulation system, which includes the cascading staircase leading up from the entrance hall and the stairs of the north entrance's vertical atrium by the movie theater.

1. Entrance hall
2. Refectory
3. Kitchen
4. Museum
5. Museum shop
6. Café
7. Lecture theater
8. Student workspaces
9. Office
10. Sound/film studio
11. ICST institute
12. IT teaching space
13. Photography workshop
14. Screening room
15. Sound studio

Toni Campus: Redevelopment

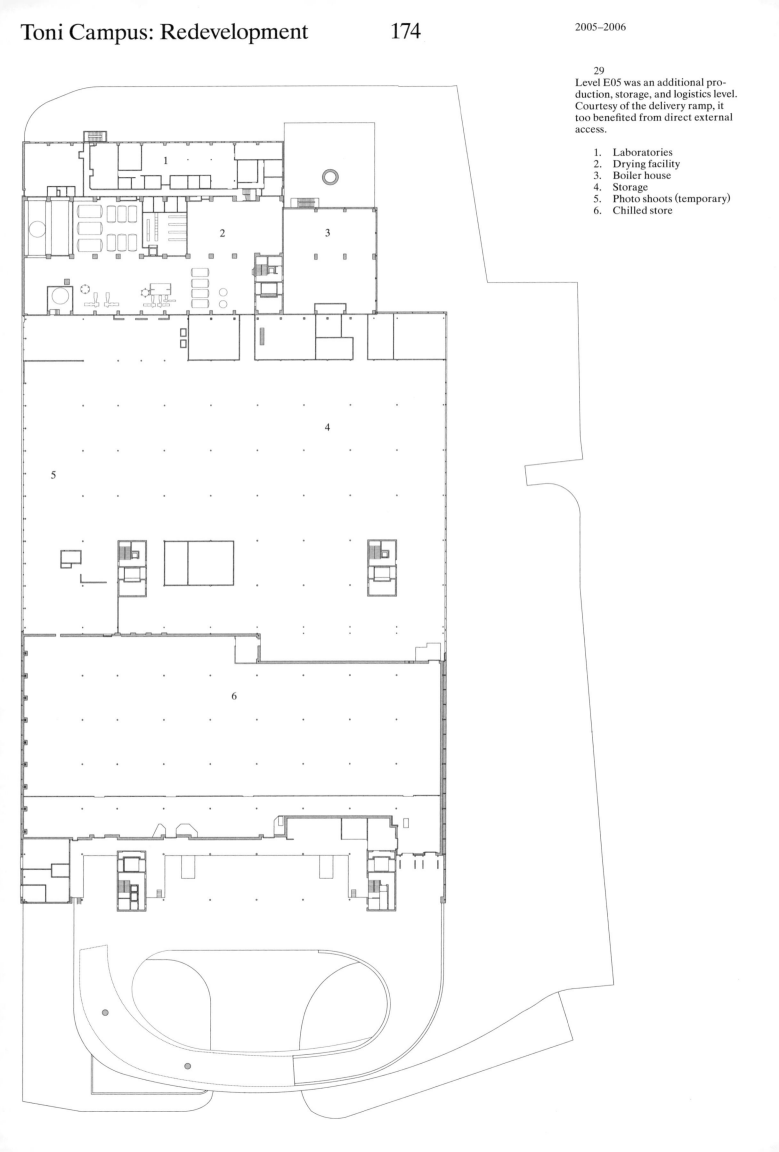

29
Level E05 was an additional production, storage, and logistics level. Courtesy of the delivery ramp, it too benefited from direct external access.

1. Laboratories
2. Drying facility
3. Boiler house
4. Storage
5. Photo shoots (temporary)
6. Chilled store

Toni Campus: Redevelopment

30
The new heart of Level E05, the mid-point of the low-rise section, is the middle landing of the cascading staircase. Along the longitudinal axis are important public facilities such as the library, the chamber music hall, and the exhibition spaces by the delivery ramp.

1. Library
2. Office
3. Teaching space
4. Middle landing, cascading staircase
5. Multifunctional space
6. Mini cascading staircase
7. Lecturers' foyer
8. Graphic design studio
9. Music teaching space
10. Exhibition hall
11. Chamber music hall

Toni Campus: Redevelopment

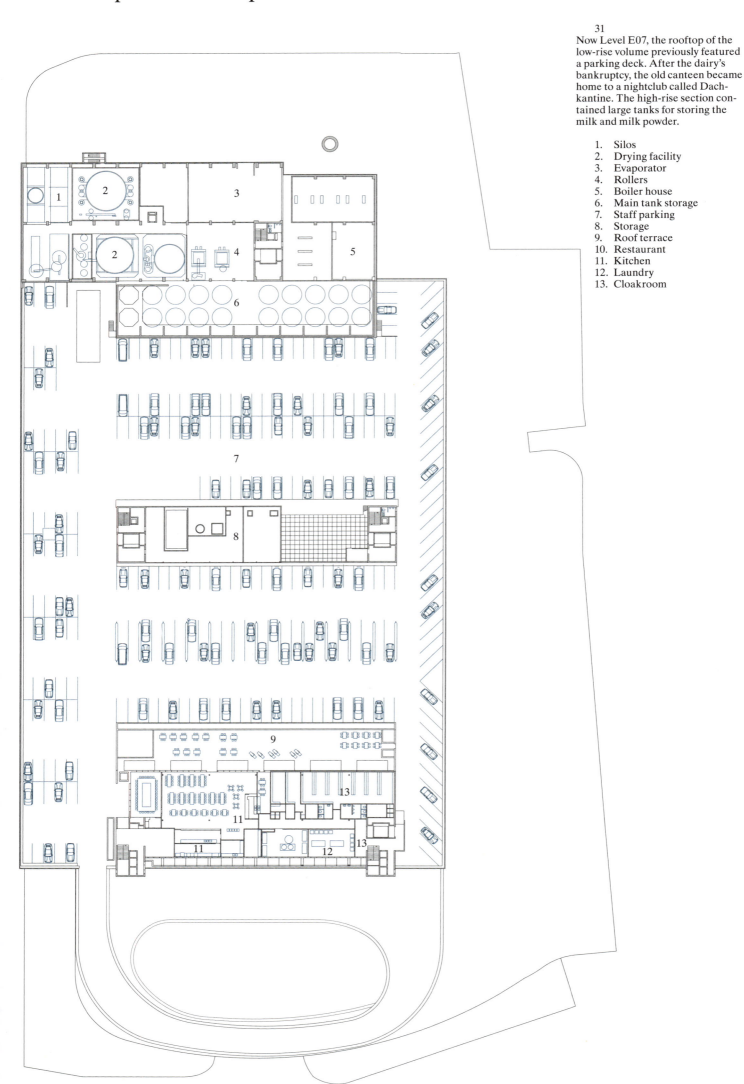

31
Now Level E07, the rooftop of the low-rise volume previously featured a parking deck. After the dairy's bankruptcy, the old canteen became home to a nightclub called Dachkantine. The high-rise section contained large tanks for storing the milk and milk powder.

1. Silos
2. Drying facility
3. Evaporator
4. Rollers
5. Boiler house
6. Main tank storage
7. Staff parking
8. Storage
9. Roof terrace
10. Restaurant
11. Kitchen
12. Laundry
13. Cloakroom

Toni Campus: Redevelopment

32
Today, Level E07 houses various usages that couldn't be accommodated within the 10 × 10-meter grid of supports or under the 6.5-meter-high ceilings. Primarily that meant the organ hall and main concert hall, but it also included ballet practice spaces, a life-drawing room, and artists' studios. The delivery ramp ends here at a covered terrace area, while the roof terrace can also be accessed via a staircase from the concert hall foyer.

1. Lecture theater
2. Compact cascading staircase
3. Teaching space
4. Student workspaces
5. Dance teaching space
6. Electroacoustic concert hall
7. Organ hall
8. Large ballet hall
9. Skylight studio
10. Gallery space
11. Large concert hall
12. Internal foyer
13. External foyer

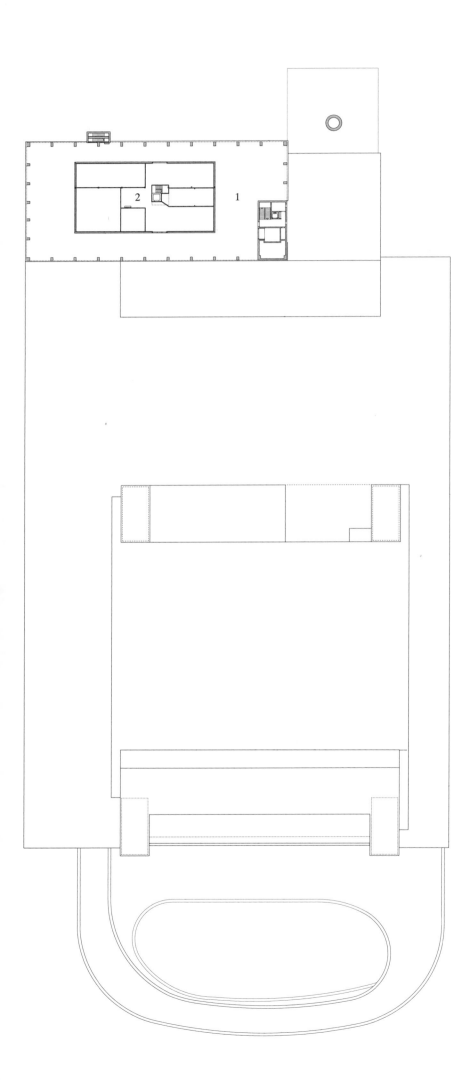

33
Level E08 marked the top of the low-rise section. The high-rise volume was two stories taller; these additional levels contained tanks and filtration systems.

1. Roof terrace
2. Filtration units

Toni Campus: Redevelopment

34
The new roof terrace on Level E08 is a valuable addition to the campus's otherwise limited outdoor space. Around a verdant inner section featuring heat-resistant Mediterranean plantings is a ring-shaped terrace that can be used for working, strolling, or just hanging out. Located within the high-rise section and benefiting from a prime location directly adjacent to the roof terrace are a nursery and communal spaces for the University of Applied Sciences.

1. Compact cascading staircase
2. Recreation area
3. Childcare
4. Office
5. Outdoor craft space
6. Fitness area
7. Terrace
8. Garden

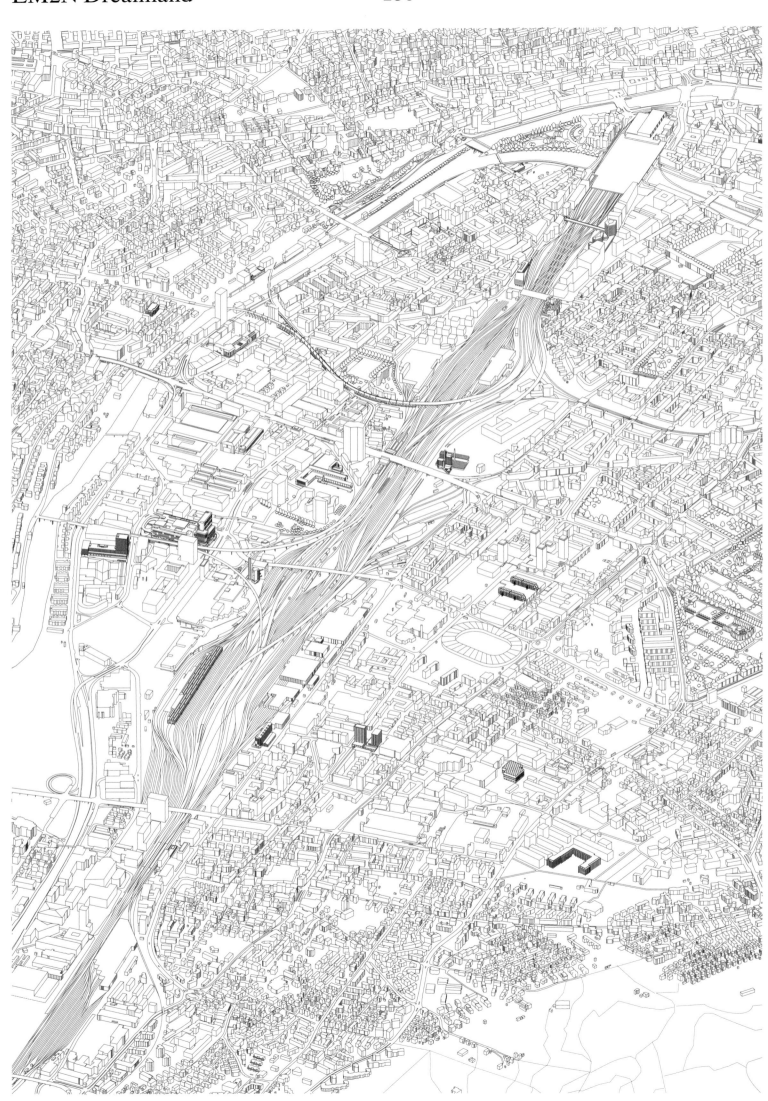

SESC Pompéia

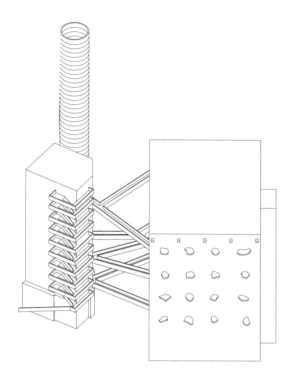

When we came across photos of this project in São Paolo, it was love at first sight—despite the fact that, or perhaps because, its architect's clever deception wasn't immediately apparent. Tasked with converting a former factory complex into a community center, Lina Bo Bardi added new-build structures to the existing industrial sheds, ingeniously disguising them as pseudo-wconversions.

Essentially, the project reflects a kind of analog design process in which new-builds first adopt the guise of archetypal industrial typologies such as a silo or a chimney only to be promptly subjected to a transformation that resembles that of an actual conversion. The amorphous openings in the sports hall tower typify this subtle strategy, offering up multiple associations. We can read them as playful, poetic, architectural symbols, and yet we are also reminded of the violent breaches made when a demolition worker takes a sledgehammer to a wall. It is precisely the random, spontaneous feel of these perforations that makes us think of an industrial silo, and has us believing this solid-concrete structure must have been retrospectively converted into a sports center. Lina Bo Bardi's SESC Pompéia is thus a cryptic blend of camouflage, mimesis, and transparency, an object lesson in how to design new-builds so that they acquire the contradictory, ambiguous, and surprising qualities of conversion projects.

Mongolian School Project 183 2008–2012

← 1   2 ↑ ↓ 3

Mongolian School Project 184 2008–2012

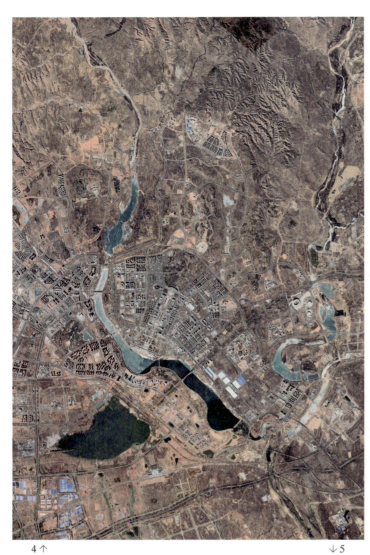

4 ↑

↓ 5

6 ↑

↓ 7

Mongolian School Project

← 1
While the Toni campus project was ongoing, we were tasked with designing a campus for a boarding school in Ordos New Town, a planned city in Inner Mongolia around one and a half hours by plane from Beijing. The two schemes had similar dimensions and the school, too, was devised as a city within a city, although this time spread out horizontally rather than densified vertically.

← 2
Encouraged by an economic boom driven by coal mining, the local authorities decided to pour money into a model city that was to be designed entirely from scratch. Private developers such as the initiator of the Ordos 100 development project got involved, hoping for rapid returns on their investments.

← 3
Within just a few years, infrastructure for several hundred thousand residents had been built. The city's streets remained empty, however; despite all the investment, no one could be persuaded to relocate.

4–7
In addition to public facilities, a new council building, and apartments, the local authorities also planned new school buildings, including a boarding school—the Ordos Mongolian Nationality High School—that would accommodate 2,000 pupils and encompass every grade from kindergarten upwards.

8
The different school stages—kindergarten, primary, and secondary—were each allocated a distinct typology, making them clearly distinguishable as individual "building blocks." All were to be accessed via communal areas that would ideally also serve as public spaces for the surrounding neighborhood, though this proved to be a somewhat naïve, Eurocentric notion. Such sites are almost always completely closed off in China, with access subject to checks. We ourselves have never set eyes on the completed campus.

9 →
Realized by a state planning agency in Beijing, the completed school diverges slightly from our design, particularly in its materiality, which deviates from our idea of a brick-and-concrete campus. Though the Ordos school is up and running, the new city's central residential district, built for around one million inhabitants, appears to still have few residents even years after completion.

8

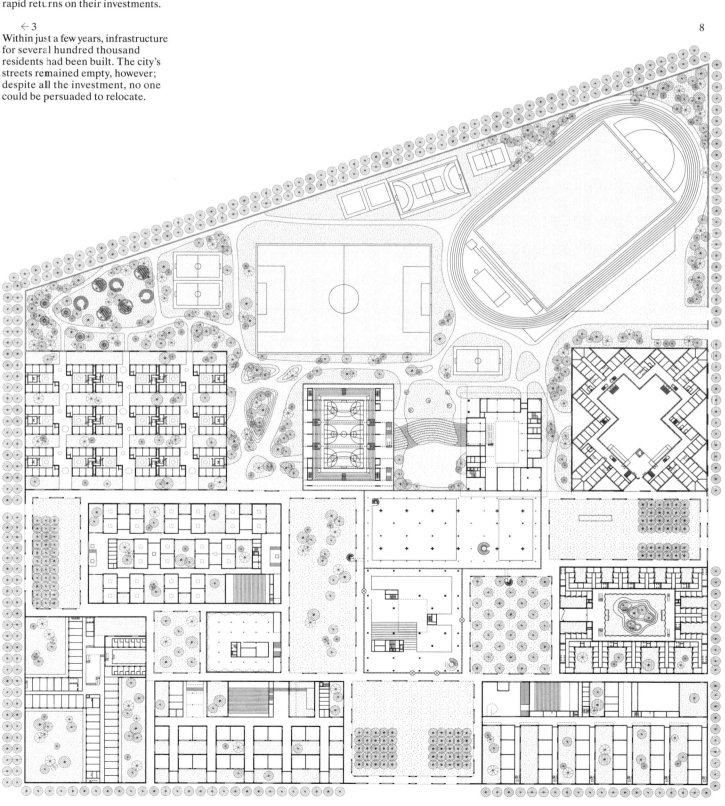

Cinémathèque suisse

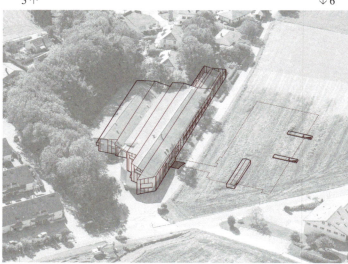

← 1 + 2
Home of the country's collective cinematic memory, Cinémathèque suisse had hitherto been housed in a cluster of barracks, a decidedly unpretentious arrangement that was more about the contents within than the appearance without. Since its founding by movie aficionados in 1943, this national film archive had always had rather makeshift premises, be it apartments, an old stable building, or a decommissioned nuclear power station. In 1992, the collection, which includes movie-making equipment, film literature, and movie posters, as well as rolls of film, was then relocated to what had previously been the premises of a book printing business in Penthaz.

3 + 4
Storage was previously the Cinémathèque's main function—the collection was simply piled up on pallets and shelves in utilitarian sheds. As it grew in size and importance, however, the existing premises became stretched to the limit and could clearly no longer meet the archive's curatorial or protective needs. The Federal Office of Culture thus decided to commission an extension.

5 + 6
For us, the modest appearance of its premises was part of the Cinémathèque's charm. Our extension project thus built on the existing structures, drawing on the utilitarian nature of those simple sheds. Today, the site comprises two distinct parts separated by a road. Whereas the public areas and workspaces were concentrated in the redeveloped and extended premises, the archive itself was housed in a subterranean new-build. The separation of storage and research functions ensures the archive material is properly protected and allows for the creation of high-quality workspaces. It was also a simple way of creating an urban ensemble that responds to the adjacent farmland while lending Cinémathèque suisse a clear aesthetic identity.

7
Cross-section.

8
The new-build is essentially an array of simple conjoined sheds. On the entrance side, the structure is cut back diagonally to create a projecting prow.

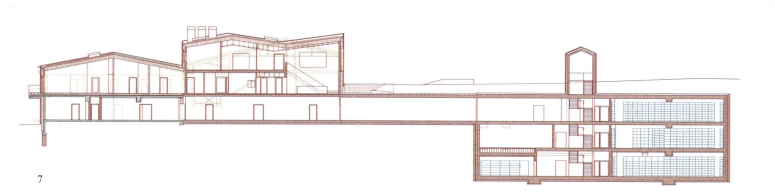

Cinémathèque suisse

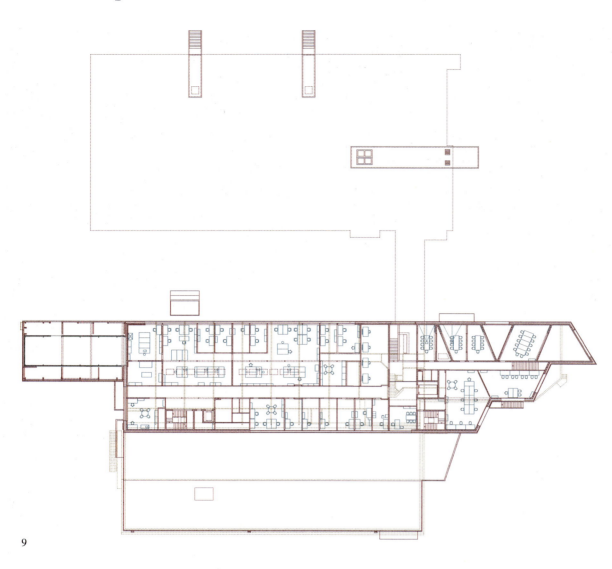

9

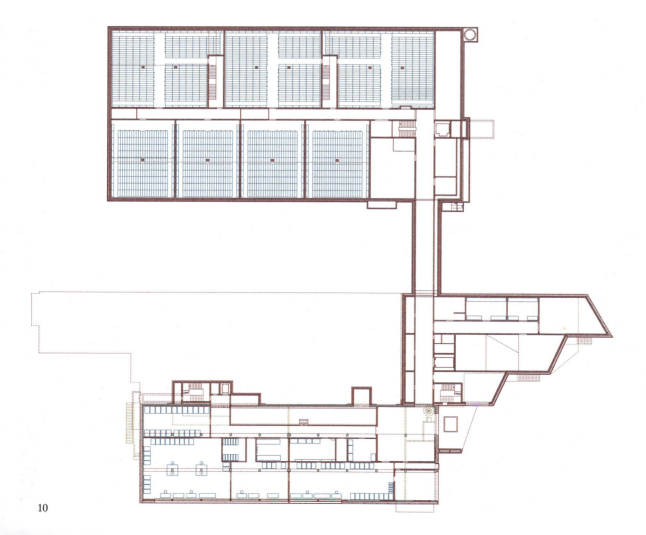

10

Cinémathèque suisse 2007–2015

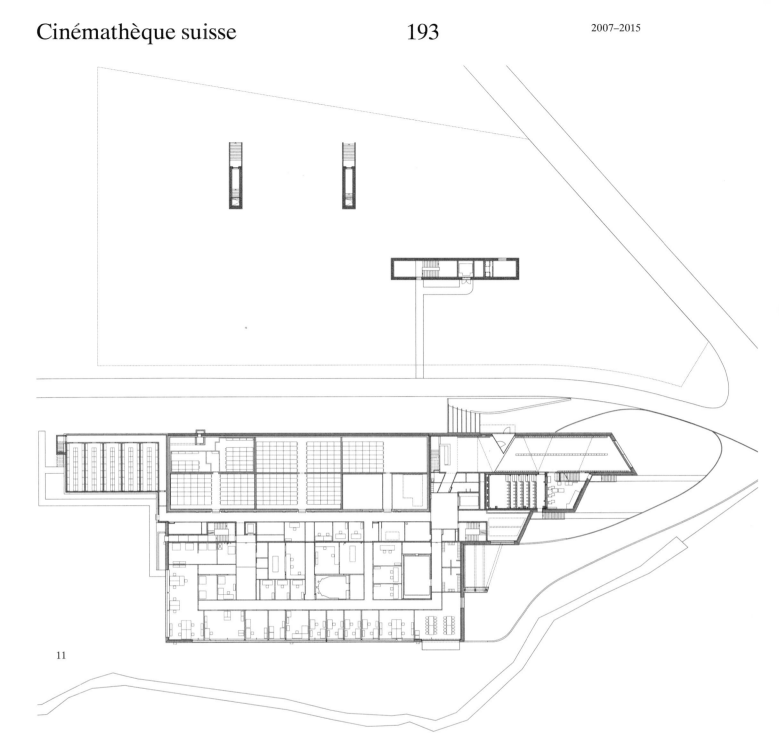

11
Upper floor plan.

9
Ground floor plan.
The compositional principle is particularly apparent in the projecting section. The main circulation route runs through the parallel crosswalls so that the spaces' serial arrangement is clearly discernible. Wherever curatorially appropriate, the workspaces are illuminated by daylight.

10
Basement floor plan.
A basement-level tunnel connects the two distinct structures.

12 →
Splitting the premises into an overground and an underground structure allowed the Cinémathèque to respond to its position at the intersection of developed land and open countryside.

Cinémathèque suisse

13 ↑ ↓ 14

13–15
Housing the permanent exhibition, the double-height entrance hall is defined by the diagonals of the prow and the geometry of the partitioned meeting rooms, which have internal windows to provide a visual link. The depths of perspective and visual overlayering apparent along the longitudinal and transverse axes call to mind cinematic effects such as montage, superimposition, and cutting.

15

Cinémathèque suisse

16 ↑

18 ↑

↓ 17

↓ 19

16–18
Cinémathèque suisse boasts a suite of dedicated rooms for the restoration and archiving of old film footage.

19
Rolls of film, movie posters, and equipment are stored in the underground archive area.

20
The public meeting rooms are screened off from the entrance and exhibition area via partial partitions; these allow the dimensions of the double-height space to remain apparent.

21
The screening room allows guests and staff to study films in a variety of formats.

22–25 →
A shell of rusted steel—an industrial material with a sensuous air—envelops the entire complex, bringing together new structures and old. The slow weathering of the metal references the archive's preservational role while also giving the ensemble its own identity. The condensed, modulated roofscape features gently sloping sections of living roof and calls to mind industrial buildings and film studios. The all-black walls of the gallery space foreground the exhibits.

20

21

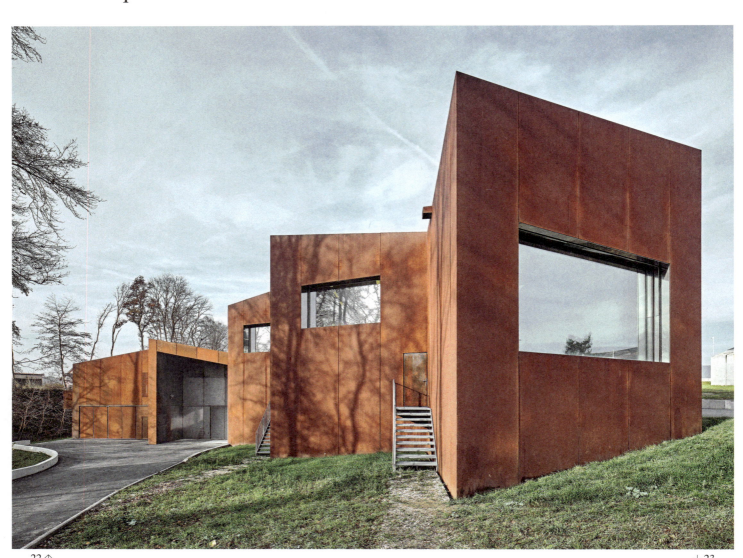

22 ↑   ↓ 23

Rosenberg

1

1
The constant repurposing and reinterpreting of what's there is a key characteristic of the city-factory. Existing structures such as industrial facilities, warehouses, office buildings, or, as in this case, a small supermarket can be test beds for new typologies and usage types. The defining factor in what such a test bed can be or do is the awkwardness or generosity of its spaces, with the productive resistance of existing buildings often leading to unconventional solutions. Frequently this process offers up unexpected spatial gifts or interesting moments of incongruence that you wouldn't get with new-builds, where the design approach tends more towards optimization.

2
This small supermarket in Winterthur boasted a 4-meter-high retail space and a basement housing a large storeroom. Demolition wasn't an option as zoning laws would have required any replacement to occupy a much smaller footprint, so, after considering the structure, we came up with a new type of residential architecture. The existing volume offered enough space to accommodate five individual homes, each accessed via a front garden and benefiting from its own roof terrace.

3 + 4
Respecting the small-scale pattern of the surroundings, the exterior has a restrained materiality that belies the diversity within. The position and size of the openings are the only clues to the units' unconventional layouts.

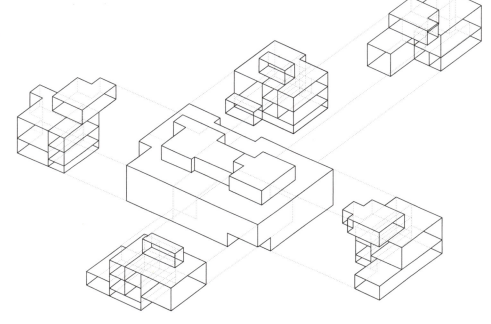

3

4

5

6

5
The existing building's open retail area inspired us to devise a loft-like interior concept, with each home featuring a double-height main space plus bedrooms on a mezzanine level.

6, 7, 9 + 10
Internal façades define how the bedrooms relate to the main space. The individual occupants were able to determine the different fit-outs, with one even opting for a full-color redesign, the concept for which was developed by artist Jörg Niederberger.

8
The new mezzanine levels make for a more dynamic layout.

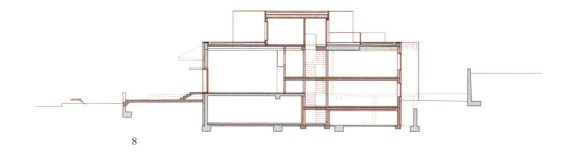

8

9

10

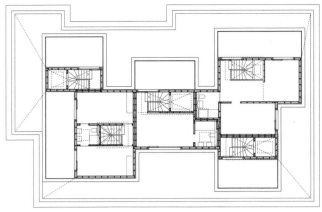

11

11–13
The plans are based on similar principles but also respond to each home's position within the existing volume. The structure now comprises four corner properties plus a middle house that extends from front to rear.

12

13

1 ↑ 2 ↓

3 ↑   4 ↓

5 ↑ 6 ↓

7 ↑

8 ↓

9 ↑ ↓ 10   11 + 12 →

School Complex Blumenfeld

2010

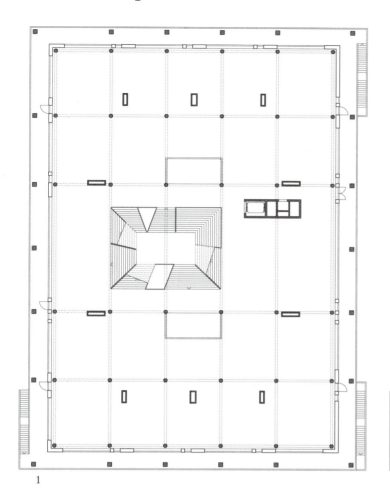

1

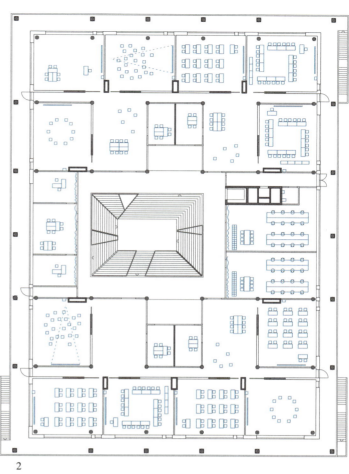

2

1–3
Schools are an ever-changing usage type, with each set of reforms bringing new educational concepts and teaching methods. At the same time, they are becoming increasingly key to the knowledge-based society with its focus on lifelong learning and continuing professional development. They thus have to be both flexible in design and easily accessible. Following on from our design for the Leutschenbach Schools, we proposed an evolution of our "school building as office block" idea.

Here, the externalization of escape routes using balconies maximizes flexibility, allowing us to design the primary internal circulation areas as a spatial sculpture without having to factor in fire regulations. With this proposal, we wanted to explore the tension between flexibility and fixity, allowing for future adaptations while also creating places that offer stability and a sense of identity.

4–6 →
Our plan was to link the different levels via a wide sculptural staircase resembling a series of tiered stands. This would serve not only as a circulation space but also as a focal point for social interaction, as a central hang-out, and a place for both performance and audience. In form, the staircase nods to familiar archetypes: the lowest level echoes the shape of a mound or pyramid, its rising sides potentially serving as tiered seating.

On the uppermost floor, the flights all lead downwards, forming an inward-facing amphitheater. On the middle level, these two spatial figures meet and create a third, enclosed space.

3

School Complex Blumenfeld

School Complex Blumenfeld 216 2010

5 ↑   ↓ 6

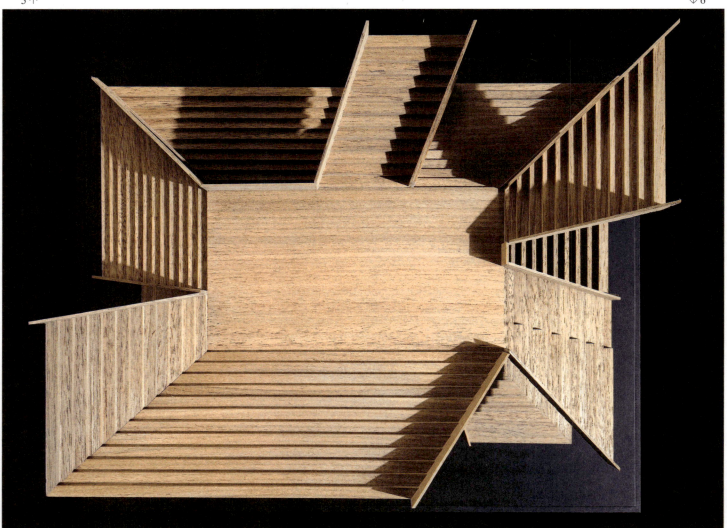

Hardbrücke Station

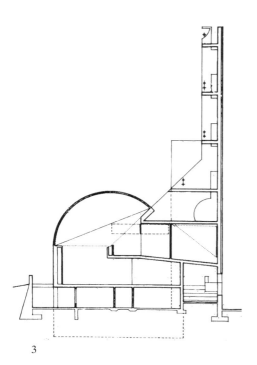

3

When Robert Venturi and Denise Scott Brown postulated their "decorated shed" theory,[A] they were attempting, via irony and subversive humor, to extract architectural potential from the everyday American buildings around them. From a European point of view, it's an approach that initially seems contrived and strained. Surely no architecture worth its salt would delegate all its ambitions to an extraneous sign, to the mere decoration of said shed? But look again and you realize it's an idea that has immense potential, one that offers the promise of freedom.

Freedom in this case means nothing less than being free from the obligation to ensure structure, interior, and programming are coordinated so precisely as to add up to a thoroughly coherent work, a work, in other words, defined by the symbiotic combination of these individual aspects. Of course, the decorated shed idea is thus a declaration of war on two fronts, challenging both the functionalist approach to design, which posits that form should follow function, and the moral ideal of truth in architectural and structural expression. There are, though, good historical reasons for this act of liberation. Spatial programming is, after all, famously fickle. These days, we can work in living spaces and live in what were office spaces, celebrate parties in converted churches, and experience art in old pumping stations. The relationship between space and use is thus a fragile one. The relationship between building and city, by contrast, would appear to be significantly more stable and fixed. Seen in this light, the decorated shed offers both stability in relation to the urban environment and flexibility in terms of usage. In plan and section, it is as open to functional appropriation as possible, while the "decorated" or sign-bearing façade can converse with its surroundings, establish historical connections, and/or offer information about the building's usage, perhaps proclaiming, as per Venturi and Scott Brown's sketch: "I am a museum!"

← 1 + 2
EM2N, Hardbrücke Railway Station Upgrading, 2007.
  Working solely with signs is often about achieving maximum effect with minimum effort. To help the much-used but well-hidden station that lies beneath Hardbrücke road bridge stand out from the urban fabric, we placed two large illuminated panels above the stairs leading down to the platforms. Facing each other across the bridge, the two panels create a virtual space that is particularly striking at night, when the surrounding darkness further enhances the signage's impact.

3
Venturi/Scott Brown, National College Football Hall of Fame, 1967.

A
Robert Venturi, Denise Scott Brown, Steven Izenour, *Learning From Las Vegas*, Cambridge, Massachusetts, 1972.

Herdern Railway Service Facility

2009–2013

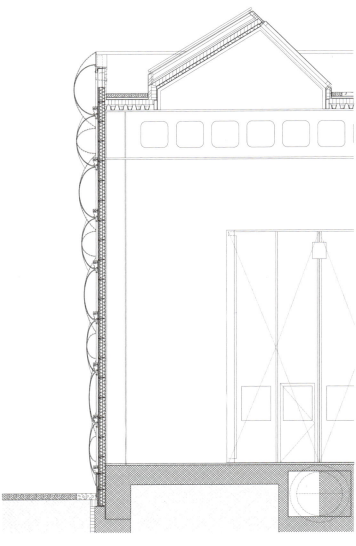

1
The Herdern Railway Service Facility forms a 600-meter-long urban perimeter right in the middle of Zurich, and marks the approach to the city for those arriving by train. At the same time, structures like this also help shape the identity of SBB as the national rail operator. But how can we use the tools of architecture and urban design to integrate such infrastructural buildings into the fabric of our increasingly densified cities? When we set about planning an extension to the Herdern Railway Service Facility, practically all of its parameters, including the pillarless structure's high ceilings, its length, and the internal rhythm of its load-bearing structure, were predetermined. Only the outer 50 centimeters, i.e. the architectural envelope facing the tracks and the city, offered any potential for design, and even then only within a narrow framework.

2 + 3
As architects, our task was merely to design the facility's façade and roof or, in the language of Venturi and Scott Brown, to simply decorate a shed. With just a few centimeters to work with, we developed the idea of a façade of deep, undulating "threads" that seem to move rhythmically as you pass by. The depth of the façade increases from bottom to top, as only the lower 4.5 meters had to respect the clearance outline of passing maintenance trains. The technical assembly and visual impact of the façade were tested using 1:1 scale samples.

4
Nodding to the track sections that continue beyond the building, the "threads" feature abruptly cut ends resembling those of extruded profiles.

5 →
Up close, the huge sculpted "threads" appear large in scale but, from passing trains, they seem much smaller. As you pass by, they seem to create a gentle oscillation that's amplified as it moves upwards.

6 →
The length of the façade elements was dictated by the spacing of the structure's uprights.

7 + 8 →
The interior of the shed design was primarily shaped by the technical dictates of rail maintenance. Only in the form of the roof was there any scope for architectural design.

9 →
The nationally recognized SBB emblem signifies the shed's user. The painted logo and the undulating surface combine to emphasize the sculpturality of the façade.

Herdern Railway Service Facility

Herdern Railway Service Facility

Herdern Railway Service Facility

Herdern Railway Service Facility 224 2009–2013

Herdern Railway Service Facility

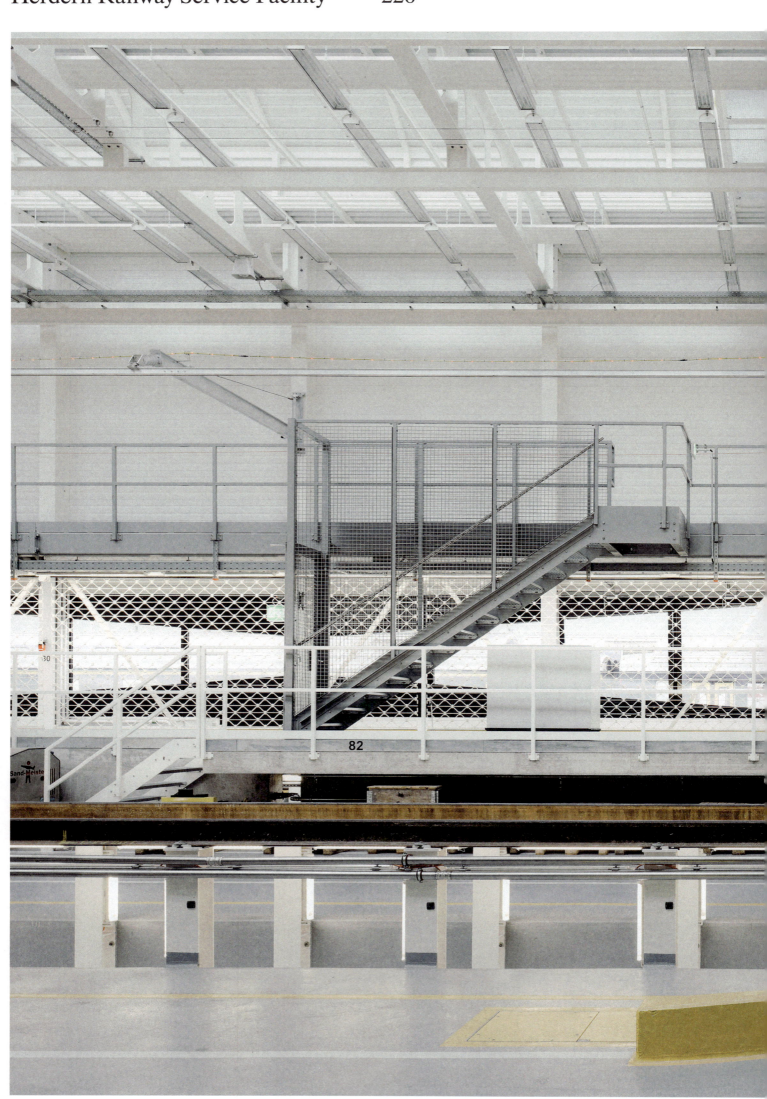

Herdern Railway Service Facility

Herdern Railway Service Facility

228

2009–2013

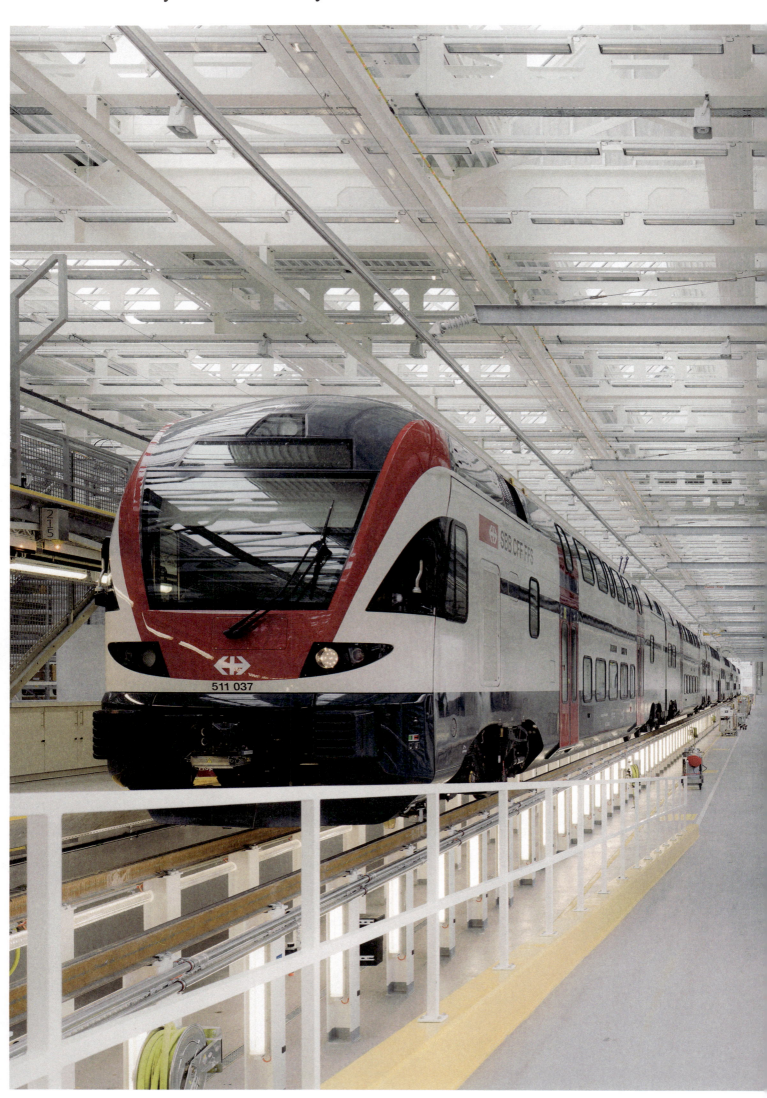

Viscosistadt

1

2

3

4

1–5
The Société de la Viscose Suisse was founded in Emmen in 1906. Initially, the factory mainly produced rayon, which was later supplanted by nylon and then by specialty fibers. Over the course of the firm's history, such changes in production always necessitated modifications to the premises. Research and production facilities were verticalized early on, with multistory research and production buildings joining the lower shed-type structures.

5

Viscosistadt 232 2011–2017

6 ↑ ↓ 7

Viscosistadt

6
The Viscosi site grew in several stages over the decades, becoming a district in its own right.

7
Ongoing densification soon created an urban atmosphere. The geometric logic underpinning the site's development set it apart from the surrounding urban realm and emphasized its separateness. The areas between the buildings performed multiple functions, serving as logistics spaces for the handling of road or rail freight, interim storage spaces, and circulation spaces for pedestrians, cyclists, and drivers.

8
The buildings' architectural language featured significant variation. As well as skeleton-frame structures of reinforced concrete with brick infill, there were also steel-frame structures and others built with solid walls. Nonetheless, the closed blocks, the restrained materiality, and the urban external spaces helped the site feel like a town in its own right, allowing it to become a kind of substitute for Emmen's nonexistent historic core.

Viscosistadt

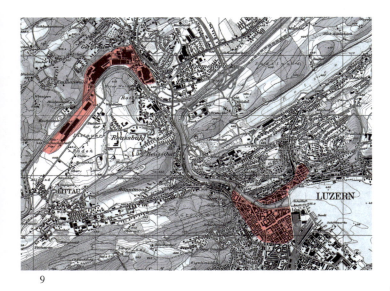

9

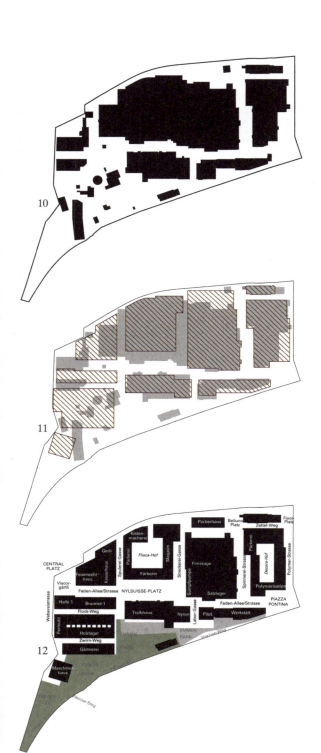

10

11

12

13

9
With regard to both their riverside location and their size, the industrial sites along the Emme bear similarities with the old town of Lucerne.

10–12
In our competition proposal, we imagined the new buildings as a continuation and reinterpretation of the existing fabric. As before, the site would develop incrementally, with new and old adding up to a stimulating whole.

13
An all-new aspect, on the other hand, was the connection to the water. A riverside park would open the site outwards into the Emme valley, creating a scenic counterpoint to the dense urban character within.

Viscosistadt

14 ↑   ↓ 15   16 ↑   ↓ 17

14–18
A model served to explore the spatial impact of the whole development. The look of the new buildings reinterpreted existing themes such as deep, rhythmic façades, restrained colors, large openings, and simple cuboid volumes.

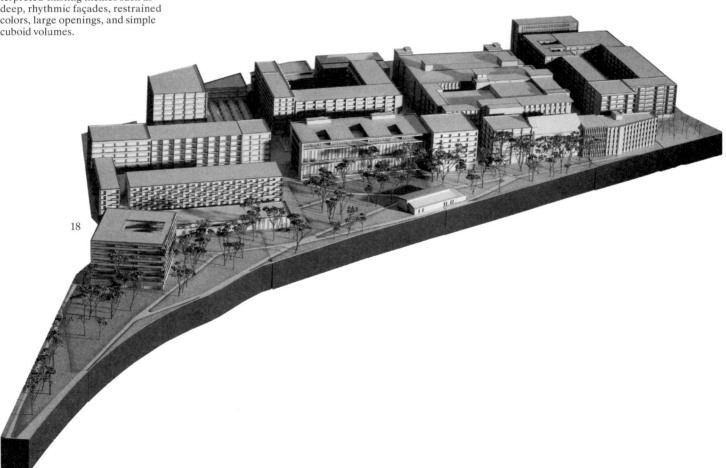

18

Viscosistadt

2011–2017

19 ↑ ↓ 20

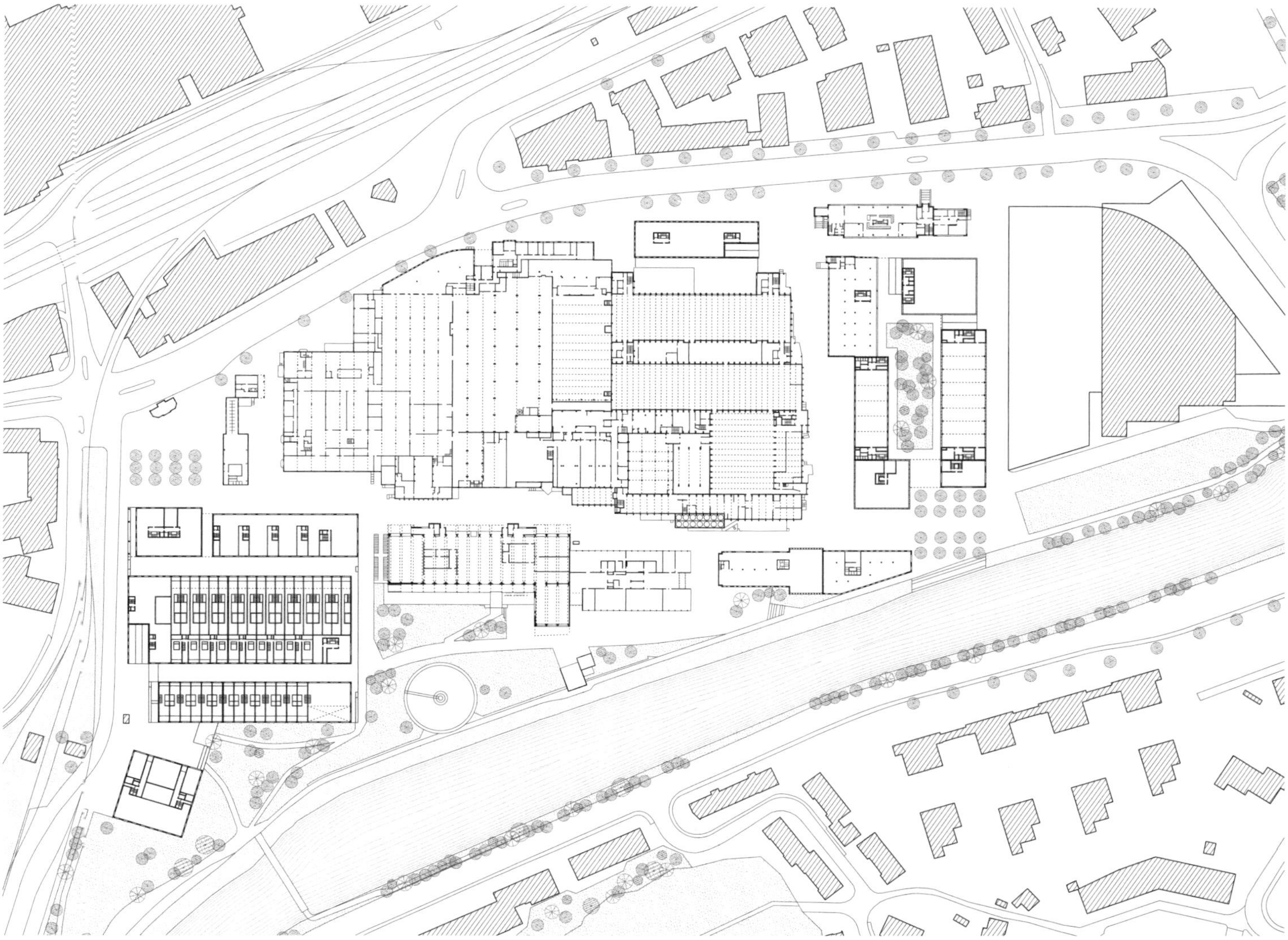

Viscosistadt

2011–2017

21 ↑

↓ 22

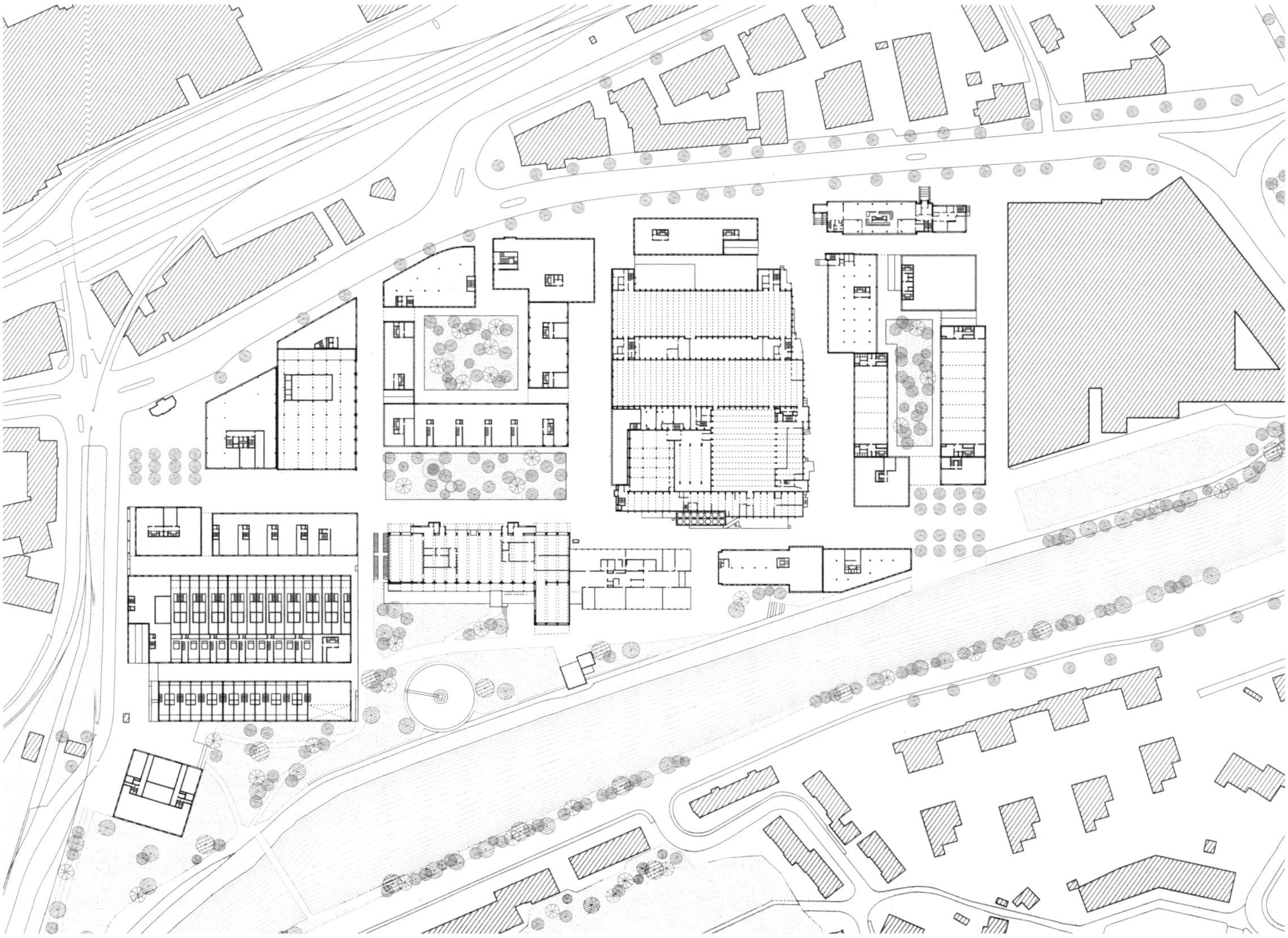

Viscosistadt

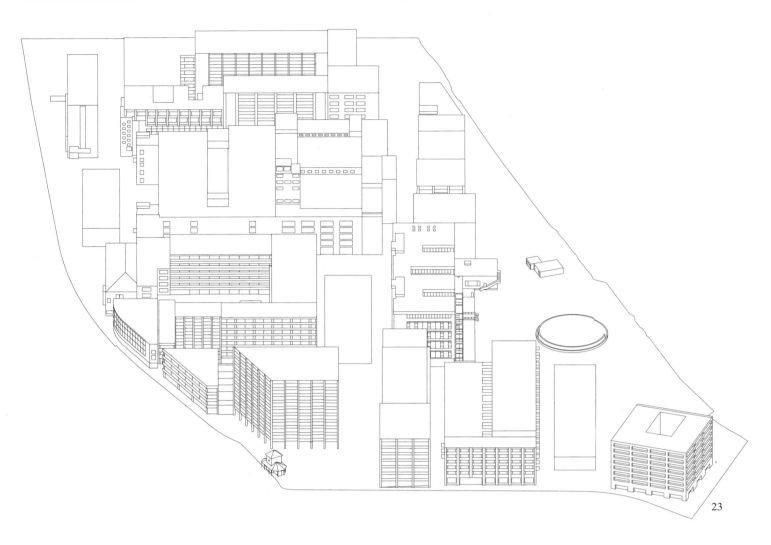

← 19–22
The redevelopment of the site was to take place incrementally over an extended period. While industrial production would continue within the core site, the outer edges would be redeveloped for commercial, educational, residential, or other usages. The overall figure would remain the same at all times and at each stage.

23
To preserve the organic, aggregate character, the master plan deliberately attempted to avoid a homogenization of the various buildings. The differing proportions of each lot, which encouraged creativity and adaptability rather than standard typologies, and the precise individual stipulations in the master plan provided highly specific starting points. Maximum eave heights were varied rather than uniform, while residential, commercial, and public usages were intermixed, thus encouraging breaks in scale and contrasts.

Engineering Building, University of Leicester

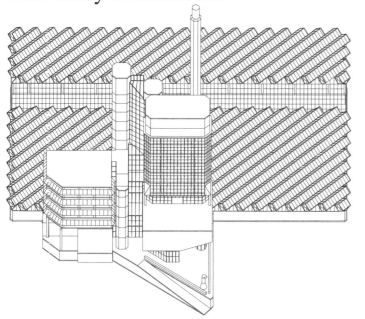

We love industrial buildings. Despite being shaped by hard-headed engineering logic, they regularly wow us with their radical forms, audacious spans, and light-filled interiors. The departure of industry from our urban centers has enabled new usages to be established in its disused sheds and blocks. Inherent in such repurposing is the joy of extravagance, the exhilaration of space, the charm of an imprecise fit. They liberate us from the need to find functionally and economically efficient solutions. By now, though, almost every suitable site has already been repurposed, leaving us once again to concentrate on the dreary task of developing precisely optimized and programmatically standardized schemes that maximize investors' returns.

Completed in 1963, James Stirling and James Gowan's engineering building for the University of Leicester showed us another way. Although it looked like a repurposed industrial conglomeration, their design was in fact a new-build, albeit one that, with its radically expressive forms, exuded the same bold spirit as great industrial architecture. By way of explanation, Stirling and Gowan pointed to the particular programmatic requirements, which included a flexibly usable, indirectly lit hall in which to set up experiments and a water tank that needed to be 30 meters above ground. Also, they contended, when building for engineers, you need to build like engineers.

Given our fondness for this spatial sculpture, this blend of rationality and irrationality, of simplicity and complexity, of technical engineering and manneristic bricolage, we're inevitably forced to ask ourselves why we can't follow Stirling and Gowan's example in our daily practice. Why don't we plan buildings that are outsize from the outset, that, precisely because of their ostensibly extravagant use of space and material, are more sustainable than economically optimized developments which may, a few years down the line, already require expensive adaptation or even demolition? What's stopping us from developing new industrial sites, places with complex densities, and spaces that don't just follow the dictates of the market, but are bigger and more adaptable than anything a marketing department would come up with?

Headquarters Roshen

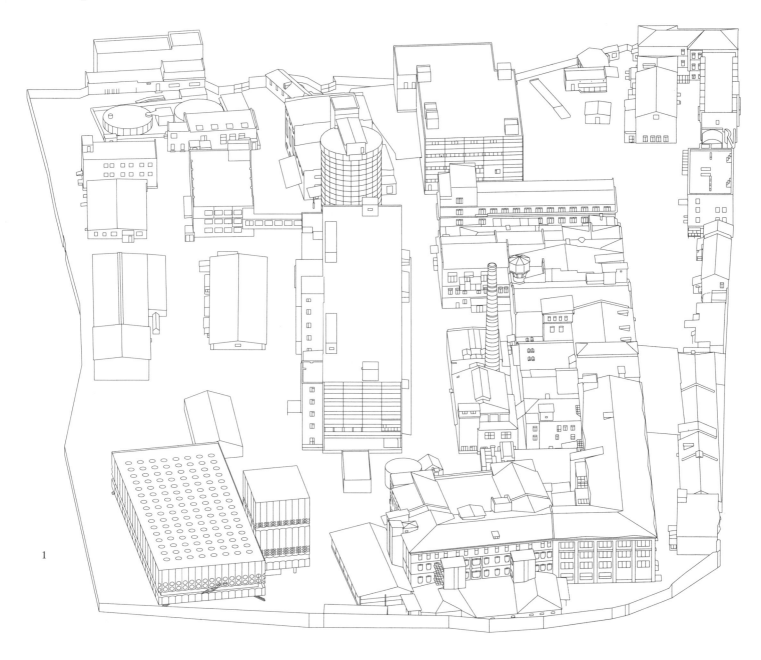

Headquarters Roshen

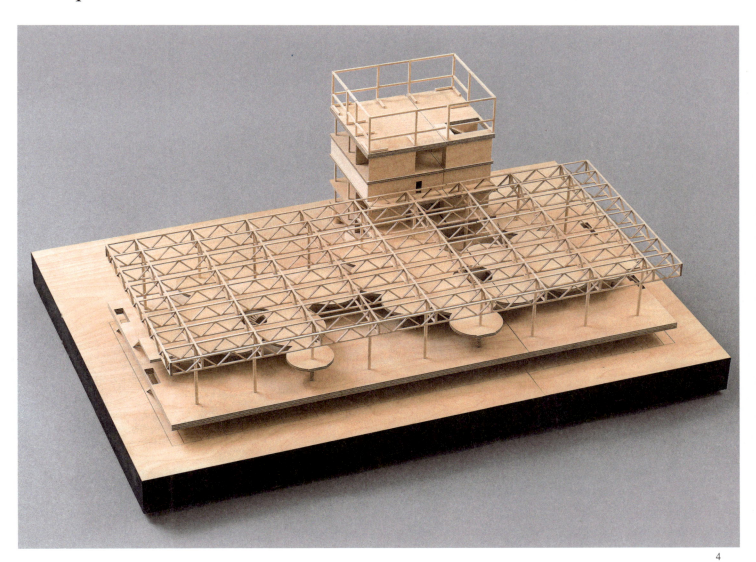

1
Before he became president of Ukraine (2014–2019), Petro Poroschenko was an oligarch with a conglomerate of companies that included chocolate makers Roshen. The firm had hitherto exported mostly to Russia and other ex-Soviet territories but had ambitions to start selling in the West. Combining a large retail store, a museum of chocolate, and innovative office spaces, the planned addition to its Kyiv headquarters would thus signal the dawn of a new era while also helping to promote the brand.

2
The only available space on this densely built industrial site was at its outer edges. Fascinated by the diversity and spatial density of the complex, we devised a hybrid of two industrial typologies, combining a large shed structure and a tower.

3
While the pillared shed with its internal gallery structure was intended for innovative workspaces, the tower would provide access, contain supporting infrastructure, and act as a symbolic street-facing branding vehicle. In addition to building services, it would also house the cafeteria and display spaces.

4 + 5
The structural model shows how the building's distinct and very different parts—tower block and pillared shed with wide-span roof and internal gallery—add up to a whole.

Headquarters Roshen

242

2012–2013

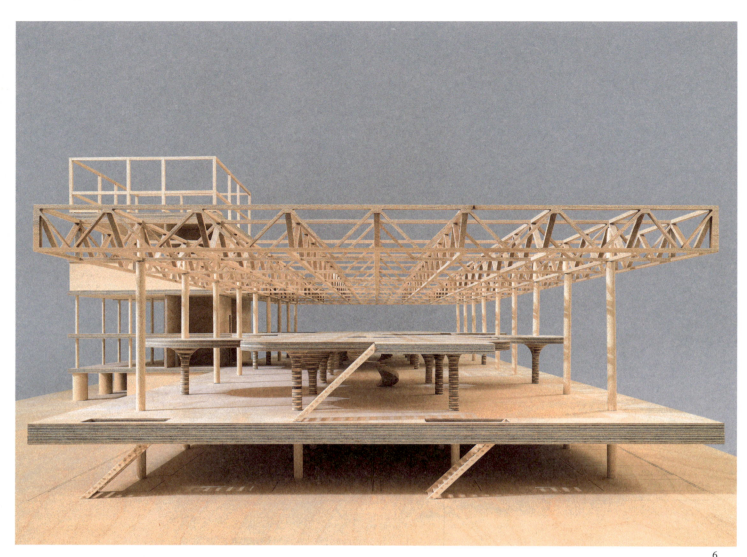

6

6 + 7
For the internal gallery, we devised an organic-looking structure resting on toadstool columns, while the wide-span shed roof was designed as a lightweight steel structure.

8–10
Plans for the ground floor and first and second stories.

7

Headquarters Roshen

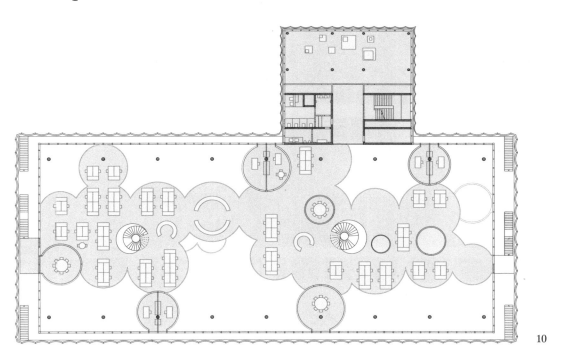

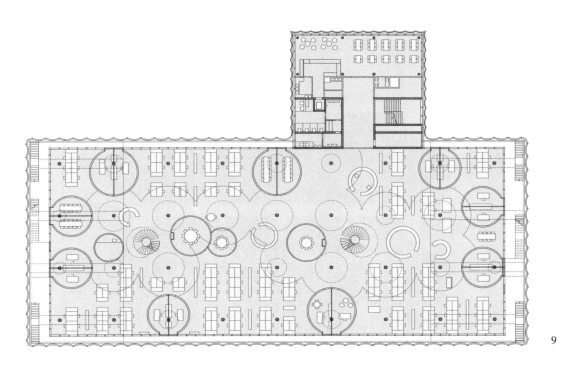

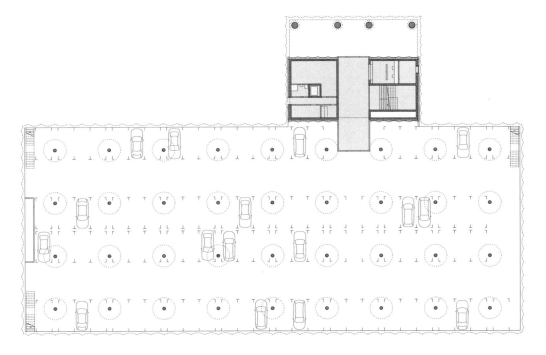

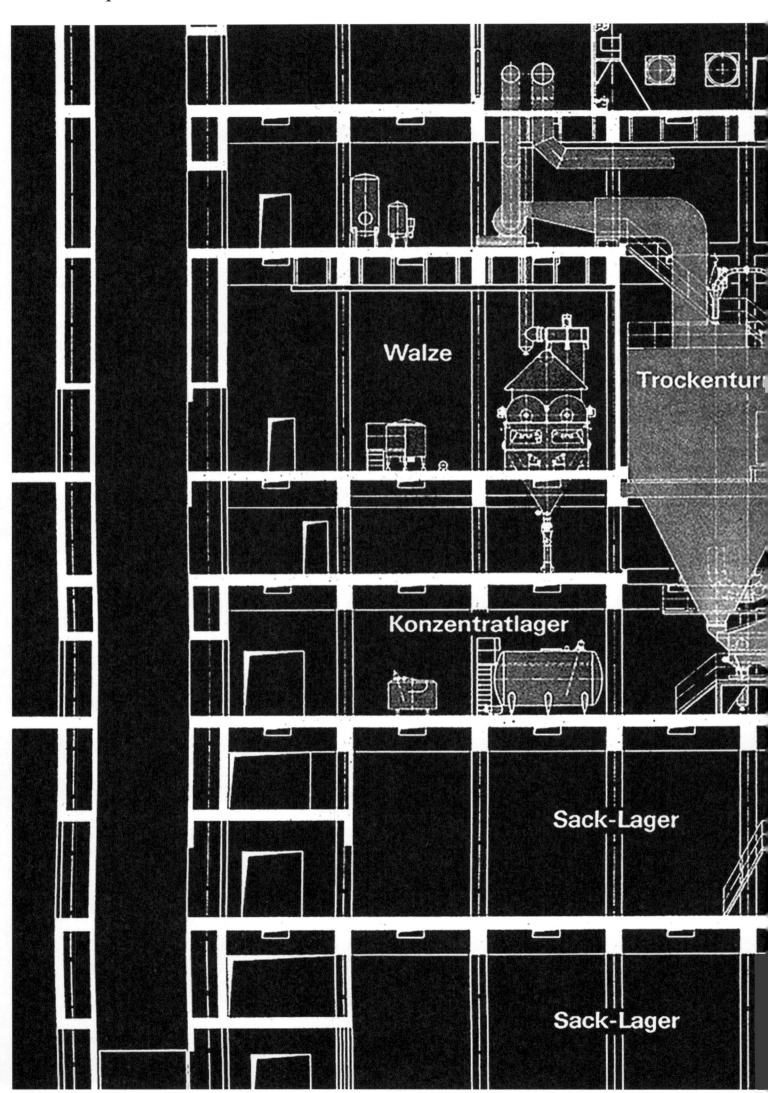

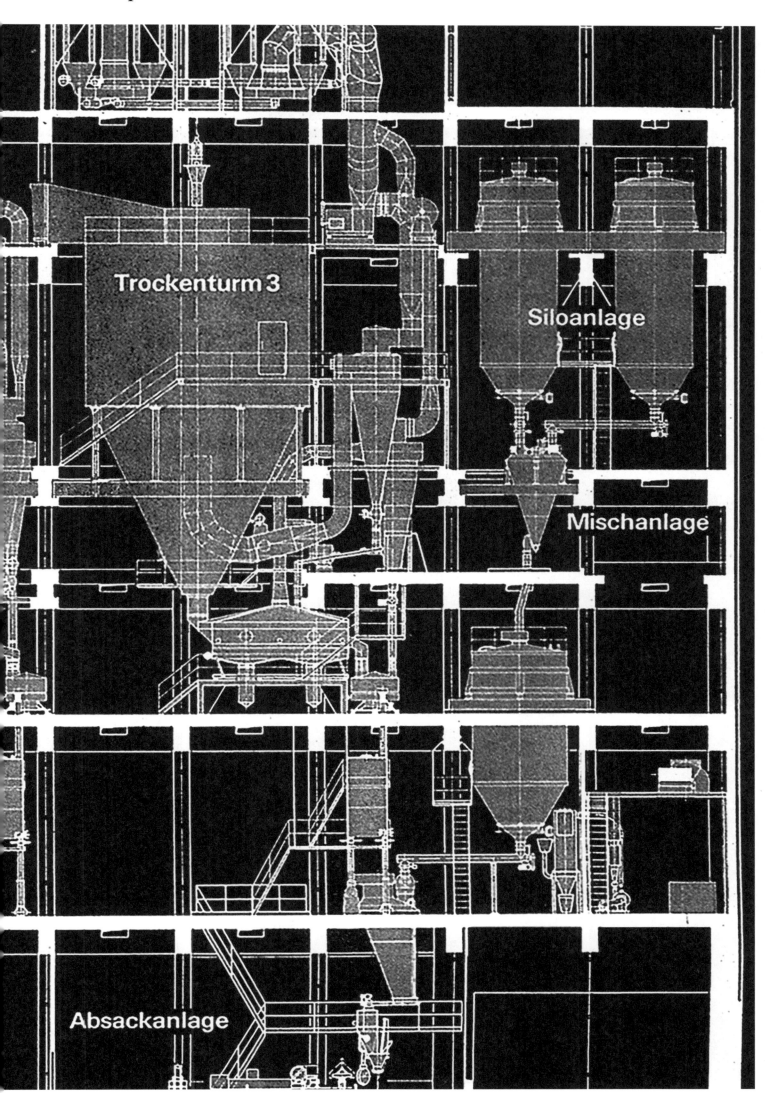

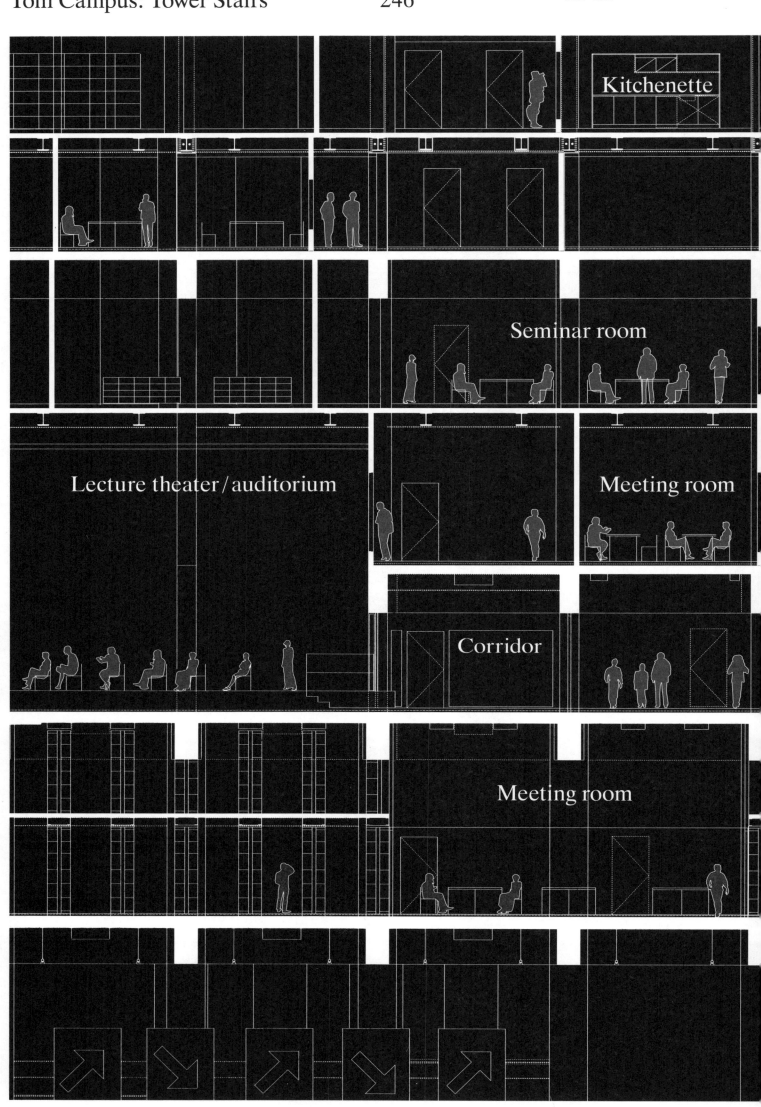

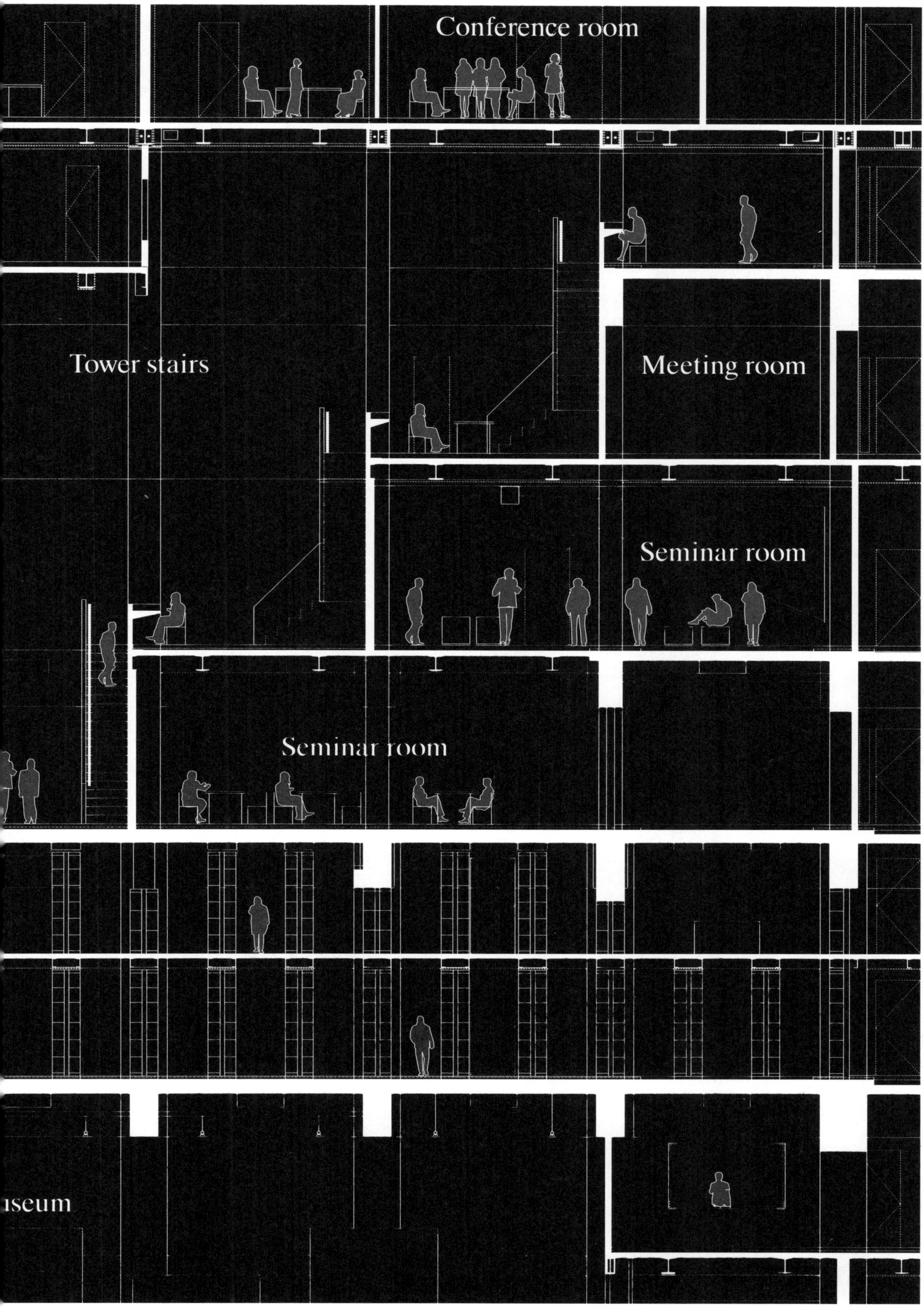

Toni Campus: Tower Stairs

Conference room

Tower stairs

Meeting room

Seminar room

Seminar room

useum

Toni Campus: Tower Stairs

Headquarters Sedorama

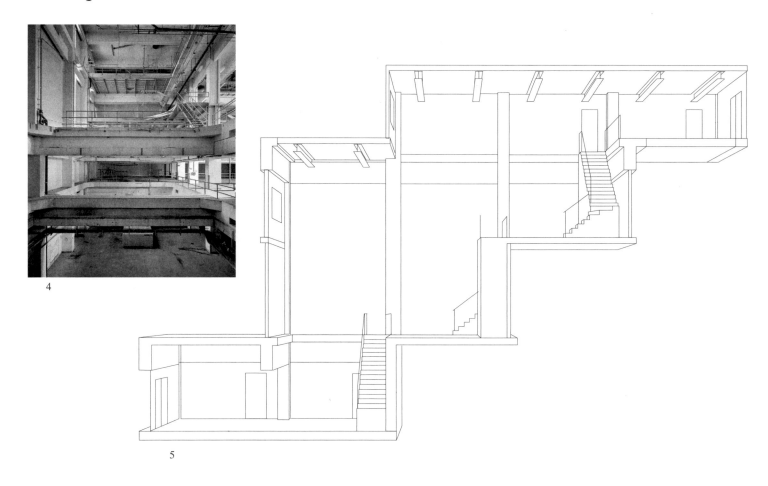

4

5

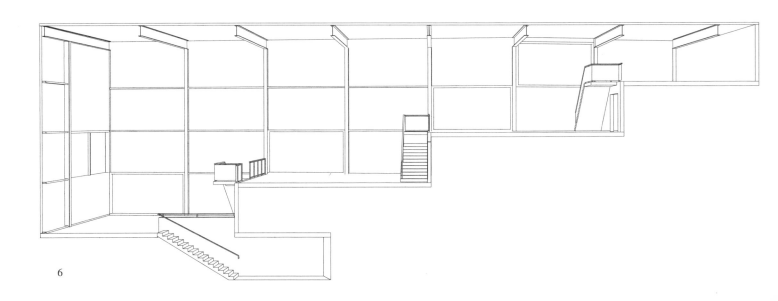

6

← 1–4
The cascading staircase of the Toni campus's tower was a response to the conditions in the existing interior. Poor light levels meant the tower's dark core didn't lend itself to spatial densification, so we instead proposed a compact cascading staircase. It performs a dual function, allowing for informal vertical circulation while providing workspaces for students on its landings. Prompted by the constraints of the site's existing fabric, this spatial arrangement has since served as a blueprint in various new-build projects. Inspiration from conversion!

5 + 6
The prototypology of the compact cascading staircase has since informed other new projects, including the new Swiss headquarters of German furniture maker Brunner. Here, it lends structure to the interior, which we split into distinct areas for storage and for display. While the storerooms and workshops decrease in size as you go up through the different levels, the showroom's spatial volume increases—maximizing space rather than surface area. The display areas can be stocked directly from the ancillary rooms.

Headquarters Sedorama

Headquarters Sedorama

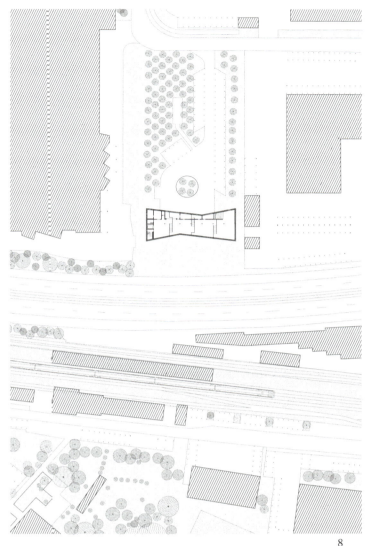

9

10

11

7
For the new headquarters of its Swiss subsidiary Sedorama, German furniture maker Brunner could offer only a limited budget. All the same, the firm wanted the premises, which were to be built right by the A1 freeway, to have an impactful look. Given the brief of maximum space at minimum cost, we built right up to the permissible height, creating a slender, elongated volume that even upstages the neighboring Schönbühl mall with its Coop supermarket.

8
Each longitudinal side of the main façade has a slightly concave kink. This not only gives the building greater presence when seen from the gently curving freeway, but the resulting void also allows for a tree-filled, noise-reduced entrance and milling area.

9–11
Standing adjacent to the A1, the almost entirely enclosed volume presents a somewhat mysterious aspect. Only the stepped arrangement of the windows offers clues to the surprises inside.

12
Model of the cascading levels.

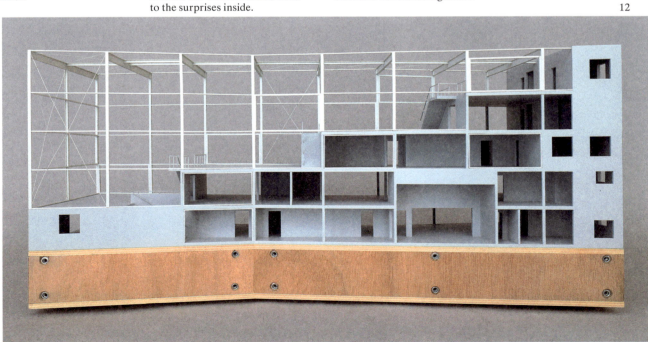

Headquarters Sedorama

252

2011–2013

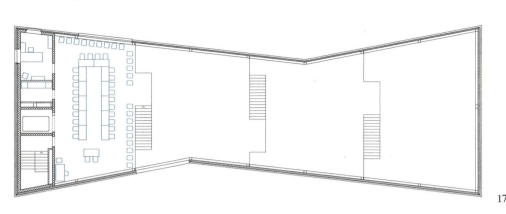

17

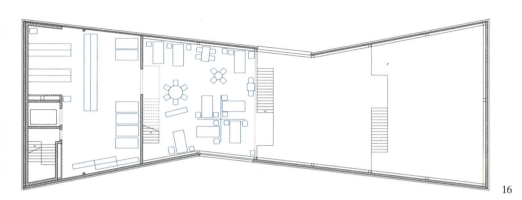

16

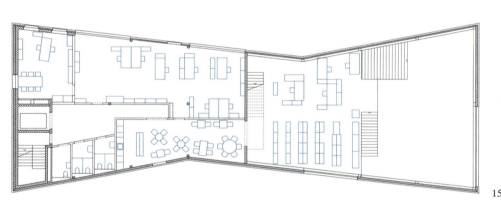

15

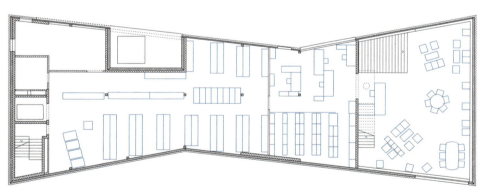

14

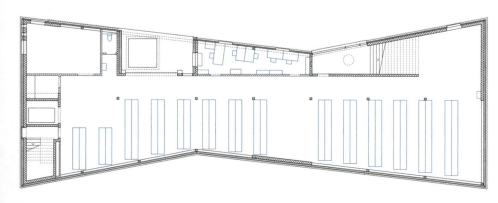

13

13–17
Plans for the ground floor and four upper stories.

18 + 19
Inside, the cascading levels have a surprisingly generous feel. A wide stair leads to the first upper floor, from where the display areas can be accessed via a series of terraced levels. Surfaces were either left bare or painted light gray, creating a neutral backdrop against which to showcase products.

20 →
The façade conceals and teases at the same time. Set into a membrane of perforated metal are large picture windows, the logical arrangement of which only becomes apparent once you're inside the building. It's a project that clearly succeeds in being both one thing and the other: spectacular yet restrained, efficiently designed yet elegantly poetic, the building oscillates between utilitarian functional architecture and eye-catching statement piece.

Headquarters Sedorama

253

2011–2013

18 ↑

↓ 19

Toni Campus: Demolition

1
The first openings provided glimpses of the tower's empty interior.

2
Where the low- and high-rise sections meet, the original structure had been almost completely opened up.

3
The thin sheet metal façade concealed a 90-meter-deep linear block.

4
At the culmination of demolition work, you could see right through the entire low-rise section. From then on, the huge block was ready to again be filled with spaces and substance.

5
Due to the vast depth of the building, five new lightwells had to be cut into the existing intermediate floors.

6
Sometimes the demolition site felt like a 1:1 scale model.

7
The demolition process revealed the low-rise section's expansive open spaces and the tower's robust concrete skeleton.

Intelligent Carcasses

Mathias Müller
Daniel Niggli

1 ↑   ↓ 2

With her mitten-versus-glove analogy, Denise Scott Brown postulated the idea that buildings work better when they are not precisely tailored to their initial usage, but rather planned with a degree of "wiggle room."[A] This loose fit may result in certain short-term inefficiencies but, in the long run, it makes for far more adaptable and future-proof spaces, spaces with potential for appropriation. The success of such an infrastructural approach depends not on buildings' refined details, but on the robustness and effectiveness of their structures and on internal qualities such as generosity, height, and good lighting. These prerequisites allow them to assimilate fit-outs for varying usage requirements.

The city-factory's emphasis on robust structures requires carcasses to be more than just unfinished buildings. These are structures that aspire to a high degree of permanence and, as such, the way they are designed has long-term consequences. We therefore need carcasses that are intelligently designed—in terms of how they impact on the urban realm, how easily they adapt to different forms of usage, and how efficiently they make use of resources. Then, of course, we also demand beauty, that our structures be aesthetic and expressive.

A prime example of this holistic approach can be seen in Marcel Meili and Markus Peter's 1991 proposal for the Alb valley in southern Germany. This architecture and urban design study envisioned augmenting existing industrial sites with a series of large-scale buildings that would result in a more precise channeling of airflows, thereby optimizing the aerodynamics of the entire valley area. In conjunction with a new park and a new irrigation system, these revised currents would help improve the urban climate in nearby Ettlingen. The new-builds were designed as expressive tectonic structures with just a few determining factors. Robust load-bearing structures, prominent circulation cores, and spatially determined conduits for technical services thus shape their architectural form. Inside, varying depths and orientations make for spaces that lend themselves to various usages.

Intelligent Carcasses

Mathias Müller
Daniel Niggli

3 ↑   ↓ 4

With their Alb valley study, Meili and Peter offered a thoughtful, multifaceted take on the issue of control. On the one hand, they devised robust structures that strive for permanence. On the other, they relinquished a degree of control, attempting to guide architectural and urban design processes solely via the creation of intelligent basic frameworks, establishing what you might call architectural microclimates that could then be left to develop autonomously. Here, architecture, infrastructure, landscape, and ecology are so thoroughly intertwined that they ultimately become mutually dependent. This deliberate pushing of disciplinary boundaries opens up new architectural potential and ensures the built environment remains fit for purpose over the long term.

A
Denise Scott Brown, "The Redefinition of Functionalism," in: Robert Venturi, Denise Scott Brown, *Architecture as Signs and Systems: For a Mannerist Time*, Cambridge, Massachusetts, 2004.

1
Glove and mitten.

2
A. B. Walker, illustration in *Life* magazine, 1909.

3 + 4
Marcel Meili, Markus Peter Architekten, study for the Alb valley, 1991.

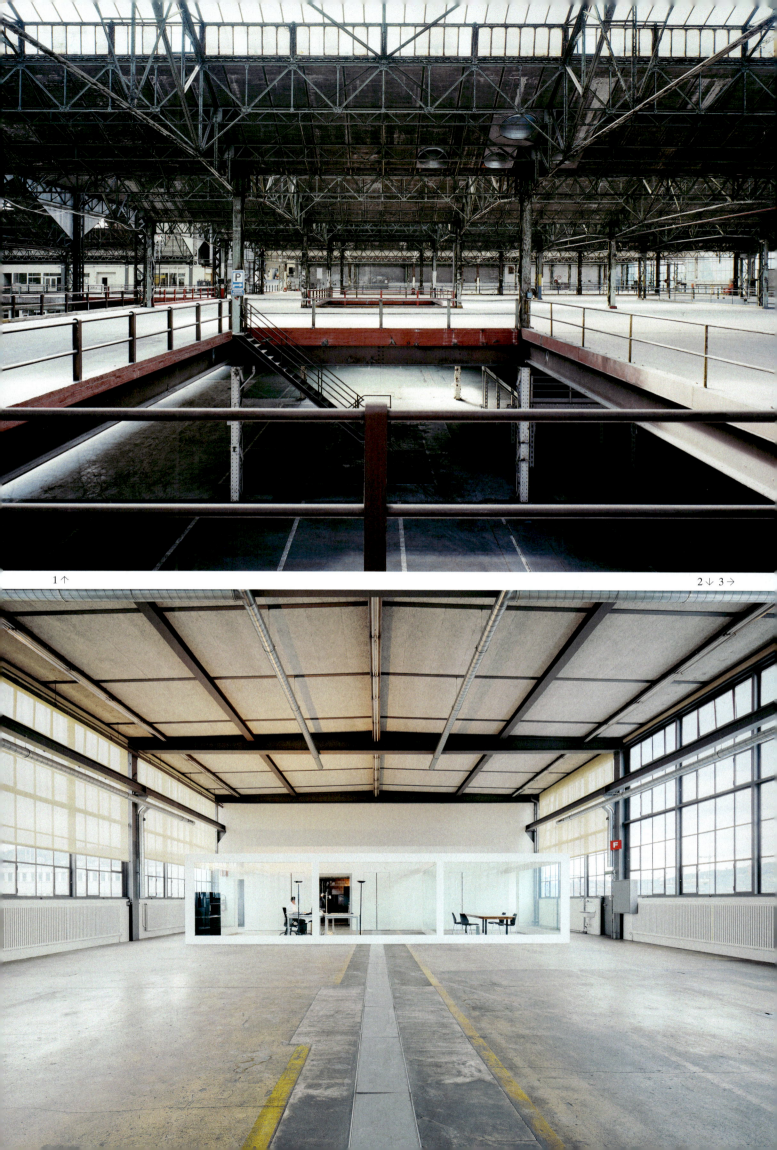

1 ↑ 2 ↓ 3 →

 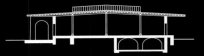 

Goods shed complex, Zurich

Magazzini Generali warehouse, Chiasso

Zellweger Luwa, Uster

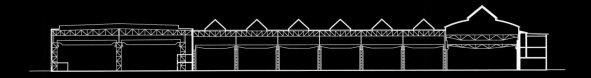

Escher-Wyss factory, Zurich

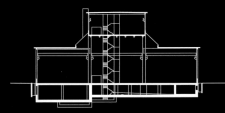 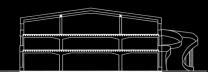 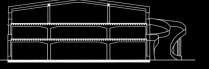

MAAG factory, Zurich

J.H. Keller AG, Zurich

Grain Warehouse, Altdorf

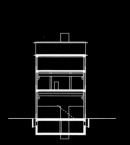 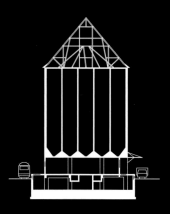 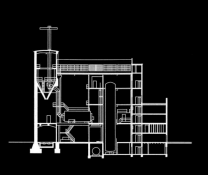

Grain silo, Altdorf

Bernoulli silo, Basel

Sulzer plant boiler house, Oberwinterthur

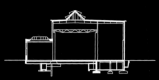

ABB factory,
Baden

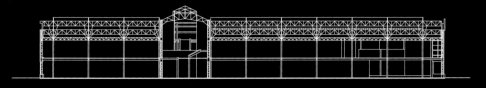

Citroën,
Brussels

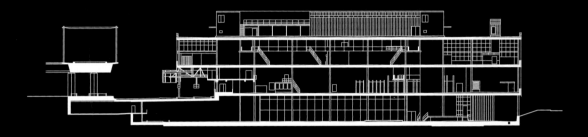

Toni dairy,
Zurich

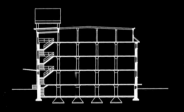

Jakobstal spinning mill,
Bülach

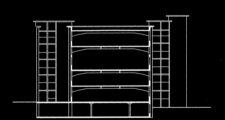

Monosuisse factory,
Emmenbrücke

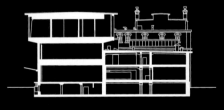

Löwenbräu brewery,
Baden

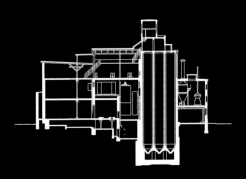

Warteck brewery,
Basel

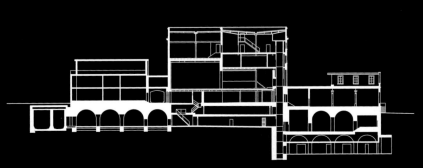

Hürlimann brewery,
Zurich

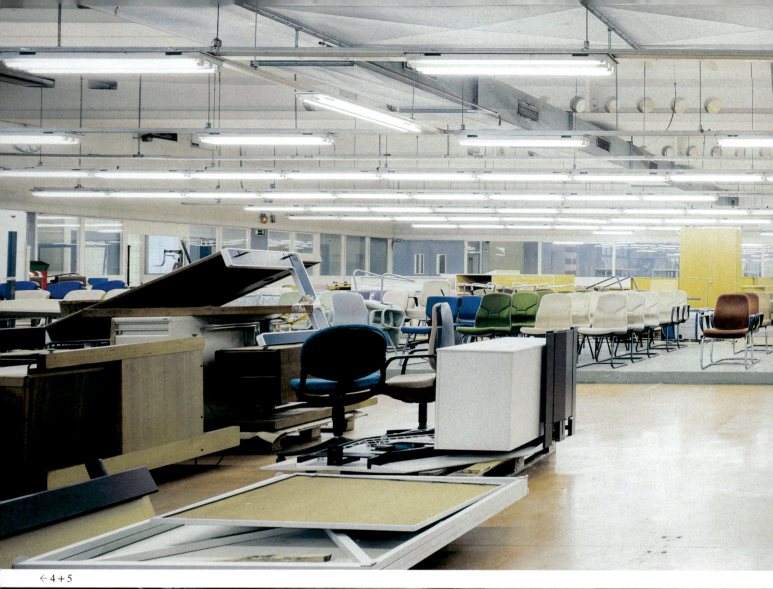

← 4 + 5

6 ↑   ↓ 7

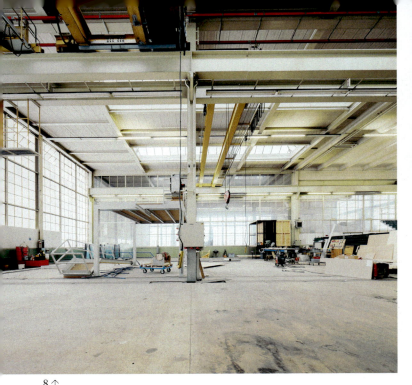
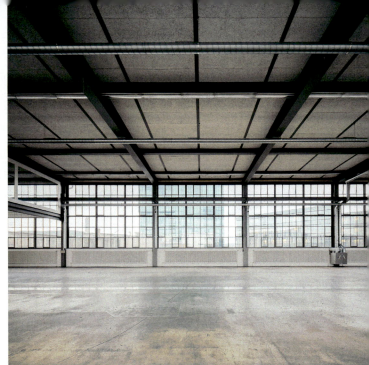

8 ↑ 9 ↑

10 ↑ ↓ 11 12 ↓

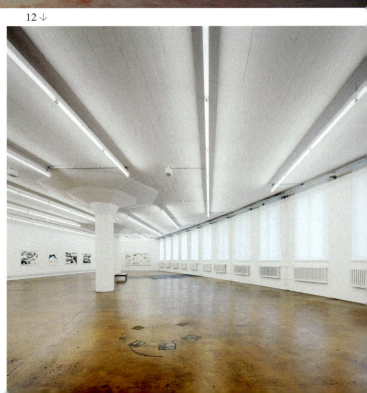

Lucerne School of Art and Design 269

Lucerne School of Art and Design

← 1
A former research laboratory and testing facility with attached high-bay warehouse, Building 745 had a striking key feature: its radical load-bearing structure. Ultralight ceiling elements, just 8 centimeters in height, were borne by gently curving supports with a 22-meter span. The positioning of stair and elevator towers at the edges of the plan maximized the available floor space, resulting in vertically stacked pillarless levels capable of accommodating a host of different usages.

2
Cross-section. Demolishing the high-bay warehouse exposed the western, river-facing façade. The large entrance hall forms a public space that links the delivery lane and the new riverside park.

3
Longitudinal section. Extremely high ceilings allow the structure to easily accommodate spaces of all sizes, from small server room up to large entrance hall.

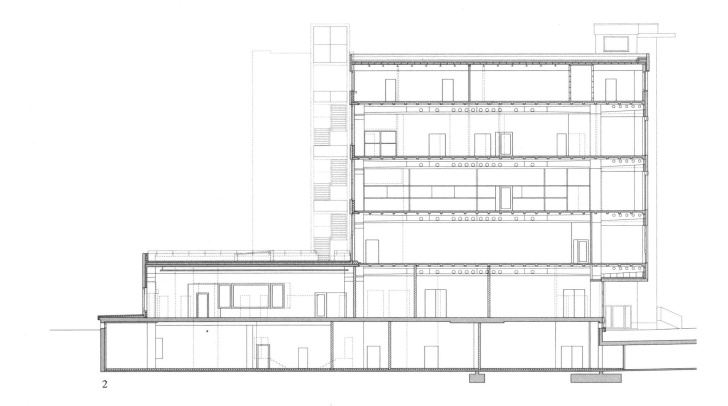

Lucerne School of Art and Design

2012–2019

4

5

4 + 5
Due to its central position within the site and its proximity to the new riverside park, Building 745 is a key element in the Viscosistadt development. Its repurposing as an art college provides a programmatic jumping-off point for the site's conversion into a mixed-used district in which public usages, residential development, and services are accommodated alongside established industrial usages. The building wasn't a designated historic monument but neither was it a teardown, its extremely capable load-bearing structure making it highly suitable for reuse.

6 + 7
The building is essentially a series of vertically stacked levels. Taking out internal walls revealed the generous, wide-span structure of prestressed supports and delicate ceiling panels.

8 →
The river-facing balcony structure not only improves fire safety but also adds usable external spaces and creates a new architectural form that identifies the building as a public amenity. The exterior's existing materials were retained wherever possible. Where new materials such as rendered thermal insulation were required, we ensured new and old would complement each other in an understated way.

6 ↑

↓ 7

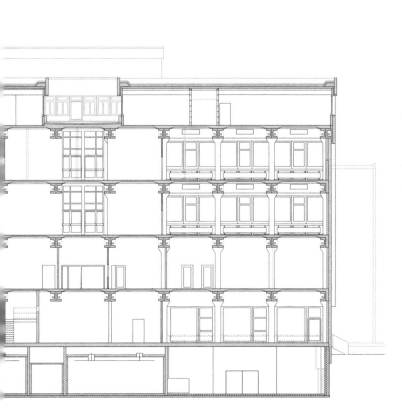

Lucerne School of Art and Design 274 2012–2019

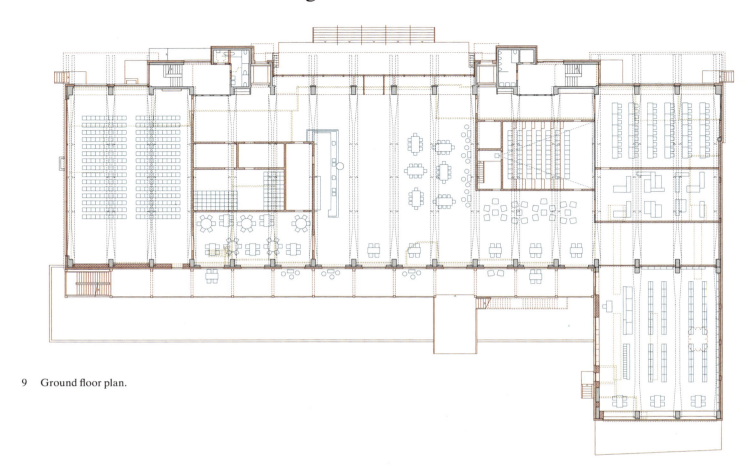

9   Ground floor plan.

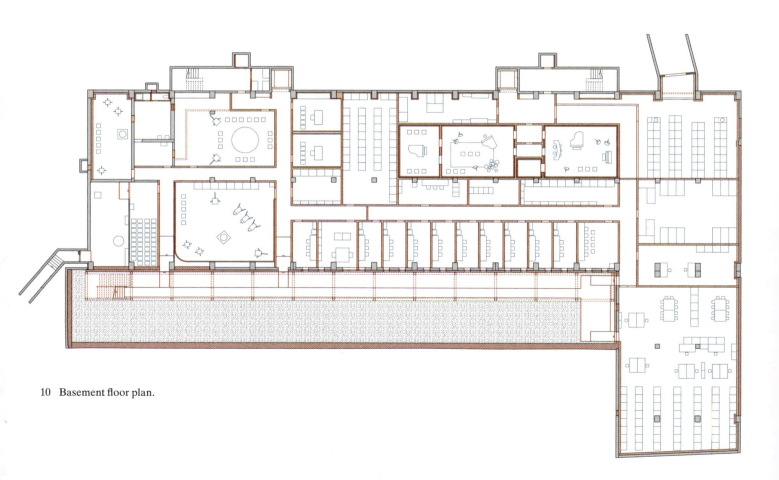

10   Basement floor plan.

Lucerne School of Art and Design

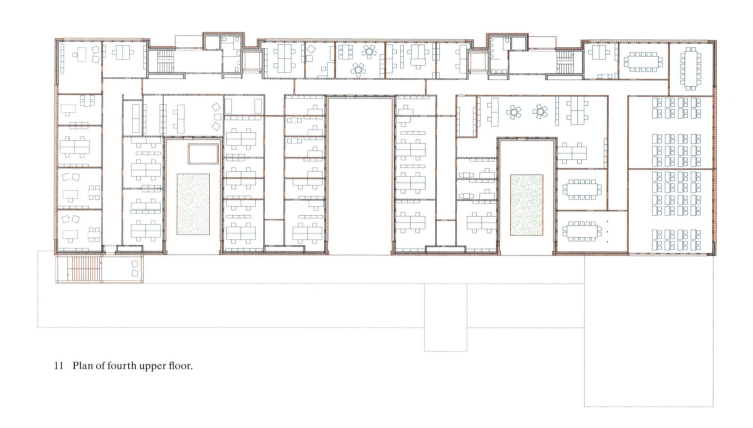

11 Plan of fourth upper floor.

9–12
Due to budgetary constraints, we limited ourselves to the most essential interventions. Circulation areas were kept to a minimum, and as many existing walls retained and integrated into the design as possible.

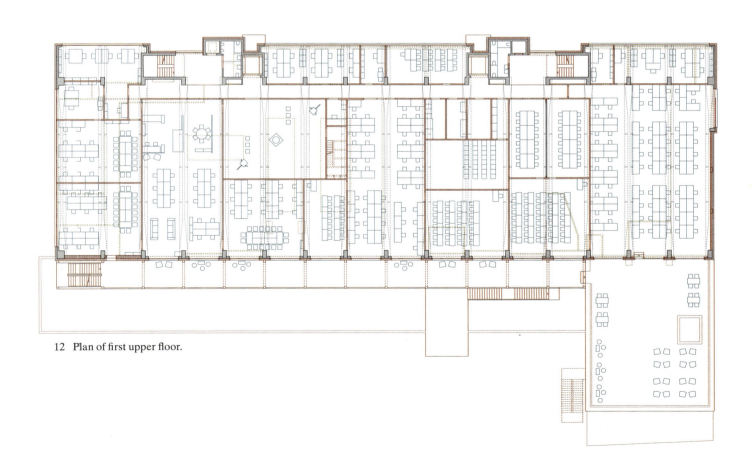

12 Plan of first upper floor.

Lucerne School of Art and Design

13

13 + 14
The large hall contains the entrance area, a café, and an exhibition space. The interior finishes take their cue from the materials that were already there, such as the distinctive yellow wood-cement floors, sections of which had to be repaired or replaced. Other than in the library, we deliberately eschewed additional colors to avoid creating interiors that were too rigidly designed. Services were also pared down, with spaces using natural ventilation wherever possible and all installations left exposed.

15 + 16
Specialist spaces such as the recording studio, editing suites, and film studio are housed in the basement.

14 ↑   ↓ 15

16

Lucerne School of Art and Design

17 ↑ ↓ 18

17, 18 + 20
The workshop spaces give the students ample scope for individual customization.

19
The retained stairwells emphasize the impressive floor heights. The flights wind their way between the stories via galleried landings.

19

20

21 →
A dark space with bold accent colors, the library was regarded as a special usage case and given a different treatment to the rest of the interiors.

Stapferhaus

1

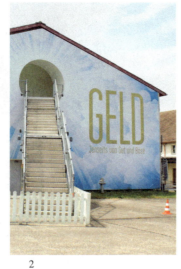

2

3

4

1–3 Lenzburg's Verein Stapferhaus had been putting on changing exhibitions at an old armory, a space that offered a high degree of flexibility, functionality, and openness. The owner, however, was planning a change of use. As a replacement venue, the foundation wanted to build new premises directly opposite the train station. For the design of the new building, we took our cue from the inventiveness with which curators had approached the previous gallery space, the radical ways they had maximized the potential of this "empty shed." Some exhibitions had even seen interventions in the building's shell, such as moving the entrance to the upper floor.

4 Given the unconventional and radical nature of previous exhibition concepts, the unpretentious typology of a shed seemed almost ideal. Our proposal thus resisted the temptation to give the new premises a spectacular exterior. Instead, we proposed a "decorated shed" that would maximize appropriability.

5 + 6 → The design featured a timber-built industrial structure standing on a floor plate and bookended by two concrete façades. The use of timber, a material that can be worked with the simplest of tools, promised a radical degree of tolerance towards exhibition-specific interventions.

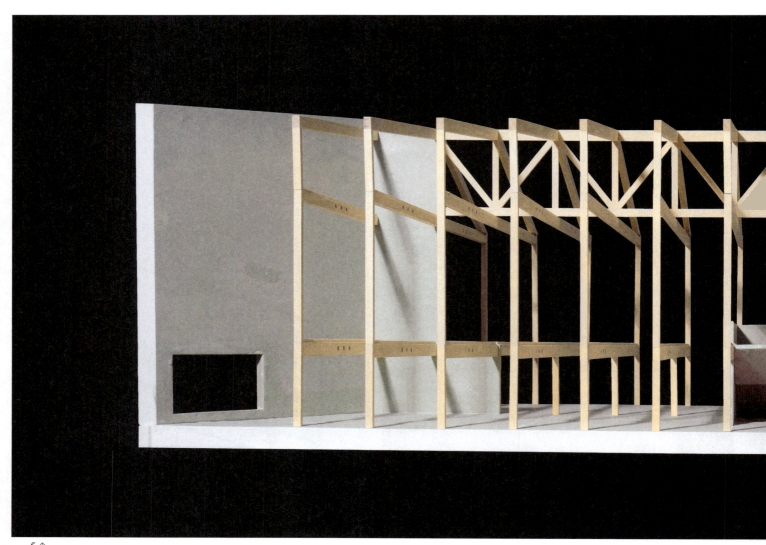

5 ↑

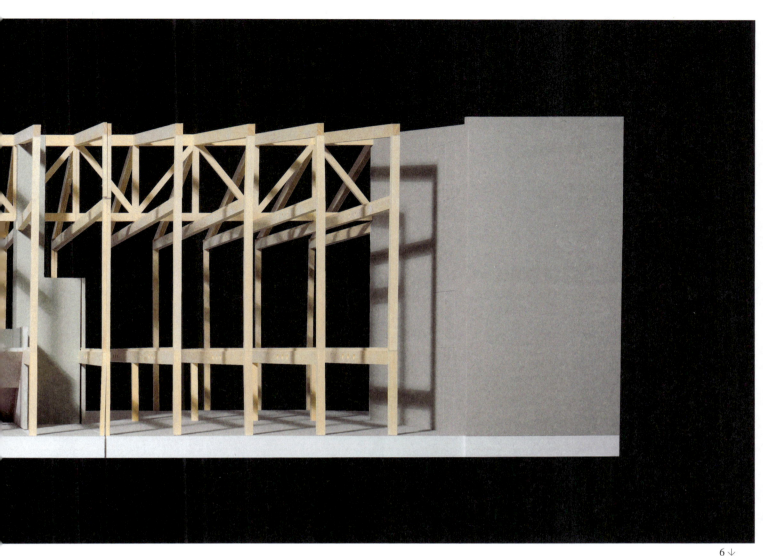

6 ↓

Stapferhaus

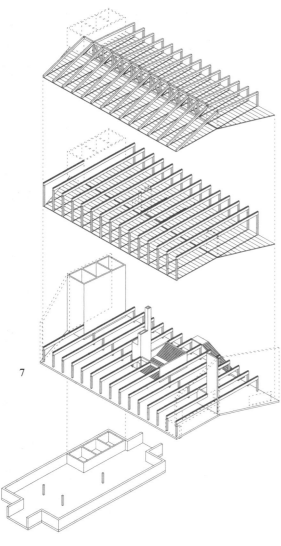

7
We devised a wide-span timber structure whose large supports bear thin ceiling elements that can be removed if required. The massy concrete staircase was intended as a spatial focal point but could also be an actor in its own right, serving as audience seating, for example. The sculptural volume combining staircase and elevator tower, meanwhile, served to link the foyer with the main gallery space upstairs, allowing exhibitions to also start on the ground floor.

8 + 9
The upper floor's pillarless shed typology was chosen for optimum flexibility regarding exhibition design. Here, visitors would have views of the surrounding area through three carefully placed windows. The attic story above would house the workshop, storerooms, and offices.

10
The main façade was conceived as a blank canvas, allowing the urban aspect of the "shed" to be tailored to the current exhibition's theme. Only the few large-format windows indicate that this could be a public building rather than just a mundane warehouse.

11
While the front was designed to emphasize the building's public character, the rear was deliberately given a more functional look, with only the large doors for deliveries and staff interrupting an otherwise closed concrete façade.

12–14
Longitudinal sections of the ground and upper floors.

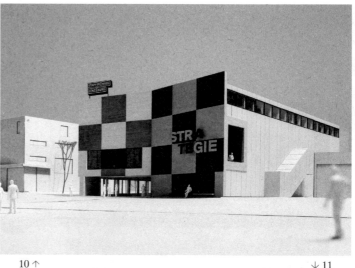

Stapferhaus

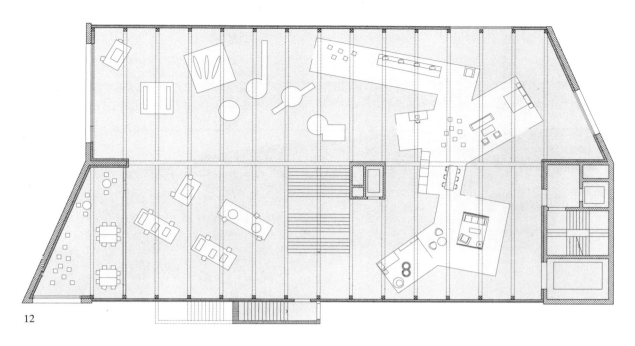

12

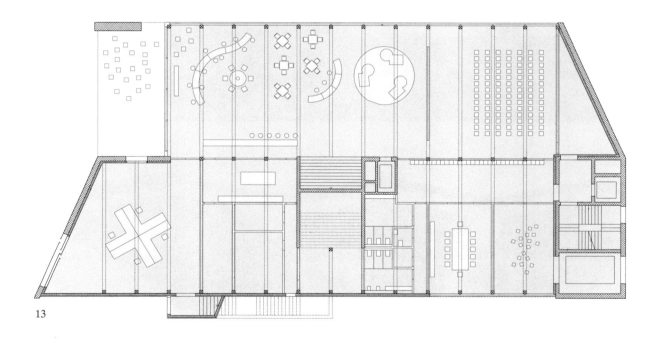

13

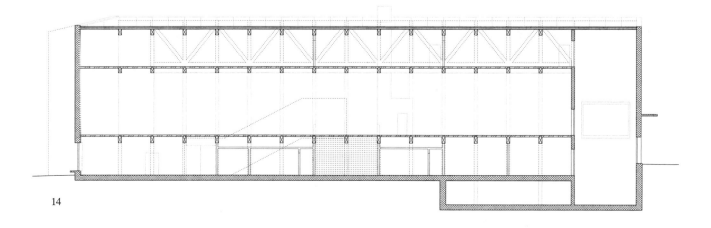

14

1 ↑

2 ↓

Long-Span Roofs

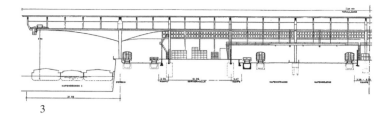

3

One of the simplest but most striking architectural typologies is the long-span roof. By which we mean not conventional building roofs but free-standing roofs that are structures and architectural forms in their own right. Generally open-sided, these latter exist merely to provide shelter from the rain or sun, spanning a space without predefining its usage. They are simple, protective gestures of unmatched immediacy. At the same time, such a canopy marks out and occupies an area, though without definitively specifying its boundaries; the space beneath is instead allowed to flow unhindered, the roof merely modifying its character. Serving to both demarcate and connect, these roofs offer potential and create possibilities. They are not prescriptive in terms of usage, making them one of the most neutral typologies around. At the same time, they make for impactful, memorable places. With their ability to bring together various smaller-scale and ostensibly incompatible elements, they are a useful typological means of lending definition to fragmented places or bringing homogeneity to disparate arrays of spaces.

1 + 2
In November 2011, we revisited the transshipment hub at Kleinhüningen docks, a place that has fascinated us since our very first trips to Basel. At this river port on the Rhine, goods are unloaded from ships and transferred to trains and trucks, a task requiring a covered transshipment and storage area. To that end, a 234-meter-long, 50-meter-wide, and 16-meter-high shed was built, the vast size of which can only really be appreciated from the air. As the first cantilevered prestressed concrete structure in Switzerland, the hub is a pioneering work. Its roof extends some 32 meters beyond the dock itself, a slender steel skeleton divides the shed below into three distinct areas, while the crane stanchions double as supports for the shallow pitched roof.

3
Longitudinal section, transshipment hub at dock I, Kleinhüningen docks, Basel, built by architects Bräuning, Leu, Dürig and engineers A. Aegerter and Dr. O. Bosshardt AG, 1953.

4
Half a village had to make way to allow the transshipment hub to be built. The arrival of port logistics brought radical changes in scale and use.

4

Heuried Sports Center

← 1
Heuried public pool, Zurich—view of the overcrowded outdoor pools and lawns, around 1975. Photo: Pro Juventute.

2
This historical map from 1930 shows the Heuried brickworks and associated claypit.

3
Zürcher Ziegeleien's steam-powered brickworks in Heuried was operational up until the 1950s.

4–6
Over the years, areas of new housing sprang up around this former industrial site. In the 1960s, approval was granted for the redevelopment of the old claypit. The aim was to provide residents with a new social hub featuring sports facilities, a community center, and a school. Between 1961 and 1965, architects Hans Litz and Fritz Schwarz thus built a sports and leisure center featuring open-air pools and two outdoor ice-skating rinks, integrating them into the artificially terraced landscape left behind by clay extraction. The combination of sports, relaxation, and leisure was considered groundbreaking at the time and, in 1968, the project was named among the winners of Zurich's Good Building Awards.

7–9
In 2008, a competition was held for the redevelopment of Heuried sports center. The open-air swimming pool was to be completely overhauled and an indoor rink added for year-round ice-skating. The extensive scheme promised to bring a new urban scale to the area. Instead of breaking it down into the numerous elements required by the brief, we opted for the forward-looking strategy of combining the various usages under one expansive roof. And instead of echoing the small-scale pattern of the surrounding neighborhood, we opted for the large scale of open-space and landscape planning.

Heuried Sports Center

2011–2015

7

8

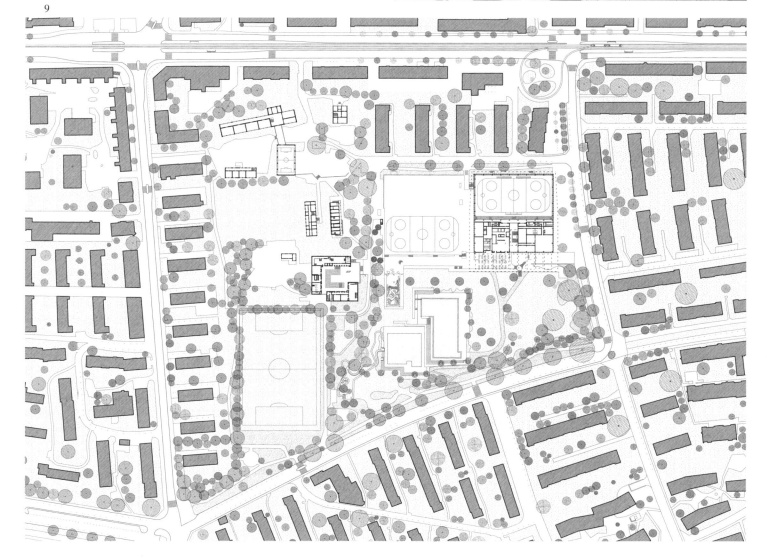

9

Heuried Sports Center

12

13

Heuried Sports Center

292

2011–2015

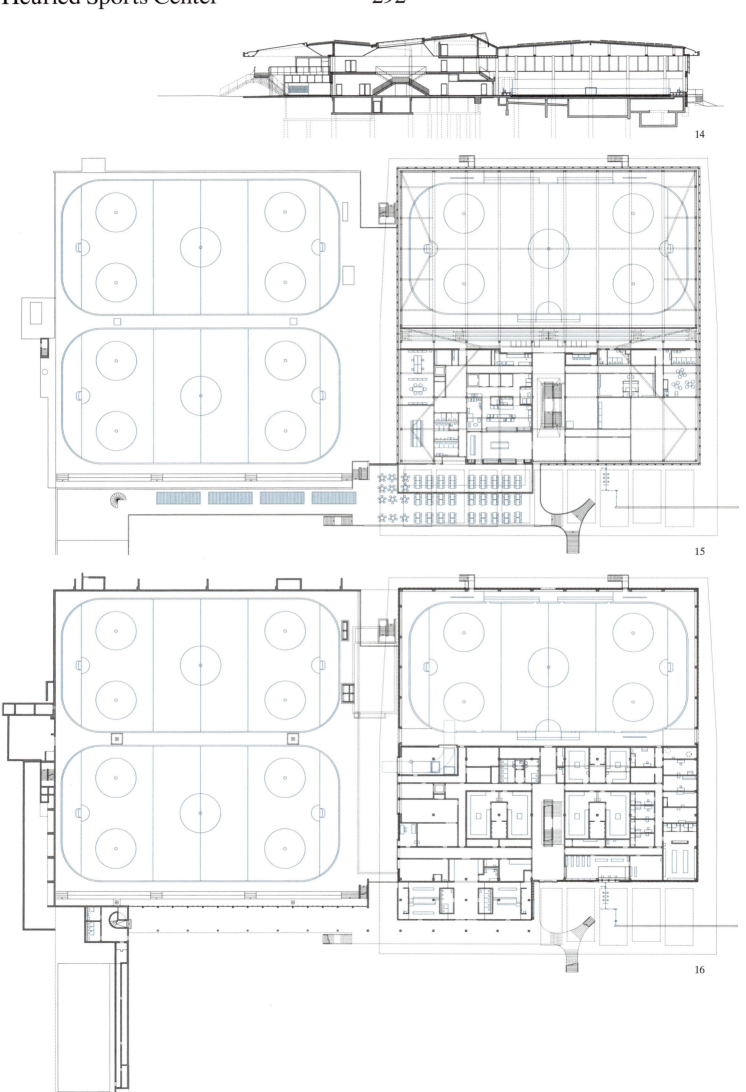

Heuried Sports Center

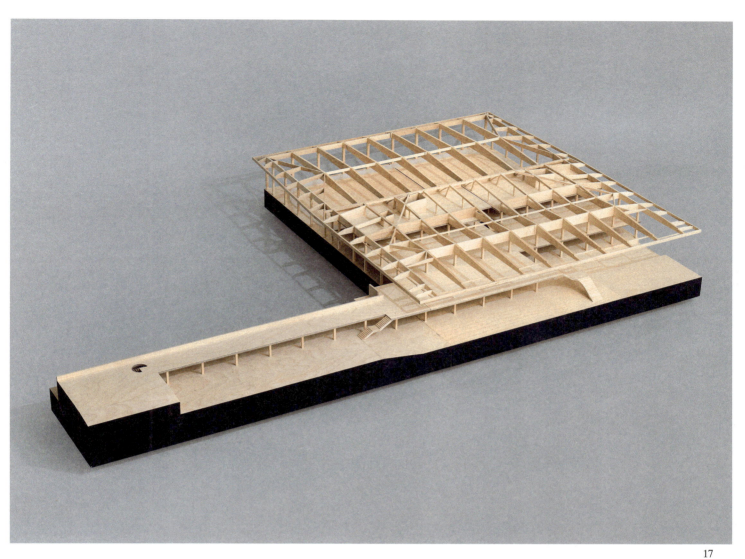

17

← 10–13
The complex is well frequented at all times of year. The indoor ice rink means skating and swimming can both now be offered in summer. The outdoor rink is only open in fall and winter.

14
Cross-section.

15
Upper floor plan.

16
Ground floor plan.

17 + 18
Our design consisted of two main elements: a plinth informed by the topography and the existing pools and lawns, and a roof with a wide overhang that projects out over the plinth. The roof creates a generous entrance area for the entire facility and helps to blur the line between outdoors and indoors, summer and winter, and water- and ice-based activities. Concrete and wood were chosen as key materials for the two elements.

19 →
Shaped by the topography of the pool terraces, the sun terrace extends to beneath the overhanging roof, while the stair bridge, which directly addresses the muscular structure of the indoor ice rink, forms a key focal point of the landscaped area. The stairs also provide access to the upper-floor restaurant, a typical feature of public pools in Zurich, from where customers can survey the activity on the lawn.

20 + 21 →
The entrance hall extends from the main entrance to the indoor ice rink. With its colored glass and mirrors, the glass skylight by art duo Wiedemann Mettler creates a kaleidoscopic effect.

22 →
An existing civil defense shelter and access to a parking garage were integrated into the new building. Designed by Bivgrafik, the signage uses timber slats similar to those of the exterior cladding.

23 →
The fencing by the entrance also references the external cladding, reinterpreting it as a spatial element.

24 →
The openness of the complex creates deliberate overlaps between outdoors and indoors and between summer and winter usages.

18

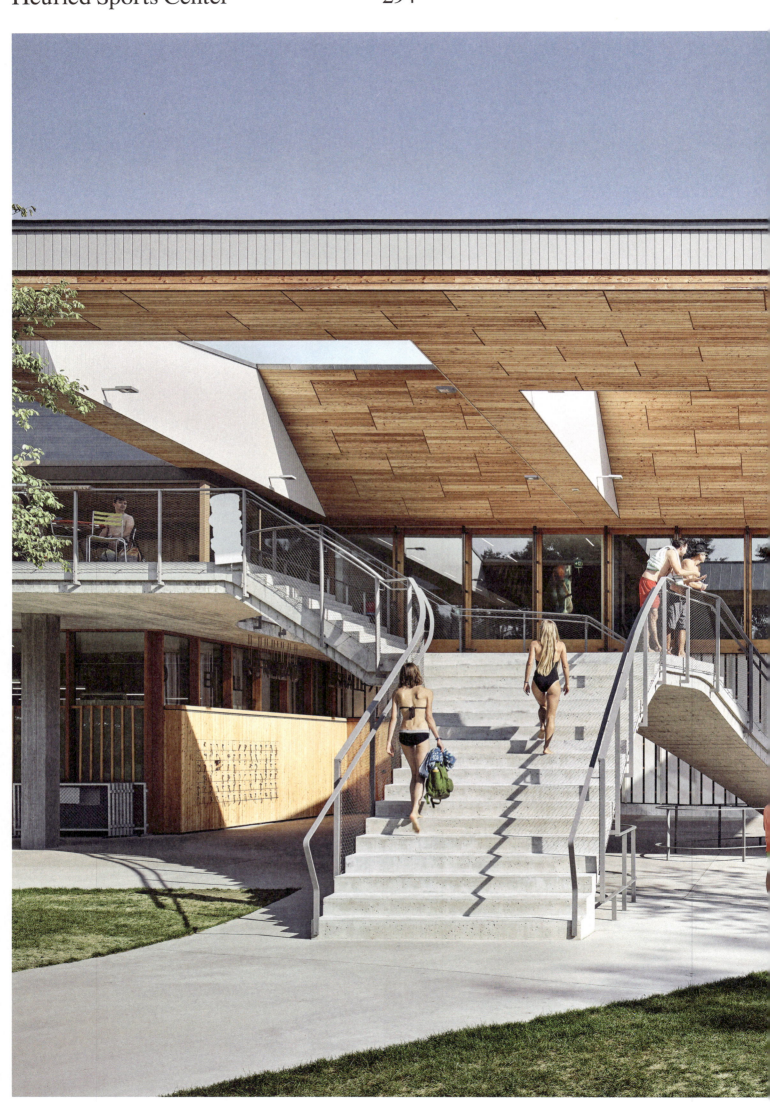

Heuried Sports Center

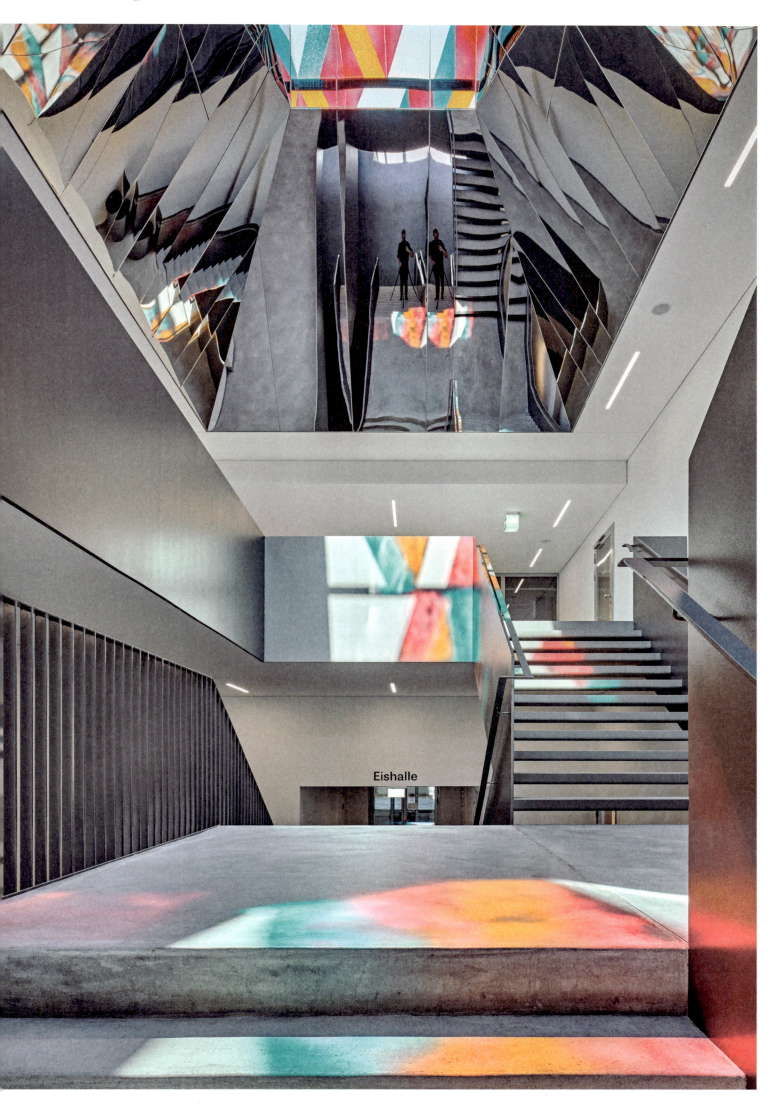

Nemausus

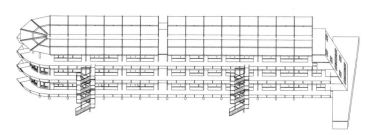

This 1987 project by Jean Nouvel in Nîmes was underpinned from the outset by a desire to counter the poverty of conventional social housing in France. Nouvel refused to accept that, compared with standard residential development, you had to radically shrink the unit size when designing social housing. Instead, he asserted that good social housing apartments had to meet three criteria: they had to be large ("a good apartment above all else means a big apartment"), easily adaptable, and affordable.[A] His ambitious aim was to provide 30 to 40 percent more space within the same budget. To meet these criteria, he took radical measures.

The buildings were designed as simple linear blocks into which various units could be inserted. Circulation areas were minimized inside, instead being concentrated on the outside. All units are thus accessed via wide double-height access galleries—walkways in the air. The large galleries on the opposite side provide balcony areas, cycle parking, and storage space. The units themselves range from single-story to duplex or triplex and are all designed as loft-style apartments. The scheme's materials, meanwhile, were strategically chosen to serve the key premise of prioritizing space over surface. It thus uses industrial components throughout and, as a result, looks rather like a giant Meccano set. Where applicable, certain statement features were integrated; for instance, 8 percent of the construction budget went on double-height industrial concertina doors, which allow the living areas to be opened up completely to the balconies. Together with the involvement of artists such as Daniel Buren, Nouvel's desire to contractually prevent tenants from painting the crude exposed concrete walls underlines that the industrial look wasn't just about economics, it was also a cultural and aesthetic statement. Of course, users' interests ultimately prevailed, meaning walls did get painted or papered and living spaces customized via fitted units or individual adaptations. Nonetheless, as an intellectual concept, Nemausus fascinates us both in its radical setting of priorities and in its typological reimagining of residential buildings as industrial blocks.

[A] http://www.jeannouvel.com/en/projects/nemausus/ (last accessed August 23, 2022).

Zugerland Verkehrsbetriebe

1
With an expanded, new-build base for its public transport operator ZBV, the canton of Zug wanted to send a clear message, namely that this is a place where the future of local public transport is taking shape. With our design, we aimed to create an open, communicative, and innovation-friendly working environment for the firm.

2
The "climate gardens" that wrap around the upper floor's offices are not only an integral part of the natural HVAC concept, they also add a calming buffer of greenery that, thanks to the primary structure's visual permeability, shapes the ambience throughout the building. In addition, they create an intersection between office spaces and outdoors.

1

3
The cross-section clearly shows the project's infrastructural ethos. The design is a series of stacked levels: a double-height bus and car parking level in the basement, a ground-floor workshop level, and office levels housed in a shed-like upper section.

4
Ground floor workshop.

5
Upper-floor offices with climate gardens.

2

3

Zugerland Verkehrsbetriebe

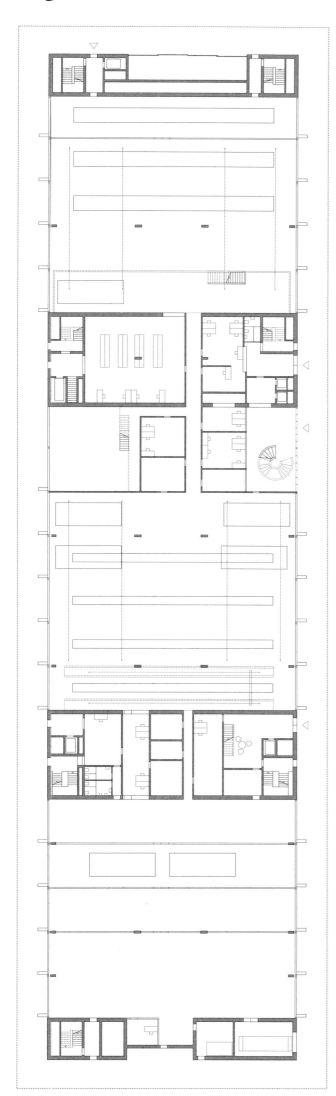
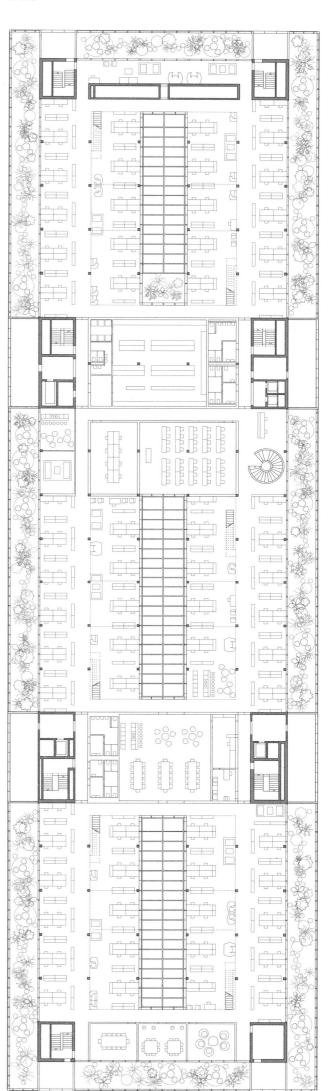

Rampenhaus Schwerzenbach

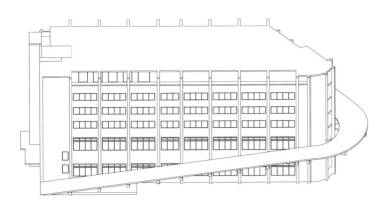

On October 30, 1960, the *NZZ* newspaper ran an article about A. Schmid & Co. AG of Schwerzenbach in its lunchtime edition, the headline of which proclaimed it to be "the largest pinsetter factory in Europe."

After studying at technical college, engineer August Schmid began making gearboxes and motors in a shed. His big break came via the registration of several patents for automated pinsetters for bowling alleys. Soon his firm had more than 150 employees and was exporting to markets throughout Europe and beyond. The architect of the new premises he then had built is not known, the only signature on the submitted plans being his own (it's entirely possible that Schmid drew them up himself in his own engineering office). It was designed in the manner of an infrastructural building. A heroic hybrid, it combined multiple usages in a single structure, with show alleys in two of the stories and workshop, parking, and living spaces in the other three. The characteristic ramp provided direct access to the parking areas on the second, third, and fourth upper floors.

Today, this iconic building is home to a martial arts center, auto repair shops, mail order businesses, and a tank maintenance firm. It may have lost its 1960s glamour, but its utopian infrastructural quality remains. The city-factory is alive and well!

1 ↑   ↓ 2

3 ↑ ↓ 4

5 ↑ ↓ 6

7–9 →

Parking Garage as Prototypology

Technological progress in matters of mobility has always been accompanied by processes of gradual adaptation to such change. Where previously human exertion had been required to tackle the monumental staircases of stately buildings, Theophil Hansen's design for the Austrian House of Lords was all about horsepower, allowing carriages to pull right up to the entrance. Its generous ramp structure around an imposing fountain was thus an architectural expression of technological progress, of outward representation, and of social standing. Konstantin Melnikov's sketch for a monumental parking garage across a Parisian bridge, meanwhile, was based on radical assumptions of convenience and safety. The design was based on the principle that cars will always go forwards and never need to use reverse. Four counterbalancing ramps, two each for entrance and exit, twist as they rise upwards, forming an expressive flying volume that is also held up by two heroic Atlas figures.

Similarly, Stanislaus von Moos used the example of Le Corbusier to show how early 20th-century architects began integrating new "utilitarian" elements into their designs, thereby expanding the typological and spatial vocabulary of architecture.[A] Corbusier was much taken with the first elevated roadway in New Jersey, which, von Moos suggests, the emblematic ramps of his own Villa Savoye had presaged a few years earlier. Later, he adopted such structures, albeit in more basic form, as defining features of projects such as the Carpenter Center (1963) or the planned but never realized congress center for Strasbourg (1964). In the early sketches for his "Plan Obus" for Algiers (1933), the freeway was even intended as a direct incubator of gigantic, linear "viaduct cities" that, overlaid across the topography and the existing urban fabric in wide arcs, would blur the boundaries between architecture, infrastructure, and urban design.

In 1953, Paul Schneider-Esleben built a parking garage in Düsseldorf that was a celebration of progress and the new motoring age, combining a spectacular transparent glass shell and ramps suspended eye-catchingly in front of the façades. The poetic openness and lightness of his design domesticizes and heroizes motoring, glorifying the car as a precious exhibit. This veneration of the stationary vehicle didn't last long, however, as can be seen in the more humdrum structures subsequently provided for parking purposes, the countless utilitarian parking

A
Stanislaus von Moos, "Hide and Seek at the Pulse of the City," in: Andreas and Ilka Ruby (eds.), *EM2N. Sowohl als auch*, Zurich, 2009, p. 199.

1
Approach to the Austrian House of Lords, competition design, Theophil Hansen, 1865.

2
Proposal for a 1,000-vehicle parking garage across the Seine in Paris, Konstantin Melnikov, 1925.

Parking Garage as Prototypology

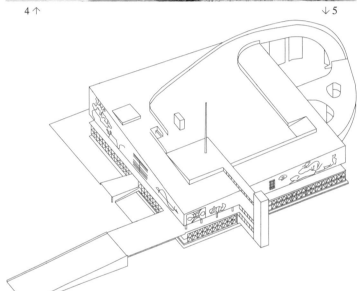

garages that were later built around German city centers.

With their Nantes School of Architecture from 2008, Lacaton & Vassal posited the idea that space is the real luxury. Their completed building provided a floor area far in excess of what was stipulated in the brief, but without incurring additional costs. The extra space was used to create lobby areas that serve as intermediate climate zones; unlike the adjacent programmed spaces, these can be used as students see fit. To create this additional square footage, the architects not only borrowed from the architectural typology of parking garages but also adopted a parking deck construction system. In a forward-looking strategy, the practice first built a parking garage only to promptly turn it into an architecture school. The radical spatial structure goes hand in hand with an equally radical circulation design. Cars, bicycles, and pedestrians are all funneled into the building via the same broad external ramp, which leads up to an expansive roof deck, branching out in various directions on the way. This *promenade architecturale* creates accesses on all levels, allowing every story, including the roof deck, to benefit from what is usually exclusive to the ground floor, namely direct ingress from the outside. This kind of co-opting of parking garage typologies or other utilitarian archetypes can have a radicalizing and liberating effect, while also serving to accelerate typological and architectural innovation. Following the motor car's remorseless takeover of our cities and the catastrophic impact that has had on the public realm, architecture is, in typically slow fashion, gradually beginning to see how infrastructural thinking can productively inform urban design and architectural discourse.

3
École Nationale Supérieure d'Architecture de Nantes, Lacaton & Vassal, 2009.

4
"Hanielgarage" parking garage in Düsseldorf, Paul Schneider von Esleben, 1951.

5
Design for a congress building in Strasbourg, Le Corbusier, 1964.

Toni Campus: In Use

Toni Campus: In Use

316

2014–…

Toni Campus: In Use

3 ↑

5

↓ 4

6

Toni Campus: In Use

← 1 + 2
The scale of the new and existing ramps is consistent with the transport infrastructure that dominates west Zurich. The north elevation's multistory ramp once allowed delivery trucks to access upper floors and staff to access the rooftop parking spaces.

3
Reinterpreted as a vertical culture boulevard, the ramp gives direct access to various levels on the new Toni campus's north elevation. In particular, it provides pedestrian access to the "Mehrspur" music venue, the main north entrance with the adjacent movie theater on Level E03, the exhibition spaces and chamber music hall on Level E05, and the main concert hall on the top floor (Level E07).

4 + 5
Below the partially extended north ramp, a new home was created for the "Mehrspur" gig venue and bar.

6
The former truck repair shop gained fame as the "Toni-Molkerei" night club. Now enlarged and vertically extended, it houses a film studio and the main theater space.

7–10
The ramp serves as a vertical extension of the public realm. With its variety of views inwards and outwards, it links the interior world of the university with the exterior world of the city, making it an intersectional area that can be actively used.

11 →
In urban design terms, the new structure has a similar impact to the original dairy, retaining its striking silhouette and distinct low- and high-rise sections. The redevelopment further exaggerated this basic outline, thus adding a bold statement at the junction of Pfingstweidstrasse and Duttweilerstrasse.

Toni Campus: In Use 320 2014–...

Toni Campus: In Use

Toni Campus: In Use

12 ↑

13 ↑ ↓ 14

12–14
The old dairy plant consisted of three stacked double-height levels, one each in the basement, raised ground floor, and upper floor. Due to the high water table, the basement level could only be partially built into the ground, giving it a single-height look from the outside. Post-redevelopment, large staircases and ramps take visitors up to Level E03, which looks down on the surrounding streets like the *piano nobile* of a grand house. Covered outdoor areas on the east and west elevations provide transitional zones between inside and out.

Toni Campus: In Use

15–18
The full-width entrance hall's staircases, bridges, and internal "streets" offer access to both the University of the Arts and the University of Applied Sciences. The area also provides a prominent location for various other usages, such as a café, the student refectory, the Museum of Design, and the two main lecture theaters.

15

16

17   18

15 + 17
Designed by Bölsterli Hitz, the multifunctional foyer furniture provides informal workspaces, spillover refectory seating, and a central meeting point. Alongside it, the earthquake-resistant wall that serves to reinforce the tower provides a blank canvas for the Museum of Design's ever-changing installations.

19 →
The café seating makes the main entrance hall feel almost like an outdoor space. The distinctive light installation by Berlin-based Realities United concentrates the light and creates areas with varying levels of illumination.

Toni Campus: In Use

20

21 ↑   ↓ 22

21 + 22
The key circulation element within the University of the Arts, the cascading central staircase rises diagonally through the upper levels, ending at the foyer of the main concert hall, from which stairs lead up to the roof garden. The staircase's generous dimensions are precisely scaled to the size of the building. It is both route and venue, its spaces allowing for creative appropriation by various internal and external users.

20 + 23
Similarly, the bridge leading to the high-rise section not only performs its actual circulatory function but is used in various other ways, too; as a balcony for spectators, for instance, or a stage for spontaneous concerts.

23

24

25

24–26 + 27 →
The cascading staircase's middle landing forms the heart of the low-rise. It opens onto the central courtyard and can be used for events of various kinds. The performative aspect of these generous circulation areas is a key programmatic and atmospheric element of the Toni campus, one that is only possible thanks to a sophisticated system of escape routes. The ability to use these areas for exhibitions, performances, lectures, and much more enables the university to host a wide range of activities within its public spaces. Staircases and access galleries thus become stages, viewing balconies, or informal meeting places.

26

Toni Campus: In Use

28

29

30

31

28–31
As well as via the cascading staircase, access to the low-rise can also be gained via the entrance hall adjacent to the north elevation's ramp. From here, a large staircase leads from Level E03 up to Level E07; along it are specific usages such as the movie theater, the chamber music hall, and exhibition spaces. The flights are set at an angle to each other to create varied spatial and visual connections.

Toni Campus: In Use

32 ↑

↓ 33

32
One story up from the cascading staircase's middle landing, the two circulation systems come together in a double-height hall. The space's café and lounge also serve as both meeting place and hang-out for the university's music students, who don't have recreation rooms or studio spaces of their own.

33 + 34
The central cascading staircase and the old external ramp both end at the mirror-clad foyer of the main concert hall. From here, another staircase leads up to the roof garden.

Toni Campus: In Use

35

35
The lofty existing spaces that formerly housed the drying silos and milk tanks were what inspired us to develop the compact cascading staircase, a vertical spatial framework for the unlit belly of the tower. It features terraced workspaces for students, but can also be used as an informal circulation route between the high-rise's various floors.

36 ↑   ↓ 37

36
At the intersection of the low- and high-rise volumes are areas that proved difficult to illuminate and to address. The creation of a vertical connecting space extending from Level E05 to the roof terrace now enables daylight to penetrate deep into the building. It also allowed for stairs that compensate for the discrepancy between the two sections' levels and provided the central library with a spectacular home.

38
Separate staircases or shared-use spaces such as double-height recreation rooms create additional circulation routes and allow for informal shortcuts.

38

Toni Campus: In Use

37 + 39–42
The numerous passageways leading off from the staircase connect up to form a dense circulatory network. They link the various programmed spaces—offices, studios, workshops, teaching and practice rooms—with the collective heart of the building. The periodic widening and angling of corridor walls creates local nodes, while generous glazing regularly provides glimpses of the adjacent interiors. Signs of use and different kinds of appropriation are apparent throughout.

39

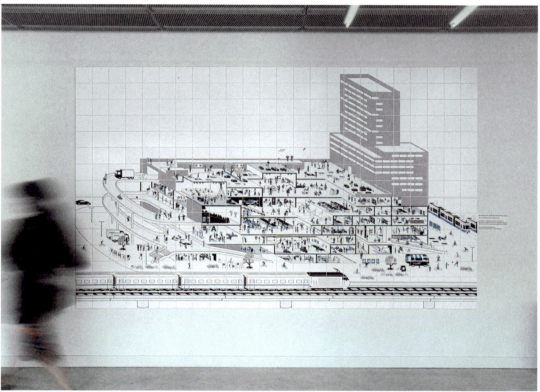

40

41

42

Toni Campus: In Use

44 ↑   ↓ 45

46 ↓

43–46
A large part of the flat roof is taken up by a garden designed by landscape architects Studio Vulkan. Featuring trees, shrubs, climbing plants, and herbs, the Mediterranean plantings in the middle of the roof make for a verdant oasis in which it's easy to forget that this is one of the most heavily built-over areas of Zurich.

47 + 48
A wide walkway runs around the top-floor façades. From here, there's access to a range of covered open-air workspaces and recreation spaces that communicate with the verdant core and the surrounding cityscape.

49 →
The edge of the rooftop walkway feels like the deck of a ship, with panoramic views of west Zurich and down the Limmat valley as well as towards the lake and Alps.

Toni Campus: In Use

47

48

Toni Campus: Cum Grano Salis II

Marcel Meili
7.5.2016

The Toni campus is a critical juxtaposition of two concepts that EM2N regards as drivers of its work: the "city-factory" and the urban realm.

With regard to the urban realm, the project is a bold gamble: it hypothesizes that one can, via a sufficiently dense concentration of attractions, change the perception and usage of that realm, bringing new life to an area that had primarily been a place of through routes and an industrial edgeland. Such attractions could include sports facilities or an event arena but, in the case of the Toni campus, the focus was on developing a cultural hub, albeit without entering into a direct functional relationship with the surrounding urban realm. The ambience of the complex is shaped by its conglomeration of functions and by the spatially intriguing redevelopment of the building's insides, which arranges those functions within what you might call "an interior city," an interior public realm. That realm owes its particular charm to the mutual proximity of various academic departments, in which the space spanning ballet, music, and fine arts is presented as a coming together of specific atmospheres and a melting pot of highly diverse student cultures. This typologically interesting repurposing of the industrial built fabric is, to borrow EM2N's own vocabulary, the "city-factory" at work.

You could call it an anti-orthodox interpretation of the urban realm. Rather than prioritizing the continuity of public spaces, the project foregrounds a kind of "urban mental mapping": in this view, our mental street map is made up of those dispersed places that we as city dwellers each use. Max Frisch articulated a similar idea back in 1953, contrasting it in his famous essay "Cum Grano Salis" with the fretwork-like attention to detail, rule-obsessed zoning, and Biedermeieresque view of the city seen in Zurich's expansion via new "neighborhoods" in the late 1940s. The idea of human scale was, Frisch felt, being misused to keep people humble. For Frisch, the city was an array of places with which to engage, of places city dwellers could seek out in order to quickly escape, as urban nomads so to speak, from the confines of their own neighborhoods. The Toni campus serves as just such a place, partly *faute de mieux* given that this one-time milk processing plant had neither a lot structure suitable for boulevard promenading nor proven economic viability as a function-oriented scheme. The project thus required completely new typologies capable of taking the city into industrial areas and distilling a positive urban vibe even from the busy transport infrastructure encircling the site. After all, urban expansion in this day and age necessarily means expanding the radius of urbanites. The city has already moved away from the cozy, small-scale existence that once characterized urban living, not least because our lifestyles have changed so dramatically now that we can commute to work on rapid public transport every morning, nip into convenience stores for essentials in the evening, then travel out to wherever our favored entertainment venues or social circle might be. For today's urbanites, cities are thus more like networks of relevant points on a map, even if those points are multiplexes on the other side of town. The locally rooted lifestyle that once imbued 19th-century streets with everyday life has virtually disappeared.

Even this new interpretation of urban life, however, has its limitations, and there's one vital issue in particular for which contemporary urban planning has yet to find a solution. Economic realities, ownership patterns, and our grimly technical view of structural design have all helped to prevent new informal spaces being found for the bars and clubs that set up in old obsolete structures, turning them into nomadic encampments that, as loci of flexibly interpreted urban realm, have added indispensable vitality to the city. With the Toni campus, the authorities have at least made an attempt in that direction, providing uncluttered new spaces for a gig venue and a bar. Efforts to anchor the complex via a series of ground-floor public usages were, however, constrained by the fact that the surrounding streets, the adjacent public realm, offered access to the tram network but not to a flowing and easy walkable neighborhood. The hypothesis, therefore, was that it is not public functions such as shops and restaurants that will shape the campus's urban character but the metropolitan vibe of its cultural attractions, be they concert venues, movie theaters, clubs, or museums.

The strength of the project lies precisely in how it strives to impose a spatially complex, functional form on the rambling "structural urbanity" of the site. With its reinterpretation of the architecture and structure of an existing industrial building, the Toni campus manages to pull off a feat of "interior urbanization." This presumably was a key premise of the design: instead of delivering a humble community center and an underused row of shops, the architects focused on various ways of maximizing urban impact and on the spatial potential of a dense

Toni Campus: Cum Grano Salis II

cluster of facilities. The kind of promenading celebrated by 19th-century Zurich has no place here.

It goes without saying that the campus succeeds in articulating this "interior city" idea in physical form, its angled internal streets permitting different usages and thus allowing for chameleon-like changes to the look and feel of its spaces. What's less obvious from the plans is that, as well as the central cascading staircase, the design also provides for numerous other vertical incisions, making the skeleton seem rather like a three-dimensional grid in which spaces with diverse functions and atmospheres are stacked vertically in almost random fashion. The incredibly dense, almost organic-looking plan with its crystalline structure of cells cannot properly reflect the directorial aspect involved in orchestrating such multifarious and unpredictable usages. The defining quality of the Toni campus, in other words, is its performative character. It doesn't just meet the needs of users; it also provides a stage for all kinds of actors.

Perhaps the limits of the campus's specific character can be seen in the fact that, while the carefully planned spatial structure benefits from a sophisticated lighting design featuring new lightwells, the new structure's ceilings and walls barely reflect the open-plan, industrial nature of the original fabric. Here, theory founders on the practicalities of the build-out. Only occasionally do you get the sense of new spaces appropriating an old structure and, at times, you're reminded more of conventional linear corridors. Moreover, all the fixtures and the inevitable, ever-present service installations mean little can be seen of that very robust industrial structure, or of the radical interventions in its original fabric. (Perhaps the art students were subconsciously aiming for such a mood with their graffiti.) Granted, the contemporary reality of budgetary restrictions, fire safety measures, building norms, and technical services requirements would have imposed significant constraints on any less rigid, more flexible kind of fit-out. Another reason for the hefty and rigid new walls was the very high levels of noise insulation that were unsurprisingly required for a building housing a music school. Fire safety regulations are a further impediment to spatially flexible interiors, insisting as they do on a largely set-in-stone system of escape routes. The fact remains, therefore, that realizing a more informal, flexible interior, one which might have been more in keeping with the usage-driven, ex-industrial nature of the complex, would, in today's world, have been an extremely difficult thing to do. Instead, numerous norms and regulations have, along with the clients' preconceived ideas, imposed a permanent, aggregated form. (This is also the reason why, ambience-wise, the tower's advertised "loft-style" apartments are not a million miles away from those of traditional Swiss housing cooperatives.) With exacting standards driving a pursuit of perfection, the campus interior has fallen prey to a typically Swiss timidity. On the other hand, any attempt to fight that tendency would, in part due to the institutional clients with their various departmental chiefs, likely have been doomed to fail. In such a complex web of decision-makers, each tends to cultivate their own individual preferences and responsibilities. In Switzerland, our built works generally strive for a sleek and risk-averse perfection that's not far removed from the obsessive attention to detail referenced by Frisch. It's these build-out standards that are the biggest threat to the many industrial structures that still have repurposing potential. Which brings us back to the city-factory: raw material for new urban realm is readily available. But to fill it with life, we would need to treat such places almost like heritage sites. They could—were it permitted—offer an urban atmosphere like no other. With its spatial framework for a conglomeration of functions, the Toni campus is a step in the right direction. If only the city-factory in this instance had a little more of the factory about it.

In the chapter on our community center for the Bäckeranlage park, essayist Max Küng refers to an "as yet unnamed novel, set to be published by Kein & Aber in fall 2016 or spring 2017" in which there's a scene that's set in the park. In fact, Max's debut novel *Wir kennen uns doch kaum* came out in April 2015, a full year earlier than the unofficial release date he announced in his piece for our City-Factory book. For its part, the latter finally made it to press in 2022 after various detours, by which time Max had already published another three books: *Wenn du dein Haus verlässt, beginnt das Unglück; Die Rettung der Dinge*; and *Fremde Freunde* (2021). What can we say? Some things just take time …

RTS Campus 342 2014

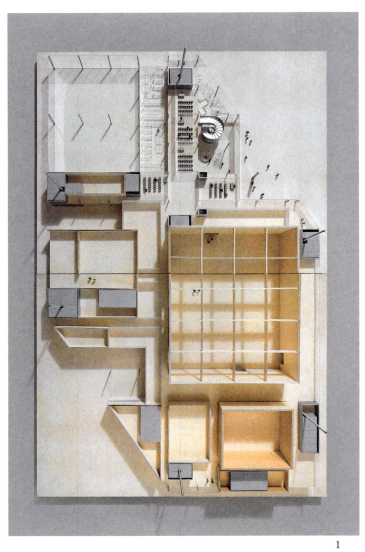

1

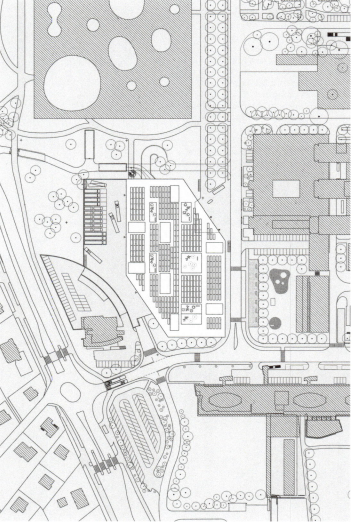

2 ↑   ↓ 3

1
We conceived the ground floor plan as a primarily logistical level, with film studios sited immediately adjacent to the main entrance and a parking garage for outside broadcast trucks to the rear. The idea was to thus bring the public into direct contact with the broadcaster's production activity.

2
For the first upper floor, we devised a wide, full-length media boulevard along which the various channels' receiving rooms are arrayed, giving an impression of the variety of RTS's output.

3
When Switzerland's national French-language broadcaster RTS decided to build a new headquarters, it chose a site on the Lausanne campus of the Swiss Federal Institute of Technology, immediately adjacent to the institute's Learning Center. Here, the broadcaster would, in line with the trend towards media convergence, produce cross-platform content for TV, radio, and online channels. Our design was based on three key goals: the building should as far as possible be part of the public realm; it should be a resilient structure capable of adapting to constantly changing use; and it should deliver high-quality workspaces while using minimal technology.

RTS Campus

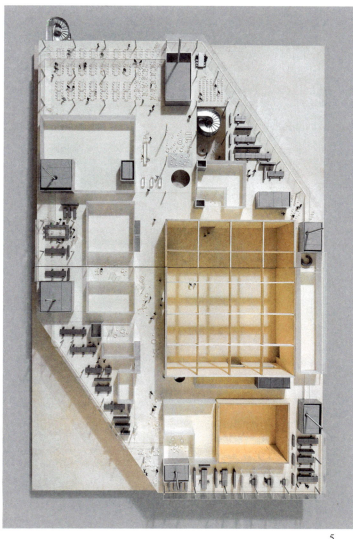

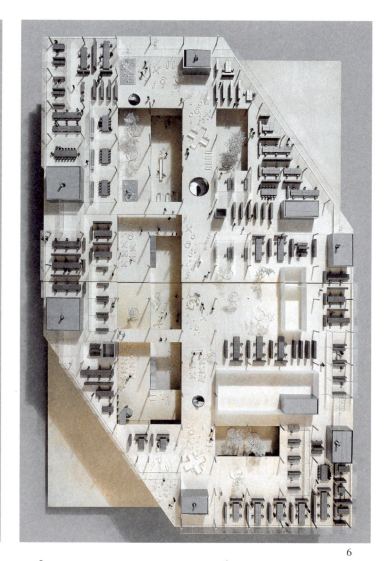

5

6

4 + 7
The sectional model reveals the open structure of the building's working environment, juxtaposing enclosed studios and internal courtyards. The building was planned as a flexible linear block whose contents can be varied over the long term.

5
For the second upper floor, we envisioned an open-plan work area to which courtyards and recessed balconies would add light and structure.

6
On the third upper floor, this would develop into a terraced interior landscape featuring light and airy workspaces thanks to large rooflights and courtyards with internal gardens.

7

HSG Learning Center St. Gallen

1 ↑

↓ 2

1
The University of St. Gallen's Rosenberg campus consisted of Förderer + Otto + Zwimpfer's exposed concrete buildings from 1963 and Bruno Gerosa's library building from 1989. To the north of these, the university wished to add a new "learning center." But what exactly is a learning center? Rather than a purely functional, spatially determined, efficiency-optimized college building, a learning center is one that offers a completely different kind of space, complementing existing buildings, offering emotionality, and helping to build identity. Its primary qualities therefore stem from its distinctness from standard university premises.

2
Buckminster Fuller's Montreal Biosphere for Expo 67 was based on a simple yet very powerful idea, namely the monospace. In this dome, a transparent membrane surrounded a spacious interior which has its own climatic biosphere and in which platforms and exhibits are housed as "objects within an object." In the monospace, there is no serial or hierarchical arrangement of spaces; instead there is just a single space in which various contents converse with each other directly. This object thus contains further objects while also conversing with the outside world. The individual objects may be varied in nature, but the space's single skin means they come across as parts of the whole.

3 + 4
The concept of "objects in an object" inspired us to devise a spatial composition intended both as an arrangement of individual spatial worlds and as an open container that can be experienced as a whole. To that end, we proposed inserting two sculptural volumes (one for the foyer, the other for concentration spaces) into the four-story shell; these would combine with the surrounding space to create a stimulating positive/negative juxtaposition.

5–8
Plans for the lower ground floor, ground floor, first upper floor, and second upper floor.

3

HSG Learning Center St. Gallen

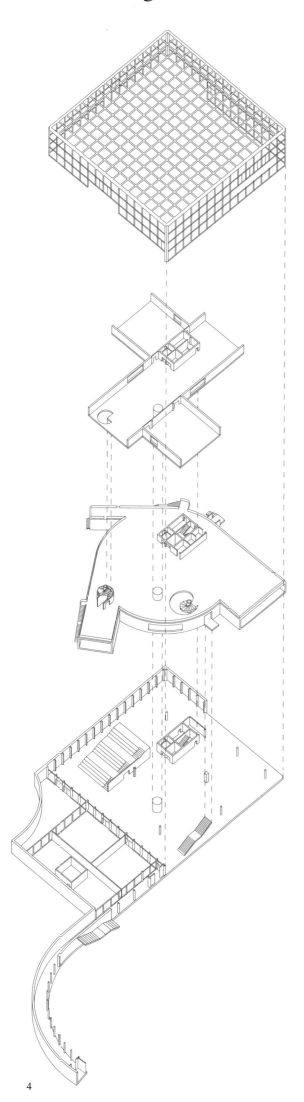

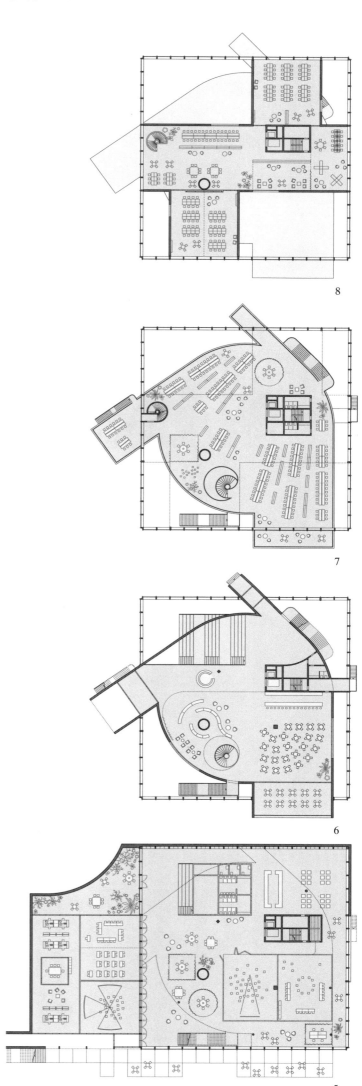

HSG Learning Center St. Gallen 347

HSG Learning Center St. Gallen

9–11
Perforations, openings, breaks in scale, and judicious circulation elements allow for surprising changes in perspective, open vistas, and cross-references, while also creating more intimate refuges. At the same time, the design ensures users always feel part of the whole, wherever they are in the building.

Natural History Museum and State Archive

Natural History Museum and State Archive

350

Natural History Museum and State Archive

1
Under the working title "Archives of Life," the Natural History Museum of Basel (NMB) and the State Archive of Basel-Stadt canton (StABS) set out to combine their collections under one roof.

2
Completed in 1899, the StABS building on Martinsgasse was Switzerland's first purpose-built archive. By the 1960s, the archive had outgrown the original premises, so an underground extension was added. Today, only around 30 percent of the archive's material can still be accessed at the main site, with the rest spread across four external depots—a logistically challenging situation. What's more, 300 to 500 meters' worth of files are added every year, further worsening this difficult situation and making a new-build unavoidable.

3
Basel's Natural History Museum was founded in 1821 but its roots lie in even older collections, in particular those of Basel-based physician Felix Platter (1536–1614) and law professor Basilius Amerbach (1533–1591). After Peter Merian (1795–1883) gifted his own collection to the museum, the decision was taken to create Basel's first purpose-built museum, the building for which was designed by Melchior Berri and completed in 1849. At first, it housed a variety of collections, but in 1879 the physics and chemistry sections were relocated to the Bernoullianum and the library then moved to a new building on Schönbeinstrasse in 1896. In 1917 the ethnological and art collections also moved out, leaving a dedicated natural history museum. Various partial renovations had previously been conducted, leading to a permanent reduction in exhibition space, but by the early 2000s the building required full-scale renovation, raising the question of whether to relocate to a temporary home or commission an all-new building.

4
Following a comprehensive exploration of options for remaining at the existing sites and an analysis of 13 possible new locations, the option of retaining the current separate premises and external depots was abandoned in favor of a combined site, with a lot by St. Johann station being chosen as the preferred location in 2012. The opening of the northern bypass in 2007 and the creation of the Novartis campus had previously accelerated St. Johann's transformation from a blue-collar neighborhood with industrial premises into a desirable residential area featuring cultural attractions and research institutions, while, from 2025, the neighboring VoltaNord ex-industrial site is set to gain a mix of homes and workplaces plus a new primary school and expansive open spaces and parks. By opting for St. Johann, the authorities hoped to further support this transformation process via the addition of two public amenities and thereby improve the quality of life around Vogesenplatz. In 2013, a design competition was launched.

5
The outline brief for the development allows for the possibility of a tower up to 40 meters tall facing Vogesenplatz. But how to decide which of the two institutions should be housed in the high-rise section? Our solution: "Neither of them!" Instead, we devised a slender, slab-like tower, an architectural landmark that would represent both institutions in the city and on the square.

2 ↑

↓ 3

4

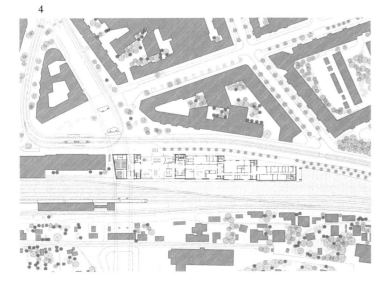

5

Natural History Museum and State Archive

2014–...

6 ↑

7 ↑

8 ↑

9 ↑

10 ↑

11 ↑

6–24
The NMB and StABS collections cover an extremely wide range of items, from church records, court documents, and maps to rock samples, skeletons, and antlers, plus all manner of wet specimens and stuffed animals.

12 ↑   ↓ 13

14 ↓

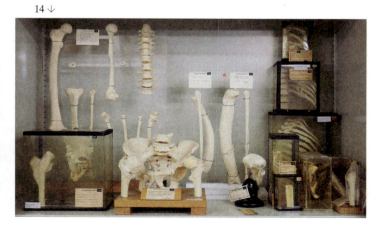

Natural History Museum and State Archive

353

2014–...

15 ↑

16 ↑

17 ↑

18 ↑

19 ↑

20 ↑

21 ↑   ↓ 22

23 ↑   ↓ 24

Natural History Museum and State Archive

354　　　　2014–…

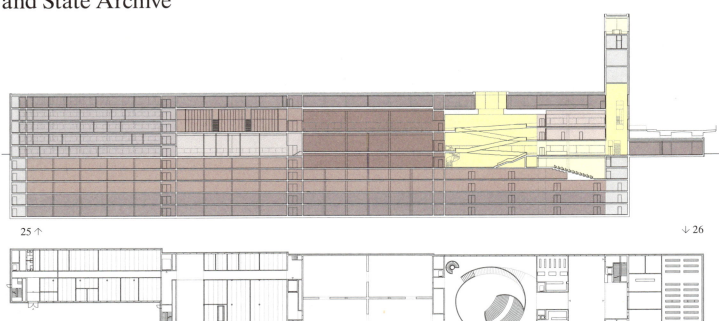

25 ↑　　　　↓ 26

25
In our proposal for the first competition phase, shown here in longitudinal section, the State Archive wraps itself around the Natural History Museum like a vertical ring, while three areas are shared by both institutions: the entrance hall, the tower facilities, and the delivery infrastructure.

26 + 27
A small shared entrance hall would direct visitors into two separate lobby areas with very distinct spatial forms: a vertical foyer for the State Archive on the top floor and a spectacular grand hall for the Natural History Museum, in which visitors can access the various exhibition spaces via circular ramps running around a central gallery.

28 + 29
After the first competition phase, the largely traditional way in which galleries and archives were arranged came in for criticism. The museum was keen to bring to life archives and other ancillary functions that would normally remain hidden, making them a central aspect of the museum experience and thus allowing visitors to experience the full range and breadth of the institution's facilities (research, workshops, taxidermy studio, library, and so on).

We thus opted to abandon the spectacular lobby, instead envisioning museum and archive as a radical linear block whose programmatically flexible double-height levels would be able to adapt to different usages. Library, workshops, and galleries could thus be freely arranged and placed in direct proximity to each other if required.

27

Natural History Museum and State Archive

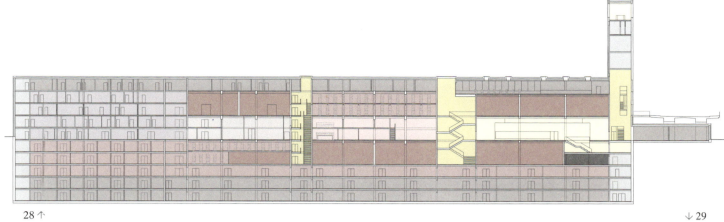

28 ↑ ↓ 29

30
We also incorporated a pair of generous vertical circulation spaces that enable visitors to take a variety of routes through the stacked levels.

31
For the State Archive, a similarly lofty circulation space was designed for the area at the base of the tower.

32 →
Museums and archives are essentially places in which to store artifacts from human and natural history. We thus interpreted the new combined premises as a giant storehouse, like the characteristic logistics buildings and warehouses along the train tracks or at Basel docks (Bernoulli's iconic Silo Tower, for instance).

33 →
The building's spaces have extremely varied requirements when it comes to ambient conditions, meaning technical services played a significant part in the project. The requisite cooling units, for instance, were all concentrated in the tower, thereby emphasizing this key conservatorial function while providing a contemporary take on the conventional cooling tower.

30

31

Natural History Museum and State Archive

356 2014–…

Natural History Museum and State Archive

Natural History Museum and State Archive

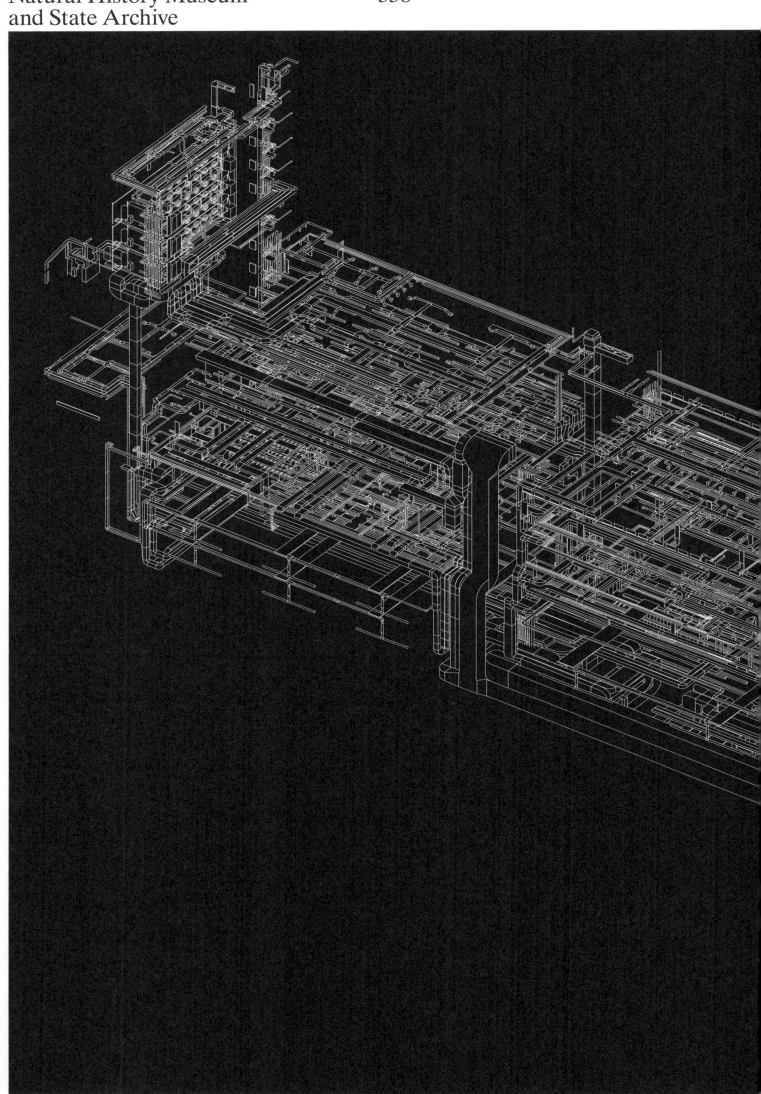

Natural History Museum and State Archive

Natural History Museum and State Archive

34
The cross-section clearly shows the stacking of double-height levels; these lend themselves to a wide range of different usages.

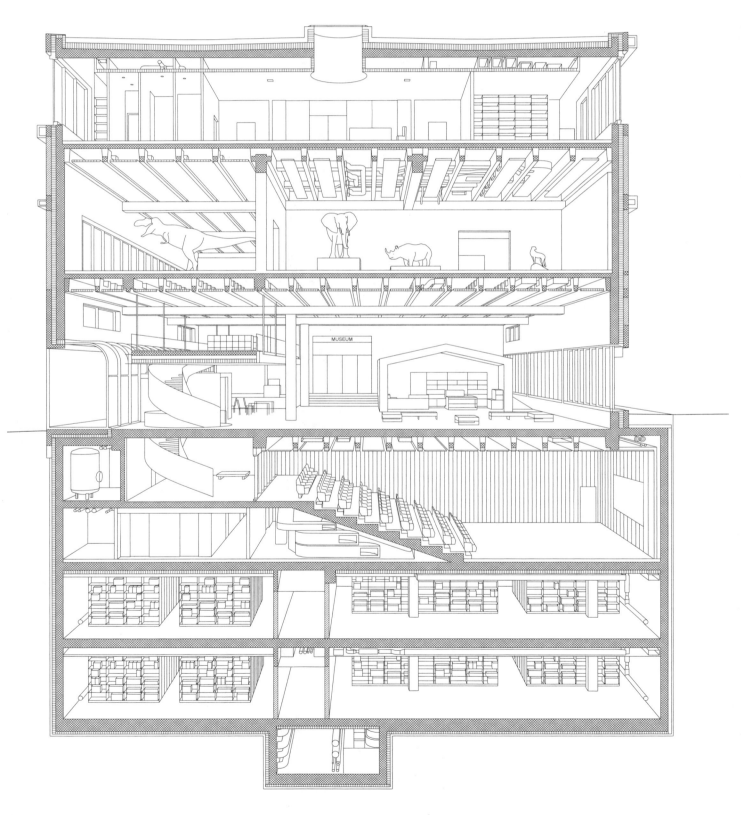

Natural History Museum and State Archive

35
The display areas span almost the entire cross-section, stretching from the middle basement to the second upper floor. The access hall will allow visitors to experience this vertical layering directly, creating visual connections between the various gallery levels.

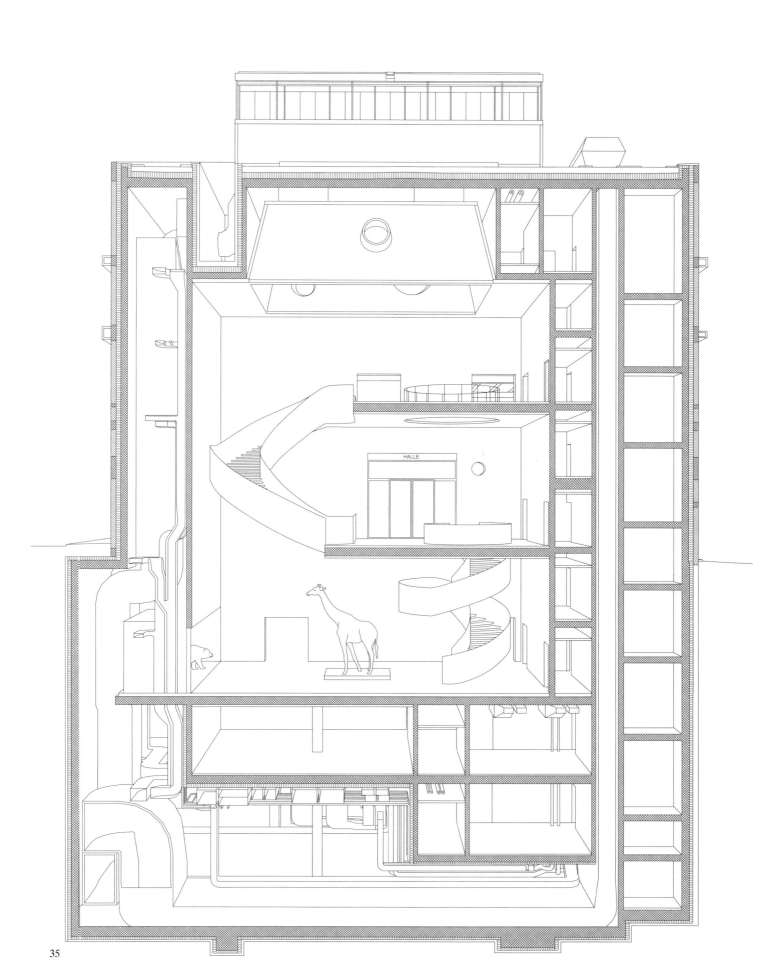

Natural History Museum and State Archive

362

2014–...

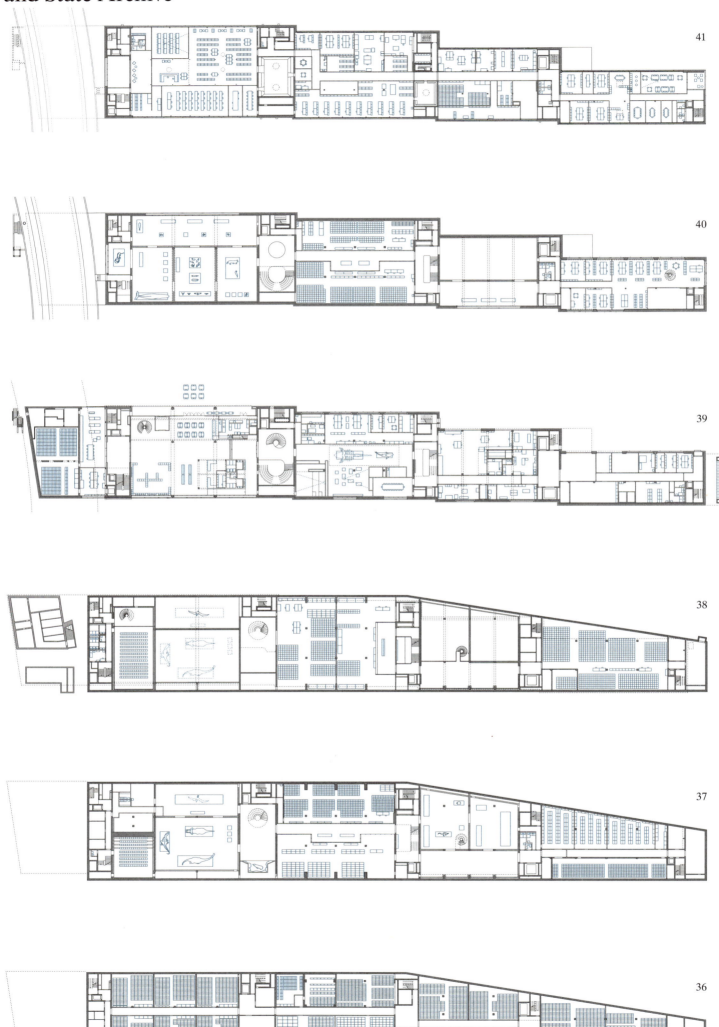

Natural History Museum and State Archive

2014–…

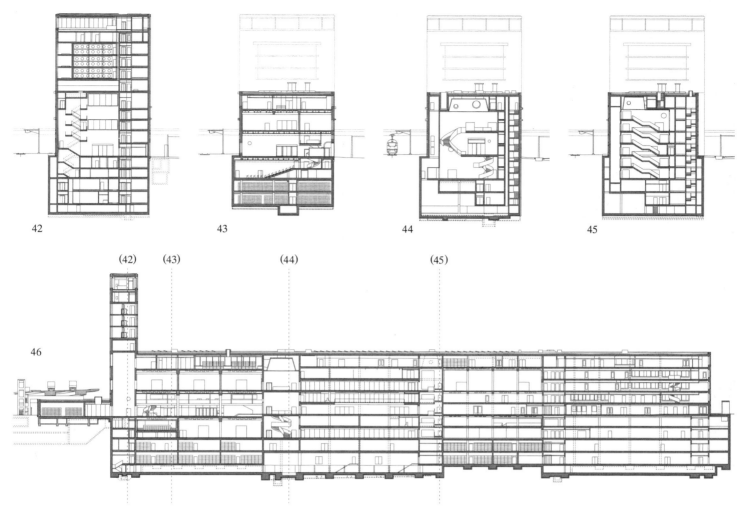

42 43 44 45

46

36–41
Plans for the third, second and first basement levels, ground floor, second upper floor and fourth upper floor.

1. Entrance hall
2. State Archive foyer
3. Building plans desk/archive window
4. Building plans archive
5. Museum foyer
6. Forum
7. Taxidermy studio
8. Workshops (museum)
9. Taxidermy, fresh specimens
10. Delivery area
11. Auditorium
12. Permanent displays
13. Geological collection
14. Mineralogical collection
15. Museum management
16. Reading room (State Archive)
17. File handling (State Archive)
18. State Archive management
19. Osteological collection
20. Permanent displays
21. Entomological collection
22. Zoological collection
23. Wet specimen collection
24. Archive (State Archive)
25. AV media
26. Archive of plans
27. Archive/library
28. Large formats

42–45
Cross-sections A–A, B–B, C–C, D–D.

46
Longitudinal section.

47 →
Akin to a geological formation, the façade will consist of solid self-supporting layers of concrete and brick. The concrete will be applied directly to the 24-centimeter-thick layers of brick, providing the window areas with load-bearing lintels for the brickwork above. The hand-crafted character of the layered façade means the building will have an industrial and urban feel.

Natural History Museum and State Archive

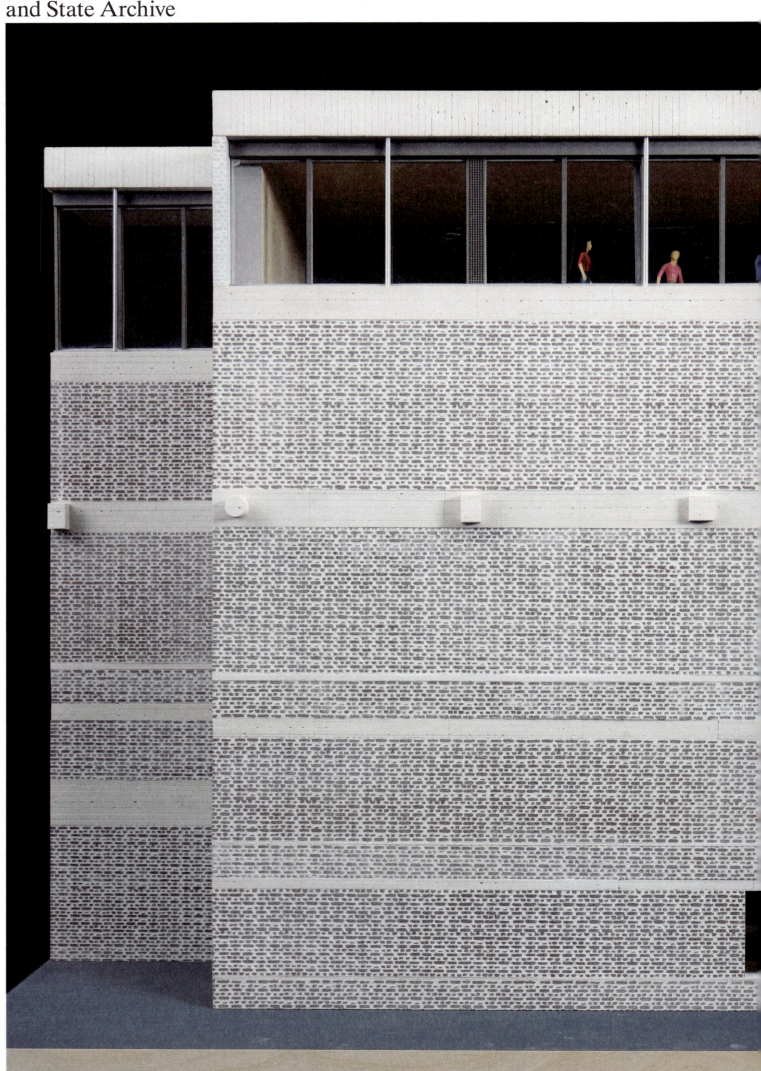

Ron Davis House, Winton Guest House

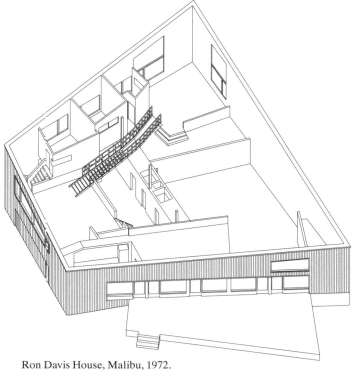

Ron Davis House, Malibu, 1972.

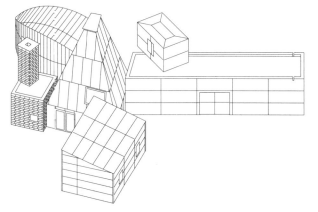

Winton Guest House, Wayzata, 1987.

From the 1970s on, Frank Gehry realized a handful of small but conceptually extremely radical Californian projects that underline how deeply he engaged with his local cultural milieu. The influence of that milieu, shaped by his numerous artist friends, on the architecture seems to have been twofold: not only did Gehry draw on aspects of a sculptor's or ceramicist's artistic process, he also started taking a phenomenological interest in the "as found" nature of the loft-like workspaces his artist friends had established in disused factory buildings or warehouses. In terms of its spaces and its atmosphere, the Malibu studio house he built for painter Ron Davis in 1968 seems to directly translate this kind of found premises into an original new-build, one that, 40 years on, would appear to have in turn served as a spatial model for the gigantic new Facebook headquarters. Completed in 1987, Gehry's iconic Winton Guest House in Wayzata seemed itself to resemble something created by a sculptor; like an artfully arranged still-life, it comprised stereometric volumes of differing materialities that merged to form a small, almost industrial-looking ensemble. The fact that it has since twice been sold, dismantled, and reassembled elsewhere merely emphasizes the building's conceptual kinship with artistic assemblages. Despite their obvious differences, these two projects show how Gehry was able to develop original and unique architecture from the close study of his own circle, with all its dissonances and contradictions. It wasn't, though, about straining to (re)produce a particular state of order; instead, it was precisely the imperfect, fragmented qualities of existing places and found objects and the constraints of budgetary or technical limitations that, in an artistically inspired process of appropriation, became the substance of the work. Like the methods of his friends Richard Serra and Robert Rauschenberg, who turned trash into art, Gehry's approach is thus avant-garde but also ultra-pragmatic.

WIN4 Sports Center

2009–...

1
Adjacent to an existing sports center in Winterthur, a private investor decided to develop a cluster for grass-roots and elite sports that would combine sports and medical facilities with athlete accommodation. The ambitious scheme comprised a pair of connectable triple-court sports halls measuring 44 × 44 meters, an 80-meter athletics track, 3,200 square meters of gym space, 120 rooms of accommodation, and a medical suite.

1

2
We decided to split the scheme into three separate volumes, one each for the sports facilities, medical facilities, and accommodation. Our proposal envisioned three loosely abutting volumes, between which would be a shared triangular entrance hall. The gym area, meanwhile, was to be housed in the roof space of the triple-court sports halls, the second upper floor of which would project out from the building and thus mark the main entrance, meeting the requirement for the gym to connect directly with the training track.

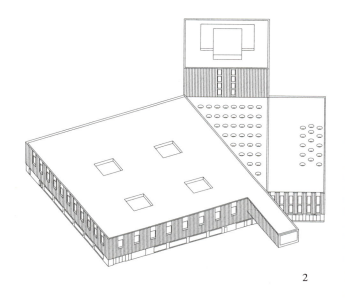

2

3
After years of planning, the scheme was deemed commercially unviable and scrapped. A new backer then stepped in and brought fresh impetus to the project. The scheme was radically slimmed down, with the two triple-court sports halls replaced by a multifunctional 2,000-seater arena, the gym resized, and a new tennis hall incorporated into the plans. Economic viability and the potential for phased development were given even greater weight. We responded to this new brief by breaking apart the ensemble and simplifying the structures of the individual volumes, while seeking to ensure each phase would result in a stimulating spatial disposition. Once the final stage was complete, two partially covered triangular outdoor spaces would unite the various buildings in a conglomerate composition.

4
The triangular, partially covered courtyard is intended as a central hub and access area for the complex.

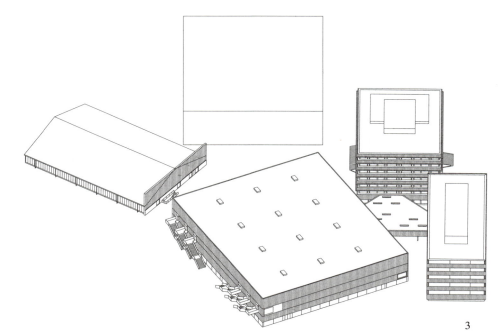

3

WIN4 Sports Center

WIN4 Sports Center

5
Ground floor plan.

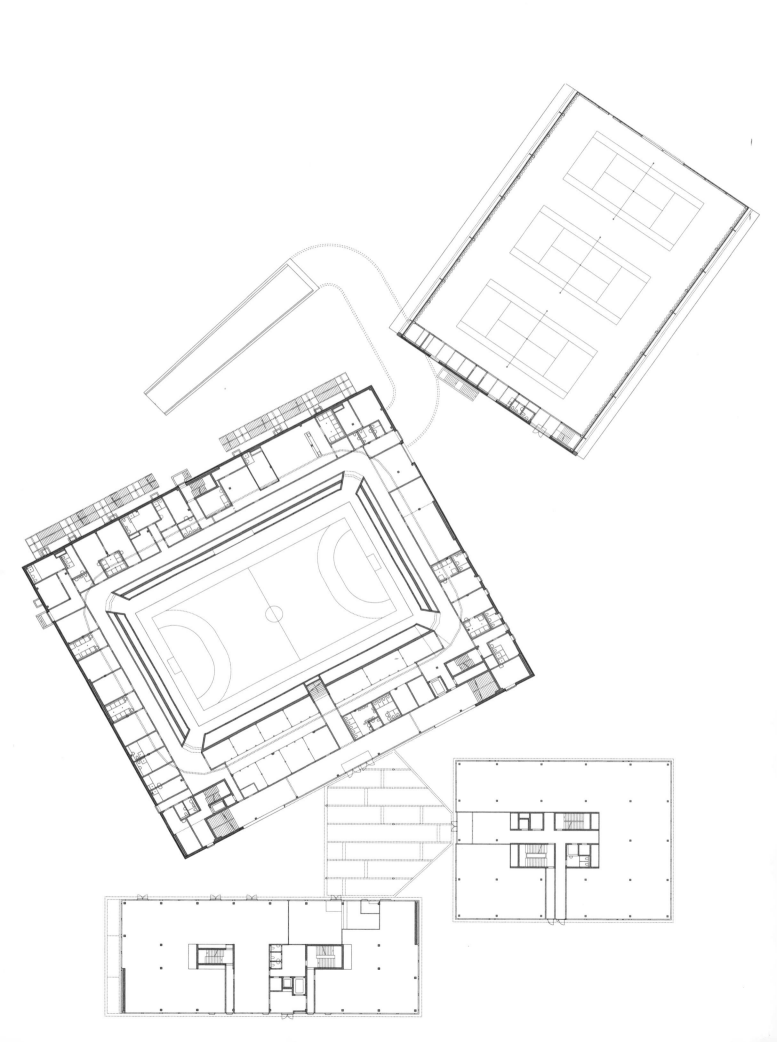

WIN4 Sports Center

6
First upper floor plan.

7 →
For cost reasons, the tennis hall was built in the form of a simple, gable-roofed industrial shed.

8 →
The sports facilities consist primarily of an arena for handball, floorball, and other indoor sports. Its radically pared-down exterior conceals an interior defined by a few bold accents, such as a red steel roof and a blue playing surface.

9 →
To ensure the tennis hall would, despite its gable roof, have sufficient visual impact to assert itself against the large arena, the gable end was visually enlarged via a semi-transparent screen of sheet metal, turning a utilitarian sheet-metal structure into a "decorated shed."

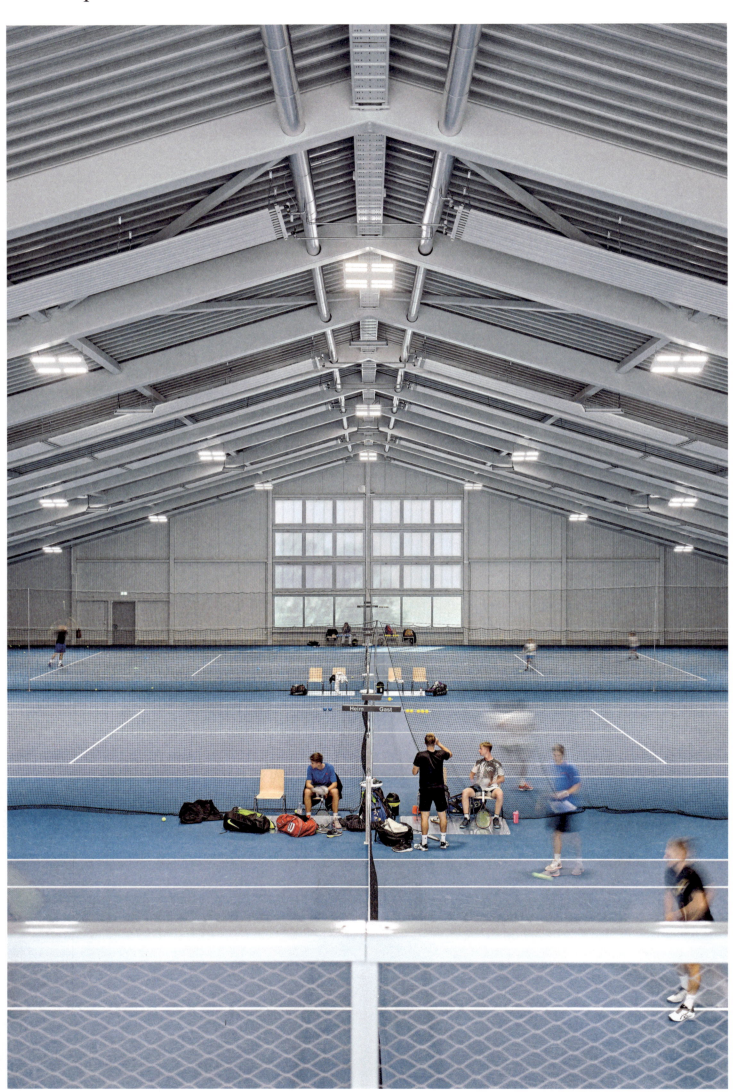

The Architect as Policy Whisperer (in Comes the Space Producer)

1

In the 34th minute of *Koyaanisqatsi*, just before all postmodern hell breaks loose, a prolific sequence of controlled demolitions unfolds. Bridges, towers, cranes, slabs; all succumb willingly and almost elegantly to an enforced sense of gravity. One of the prime detonation victims is the 1954 Pruitt-Igoe housing estate in St. Louis, conceived by World Trade Center architect Minoru Yamasaki. America's most infamous public housing project had survived a mere 18 years until its iconoclastic erasure. Adding to the civic drama, architectural theorist Charles Jencks used the event to substantiate his axiomatic pitch for postmodernism's kick-start, announcing that "Modern architecture died in St Louis, Missouri on July 15, 1972, at 3.32 pm (or thereabouts),"[A] the moment of Pruitt-Igoe's dynamiting. Was Jencks's imposed celebration of the Modern End just an epitaph for the sake of unproven novelty? And what kind of societal impact should or could architecture generate based upon such an overextended cryptolect?

Some More Endings in Architecture

During an untitled lecture at the Architectural Association on April 8, 1989, Daniel Libeskind, the then self-proclaimed non-building architect, enunciated an altogether more salient end. Having bombarded the audience with rapid fire semantic intricacies, Libeskind almost uneventfully declared: "I certainly feel that we are at the end of architecture, it's basically over." The audience smirked, seemingly content at having witnessed such a visionary and arcane cant. What if the gathering had known then that 25 years later all this soothing rhetoric of the apocalyptic would vaporize into countless outlandish icons, often for false flag politics?

Fast-forward to June 9, 2014. A *Dezeen* interview given by the 81-year-old Peter Eisenman on the occasion of the 14th Venice Architecture Biennale, an edition curated by Rem Koolhaas and AMO. Through his account of the show Eisenman seems more interested in the totemic figure of Koolhaas than the content itself. He states: ". . . Koolhaas has presented the Biennale as *la fine* [the end]: 'The end of my career, the end of my hegemony, the end of my mythology, the end of everything, the end of architecture'." Eisenman's as well as Koolhaas's coquettish dealings with the end of architecture seem—yet again—extremely haphazard and off-hand. Their fixation reveals, if anything, the recurrent sclerosis of the 20th-century architect at the brink of the 21st century, a generation that has swapped effective societal impact for the bemusing impact of the mythical cultural figure. Eisenman concludes the interview by stating how important it has been to have lived "in the time of Rem."

Barely a month earlier Frank O. Gehry had received the prestigious Spanish Prince of Asturias Award. During the press conference to announce the award, an *El Mundo* journalist asked Gehry what he thought of people who accused him of creating architecture for show. The jet-lagged architect squinted, paused bewilderedly, then pontifically raised his middle finger. The ultimate embodiment of the architectural figure's imperial overstretch.

The Good Architect, the Bad Architect

Architecture, as an inherent social and economic by-product, cannot simply be assumed to be "over with." Especially not by architects. However, what this dallying might conceal is perhaps a more urgent understanding that the very position of the architect within society is on the verge of a fundamental recalibration. Over the past century the discrepancy between the practice of the "cultural architect"—the so-called *good* architect—and that of the "commercial architect"—the *bad* one—has grown incrementally. The former burying themselves ever deeper into a self-inflicted and often autistic *de profundis* belief system, the latter offering just enough "architecture" to please the public and just little enough not to upset the financial balance of the building developer. *In fine* both antagonistic positions have ceased to be productive, if ever they were.

The current societal challenges for the contemporary spatial practitioner bear virtually no comparison with those of 50 or even 20 years ago. A cataclysmic growth in population and the ever-widening schism between powerful and vulnerable cultures have rendered the practice of spatial intelligence ever more urgent. Playtime seems well and truly over with. Now is the moment for architecture to re-engage itself with the politics and critical mass of the common good—the public good. How can the architect transform into a spatial professional that can and wishes to engage with social reality and all its adherent strategies of policy making? This question has become ever more pressing in an era when public policy makers seem to have run out of ideas, baffled by society's complexity, and have abdicated responsibility in favor of the doctrine of private enterprise.

A Servant's Prestige

The apparent challenge in architecture is that its societal urgency and credibility have always been derived from the development of technological building principles. The invention of air-conditioning aside, the discovery of iron-reinforced concrete in 1853 was the last major revolution in construction technology. Not only did it give rise to a new societal and spatial imagination, it also opened up a path for architects to reinvent their role and position within society. The career of the architect and entrepreneur Auguste Perret (Brussels, 1874–Paris, 1954) is an interesting case in point. Apart from being a prolific designer, Perret very early on saw the commercial and civic possibilities of reinforced concrete, cofounding the Perret Frères, architectes, constructeurs, béton armé company in 1905. As "constructor-architects" the Perrets managed to surpass the then formalistic limitations and dogma of the architectural trade, offering an all-encompassing technological service, working as architects in their own right while also executing work for such designers as Henry van de Velde. This both/and attitude of an economically driven artisanship—the attitude of the "servant's prestige"—was somewhat of an exception in the architectural field, where the pursuit of private

1
Frank Gehry at the press conference for the Prince of Asturias Award, October 23, 2014.

2
Makeshift residences line the Bassin de Commerce, c. 1950. In the background is Auguste Perret's ISAI housing complex.

The Architect as Policy Whisperer

2

practice and the personal signature remained the ultimate proof of apparent professional success.

Auguste Perret not only excelled through his constructor's logic and social poetry. In his testamentary volume *Contribution à une théorie de l'architecture* (1952), he also expressed a profound understanding of the wide-reaching impact and urgency of architecture in society. The very first page of this pamphlet reads: "*Mobile ou immobile, tout ce qui occupe l'espace appartient au domaine de l'architecture.*"[B] This one sentence perhaps describes the essence of a modern and even contemporary architectural sensibility, promoting architecture as a proactive trade rather than as a reactive form of expression. Perret implies that all (political) decisions will turn into architecture, so one had better come prepared and act preemptively. Through his all-embracing writings and practice, Perret managed to establish the idea of the architect as a pivotal civic and political figure—a professional without whom society cannot properly evolve.

Policy Whispering as a New Architectural Nexus

During the 1960s and 1970s strong and omnipresent public works departments were established throughout western Europe. Many of these departments served the public cause, employing architects as proactive civil servants. Some of the prime examples of these were the Greater London Council, the Stadtbaurat in Berlin, the Dutch Rijksgebouwendienst, and the Public Works Department of Amsterdam. This short-lived period of public political engagement with architecture proved the enormous potential of deploying spatial strategies and architectures as societal tools for policy making. However, the ever-increasing levels of public debt and macroeconomic dislocation experienced during the 1970s and 1980s pushed policy makers towards the formation of opportunistic public–private partnerships (PPP). From the early 1990s onwards this cunning debudgeting strategy has had a dramatic impact on the role of architecture within society, because with it the public client (and the public initiative) has virtually disappeared. To this day the practice of PPP is still rising in popularity, reflected in an ever more impotent and mute public power, as well as an increasingly marginal position for the architect. The contrast with Perret's central figure—the architect as an enabler—couldn't be more stark.

"Architecture finds itself in the paradoxical situation of being more popular than ever before while at the same time being exposed to total decline […]. Yet never before have architects had so little influence on the actual work of constructing buildings."[C] In addition, it could be argued that architects have never had so little influence on the making of society altogether. However, this ascertainment shouldn't give rise to gratuitous lamenting. On the contrary, it should help the architectural discipline to open up to new ways of practicing. Perhaps it's finally time to cast off the burdensome shell of the crypto-figure that is the private architect, with their false need to affirm themselves personally in the work. Society's complexity calls for a spatial practice that can act as a catalyst for societal programs, rather than for producing and showcasing the one-off spectacle. Perhaps the architect has become too slow, too heavy, and too duplicitous to adequately serve society.

The relevant task ahead for the architectural discipline—as a theoretical environment, an educational model, and an effective building practice—is to seriously question when architecture could come into play within the process of forming society. Is its role simply to answer a brief, or can it prefigure this brief—or even the client, for that matter? How preemptively can architecture actually perform, beyond the mere reflex of troubleshooting and commercial promotion? How unsolicited can architecture act? Not that there's a need for faint copies of the 1970s and 1980s public works departments, with architects directly working within government. But there is a requirement for architects that wish to engage with policy making, offering their architectural imagination in service of critical areas such as collective housing, health care, energy landscapes, and infrastructure. Architects that are able to understand and convey that their profession can be a tool for societal invention, not merely a social construct in itself.

The real question, then, might be: Can contemporary architects become policy whisperers, employing their architectural intelligence to the full by integrating their design skills with the policy intelligence at hand? It might therefore be productive and even refreshing to briefly revisit a particular feature of the earlier public works departments: a corps of rather anonymous yet ambitious architects bound by strong collective aspirations. It couldn't harm architects to regain some of this anonymity, to become more like enabling authors instead of characters in command of their "personal" visual language. Authors that are able to reassess the ethos and societal value of architectural work all together, building up a truly equitable practice of architecture, a field which up to this day has been largely overlooked and left uncultivated. A field inhabited by bridging figures rather than solipsistic architectural characters; spatial professionals acting as producers rather than ultimate creators; specialists who challenge clients to achieve the maximum societal benefits rather than perform as their private architectural jester. Policy whisperers that are willing to move beyond the antiquated model of the architect, venturing into the meaningful domain of the production of space.

A
Charles Jencks, *The Language of Post-Modern Architecture*, New York, 1977.

B
Whether mobile or immobile, everything that occupies space belongs to the domain of architecture.

C
Harry Gugger, Aurelie Blanchard, *Swiss Lessons: Teaching and Research in Architecture*, appendix, EPFL, Zurich, 2014.

1
In the exhibition *Together! The New Architecture of the Collective* for Vitra Design Museum, we worked with Ilka and Andreas Ruby to reconsider the past, present, and future of collective living and its relationship with the urban realm.

2
Using specially made models of interesting case studies, we assembled a vision of a fictitious city, focusing chiefly on programmatically diverse internal and external spaces that make a wider contribution to the urban realm, i.e. that are not just housing but also sites of social interaction.

3 →
The inhabitants of this city live their lives not just in their homes but also in the public and semi-public realm, just as the public realm not only spans outdoor areas but often extends into buildings, too.

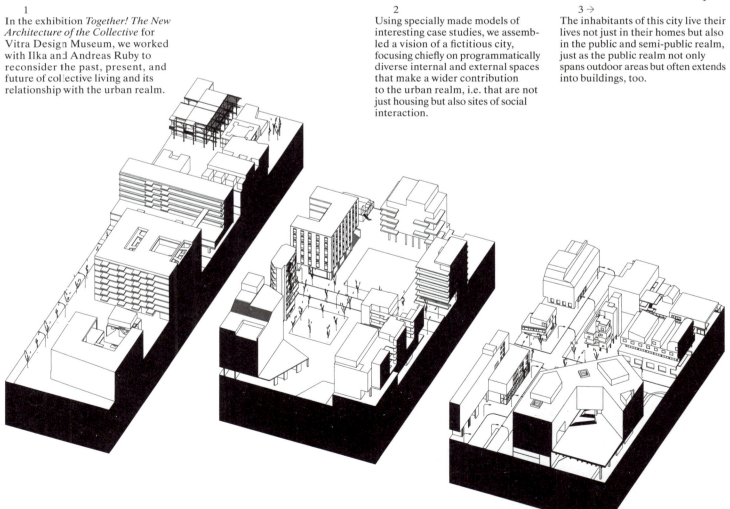

Together! Exhibition

1 ↑

↓ 2

3 ↑   ↓ 4

5 ↑ ↓ 6

7 ↑

↓ 8

9 ↑ 10 ↓ 11 →

12 ↑   ↓ 13

16 ↑   ↓ 17

18 ↑   ↓ 19 20 →

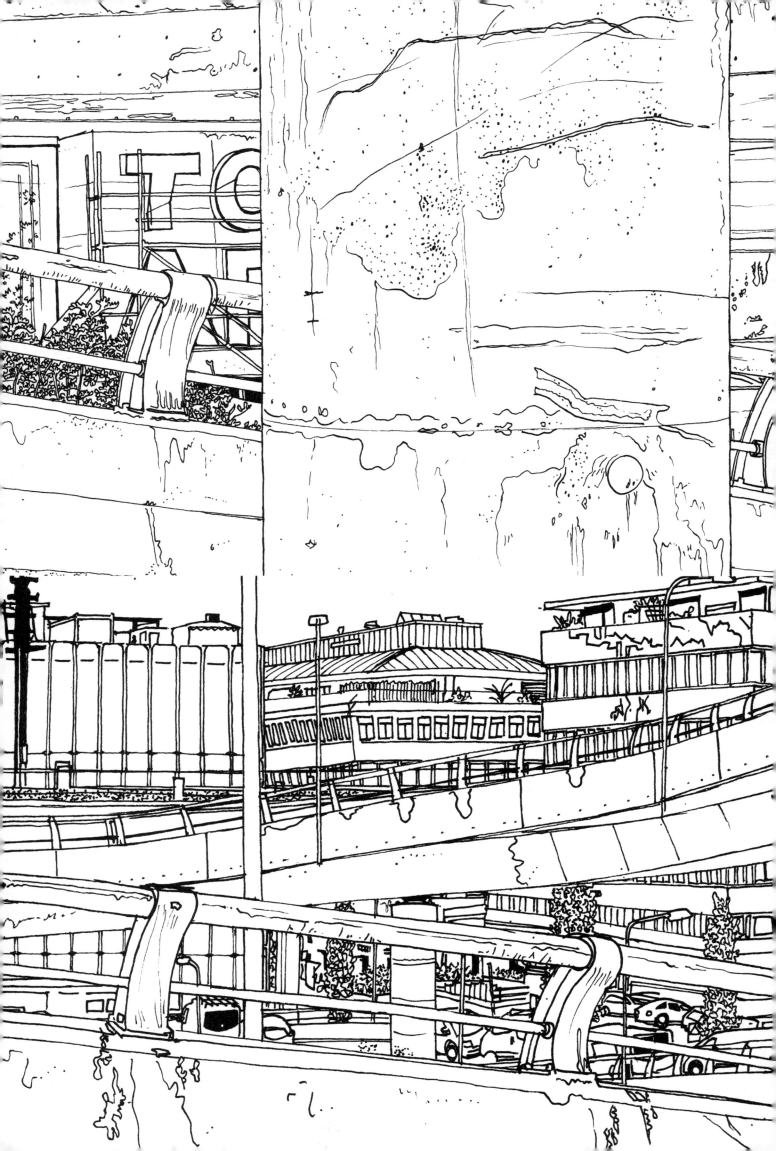

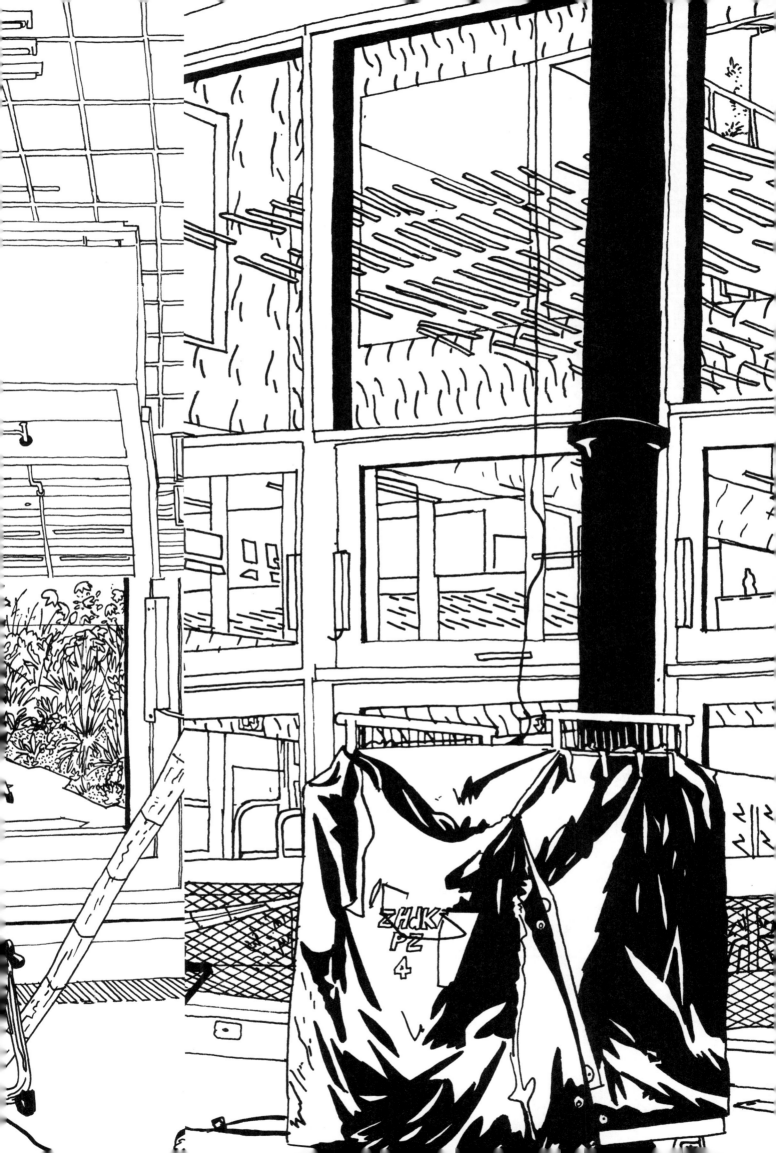

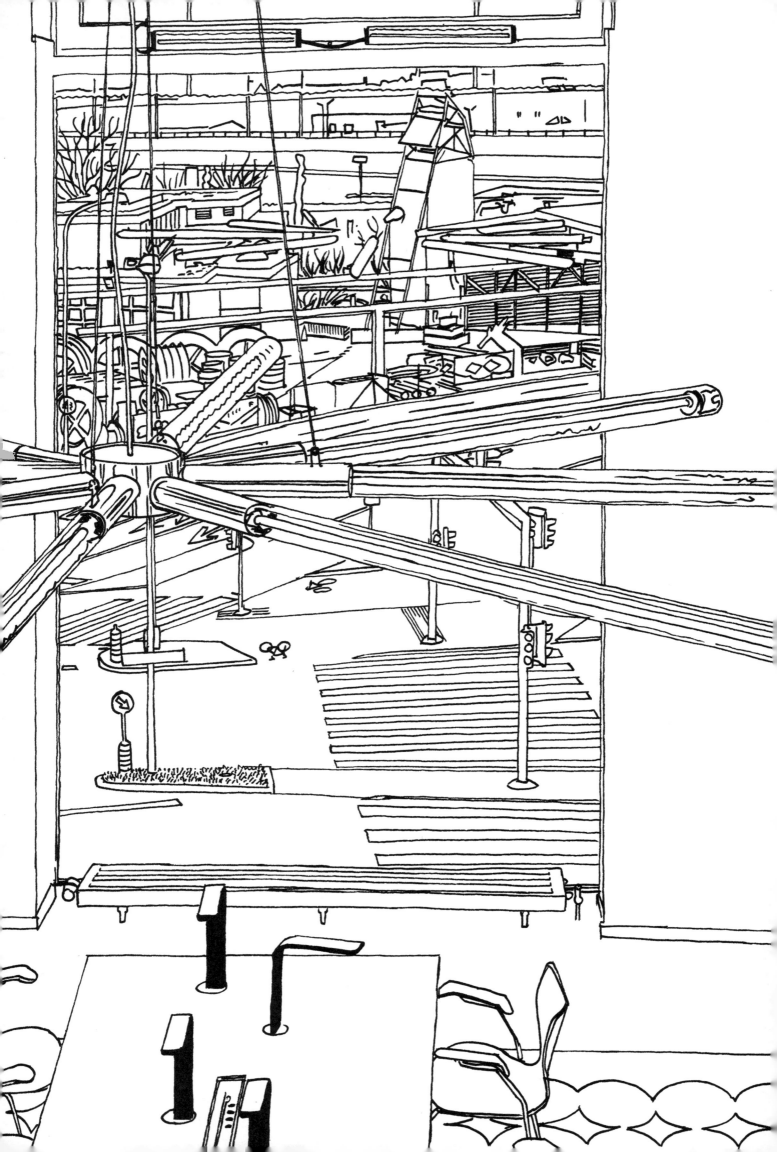

In his writings, Austrian architect Hermann Czech has tackled subjects including urban design, space and building design, and methodology and culture. A key aspect of this written output is the concept of transformation. For Czech, transformation as a cultural practice is always contingent on a capacity for appropriation and interconnection. After all, cities generally develop via overlayering, via the ongoing extension, conversion, and redevelopment of existing structures, taking into account their individual hierarchies and time horizons. In Czech's thinking, this concept of urban transformation is also emblematic of the periodic renewal and change that society as a whole inevitably undergoes.

At the same time, he puts transformation at the heart of his conception of architecture, regarding everything as a form of transformation. Wherever architects build, they are never starting from scratch; every intervention therefore represents the transformation of what is already there. Czech's idea of design as a process of transformation is probably the most radical counterargument to the notion of design as a one-off act of creative brilliance.

In transformation projects, the existing fabric is more than just context. Merging with the intervention to become an integral part of the new solution, it is what you might call "hypercontext". The manipulated object itself helps to shape the new reality, framing perceptions of the now modified site. Fabric and addition combine indivisibly to form a new whole. For architects, all this serves to both challenge and push the boundaries of established architectural conventions.

Once function and form have become disentangled, an existing building can no longer be remodeled along purely functionalist lines. As outlined in Aldo Rossi's writings on permanence, the form created for a building's original usage often survives long after that usage has ceased. Inevitably, the close correlation between structure, exterior, interior, and programming encapsulated by the modernist dogma of "form follows function" then no longer applies. With transformation projects, that precise fit is replaced by a multilayered, elastic relationship between form and function. The new usage interprets and inhabits the existing form. At the same time, the stubbornly resisting fabric challenges the new requirements being asked of it. Often it's not just the built fabric that ends up being transformed; programming, too, has to adapt, with new usages having to reach a compromise with existing spatial conditions. The resistance exerted by the built fabric frequently forces architects to try out spatial and typological ideas that wouldn't be considered for a new-build project. In other words, the imperfect fit between form and usage provides us with a wonderful opportunity for experimentation. The superimposition of a new idea on a built status quo can lead to spatial solutions that would be unimaginable without the resistance of the existing fabric. Conversions thus often give rise to genuine architectural innovations that open up new spatial and typological possibilities.

Ultimately, Czech's philosophy is based on the idea that design is also a means of perceiving reality. For his part, Marcel Meili compares the profession of architecture with that of an author. Both, Meili asserts, pay close attention to the world around them in order to give form to their observations.

Everything is Transformation

The adaptation of existing structures or spaces is, along with the realization of imagined spatial concepts, one of the fundamental capacities of architecture. It is thus from the overlayering of reality and imagination that architecture derives its transformative power.

Mathias Müller
Daniel Niggli

KANAL, Brussels 2017–…

2

3 ↑   ↓ 4

← 1
The empty Citroën dealership awaiting new usage.

2–11
In the early 1930s, seeking to expand into Belgium, carmaker André Citroën commissioned a huge Brussels dealership on Place de l'Yser, just outside the city center. The canal-side building was completed in only five months, between September 1933 and February 1934. Citroën himself, though, didn't get to see it open its doors the following year.

2–6
The high showroom facing Square Sainctelette was like a cathedral of motoring, the multistory space with its all-glass frontage and elegantly tiled floor displaying vehicles as though they were sacred treasures.

7–11
The repair shop behind the showroom had three entrances. Customers drove in through the doors on Quai de Willebroeck then, once their car had been serviced, exited via the opposite door on Quai des Péniches. The entrance on Quai de la Voirie was used for parts deliveries. At first, entire cars were assembled here from components but, before long, the garage was concentrating solely on servicing, with services always following a set sequence: first a wash, then the oil change, then a brake service, then wheel balancing. The garage also had its own auto-glass service, body repair shop, and a workshop for larger-scale repairs.

5

6

KANAL, Brussels 2017–...

7

8

9

10

11

KANAL, Brussels

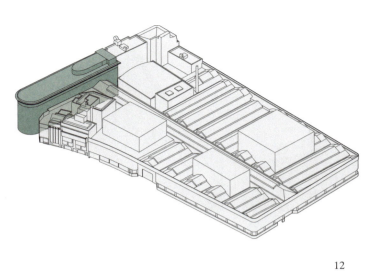

12–14
Trust in what's there: our approach was shaped by optimism and a faith in the existing building—in other words, we wanted to fully engage with the historic fabric. Five key principles underpinned the project's design, the first being that the old showroom already offered a prominent urban face that simply needed restoring to its former glory.

15–17
Prominent circulation: linking the two main levels, the existing cruciform circulation system will form the backbone of the new complex. The main route network will link this cultural hub with the surrounding urban fabric in a natural way. Additional secondary and tertiary pathways will provide a variety of routes, allowing visitors to wander around the building as they might stroll around a town.

KANAL, Brussels

18

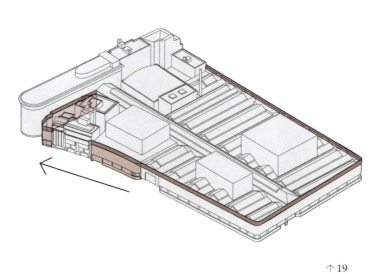

↑ 19

20 ↑   ↓ 21

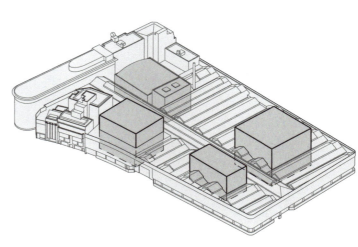

↑ 22

18 + 19
Enhanced connections: by emphasizing horizontality via a replacement new-build on Quai de Willebroeck plus iArt's wraparound electronic frieze, the proposal aims to create as close a visual and physical link between workshop and showroom as possible, thereby echoing Citroën's original vision.

20–22
New insertions: three vertically organized volumes will be inserted into the horizontal structure; the spaces within will meet highly specific climatic, acoustic, and structural needs, thus complementing the semi-air-conditioned spaces of the existing premises.

23 + 24
Places of production: learning and doing are to be central to the visitor experience. Studio and workshop spaces will thus be a key aspect of the complex and hence located at visible locations, such as by the route into the museums or along the main circulatory axes.

← 23

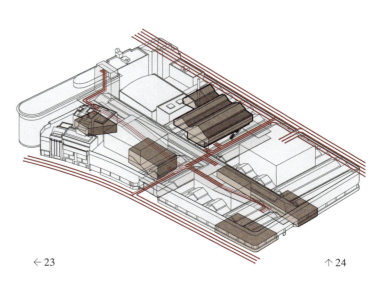

↑ 24

KANAL, Brussels

2017–...

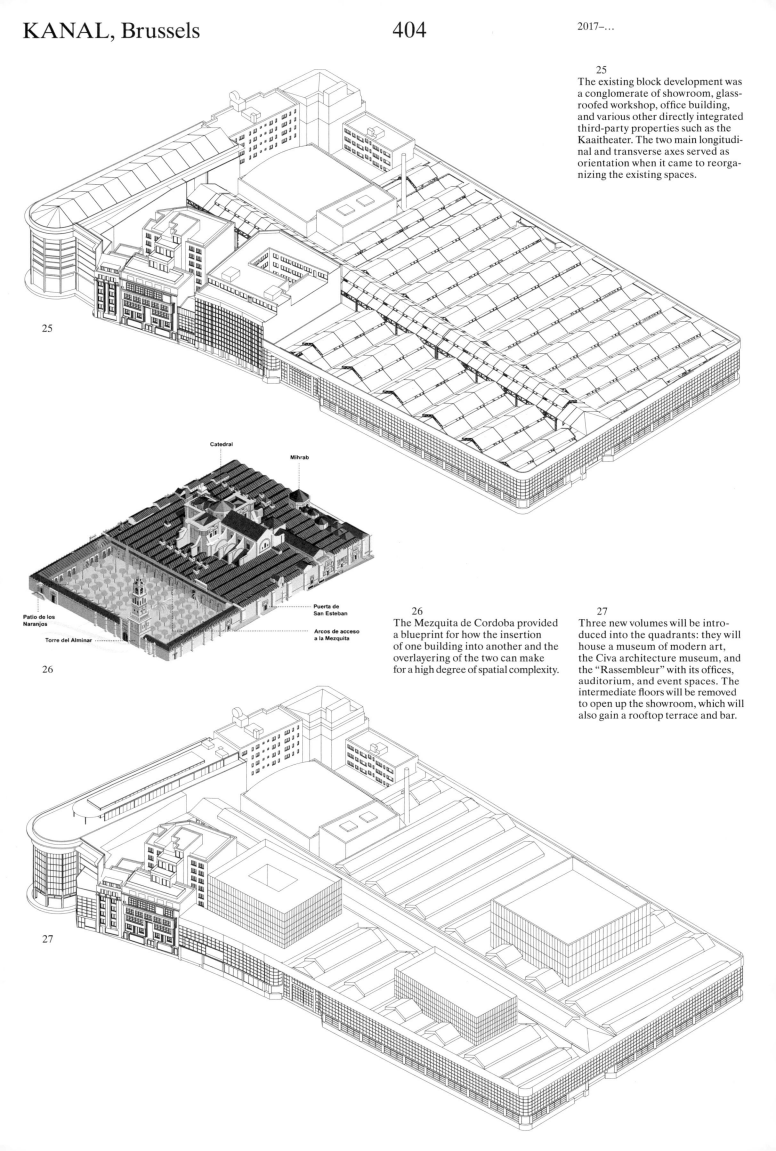

25
The existing block development was a conglomerate of showroom, glass-roofed workshop, office building, and various other directly integrated third-party properties such as the Kaaitheater. The two main longitudinal and transverse axes served as orientation when it came to reorganizing the existing spaces.

26
The Mezquita de Cordoba provided a blueprint for how the insertion of one building into another and the overlayering of the two can make for a high degree of spatial complexity.

27
Three new volumes will be introduced into the quadrants: they will house a museum of modern art, the Civa architecture museum, and the "Rassembleur" with its offices, auditorium, and event spaces. The intermediate floors will be removed to open up the showroom, which will also gain a rooftop terrace and bar.

KANAL, Brussels

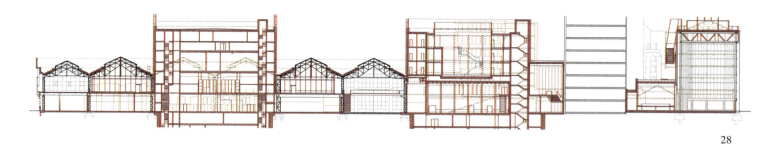

28

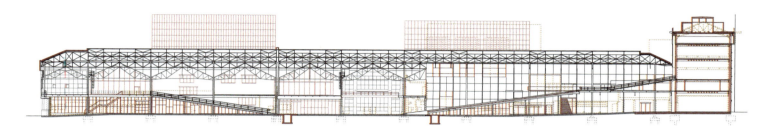

29

30

28–31
Longitudinal and cross-sections. The long ramp along the longitudinal axis will provide access to the first upper level and to the upper floors of the showroom. The new volumes are designed to fit into the main space with almost surgical precision.

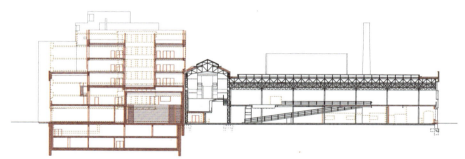

31

KANAL, Brussels 406 2017–...

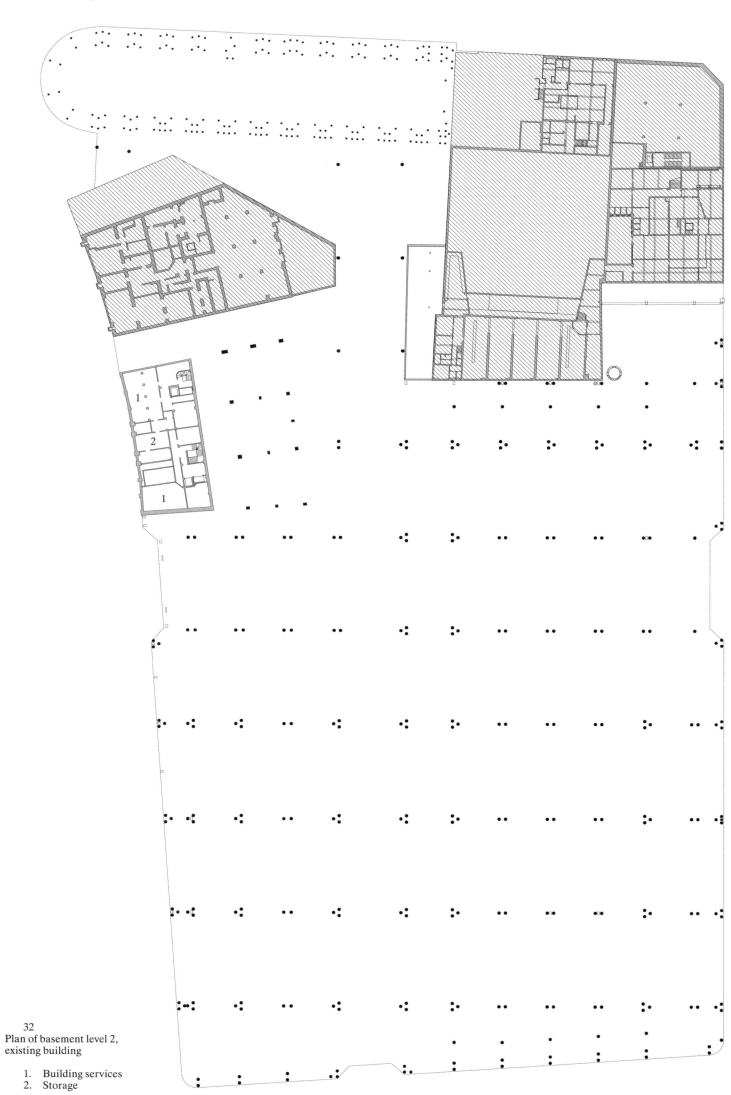

32
Plan of basement level 2,
existing building

1. Building services
2. Storage

KANAL, Brussels

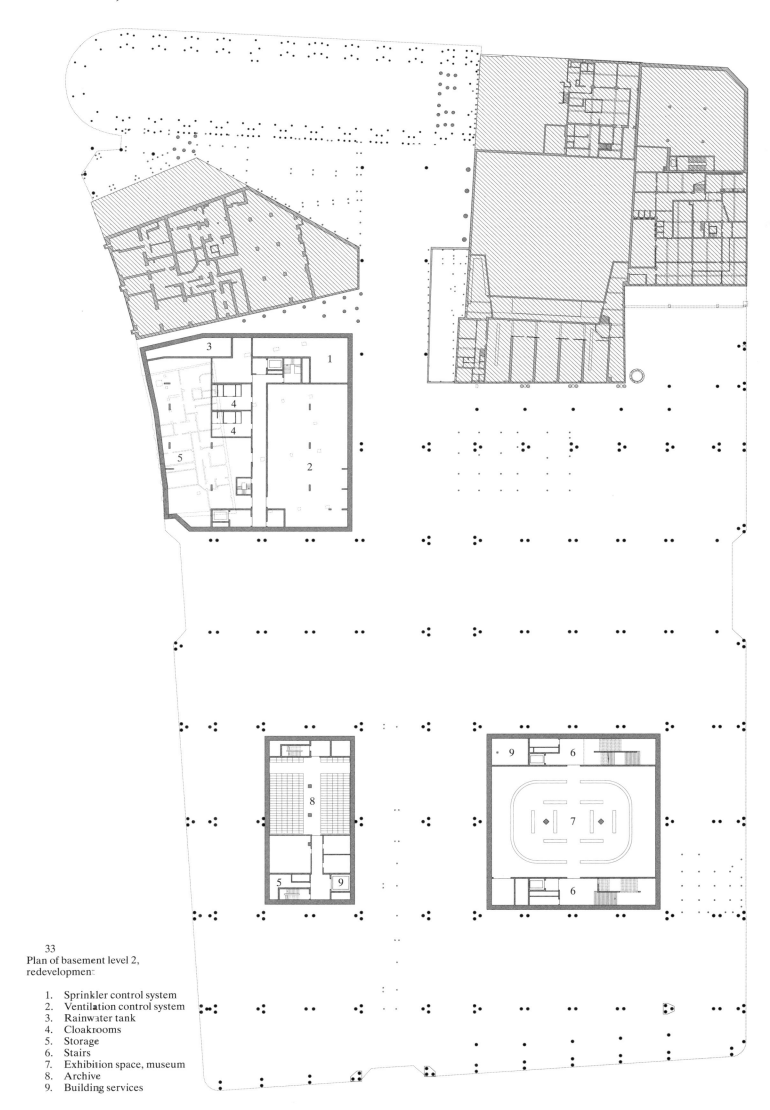

33
Plan of basement level 2, redevelopment

1. Sprinkler control system
2. Ventilation control system
3. Rainwater tank
4. Cloakrooms
5. Storage
6. Stairs
7. Exhibition space, museum
8. Archive
9. Building services

KANAL, Brussels 408 2017–…

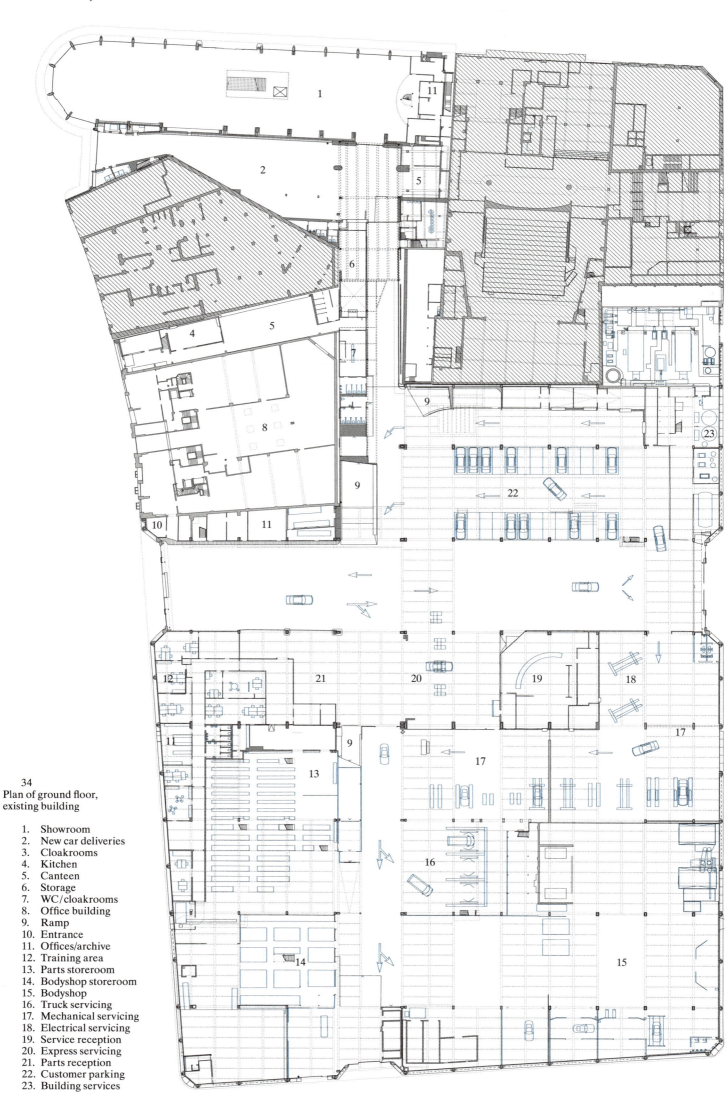

34
Plan of ground floor, existing building

1. Showroom
2. New car deliveries
3. Cloakrooms
4. Kitchen
5. Canteen
6. Storage
7. WC/cloakrooms
8. Office building
9. Ramp
10. Entrance
11. Offices/archive
12. Training area
13. Parts storeroom
14. Bodyshop storeroom
15. Bodyshop
16. Truck servicing
17. Mechanical servicing
18. Electrical servicing
19. Service reception
20. Express servicing
21. Parts reception
22. Customer parking
23. Building services

KANAL, Brussels

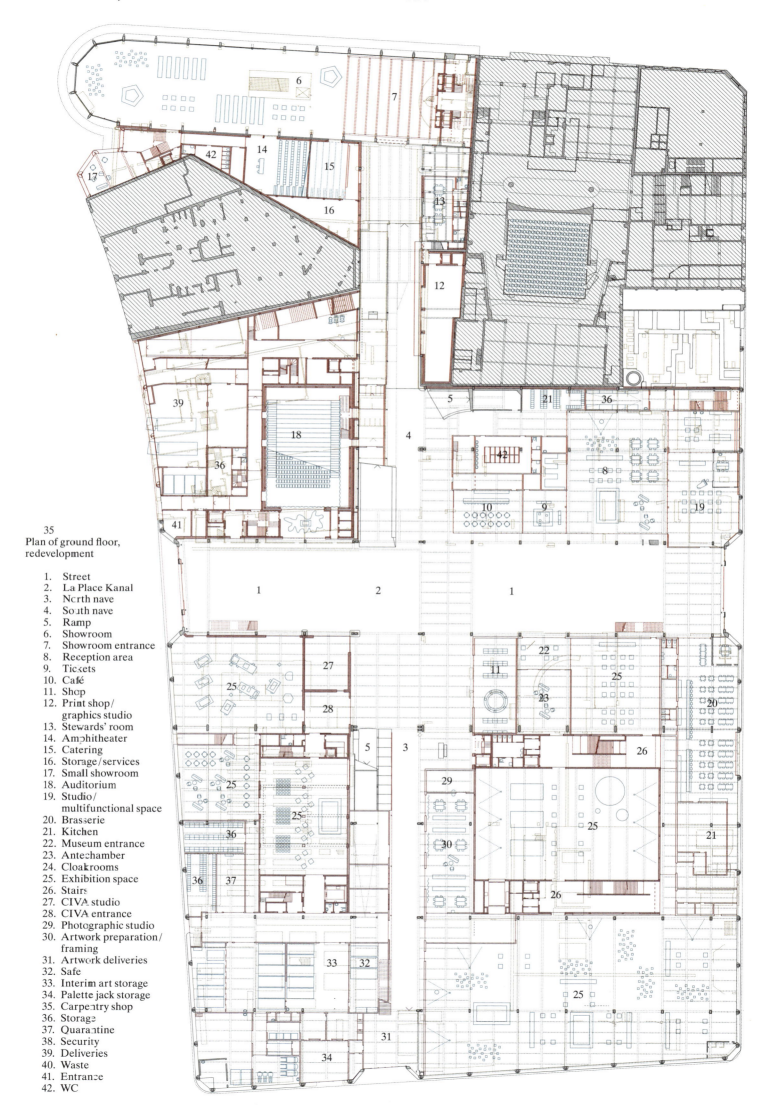

35
Plan of ground floor, redevelopment

1. Street
2. La Place Kanal
3. North nave
4. South nave
5. Ramp
6. Showroom
7. Showroom entrance
8. Reception area
9. Tickets
10. Café
11. Shop
12. Print shop/ graphics studio
13. Stewards' room
14. Amphitheater
15. Catering
16. Storage/services
17. Small showroom
18. Auditorium
19. Studio/ multifunctional space
20. Brasserie
21. Kitchen
22. Museum entrance
23. Antechamber
24. Cloakrooms
25. Exhibition space
26. Stairs
27. CIVA studio
28. CIVA entrance
29. Photographic studio
30. Artwork preparation/ framing
31. Artwork deliveries
32. Safe
33. Interim art storage
34. Palette jack storage
35. Carpentry shop
36. Storage
37. Quarantine
38. Security
39. Deliveries
40. Waste
41. Entrance
42. WC

KANAL, Brussels

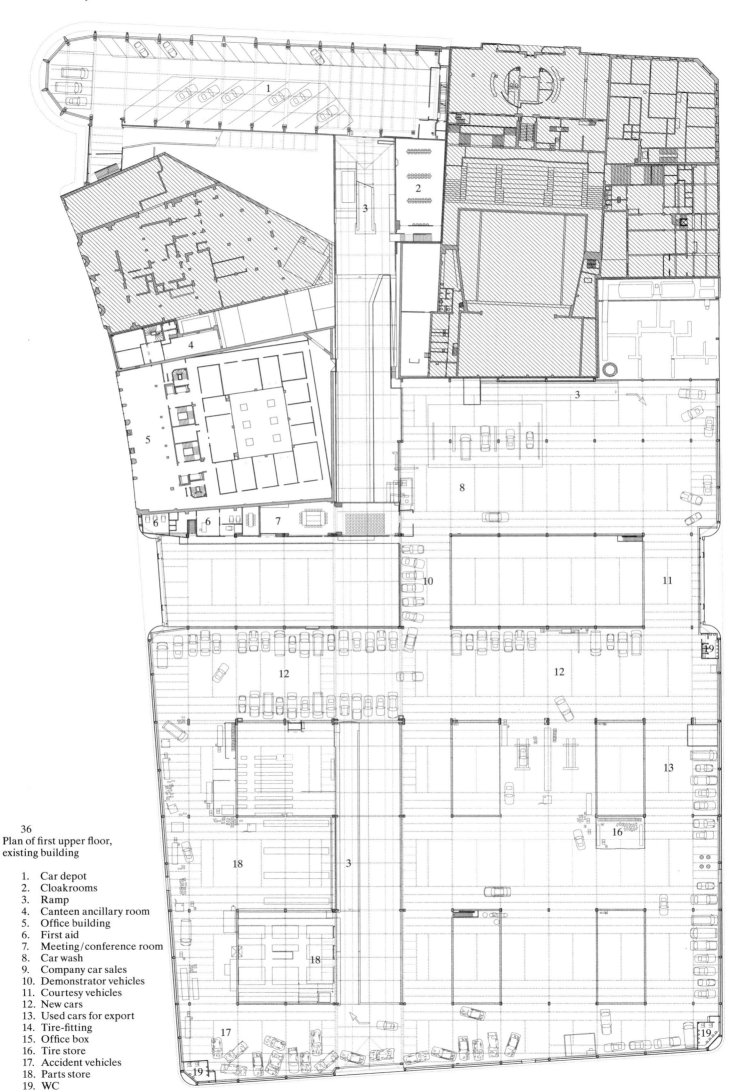

36
Plan of first upper floor, existing building

1. Car depot
2. Cloakrooms
3. Ramp
4. Canteen ancillary room
5. Office building
6. First aid
7. Meeting/conference room
8. Car wash
9. Company car sales
10. Demonstrator vehicles
11. Courtesy vehicles
12. New cars
13. Used cars for export
14. Tire-fitting
15. Office box
16. Tire store
17. Accident vehicles
18. Parts store
19. WC

KANAL, Brussels

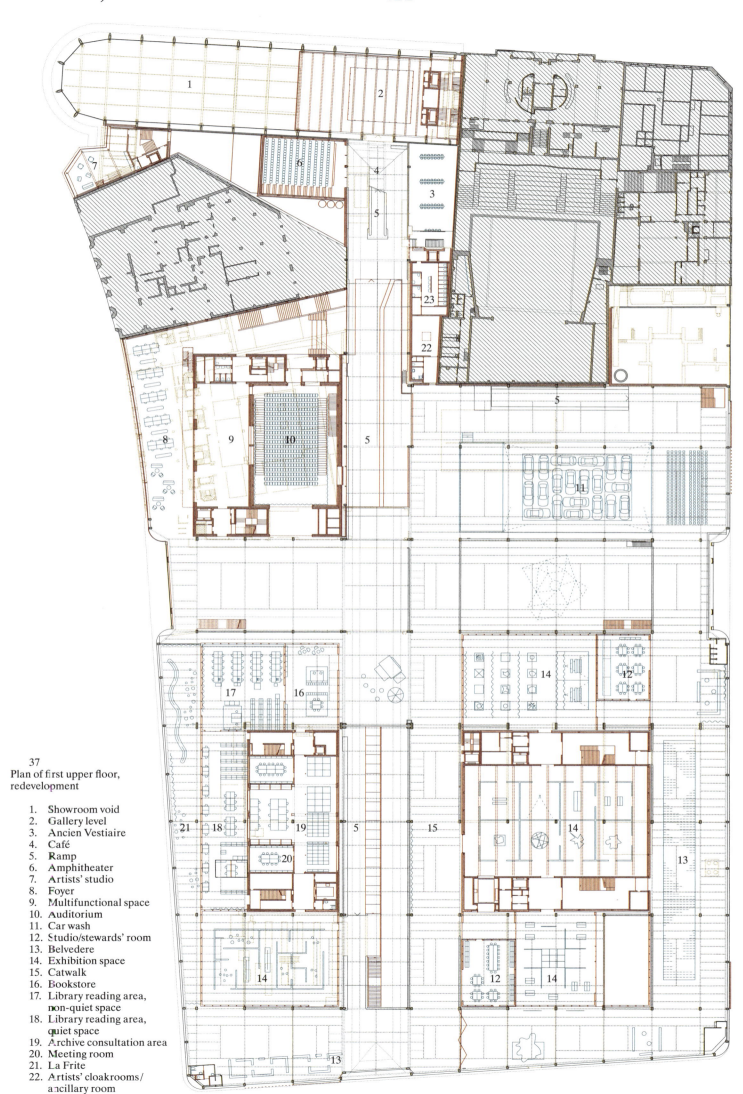

37
Plan of first upper floor, redevelopment

1. Showroom void
2. Gallery level
3. Ancien Vestiaire
4. Café
5. Ramp
6. Amphitheater
7. Artists' studio
8. Foyer
9. Multifunctional space
10. Auditorium
11. Car wash
12. Studio/stewards' room
13. Belvedere
14. Exhibition space
15. Catwalk
16. Bookstore
17. Library reading area, non-quiet space
18. Library reading area, quiet space
19. Archive consultation area
20. Meeting room
21. La Frite
22. Artists' cloakrooms/ancillary room

KANAL, Brussels 412 2017–...

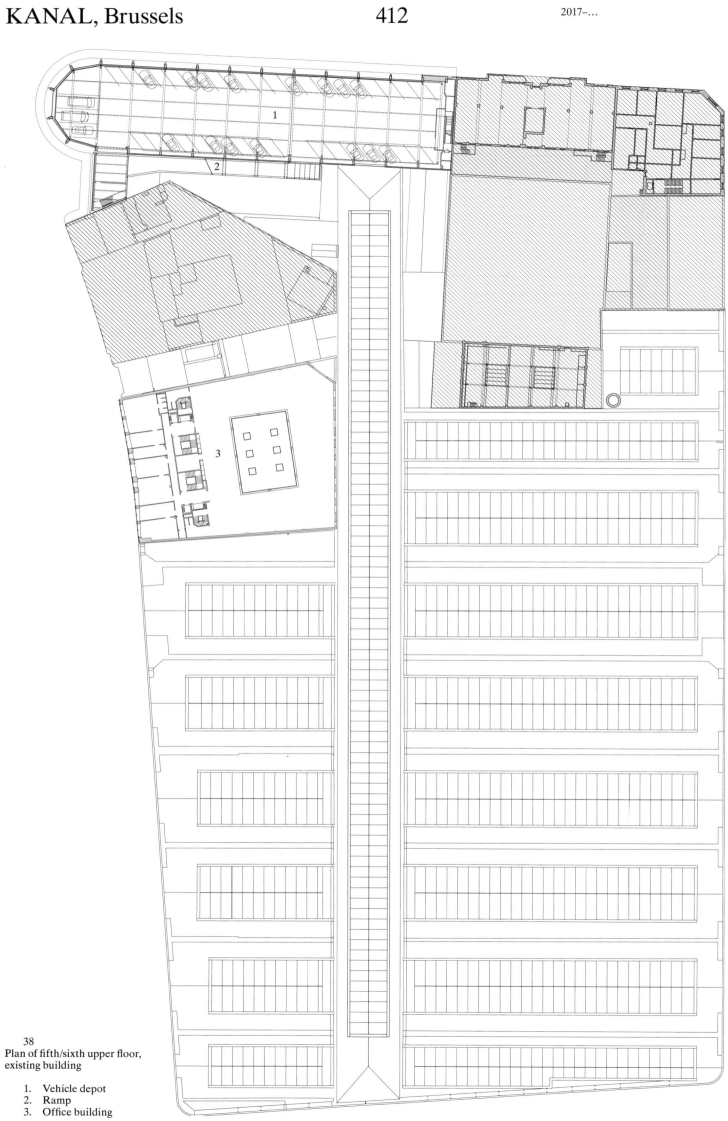

38
Plan of fifth/sixth upper floor,
existing building

1. Vehicle depot
2. Ramp
3. Office building

KANAL, Brussels   413   2017–…

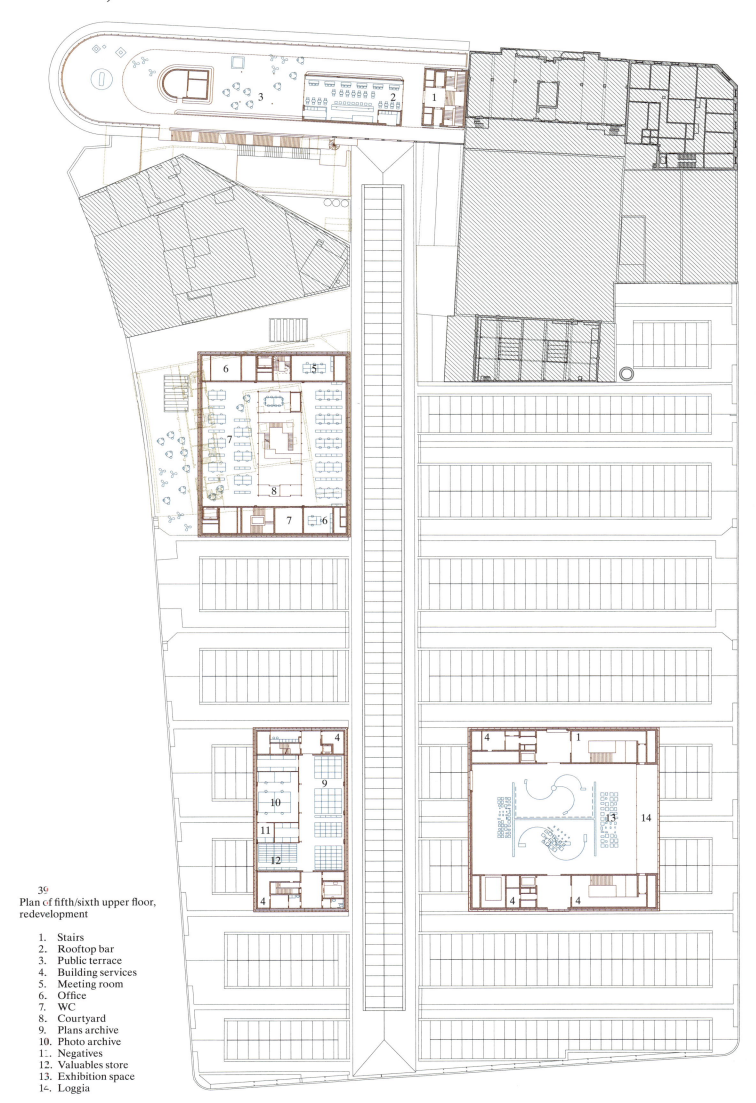

39
Plan of fifth/sixth upper floor, redevelopment

1. Stairs
2. Rooftop bar
3. Public terrace
4. Building services
5. Meeting room
6. Office
7. WC
8. Courtyard
9. Plans archive
10. Photo archive
11. Negatives
12. Valuables store
13. Exhibition space
14. Loggia

KANAL, Brussels

414

40 ↓
Ground floor plan with
surrounding street plan

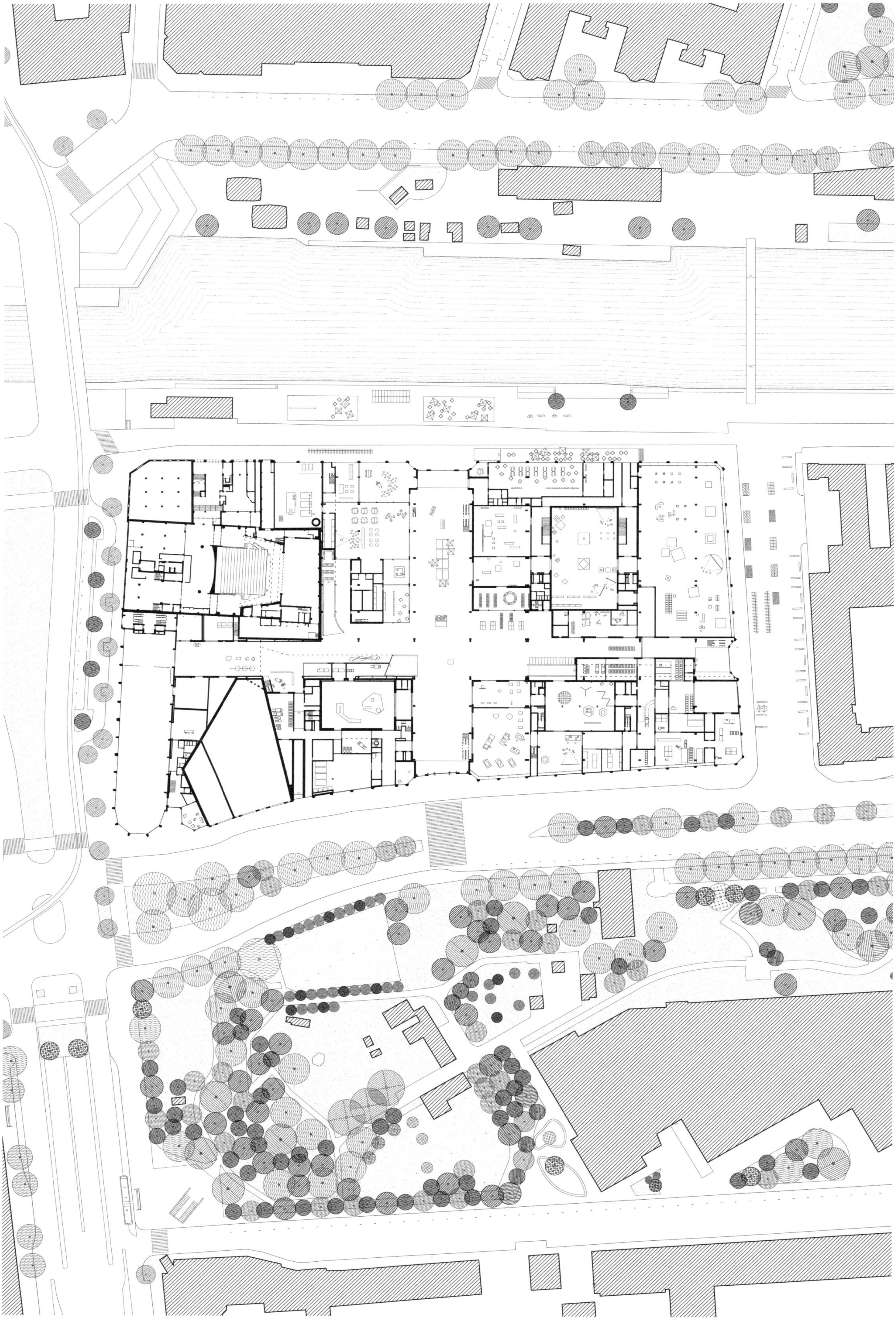

Office and Commercial Building Binzstrasse

Office and Commercial Building Binzstrasse

2 ↑   ↓ 3

Office and Commercial Building Binzstrasse

2017–2023

← 1

Situated close to central Zurich, the Binz business park is a microcosm within the city. Formerly a claypit serving the local brickworks, the site is cut off from the city by steep banks on three sides, only opening out towards the city center on the valley side. Strict zoning regulations prevent the area from becoming an upscale residential neighborhood, instead permitting offices and other commercial usages plus a certain proportion of services. Over the years, a mixed ecosystem has thus developed in which old and new industries, offices, commercial enterprises, and services sit alongside event spaces and restaurants.

2 + 3

Adjacent to the Supertanker development, a new office and commercial building was planned for a vacant lot that had previously been used for car parking. The complex regulatory framework led us to devise a structure whose rear courtyard-facing aspect would taper in a series of terraces. This theme of planted terracing also recurs in modified form on the street elevation.

4 ↑

↓ 5

4 + 5

The sectional model clearly shows how the building's façades and structure follow the outline dictated by the regulatory framework. The south-facing rear terraces are significantly larger than those on the north-facing balconies overlooking the street. The load-bearing structure comprises concrete supports and a prefabricated ribbed concrete ceiling with binders.

6 + 7 →

The balconies and terraces to the front and rear add outside space to the interiors. The vertical tapering is also apparent within, especially in the double-height hall that connects the second and third upper floors.

Office and Commercial Building Binzstrasse

Office and Commercial Building Binzstrasse

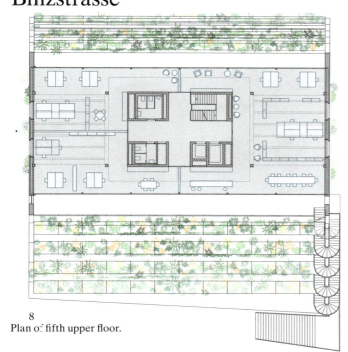

8
Plan of fifth upper floor.

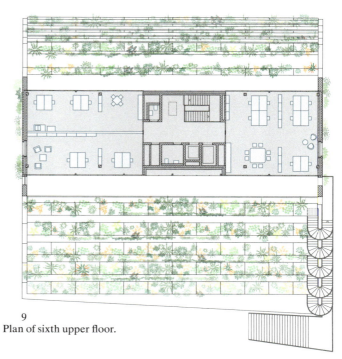

9
Plan of sixth upper floor.

10
Plan of third upper floor.

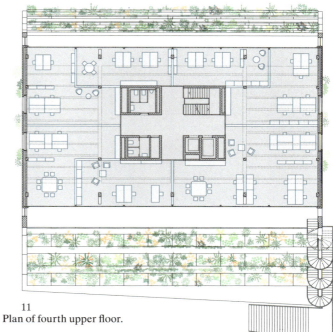

11
Plan of fourth upper floor.

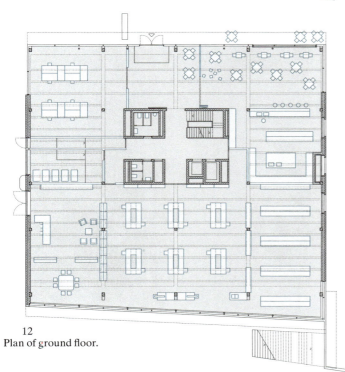

12
Plan of ground floor.

13
Plan of first upper floor.

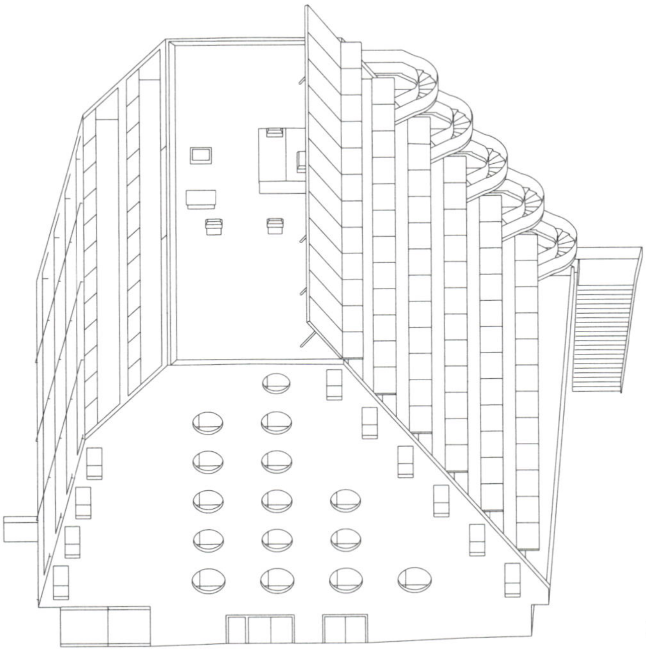

Office and Commercial Building 420 2017–2023

14

14–42
An external staircase connects the courtyard-facing terraces and provides additional access. Lattice-work projections serve as trellises for various climbing plants that will lend shade in summer months.

43 →
The courtyard elevation features a projecting external staircase that offers spectacular views of the surrounding neighborhood.

15
Amelanchier ovalis

16
Aristolochia macrophylla

17
Berberis stenophylla

18
Berberis vulgaris

19
Chamaecytisus purpureus

20
Clematis alpina

21
Clematis montana

22
Colutea arborescens

23
Cytisus scoparius

24
Daphne cneorum

25
Dorycinum hirsutum

26
Hedera helix

Office and Commercial Building Binzstrasse

27
Hippocrepis emerus

28
Hydrangea anomala

29
Jasminum nudiflorum

30
Lonicera japonica

31
Parthenocissus quinquefolia

32
Parthenocissus tricuspidata

33
Pinus mugo

34
Prunus fruticosa

35
Prunus tenella

36
Raphanus sativus

37
Rosa glauca

38
Rosa rubiginosa

39
Rosa villosa

40
Schizophragma hydrangeoides

41
Sorbus chamaemespilus

42
Taraxacum officinale

Office and Commercial Building Binzstrasse

Rampenhaus Schwerzenbach Revisited

← See pages 22 and 304

1
The sensation of phantom pain is back (see page 22), but this time the source is much more specific: the sight of the newly amputated Rampenhaus in Schwerzenbach causes us almost physical pain.

2
For us, Schwerzenbach's Rampenhaus has long been a source of inspiration, and perhaps also of silent reproach: if non-architect August Schmid was able to create such an iconic building for entirely pragmatic ends, why have we not managed to come up with something similarly radical? Acquaintances have often asked about this find and, in the fall of 2007, one of our colleagues decided to take a look for himself.

3
Backed up by photographic evidence, his report was deeply distressing. The spectacular ramp had been brutally amputated! A new owner had evidently had it summarily removed, closing off the upper floor accesses and hastily covering the wounds with sheet metal.

New Housing on Briesestrasse

New Housing on Briesestrasse

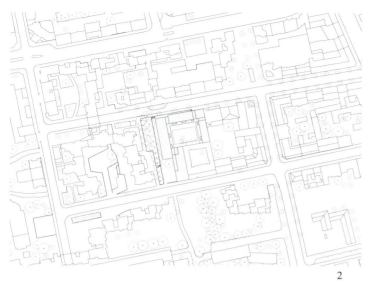

1 + 4
Briesestrasse in Neukölln, Berlin, features a variety of very different architectural styles, encompassing both 19th-century buildings and modern developments from the 1960s, '70s, and '80s.

2
Neukölln's perimeter blocks largely survived World War Two intact but, in the 1960s, their densely built courtyards were deemed unsanitary. Rollbergviertel, the area to the west of the project site, was thus cleared and redeveloped, with perimeter blocks eschewed in favor of a typology that let in more light and air, and in some cases spanned multiple streets. Our project incorporated aspects of both these building types, embedding them in a new kind of perimeter development that would mediate between the two typologies.

3
The existing parking garage on the site had low floor-to-floor heights that made it unsuitable for residential redevelopment. The competition brief thus stipulated a new-build.

5 →
Ground floor plan.

6 →
Arranged around a peaceful courtyard, the new buildings echo the varying height and geometry of the surrounding buildings. On the Kienitzer Strasse side is a small public forecourt, alongside which are studios and a café.

7 →
First upper floor plan.

8 →
The apartments (comprising small units of 40 square meters and upwards plus large cluster units of up to 300 square meters) are accessed via external galleries overlooking the planted courtyard. Each unit has at least one outdoor space either directly by the courtyard or on the access gallery. Many also have a small street-facing balcony or an additional outdoor seating area.

New Housing on Briesestrasse

New Housing on Briesestrasse

2015–2020

7 ↑ ↓ 8

New Housing on Briesestrasse

9 ↑   ↓ 10

11

12

13 ↑   ↓ 14

New Housing on Briesestrasse

15 ↑   ↓ 16

17 ↑   ↓ 18

19 ↑   ↓ 20   21 ↘

9
Access gallery, seventh upper floor.
10
Access gallery, fifth upper floor.
11
View from a balcony, fifth upper floor.
12
The ground floor studios have their own outdoor seating areas; the upper floor apartments have private balconies.
13
Courtyard-side studio apartment.
14
Covered courtyard-facing outdoor areas on the ground floor.
15 + 17 + 19
Two-bedroom apartment, seventh upper floor.
16
Two-bedroom apartment, fifth upper floor.
18
One-bedroom apartment, fifth upper floor.
20
Three-bedroom apartment, fifth upper floor.
21
Two-bedroom apartment, sixth upper floor.
22 →
The external galleries are not just an efficient means of providing access given the large number of small units, they are also a way of extending living space and facilitating interaction between inhabitants.

New Housing on Briesestrasse

Office Block as Typology

Mathias Müller
Daniel Niggli

The office block is one of the key typological innovations in late 19th-century architecture. In his book *S, M, L, XL*, Rem Koolhaas even claimed that the radical US iteration, with its "typical plan" offices, was an expression of the fundamental ideological differences between the Old World and the New (i.e. between Europe and America).[A] As "architecture without qualities," the typical plan provides generic, fluid, and decontextualized accommodation for the formless and abstract program of "business." With business no longer requiring a particular kind of space (or even any space) or translating into any specific form, 21st-century society is, however, increasingly turning away from the typical plan. Indeed, in a reversal of the old adage "form follows function," the most attractive and innovative offices are now found in one-time industrial buildings—warehouses, breweries, converted sewage treatment plants—disused swimming pools, and even in old churches. The resulting office typologies are in turn influencing the design of new-build office blocks, shaping their spatial, structural, and atmospheric characteristics. In a paradoxical inversion, today's office block concepts are thus drawing on essentially obsolete typologies and building types.

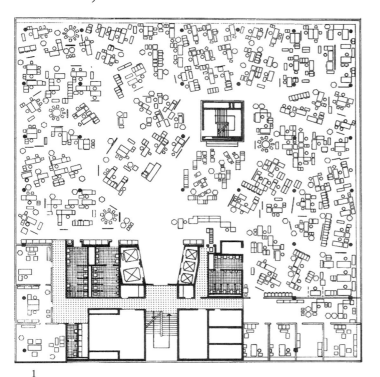

1
Osram headquarters, Munich, Walter Henn, 1965: offices as radical open spaces in which furniture becomes the chief determinant of interior zoning.

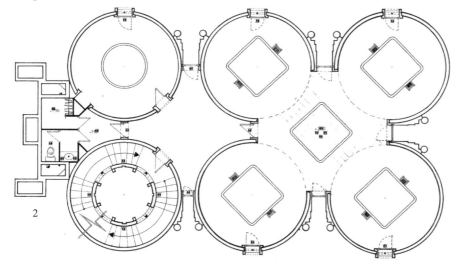

2
In the early 1970s, architect Ricardo Bofill bought a ruined cement factory and set up his practice in its disused silos. It's a project he continued to develop and adapt up until his death in 2022.

A
OMA, Rem Koolhaas, Bruce Mau, *S, M, L, XL*, New York, 1995.

Office Block as Typology 432 3↓

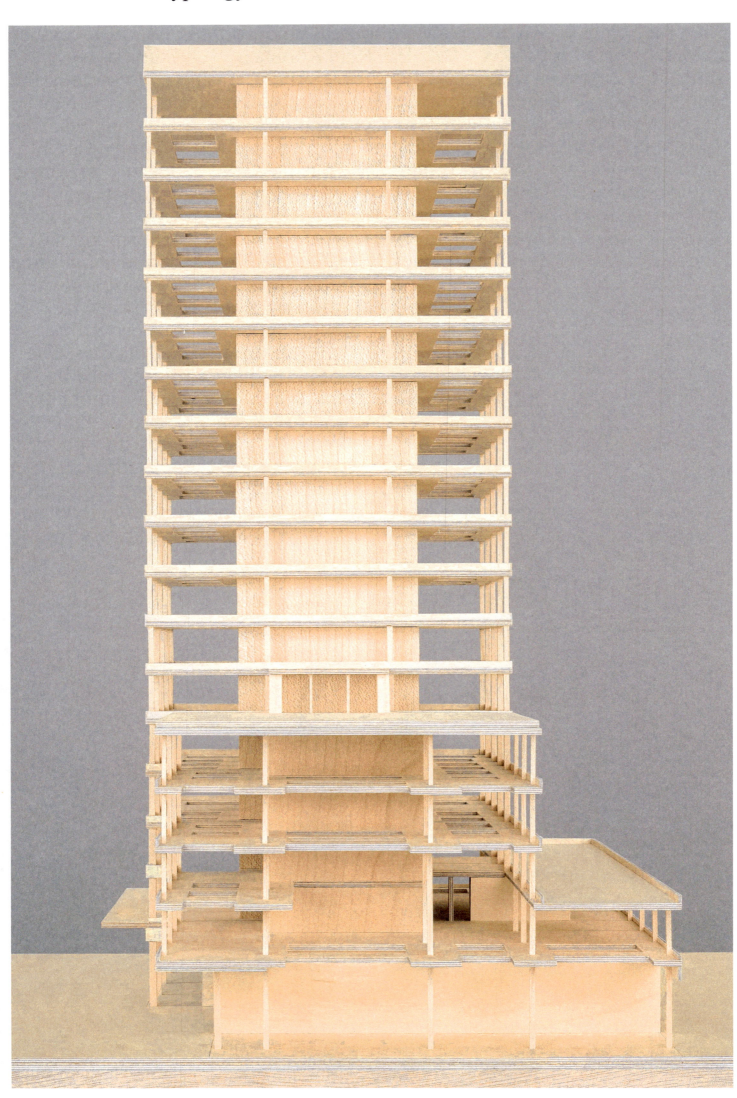

Office Block as Typology

3
For the new Atmos office building in Zurich, which was to replace a highly dysfunctional late-1980s speculative development with a structural vacancy rate of 50 percent, we took our cue from the spatial configurations of industrial conversions such as the Toni and Maag sites. If these complexes with their great variety of spaces are so popular with their users, then surely our new-builds should offer similar spatial, structural, and atmospheric qualities inside and out. The Atmos project was thus designed and engineered so that large openings could be made in the center of each ceiling section on every floor, tower included, thus allowing for vertical connections between the different stories. The building's intelligent carcass thus offers scope for appropriation and adaptation, opening up a wide range of possibilities.

4
The new-build offers a variety of very different spaces. The double-height hall spanning the first and second upper floors, for instance, is extremely deep yet receives ample daylight thanks to its basilica-like form. Together with the optional vertical openings, the ability to densify the building's high-ceilinged spaces via inserted platforms offers significant potential for individual customization.

5
Spillmann Echsle's build-out for footwear firm On Running made full use of this potential, inserting a staircase into the tower that connects the ground floor with all the upper floors.

6
Large folding doors open the ground floor up to the outside, allowing vehicles to drive in and move around the 5-meter-high spaces.

7
Work for the new On Running staircase started with the opening up of the carcass's ground floor ceiling.

8
For the Scandit headquarters, architecture practice HelsinkiZurich also exploited the potential for densification, inserting additional lightweight platforms and adding partial ceiling openings to create internal connections and sight lines.

Office Block as Typology

9–11
Plans for the fifth upper floor, first upper floor, and ground floor.

12
In addition to a kitchen and common room, the fifth upper floor features a densely planted roof garden that can be used by all tenants. This shared space is accessible from all three sections of the complex.

13
Our idea to create a public pocket park (designed by Studio Vulkan) with a small-scale restaurant pavilion helped to persuade planning officials to approve a scheme featuring a tower. The value of closely interlinked indoor and outdoor spaces is another lesson learned from our study of good industrial sites.

Office Block as Typology

12 ↑

↓ 13

Office Block as Typology

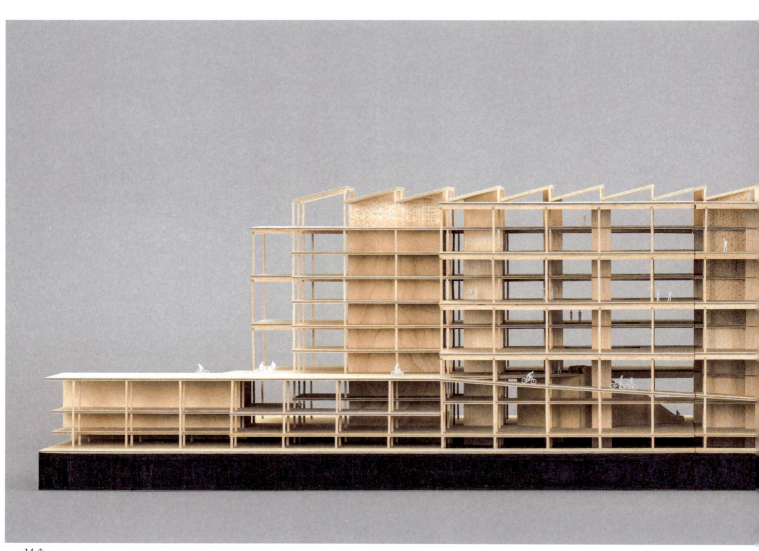

14 ↑

Office Block as Typology 437

↓ 15

Office Block as Typology

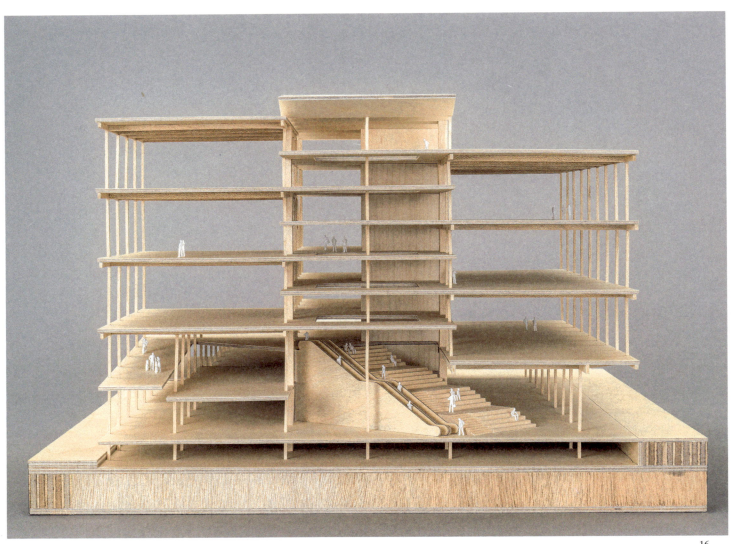

← 14 + 15
For our winning proposal in a 2019 competition to build an office block in Stavanger, we worked with Ghilardi + Hellsten Architekter to devise double-height workspaces that took their cue from warehouse typologies. By integrating a bicycle highway and large staircases, we also put public circulation routes at the heart of our design.

16
The middle section of the tripartite block houses supporting infrastructure and circulation spaces for the two vertically stacked double-height office levels, which can be retrospectively densified and customized via galleries and other insertions.

17
Our proposal for the QH Track project in Berlin's Heidestrasse development zone also used a warehouse typology to counterbalance the monoculture of uniform, standardized office spaces. Featuring a string of 11- to 14-story towers interspersed with five-story "warehouses," the complex is due to form the perimeter of the new Europacity district, flanking the busy rail approach to Berlin's central station.

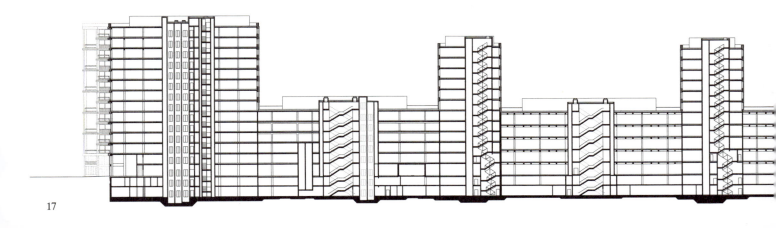

Office Block as Typology

18 + 19
In the "warehouse" sections, deep plans will combine with 4-meter-high ceilings and recessed loggias to create contemporary yet timeless workspaces.

20
An internal atrium is planned for one of the two "thick" towers, allowing for an open-plan officescape with double-height balconies.

21 →
The skyline of tower blocks and "warehouses" will create a new built perimeter alongside the tracks.

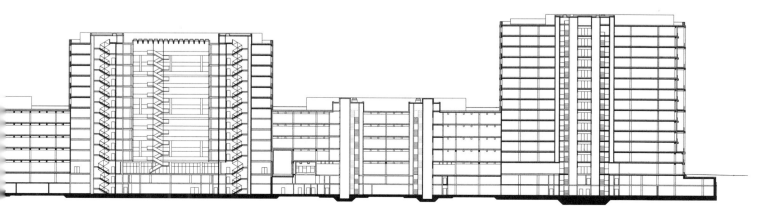

Koch Campus

1
A former industrial site owned by Swiss banking giant UBS, the Koch campus was occupied by activists in 2013. Events such as gigs and parties then led to noise complaints from local residents but, as the owners declined to pursue legal action, the squatters were able to remain. After the site's sale to the city of Zurich, a master plan was developed and housing co-ops and investors were invited to participate in a competition of ideas. Four parallel design competitions were then held for two mixed-used residential developments, an office building, and an urban park.

2
Working within the narrow outline plan, our design for the office building attempted to manipulate the planned simple structure so that its large volume would be sensitively incorporated into the urban setting but still offer a distinctive form. We thus proposed creating two notched corners at opposite ends of the square block, creating a striking presence alongside the new park and allowing light to better penetrate the deep plan. For the materials, we deliberately chose simple, cost-effective options such as concrete, exposed OSB, and roofing felt as exterior cladding.

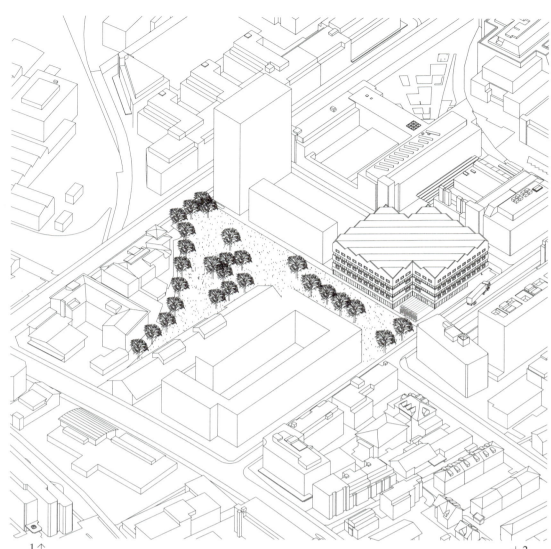

Koch Campus

3 ↑   ↓ 4

5 ↑   ↓ 6

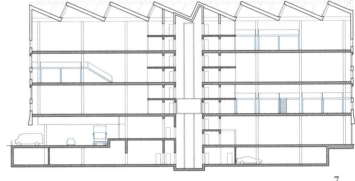

7

3
In our design, a glazed sawtooth roof illuminates the top floor, while the double-height office spaces are lit by large, high-level ribbon windows with punched openings below. The façade thus presents a modified version of the sectional view.

4
The ability to insert galleries into the high-ceilinged spaces allows a range of spatial configurations to be created.

5
Without insertions, the spaces would lend themselves to commercial or light industrial uses, while their height would also enable them to accommodate split-level vertical configurations of storage, archive, and office spaces.

6
Adding galleries along the façade walls would create a high space at the heart of the plan—perhaps for the central hub of a coworking space. A reception area and meeting or relaxation room could all be sited here.

7
Our proposal stacked three double-height levels above an extra-high ground floor.

Koch Campus

8 Top floor plan showing the diagonals of the sawtooth roof.

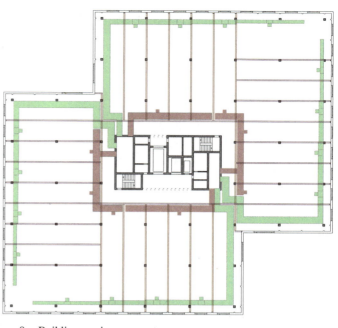

9 Building services concept.

10 Middle level plan featuring a variety of commercial units.

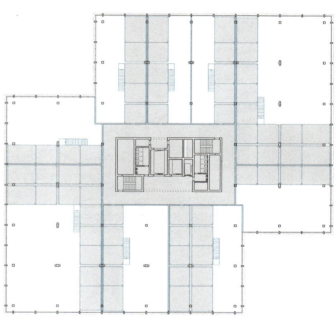

11 Modular ceiling openings and grids for galleries.

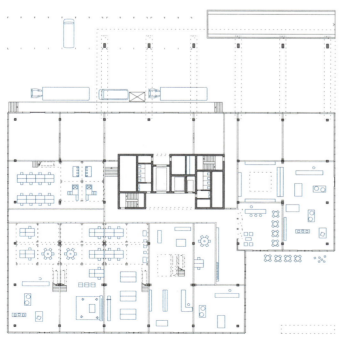

12 Possible ground floor configuration incorporating a restaurant, commercial units, and central delivery area.

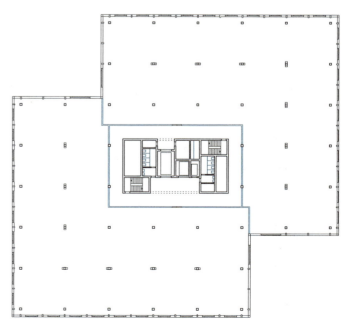

13 Possible configuration of mezzanine galleries.

KANAL Brut

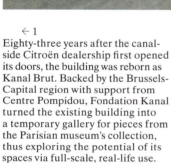

← 1
Eighty-three years after the canal-side Citroën dealership first opened its doors, the building was reborn as Kanal Brut. Backed by the Brussels-Capital region with support from Centre Pompidou, Fondation Kanal turned the existing building into a temporary gallery for pieces from the Parisian museum's collection, thus exploring the potential of its spaces via full-scale, real-life use.

2
Visitors in the repair shop's transverse shed, which formed the entrance hall on the Quai des Péniches side.

3
Florian Beigel and Philip Christou's installation *RE-BUILDING CASS, The Little City inside the Building* served as premises for a temporary café and museum shop.

4
Theatrical performance directed by Roméo Castellucci.

5
Franz West's *Auditorium* sculpture in the repair shop, April 2019.

6
Jean Tinguely's sculpture *L'Enfer, un petit début*, June 2019.

7
Performance *Stop Kanal* by Bowling Brands, part of the Kanal Festival in June 2019.

8
Jean Prouvé's *Maison Tropicale* exhibited on the repair shop's upper level, June 2019.

9
Performance by Company du Zerep on the upper level, June 2019.

10
Fundraising initiative "Origami for Life" by Charles Kaisin, April 2020.

11
Ross Lovegrove's *Liquidkristal* pavilion on the upper level, June 2019.

12
Miscellaneous Folies exhibition by Cédric Libert, Benjamin Lafore, Sébastien Martinez-Barat, and Michel Mathy, June 2019.

KANAL Brut

2018–2019

8

9

10

← 11

↓ 12

Uster Culture Center

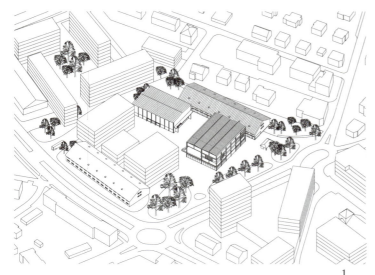

1

2 ↑ ↓ 3

1 + 2
Built in 1938 by the federal government, the Uster arsenal was decommissioned in 2005. In 2017, part of the site was bought by the local authority, with the rest remaining in the hands of Armasuisse, the Federal Office for Defence Procurement. From 2007 on, the site hosted a range of cultural activities, parties, eateries, and even an open-air festival. In 2017, a master plan developed by Morger + Dettli Architekten came into effect. While the Armasuisse-owned western section was to be developed for housing, the local authority-owned eastern section was the subject of a competition for an arts center.

3 + 4
We developed a proposal that spreads the specified functions across the existing arsenal building and the two additions. As the scheme's programming needs hadn't yet been definitively decided, we opted to leave the upper floors of the old arsenal building largely untouched and convert the ground floor into a foyer for the two new-build additions. Our design for the latter gave the "Stadtsaal" building a partitionable interior and a façade that can be opened up to the outside, while the "Kulturregal" was conceived as a combined two-screen movie theater, cabaret venue, gallery, and restaurant. The area between the three buildings is envisioned as a venue for various cultural events. The Stadtsaal building could also be opened up to the courtyard, enabling it to host outdoor concerts, for instance.

5 + 6
To ensure it would have the urban presence envisaged in the master plan and represent the site as a whole, we planned the "Kulturregal" building on a larger scale than required by the scheme's programming needs, thereby helping to create clearly defined outdoor spaces. We also devised open-fronted levels that create a kind of walk-through sculpture while allowing for spontaneous, temporary usages. Should additional functions be required in future, the structure offers the potential for temporary or permanent densification.

7 + 8 →
For the Kulturregal, we planned publicly accessible terraces that add internal outside space and offer scope for various forms of appropriation, being suitable for changing usages such as exhibitions, installations, performances, or movie screenings.

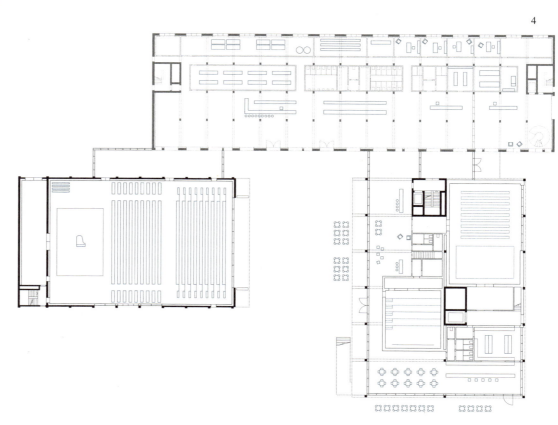

4

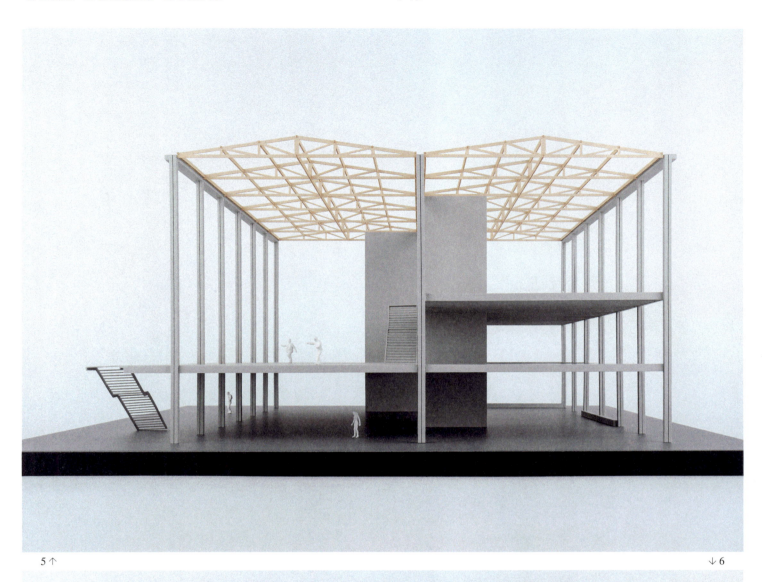

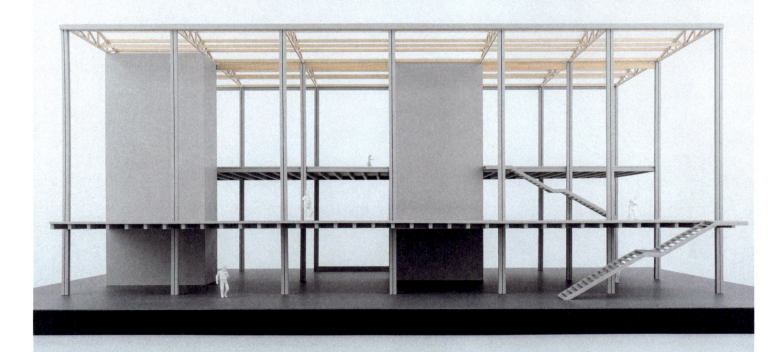

Uster Culture Center 450 2019–…

Maag Campus

When we moved our practice from Selnaustrasse in central Zurich to the Maag campus in 2004, we were following a decade-old trend. In the structural transition of the 1990s, traditional industries deserted west Zurich and new tenants in search of affordable premises, including freelancers, creatives, and nightclubs, moved into the recently vacated spaces. Following the closure of the Steinfels, Schoeller, and Sulzer-Escher-Wyss industrial sites, the remaining production units of gearbox manufacturer Maag also gradually moved out of District 5. Well-connected thanks to the proximity to Hardbrücke station, this centrally located, hitherto inaccessible site was suddenly back in play, opening up a world of new possibilities: before long its empty sheds and office blocks had filled up with new occupants—not just architects, engineers, and designers, but also an event venue, the workshops of bagmaker Freitag, various art galleries, and much more besides. The old canteen, meanwhile, continued to offer diners massive yet ridiculously cheap portions of Wiener schnitzel. Soon a church also joined the new arrivals, its congregation flocking from Hardbrücke station to Saturday morning services just as the last of the club-goers, exhausted after a night of dancing, headed the other way. When the one-time office and production spaces by the station became available at affordable rents, we quickly snapped up a 4-meter-high unit that had probably been used as a drawing office. In terms of atmosphere, it was part office and part workshop. There were large, north-facing windows overlooking the courtyard, a lack of direct sunlight, and high ceilings that allowed heat from the computers to drift upwards, meaning the interior stayed pleasantly cool in summer. Other architects and designers had also set up shop on our floor and, whenever we visited their studios and offices, we were struck by how varied the premises' spatial and locational characteristics were: a view of the train tracks here, a rooftop seating area there, spaces with large doors enabling them to open up to the courtyard, others with double-height ceilings and installed containers serving as meeting rooms, others still that had outdated fixtures and awkward shapes, plus huge, unheated open spaces that delivery vehicles could drive right into. In the courtyard below, we could watch the to-ing and fro-ing of a crate-making and removals firm's forklifts. When a large model needed delivering, we could just park our rental van in the courtyard and use the large goods elevator. We could do noisy, messy work—such as model-building, drilling, sawing, painting, or spraying—without causing any trouble, thanks to the very forgiving industrial surfaces and the underlying noise levels generated by similar activities throughout the building. Of course, this halcyon situation couldn't last. While we were still making the most of our studio space, preparations for the redevelopment of the site and adjacent areas were already underway. According to a master plan drawn up by a working group

Maag Campus

comprising Diener & Diener and Boesch Architekten, that redevelopment would largely consist of new offices and homes. Once a start date for the construction of Gigon Guyer's Prime Tower and Platform building had been set, our days at the old factory were numbered, and so we relocated to a profit-maximized, space-efficient 1960s office block on Langstrasse. The microlocation was great—we were surrounded by restaurants, cafés, and takeout joints—but we badly missed the spatial, atmospheric, and performative qualities of the Maag site's rough-and-ready spaces.

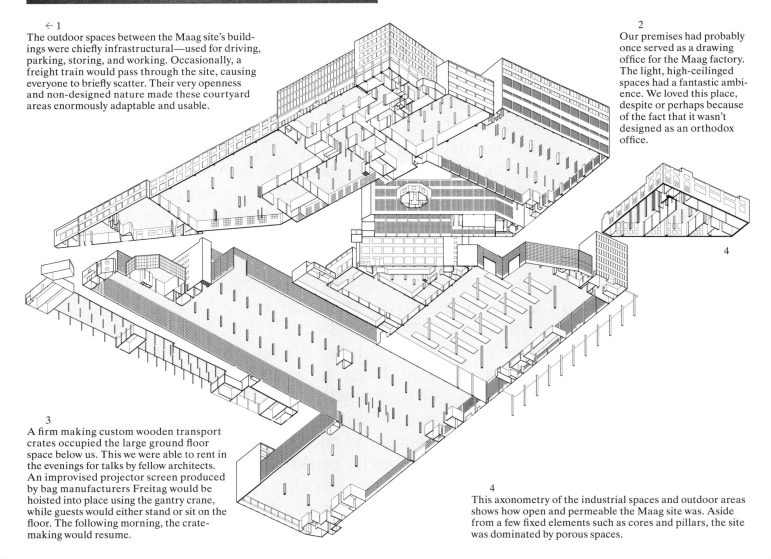

1
The outdoor spaces between the Maag site's buildings were chiefly infrastructural—used for driving, parking, storing, and working. Occasionally, a freight train would pass through the site, causing everyone to briefly scatter. Their very openness and non-designed nature made these courtyard areas enormously adaptable and usable.

2
Our premises had probably once served as a drawing office for the Maag factory. The light, high-ceilinged spaces had a fantastic ambience. We loved this place, despite or perhaps because of the fact that it wasn't designed as an orthodox office.

3
A firm making custom wooden transport crates occupied the large ground floor space below us. This we were able to rent in the evenings for talks by fellow architects. An improvised projector screen produced by bag manufacturers Freitag would be hoisted into place using the gantry crane, while guests would either stand or sit on the floor. The following morning, the crate-making would resume.

4
This axonometry of the industrial spaces and outdoor areas shows how open and permeable the Maag site was. Aside from a few fixed elements such as cores and pillars, the site was dominated by porous spaces.

Hammerbrooklyn

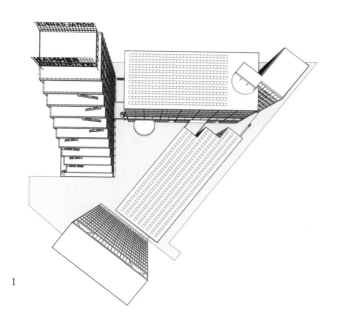

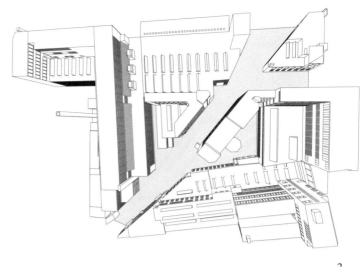

1 + 2
Hammerbrooklyn is a project planned for a central Hamburg site next to the Deichtorhallen gallery complex, opposite the Oberhafen creative quarter and the headquarters of news magazine *Der Spiegel*. According to the competition brief, it's a place where the future of work will become reality. We therefore asked ourselves: What kind of place would we want to work in? The first thing that came to mind was the Maag factory site where our office used to be. Its spaces were generously dimensioned, varied in form, rough and ready, and open for appropriation, while outdoor areas had an urban, flexible feel. We christened it the City-Factory.

3
The Hammerbrooklyn project is to be realized in stages. The first stage will involve the construction of a waterfront pavilion called the Hammerbrooklyn Box. It will provide an information point for the development and a venue for workshops to kick-start the project.

Hammerbrooklyn

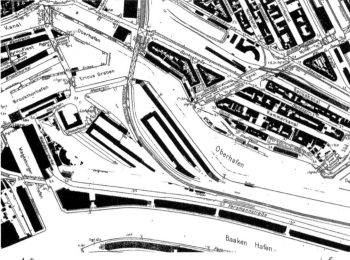

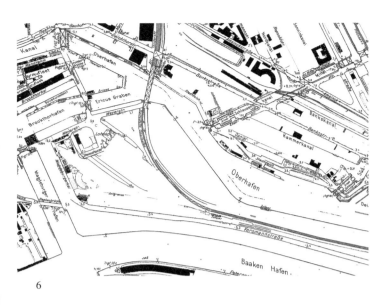

4 ↑   ↓ 5   6

4 + 5
Up until World War Two, this was a residential area for dockworkers.

6
Almost totally destroyed during the war, Hammerbrooklyn was subsequently redeveloped with industrial and commercial buildings. Today, the project lot belongs to the neighboring wholesale market, a place where banana-ripening and pallet-washing takes place alongside research on soilless vegetable-growing.

7
In our competition proposal, we grouped three distinct, muscular buildings around a courtyard, creating a captivating ensemble: the stepped Stairway Building, the Kontor Building with its open first upper floor, and the Gallery Building with a façade of double-height winter gardens.

8
Rather than devising a homogeneous trio, we proposed a disposition that would offer both narrow and broad spaces, clear sight lines, and an open aspect on the Oberhafen and Billekanal side. The intention was to create an urban ensemble that isn't harmonized or polished, instead translating the site's contradictions and geometric constraints into a state of permanent tension.

9
Our design comprised three large but simple skeleton-frame timber structures. Double-height spaces were planned for the Gallery Building and the Kontor Building's first upper floor, allowing for the addition of internal galleries to further structure and densify the spaces. The trio's first upper floors were all connected up to create a shared, semi-public area.

10 →
Neither a mall nor a campus, Hammerbrooklyn is intended as a new urban quarter, a place where the urban realm extends into the space between the buildings. Similar to industrial sites, the simple, robust, and flexible outdoor areas will have no fixed functional assignment or zoning. Even the greenery will be movable if the seasons or specific occasions require.

7

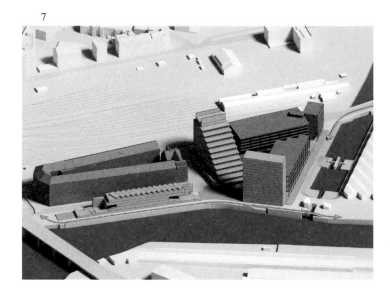

Hammerbrooklyn 2019–…

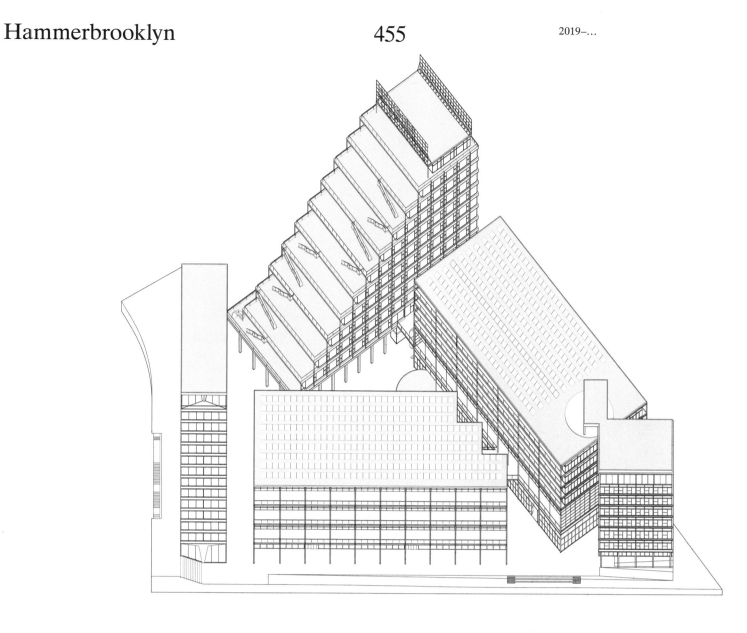

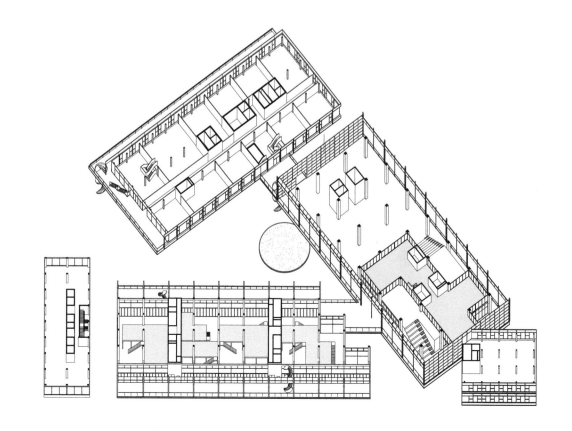

Hammerbrooklyn

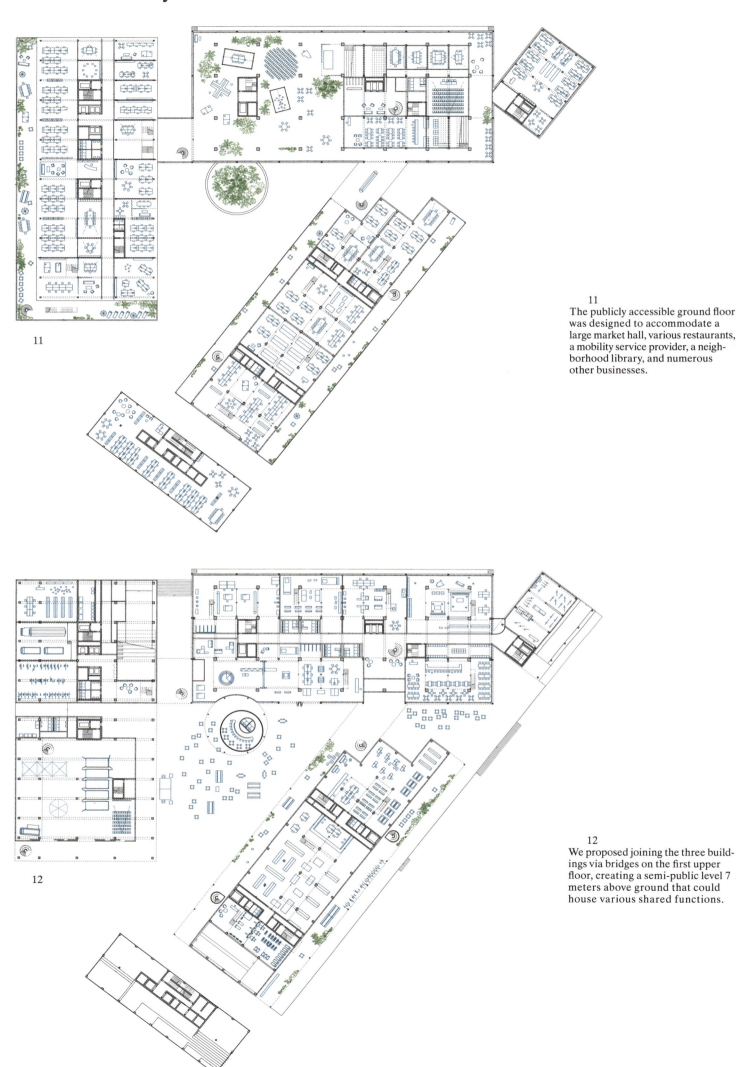

11
The publicly accessible ground floor was designed to accommodate a large market hall, various restaurants, a mobility service provider, a neighborhood library, and numerous other businesses.

12
We proposed joining the three buildings via bridges on the first upper floor, creating a semi-public level 7 meters above ground that could house various shared functions.

Hammerbrooklyn

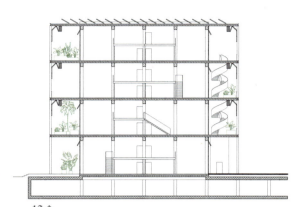

13 ↑

15 ↑   ↓ 16

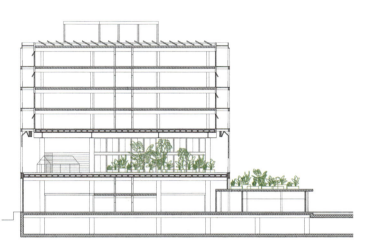

↓ 14

13 + 15
We planned the Gallery Building as a vertical stack of double-height open spaces with full-height "climate gardens" on each side. Depending on the season, the latter can serve as open or closed extensions to the interiors and be used as milling areas or workspaces. The high-ceilinged main spaces allow for partition and the insertion of internal galleries, enabling bespoke loft-like premises to be created for small or large firms.

17 ↑   ↓ 18

14 + 16
Together, the Gallery Building and Kontor Building were designed to form Hammerbrooklyn's urban perimeter. The first upper floor was envisioned as a multi-use area featuring a café, a small conference center, and open spaces for all kinds of events, with conventional offices spread across the remaining upper levels.

17 + 18
Featuring a terraced façade, the Stairway Building was conceived as a vertical extension of the public realm, with publicly accessible external stairs leading to a top-floor restaurant. In addition, an internal cascading staircase was planned as an intermediate space between offices and public areas. The ground floor was devised as a market hall accommodating a wide range of usages.

19–21 →
The Hammerbrooklyn project brings together various muscular, robust typologies. Each building works on its own but also converses with its neighbors, adding up to a place that's more than the sum of its parts.

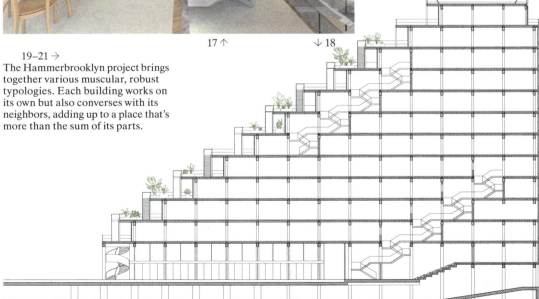

Hammerbrooklyn

460

2019–...

19 ↑

↓ 20

The Beauty of Chaos

Mathias Müller
Daniel Niggli

"I hope to have the opportunity to hear how you in Switzerland, a country that has constructed cities that are beautiful in a more widely accepted sense, view this theory of Tokyo."[A] This was how Kazuo Shinohara concluded a brief correspondence with Jacques Herzog and Pierre de Meuron in 1998, a correspondence in which he outlined his hypothesis that "the contemporary city can only express the beauty of chaos." We don't know whether he ever got a response, so perhaps this text can be seen as an effort to provide one.

Shinohara is generally viewed as a designer of masterly one-off buildings. What's less widely known is that, from the outset, his approach was founded on two key cornerstones: the rigorous examination of the individual building's architectural potential on the one hand and the reality of the modern Japanese city on the other. The three tenets Shinohara postulated in 1961 in an article in the magazine *Shinkenchiku* underline the dual approach:

1. "The space of a house must be as large as possible."[B]
2. "A house is a work of art."[C]
3. "The expression of modern townscape must be found in the beauty of chaos, and not necessarily in that of harmony."[D]

Shinohara articulated these principles at a time when Japan found itself at a cultural turning point. Defeat in World War Two had left it almost completely destroyed but, in the 1960s, the country's economy began to boom as it embraced Western consumer culture and faith in technology. Largely devastated by bombing, Tokyo offered young avant-garde architects a clean slate on which to realize their modern vision.

Shinohara had doubts as to whether cities could really be planned. In the mid-1960s, he gradually came to the conclusion that neither Japanese tradition nor modern Western theories allowed for a proper understanding of the city of economic and technological progress. He expressed his reservations with reference to a term that had no place in the new technocratic planning culture: beauty. "There is a certain beauty in districts never intended for (aesthetic) appreciation, while beauty does not exist in modern communities in which individual houses were designed to be beautiful."[E]

On his travels around the then rapidly growing Tokyo, Shinohara discovered a new form of city that was developing based on the old pattern of small-scale lots. He was fascinated by the chaotic and seemingly irrational growth of an artless city of huddled together houses that seemed to have nothing to do with each other yet formed an urban landscape which, in his eyes, was more dynamic and vibrant than his contemporaries' grand Metabolist projects. At the time, chaos and irrationality were seen in negative terms but, for Shinohara, who initially studied mathematics, they were simply phenomena to be explored. With his mathematically trained mind, he viewed the city as an abstract system determined by an infinite number of functions and function spaces.[F] Finding one coherent solution for such a hypercomplex system was, he reasoned, simply not possible.

Growing complexity accompanied by a loss of political control would ultimately lead to cities that manifested disorder rather than order.[G] For Shinohara, chaos therefore represented a productive basic condition and acted as a necessary catalyst for the creation of vibrant and viable cities—a phenomenon he described as "progressive anarchy."[H]

Unsurprisingly, Shinohara prophesied that European cities, too, would eventually have to experience this state of chaos. Written during a two-month stay in Vienna, his essay "Wien und Tokio" compares these two different urban models, adding the concept of "open and closed systems" to his hypothesis.[I] Having abandoned uniformity, Tokyo has become an open city, he writes, whereas Vienna represents a closed system. Openness, however, is essential if large cities are to remain vibrant and viable over the long term. Such a dispassionate view of reality produces a different conception of beauty, one that sees beauty in vitality, contrasts, and disunity, or even in the absence of reminders of the past. Diametrically opposed to the conventional European perspective, this attitude ultimately results in a potentially explosive juxtaposition: freedom versus control.

Shinohara also used the word "savagery" to characterize Japanese cities, and the martial undertone of that term quite accurately reflects the battle between unruly forces playing out across our cities. In this "savage" context, form-finding can take contradictory directions, control can be elusive, and randomness can serve as a design tool. In projects such as Shinohara's House in Uehara and House under High-Voltage Lines, not only are internal and external contradictions allowed, they are key drivers of the architecture. It is somewhat paradoxical that these theories and reflections on the city come from an architect whose built oeuvre consists largely of single-family homes, but then, for Shinohara, such homes, the smallest units of urban development, are a microcosm of the wider tension between individual and society.

Tradition is the Starting Point, Not the Destination

Around that time in Europe, Aldo Rossi offered a similarly radical dissection of urban architecture. Rossi's exploration of the history of European cities and their lines of fracture, however, led him to draw conclusions that were diametrically opposite to Shinohara's. For Rossi, the city was a collective project and thus the sum of its rational and irrational imperatives, a built piece of architecture. His belief in the indivisibility of the city represented a fundamental critique of the functionalism of modern urban development. With his morphological approach, he reconnected theory with history, employing the notion of "type" as a key conceptual instrument for bringing analysis and design practice together. Types, after all, are the repository of the collective memories that preceded the creation of the form. On the other hand, as Ulrich Schwarz notes, when this utopia of form with its amalgam of history, diffuse memories, longings, and ideology encounters the unloved reality of actual urban development, it instinctively reacts with a "way things have always been" attitude.[J] And that brings us back to where we began, to what Shinohara inquired of Jacques Herzog and Pierre de Meuron. For their part, Herzog and de Meuron, who had studied under Aldo Rossi at the Swiss Federal Institute of Technology, soon recognized the limitations of applying their Italian tutor's theoretical construct to

---

A
Kazuo Shinohara, "The Mechanism of Fiction Never Stops Functioning," in: *SD (Supesu desain)* 2/1998, p. 115.

B
Shin-Ichi Okuyama, "Worlds and Spaces: How Kazuo Shinohara's Thought Spans between Residential and Urban Theory," in: *2G* 58/59, 2011, p. 36. He quotes Shinohara as follows: "Seikatsu kukan no atarashi shiten o motomete" ("Seeking new viewpoints about living space"), *Shinkenchiku* 36, 1/1961, p. 105.

C
Kazuo Shinohara, "Jutaku wa geijutsu de aru" ("A house is a work of art"), in: *Shinkenchiku* 37, 1/1962, p. 77.

D
Kazuo Shinohara, *Jutaku Kenchiku (Residential Architecture)*, Tokyo, 1964, p. 103.

E
Ibid., p. 102.

F
Kazuo Shinohara, "Toward a Super-Big Numbers Set City and a Small House Beyond" (2000), in: *2G* 58/59, 2011, p. 280.

G
Ibid., p. 284.

H
Kazuo Shinohara, "Auf dem Weg zur Architektur," in: *Baumeister* 11/1984, p. 49.

I
Kazuo Shinohara, "Wien und Tokio," in: Institut für Wohnbau, and Tadao Andō (ed.), *Bewohnbare Architektur*, Vienna, 1990, p. 92.

J
Ulrich Schwarz, "Dieses ist lange her," in: *Archithese* 3/2014, pp. 34–39.

The Beauty of Chaos

1

specific local circumstances and thus used a significantly broader lens for their own urban explorations.[K] Where for Rossi architecture was ultimately an embodiment of memory that aimed to achieve historical continuity, Shinohara gradually turned away from traditional architecture and cities and their cultural associations, moving from a historically defined approach, in which architecture is practically a universal distillation of timeless substance, to one that is thematically defined. At Tokyo's Shibuya Station, for instance, he saw the absence of reminders of the past as an explicit quality. Born simply out of local mobility and trade requirements, it's a place that stands alone as a radically new kind of architecture and urban realm. Let us, then, briefly set aside the clichéd images of what Shinohara describes in his letter to Herzog and de Meuron as our "beautiful cities in a more widely accepted sense" and take a dispassionate but empathetic look at the reality of contemporary European cities. At their peripheries and in their agglomerations, Shinohara's unruly forces have long since been at work, despite a dense web of regulations and planners' attempts to impose order. Eight years before Shinohara's correspondence with Herzog and de Meuron, architectural journal *Archithese* published an issue entitled "Neue Ansichten – Dirty Realism" that contained an essay by Fritz Neumeyer with the eloquent title "Realität als Disziplin,"[L] in which the author described how the unstoppable march of industrialization and the associated reorientation of architecture had transformed our cities (this, ironically, just a few years before he became a theoretical apologist for the traditional European city). As a reaction not least to Rossi-influenced historicism, he urged that contemporary urban architecture should be viewed not merely in terms of the historical imperative but as a tool for perceiving and constructing contemporary reality.

In that context, it's worth asking whether Rossi's concept of "type," which chiefly derives its legitimacy from history (not that it needs to), has any relevance as a practical concept for today's reality. Marcel Meili, for instance, regarded type more as an epistemological than an architectural tool—i.e. one that can help us assess the invisible qualities of broader cultural processes. Crucially, this involves seeing architecture not just as "evidence of the historicality of a city that is not our own," but as a medium for shaping the whole.[M] Viewing architecture as a perceptual lens or transformative tool can certainly help us better understand Shinohara's work. From the various phenomenologically influenced "crevice spaces"[N] of his second style to the later House in Uehara, that work seems to lead inevitably to his Centennial Hall at Tokyo Institute of Technology. Indeed, it's here that the final leap from perception machine to urban machine takes place: the Centennial Hall is both technoid and mysterious, heroic and industrial, eloquent and silent; it is intangible yet present—a true Tokyo icon. By freeing himself from Japanese tradition and embracing the idea of architecture as artistically autonomous and rooted in contemporary urban reality, Shinohara also shifted from an "interpretative art"[O] approach to one that sees architecture as a medium. With nostalgically tinged visions finding favor once more, such a resolutely contemporary attitude could provide a particularly timely blueprint for addressing complex urban realities without harking back to the past. Then, rather than idealizing what was perhaps there before, we could take what's there now and use it as material for our own "ModernNext,"[P] for a city of tolerant coexistence, of programmatic, typological, and architectural freedom—the European city of the future.

K
Philip Ursprung, "Genealogie – Aldo Rossi und Herzog & de Meuron," in: *Tec21* 25/2011, p. 31. See also: Marcel Meili, "Ein paar Bauten, viele Pläne," in: *Werk, Bauen + Wohnen* 12/1989, pp. 26–31.

L
Fritz Neumeyer, "Realität als Disziplin. Grossstadtarchitektur und urbane Identität," in: *Archithese* 1/1990, pp. 22–27.

M
Marcel Meili, "Probleme unserer Entwurfsarbeit," Harvard Lecture, July 2002.

N
Kazuo Shinohara, description of The Uncompleted House, in: Kazuo Shinohara, *Kazuo Shinohara*, Berlin, 1994, p. 32.

O
Fritz Neumeyer, "Realität als Disziplin. Grossstadtarchitektur und urbane Identität," in: *Archithese* 1/1990, pp. 22–27.

P
Seng Kuan (ed.), *Kazuo Shinohara: Traversing the House and the City*, Zurich/Cambridge, Massachusetts, 2022. Excerpt available online at: https://www.gsd.harvard.edu/2021/05/excerpt-from-kazuo-shinohara-traversing-the-house-and-the-city-by-seng-kuan/

1
Like an airship rising above the urban bustle, the hemisphere atop Shinohara's Centennial Hall (1987) is an iconic feature of Tokyo's Institute of Technology. The building as a whole is an "urban machine," a concrete yet intangible expression of the city's chaotic fabric. Photo: Tomio Ohashi.

Oerlikon Sports Center

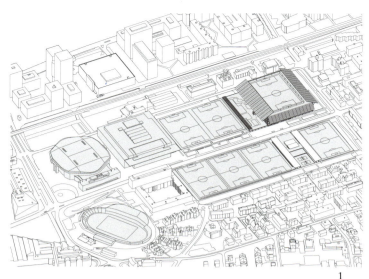

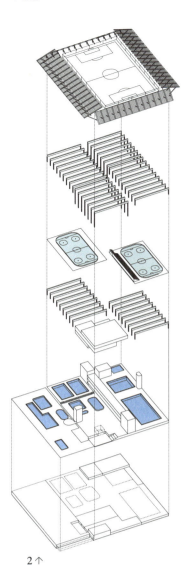

1
In 2020, the city of Zurich launched a competition to build a new sports center in Oerlikon. The intention was for the scheme to bring together the facilities of a district swimming center (various indoor pools, outdoor pool, sauna, massage and gym facilities, restaurant, center management) with those of a local ice rink (two indoor ice rinks plus locker rooms), while also incorporating a maintenance yard and seven playing fields. With its exceptional size and unique makeup, it's a project of citywide significance and one that will add a new focal point to the urban realm, combining with the indoor arena and the exhibition center to form an array of large-scale public amenities that deliberately stand apart from the grain of the surrounding residential areas.

2
The scale of the scheme and the limited available space led us to vertically stack the different functions, with the ground floor combining entrance area, technical services, parking, and maintenance yard, the floor above housing the indoor and outdoor pools, the next level, a further 7 meters up, containing the ice arena, a second ice rink, plus gymnastics and workout areas, and the rooftop featuring an all-weather pitch. Basement spaces, on the other hand, were kept to a minimum in order to maximize sustainability.

Oerlikon Sports Center

466

2020–2021

Oerlikon Sports Center

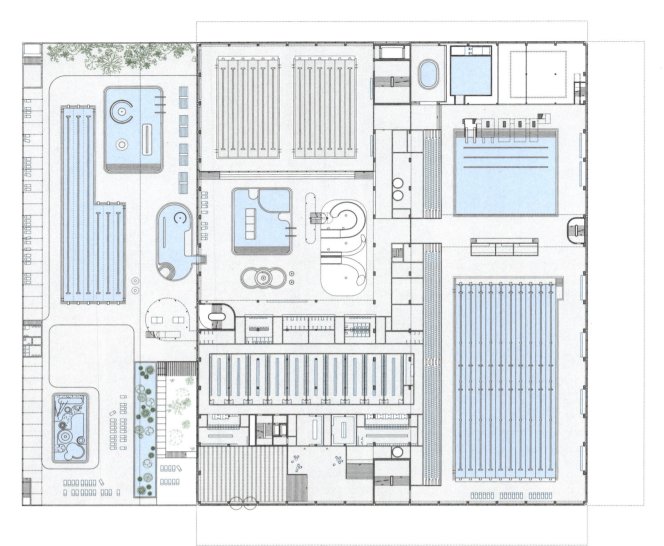

5 ↑   ↓ 6

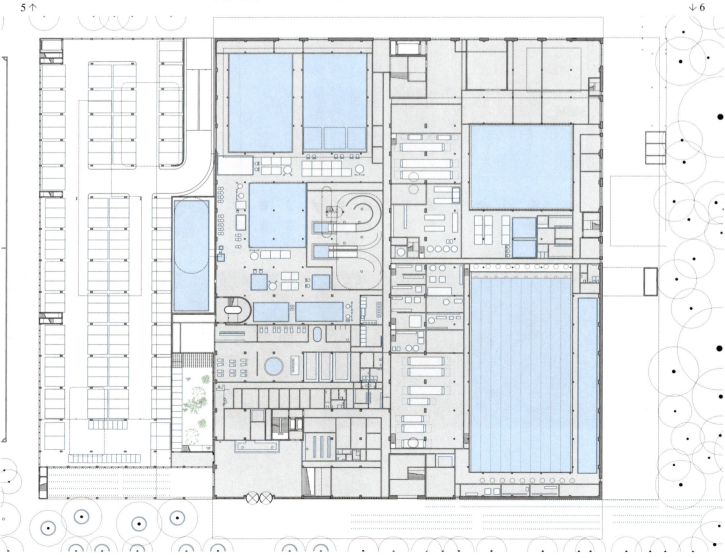

Oerlikon Sports Center

← 3
Swimming pools and ice arenas are not generally bywords for sustainability, but we actively embraced this challenge. The vertical stacking of sports facilities involving large spans, high loads, and dynamic usage meant an all-timber load-bearing support structure was not practicable due to the structural dimensions required. It did, on the other hand, make sense to try to generate as much energy as possible on site—so we devised a bespoke solar array.

← 4
As the rooftop was earmarked for a pitch, we developed large solar sails that would generate energy, provide shade, and create covered transitional areas and milling spaces around the building. They were also a way of breaking up the vast bulk, adding spatiality to the boxy volume, and creating a more intimate scale. Visually, these four sails come together to form a huge roof-like addition, the structural logic of which calls to mind traditional wooden roofs. At the same time, their unique visual language served to give the design an identity all its own.

5
Plan of first upper floor.

6
Plan of ground floor.

7
Plan of second upper floor.

Oerlikon Sports Center

8
Plan of fourth upper floor.

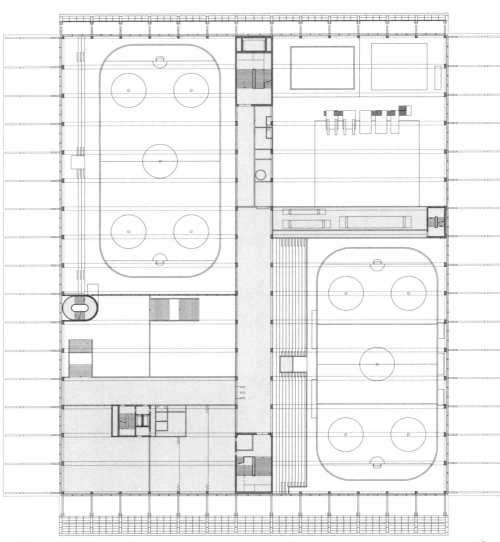

9
Plan of third upper floor.

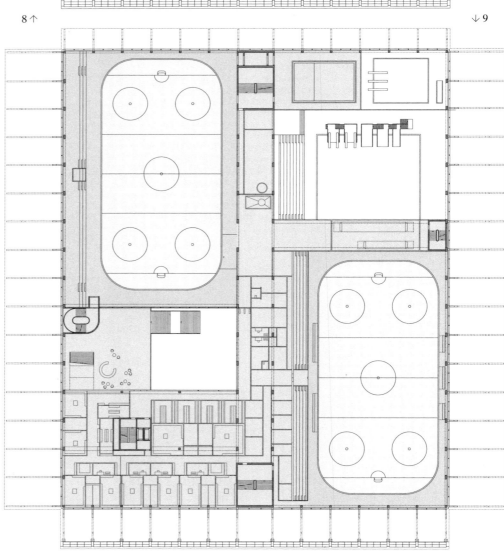

Oerlikon Sports Center

10
Rooftop from above.

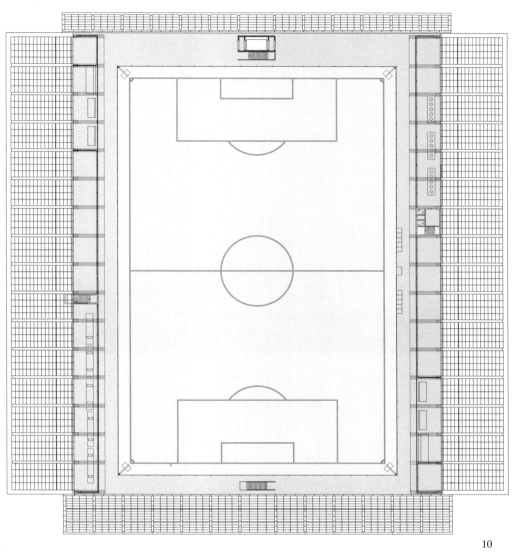

11 →
We chose cast-in-place concrete for the plinth and reinforcing cores.

12 →
For the concrete load-bearing structure, we devised a system of prestressed wide-span binders resting on prefabricated pillars, with a ribbed ceiling-style secondary support structure between the main binders.

13 →
Wherever possible, we planned to use composite wood-and-concrete ceilings, thereby significantly reducing both the ceilings' overall weight and their embedded energy consumption. Where particularly high vibration resistance was required, we switched to conventional prestressed concrete ribbed ceilings. The façade and the solar sails, meanwhile, were conceived as all-timber structures covering an area of some 4,000 square meters.

14 →
In conjunction with the topography of the pools and upright cores, the plinth offered a muscular aesthetic of its own.

Oerlikon Sports Center

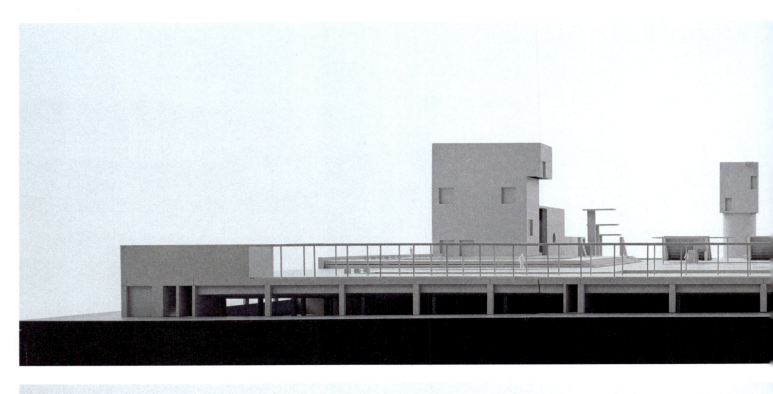

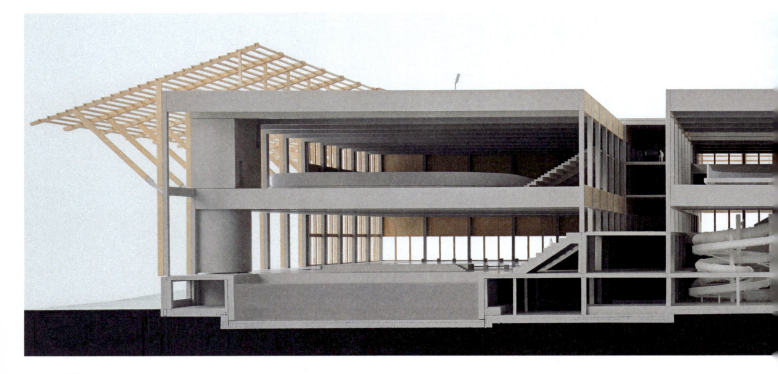

Oerlikon Sports Center

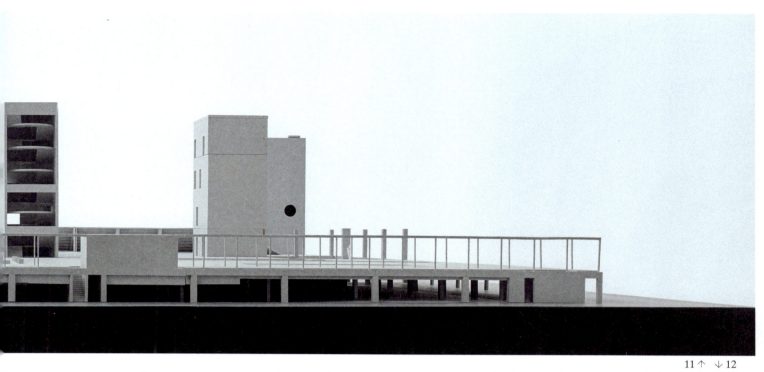

Oerlikon Sports Center

Plea for a City of Tolerant Coexistence

Mathias Müller
Daniel Niggli

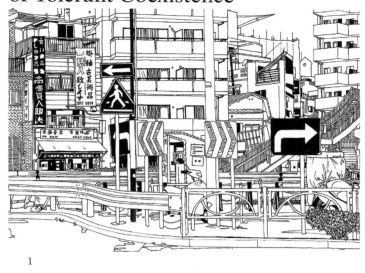

1

"We need to relinquish the idea of a homogeneous city in which every relationship is determined by some coherent overall system. The notion of foreground and background only makes sense in conjunction with an overarching dialectic structure."[A]

Architects regularly complain that we find ourselves in an age of randomness and formal excess, an issue recently addressed by Philipp Esch in his intelligent essay on the critical relationship between foreground and background. Obviously, in a Swiss context, you could counter that these are very much first world problems; nonetheless, there is a perception that the quality of our built environment has declined, something that is, in our view, attributable to the enormous spatial and socioeconomic upheavals of recent decades. While the forces thus unleashed have also affected the fabric of the urban core, the real transformation has taken place at the periphery, in the agglomerations of ill-defined suburban areas.

That the technocratic concepts of modern spatial planning seem incapable of counteracting these trends and shaping identity is a familiar complaint, one that has been a key aspect of critical postmodern discourse since the 1960s. Instead of offering up alternatives, however, such criticism has often gone hand in hand with a nostalgia for the certainties and aesthetics of the traditional city.

And yet this spatial transformation of our environment has not happened for no reason or in arbitrary fashion, even if the built reality may suggest as much. On the contrary, it is the consequence of a very precise conjunction of political, economic, and urban-planning mechanisms[B] whose attempts to impose order via tortuously negotiated processes tend paradoxically to result in disorder instead. Seen in this light, today's urban development is an unflinchingly honest representation of the real-world forces at work in our democratically legitimated pluralist society. The affliction from which our cities are suffering is not therefore the boundless ego of our designers, but our tendency —in Switzerland at least—to cater to narrow interests at the expense of effective spatial and urban planning.

In his "Letter from Zurich" from 1988, Marcel Meili highlighted a dilemma that Swiss architects have been wrangling with ever since: in a society that is fragmenting into more and more subcultures and different audiences, architecture inevitably finds it difficult to pursue an overarching narrative.[C] And just as they are unable to agree on shared values, architects also no longer agree on what the city is and should be.

While architecture and urban planning thus remain paralyzed, the world around us is becoming more fluid. Our urban cores may have

[A] Philipp Esch, "Lob des Hintergrundes. Vom Missverständnis, die Architektur gewinne an Bedeutung, je mehr Aufmerksamkeit sie beansprucht," in: *Werk, Bauen + Wohnen* 6/2020, pp. 38–40. The response printed here was first published (in German) in: *Werk, Bauen + Wohnen* 11/2020, p. 41.

[B] Marc Angélil et al., "1 m²/sek. 08/15," in: Marc Angélil, Michael Hirschbichler (eds.), *Abecedarium zur Peripherie*, Berlin, 2013, pp. 39–61.

[C] Marcel Meili, "A letter from Zurich," in: *Quaderns* 177/1988, available in German at: https://www.meilipeterpartner.ch/media/medialibrary/2013/07/1988-Ein_Brief_aus_Zürichmit_Cover-MM.pdf (last accessed May 6, 2022).

1
Everyday visual chaos in which the mundane and the high-value, the permanent and the transient have equal weight, Ingo Giezendanner/ GRRRR: Showa-dori 4, Tokyo, May 2016

become ossified museum pieces but, all around them, opposing forces have collided to create new kinds and forms of spaces. In this context, Meili sees traditional urban analysis as being shaped less by scientific fact than by yearning.[D] He concluded that those then studying under Aldo Rossi in Zurich must have understood little if they no longer viewed architecture as a medium, but rather as evidence of the historicality of a city that was not their own.

But the dynamic of economic development isn't interested in sentimentality. The impact of forces such as globalization, tertiarization, societal individualization, and the commercialization of everyday life on our surroundings is far greater than that of any architectural "ism." While architecture struggles to come to terms with these forces, real life goes on—and often at places that seem to have nothing to do with architecture.

"Culture is the death of something." In his essay "Hot Places, Cold Places," historian Karl Schlögel used this apodictic statement to describe the physical and atmospheric transformation of a non-place into a place.[E] In Schlögel's eyes, "hot" or "fluid" non-places are those characterized by their usage, be they the public transport hubs that daily waves of commuters transform into teeming anthills, or a gravel lot that only comes to life as an occasional venue for markets or fairs.

Such places, says Schlögel, know no time but the present; here, the city is reinvented from scratch every day. Once rigidification sets in, they enter a "cold" phase. At best, they might still be able to draw on that original energy; at worst, they end up as museums in which an impression of vitality has to be created.[F]

Schlögel's observations allow us to redefine the characteristics of our urban background, to consider it not through the lens of psychological perception but in performative terms. Background can thus be defined as an open container (deliberately constructed or otherwise) in which things might happen.

Seen in this light, such "hot" places could be viewed as the ultimate background spaces. "Cold" places, on the other hand, can be said to assume the characteristics of foreground spaces. Their purpose is to offer outward representation, to generate meaning, and to make the past tangible via permanent forms.

Cities are characterized by simultaneity, with contradictory and sometimes incompatible elements existing side by side and on top of each other. They never consist merely of one level, layer, or idea. These unspectacular realities are echoed in the drawings of Zurich-based artist Ingo Giezendanner, better known by his pseudonym GRRRR. Thanks to his particular illustration style (black pencil lines of uniform thickness), foreground and background merge to create a single level. Built or ephemeral, ordinary or prized: every component of the urban realm is lent equal weight. Hierarchies thus dissolve, everything counts equally, and we see the city as it is used.

[D] Marcel Meili, "Probleme unserer Entwurfsarbeit," Harvard Lecture, July 2002, available in German at: https://www.meilipeterpartner.ch/media/medialibrary/2013/07/2002-Harvard_Lecture-MM.pdf (last accessed May 6, 2022).

[E] Karl Schlögel, "Hot Places, Cold Places," in: idem, *In Space We Read Time*, Bard Graduate Center, 2016, pp. 242–52.

[F] Ibid., p. 298.

Japanese architect Kazuo Shinohara based his "synchronic city" theory on similar observations, specifically on a comparison of European and Japanese cities and their different urban models and historical layers. Later, he declared that only by embracing the beauty of chaos could contemporary cities remain vibrant, adaptable, and resilient.[G]

The chaos of the city was also appreciated by Viennese architect Hermann Czech, whose statement "Architecture is background. Everything else is not architecture" is referenced by Esch. For Czech, chaos was a metaphor for urban forms not encompassed by conventional notions of the traditional city. Instead of relying on clear dualities such as transportation versus settlement, he thinks in terms such as emptiness, nothingness, intermediate space, or otherness. Interestingly, Czech also thought cities old and new should cherish the utopian potential of chaos in order to remain open to further development.[H]

Like Czech and Shinohara, we believe that an intellectual shift is required, that moving away from traditional ways of thinking towards an artistically autonomous, conceptual view of architecture rooted in the reality of synchronic cities would allow us to creatively address today's urban landscapes.

The challenge, however, is twofold: while some urban areas will inevitably have to deal with issues of rigidification, others are likely to experience a controlled form of fluidification. As a result, we will need strategies that can cope with dissonances, breaches, and permanent transformations. We need to relinquish the idea of a homogeneous city in which every relationship is determined by some coherent overall system. The notion of foreground and background only makes sense in conjunction with an overarching dialectic structure, such as "transportation vs settlement."[I] Where no such structure exists—i.e. almost anywhere outside urban cores—the distinction between foreground and background breaks down and individual objects with their respective strengths and weaknesses take center stage.

In dissonant urban landscapes where there is no overarching system, the framework conditions for new projects have to be redefined each time, based on the specific forces in play at that particular site. As long as that remains the case, the much-maligned "negotiated urbanism" approach will still be with us. Here, architectural considerations, which generally carry less weight than political, financial, or legal factors, have to be either pushed very aggressively or slipped in very surreptitiously. In order to tease out the hidden qualities of each place, we need creative ideas that result not in imported, standardized solutions but in bespoke, site-specific concepts. In contrast to spatial planning decisions, such isolated interventions may only have a local impact, but they can at least inject a targeted dose of urbanism or provide identity-building focal points.

Two examples of where that has happened are Schneider Studer Primas's redevelopment of the Zwicky campus in Dübendorf and Peter Märkli's master plan for the Zhwatt quarter in Regensdorf. Taking the existing fabric as their starting point, both represent innovative

---

G
Mathias Müller, Daniel Niggli, "Schönheit des Chaos. Plädoyer für eine Stadt des toleranten Nebeneinanders," in: *Werk, Bauen + Wohnen*, 12/2015, pp. 38–41.

H
Hermann Czech, "Elemente der Stadtvorstellung," in: idem, *Zur Abwechslung*, Vienna, 1996, p. 136 (first published 1977).

I
Ibid., p. 132.

transformations, providing novel forms of housing and workspaces. Of course, such projects can only come to pass with the aid of clients whose sense of cultural responsibility goes beyond the mere creation of Excel spreadsheets. If these "in-between" urban islands are to be successfully connected up, moreover, much needs to be done to bolster the unbuilt realm, be it public open spaces, transport routes and connecting spaces, or even urban agriculture spaces.

Urban cores, too, are facing a whole new set of problems, with internal densification inflaming debates around gentrification and heritage conservation. Here, important background qualities are coming under severe pressure, with recesses, voids, and wastelands as well as built and unbuilt "fluid" spaces all acutely at risk. These are critical to the socially, culturally, and financially "weak" usages that, as a key part of lively, mixed, and innovative urban living, enable the city to be "reinvented from scratch every day."

In recent decades, Zurich has placed great emphasis on building housing, but this development has not come via the densification or optimization of the hybrid city; instead it has, both in architectural and urban design terms, been more in the form of new-build housing projects. For all the quality of their designs, it is notable that the focus on increasingly complex and sophisticated floor plan typologies has paradoxically also cemented their monofunctional, residential use. Once set in stone, this functional circumscription of what could otherwise be mixed neighborhoods will likely prove difficult to reverse.

In both old and new urban areas, the increased fragility of the contextual framework means architectural creation is set to play a more central role once again. Marcel Meili described that creative process as the bringing together of perception, analysis, and design in order to give form to hidden structural attributes.[J] For Berlin-based architect Konrad Wohlhage, every architectural object is a location- and meaning-specific distillation of urban life, one that, by itself becoming a piece of the urban fabric, in turn enhances the city around it. Each built object is an architectural reflection of the city, which is thus continually generating reflections of itself.[K] If we take this reciprocity between city and building as read, then issues of foreground and background become relative. At the same time, all urban stakeholders—from investors to residents to local authorities—share responsibility for codeveloping the city. Perhaps, then, it's not always such a bad idea for architecture to simply "stand there keeping quiet." On the other hand, it could also do much more: making an active, intelligent contribution to the debate would be a good place to start.

[J]
"If, rather than putting the object first, a project is able to prioritize the intention to give form to unseen structural attributes, then perception, analysis, and design can start to coalesce.", Marcel Meili, *Challenges of Our Design Process,* unpublished lecture manuscript, Harvard, July 2002.

[K]
Konrad Wohlhage, "Das Objekt und die Stadt," in: *Arch+* 105/106, 1990, pp. 51–57.

Emptied Typologies: Frameworks for Something Else to Happen

Having been given the last word, so to speak, allow me to begin these "concluding" remarks by questioning a proposition made at the very beginning of this book, summed up in the seemingly provocative statement "*degré zéro* versus context," which—even when taken with a grain of salt, *cum grano salis*—seems to miss the point entirely. It is less the bias in favor of "context" and the one expressed against "*degré zéro*" that causes irritation, and more the carefully placed term "versus" between what we're given to believe are binary opposites. They are not—on the contrary!

Looking at the work of EM2N, one could make the case that one term engenders the other, in a mutual interplay by which the work's contextuality as cultural artifact is very much produced by its zero-degree condition, and vice versa. Acknowledging that the term *degré zéro* was introduced in literary criticism (by none other than Roland Barthes, some time ago) to describe a neutral mode of writing, colorless and devoid of particular stylistic references, one might argue that, when applied to architecture, a range of possibilities emerge—tenuous analogies and line-for-line correspondences between fundamentally different art forms (i.e. architecture and literature) notwithstanding.[A]

White Writing

The strategic reduction of architectural means lays open (in its vigilant avoidance of overdetermined signifiers and predetermined meanings) a field of interpretations from which particular "readings" might unfold in the process of deciphering the work. Call it a form of "zero-degree writing" or "white writing" that instigates the construction of meaning by those involved in the act of reading.[B] Or call it an "open work," in which the reader partakes, via negotiations with the text at hand, in the production of said work; one, in other words, begetting acts of appropriation while prompting collective and shared authorship in the process.[C]

White writing is accordingly the response to a thorough understanding of an emblematically contextual condition. Conceding to the notion that the expression "white writing" has been attributed to Jean-Paul Sartre, presumably in response to his reading of Albert Camus's novel *L'Étranger*, one might venture to claim, albeit with a sense of humor, that EM2N is the "Camus" of our time.

Literary references and irony aside, the question arises of how a zero-degree architecture is indeed deployed to become in effect culturally contextual. One of the clues offered by EM2N is their reference to a generic type form—namely, the factory—as key ingredient in the production of cities, as highlighted by their use of the compound expression "Stadtfabrik," or "city-factory," for the title of this book. In its performative potential, the factory constitutes, both as product and process, the site of urban, socio-spatial production. It is in this respect that the factory, without actually naming its specific outputs, comprises a kind of zero-degree, white-writing infrastructure that can be filled with meaning when appropriated by current and future inhabitants. Though undoubtedly designed, the building as factory constitutes a type form almost emptied of particular signifiers, yet open to interpretation. To put it differently, EM2N engages in the design of the "unfinished," while still managing to address the production of buildings and urban ensembles as architecture.

Empty Type

Foregrounding the interaction between physical and social aggregates, between structure and use, between what is "determined" and what is left "undetermined," between "formality" and "informality," the "generic" and the "specific," their buildings are conceived, and thus designed, as scaffoldings anticipating their prospective transformation, as support systems for yet unanticipated uses to unravel. Of interest here, from a theoretical point of view, is the notion of what has been called "emptied typologies"—in this case, an architectural type form derived from factory buildings that can be seized by users in time and as life unfolds.[D]

Their structures offer frameworks for "undesigned" activities, possibly in analogy to the speculative project for the city of Detroit by Michael Meredith and Hilary Sample (founders of MOS Architects in New York), who, having coined the expression "emptied typologies," purposely exploit the inherent flexibility of parking garage structures not only to frame a "low-rise, high-density development—produced through the loose arrangement of empty types, frameworks, and open spaces—to connect existing conditions with the new urban fabric," but most importantly "for something else, imagined by someone else, to happen." Within the physical structure, they further write, "apartments, stores, coworking spaces, museums, greenhouses, chess clubs," and so forth "produce a density of possible relationships."[E]

A
See Roland Barthes, *Writing Degree Zero*, trans. Annette Lavers and Colin Smith, New York: Hill and Wang, 1968.

B
For more on the term "white writing," or "écriture blanche," see Susan Sontag's foreword to the English edition of *Writing Degree Zero* (ibid., pp. xvi and xvii). Sontag ascribes the expression "écriture blanche" to Jean-Paul Sartre, referencing his review of Albert Camus's novel *L'Étranger*, though Sartre himself didn't use this exact term; see also Jean-Paul Sartre, *Explication de L'Étranger*, Situations I, Paris: Librairie Gallimard, 1947.

C
For more on the term "open work," see Umberto Eco, *The Open Work*, trans. Anna Cancogni, Cambridge, Massachusetts: Harvard University Press, 1989.

D
For more on the term "emptied typologies," see Michael Meredith, Hilary Sample (MOS Architects), *A Situation Constructed from Loose and Overlapping Social and Architectural Aggregates*, Baunach: Spurbuchverlag, 2016, p. 95.

E
Ibid., pp. 95–98.

Emptied Typologies

Likewise, the Nantes School of Architecture by Anne Lacaton and Jean-Philippe Vassal is based on similar objectives, with the design adopting the structure of freeway construction as rough armature and emptied type form to create what has been called "a veritable education factory," with plenty of unassigned spaces, each labeled *"espace libre appropriable,"* to be used as students and members of the faculty see fit. "Acknowledging that functions and relationships change over time," architecture cannot, as stated by the architects, be "too prescriptive."[F] Their building is an instrument to be used. Moreover, should the primary function of the building change, they maintain that it could be appropriated for other uses, giving credence to their dictum, "Never demolish, never remove or replace; always add, transform, and re-use!"[G]

Common to these examples, including countless EM2N projects, is the treatment of public space as a continuous infrastructure that infiltrates architecture and thus softens assumptions between what is normally perceived to be inside or outside. From the ground floor level (that is often defined by uninterrupted tarmac), to its extension into a network of circulation spaces (that runs both vertically and horizontally through the building), to collectively shared roof terraces for social gathering (that crown the structure as *toit-jardin*), public spaces complement the frame offered by the load-bearing system—the latter in itself considered an essential armature of the civic realm.

Whether factory, parking garage, or freeway constructions, their deployment via typological transfers to the domain of architecture does not by any means constitute a free pass to unrestricted action, a free-for-all where anything can happen, or, at its worst, promote a *laissez-faire* mentality, which some developers might welcome. Quite the opposite, EM2N's projects are provocative and farsighted inasmuch as they reframe architecture in view of its performative potential, one countering prevalent approaches to professional practice today that are driven by a priori formal expression of the final building as "finished" artifact, if not as commodity per se. In a similar vein, their approach to what might be considered an open work does not relinquish authorship to market forces in play. Absolutely not.

Minor Architecture

As one might expect, the design of open structures requires a mode of intensified authorship, albeit one that is somehow restrained and does not foreground the author as such. What has been called "the death of the author" gives tribute to the art form itself—suppressing the "me" of the Author (with a capital A) "in the interest of writing," be it concerning the production of a text or of architecture.[H]

We encounter here, as exemplified in the work of EM2N and others, a movement toward what could be termed a type of "minor architecture" (without a capital A), which offers a network of robust spaces and structures, punctuated by public facilities, circulation systems, mechanical equipment, and so forth, arranged and constructed to form the building's primary framework, one purposefully designed to engender unanticipated situations—nested, aggregated, multiple, loose, overlapping, entangled, and at times running against the grain of the original armature.[I]

The concept of a minor architecture as practice overturns and accordingly deterritorializes time-honored conceptions of Architecture (with a capital A) as a discipline and pure art form, accepting—by being unfinished and seemingly undecidable—the messiness of daily life and the disorderliness of our actual condition in the world. EM2N's work is revolutionary inasmuch as it aims to define—and thus design—the conditions for radically heterogeneous social and spatial assemblages to emerge. It is to this end that their experiments aspire to identify the potential of an architecture (without a capital A) as a procedure in action, one vitally dedicated to life.

[F]
Catherine Slessor, "Nantes School of Architecture by Lacaton & Vassal, Nantes, France," in: *The Architectural Review,* 6/2009, p. 68.

[G]
Ilka Ruby, Andreas Ruby, Anne Lacaton, Jean-Philippe Vassal, Frédéric Druot, *Plus—Large-Scale Housing Developments: An Exceptional Case*, Barcelona: Editorial Gustavo Gili SL, 2007.

[H]
See Roland Barthes, "Der Tod des Autors," in: Fotis Jannidis et al. (eds.), *Texte zur Theorie der Autorschaft*, Stuttgart: Reclam, 2000, pp. 185–197.

[I]
On the term "minor literature," see Gilles Deleuze, Félix Guattari, *Kafka: Toward a Minor Literature*, trans. Dana Polan, Minneapolis: University of Minnesota Press, 1986.

Authors

Mathias Müller
*1966
Architect (ETH BSA SIA); cofounded EM2N with Daniel Niggli in 1997.

Daniel Niggli
*1970
Architect (ETH BSA SIA); cofounded EM2N with Mathias Müller in 1997.

Medine Altiok
*1974
Architect (AA BDA SIA) with practices in Zurich and Aachen.

Caspar Schärer
*1973
Architect (ETH SIA), writer, and spatial planner; lives and works in Zurich.

Marc Angélil
*1954
Architect (ETH BSA SIA), principal of agps architecture in Zurich and Los Angeles, professor of architecture and design at ETH Zurich from 1997 to 2019.

Max Küng
*1969
Author and journalist; reporter and columnist for the *Tages-Anzeiger* magazine since 1999.

Marcel Meili
1953–2019
Architect and author; cofounded and ran Zurich-based architectural practice Meili, Peter Architekten with Markus Peter.

Peter Swinnen
*1972
Architect with his own Brussels-based practice. Served as architect to the Flemish government from 2010 to 2015.

Current Staff
(As of January 1, 2023)

Alexander Arregui Leszczynska
Tom Bauer
Catarina Bello
Max Blake
Baptiste Blot
Björn Böök
Jelena Bottani
Christof Braun
Dario Bruhin
Jayden Brüllmann
Tomasz Bulczak
Melih Dilsiz
Matteo Donghi
Bernd Druffel
Joey Frei
Jana Galovic
Katja Gockel
Guido Greco
Nadia Haslimeier
Nils Heffungs
Joshua Henn
Kateryna Isakova
Jean-Baptiste Joye
Mathias Kampmann
Damir Karakaš
Judith Kimmeyer
Raphaël Klucker
Olga Konovalova
Henrike Kortemeyer
Jochen Kremer
Emmanuel Laux
Lars Leonard Müller
Verena Lindenmayer
Minka Ludwig
Andrea Malagnino
Bartłomiej Markowski
Kamile Medolago
Sivan Melamed
Silvia Miralles Pérez
Agata Morawczyńska
Coralie Placide
Kseniia Ponomar
Sandra Quirós Navas
Maria Remma
Kerstin Rienecker
Björn Rimner
Jonas Rindlisbacher
Olivia Rudolph
Maria Savastano
Sabine Schirmer
Malte Schoemaker
Jakob Scholl
Gerry Schwyter
Dániel Simoncsics
Susan Singer
Domenico Spagnolo
Anna Stevenson
Marina Stoynova
Kristina Strecker
Marcin Szczodry
Vera Theler-Jeiziner
Thibault Troesch
Caroline Vogel
Henriette von Flocken
Virginia Zaretskie
David Ziegler
Jonathan Zimmermann
Christof Zollinger

Former Staff

A
Christoph Abächerli
Peter Abele
Riccardo Acquistapace
Eirini Afentouli
Onur Akin
Güley Akin
Güley Alagöz
Roman Albertini
Medine Altiok
Emmanuel Álvarez Sánchez
Isabel Ammann
Sebastian Andersson
Andri Andrésson
Jan Francisco Anduaga
Marius Annen
Gisele Antunes Gloor
Vanja Arzner
Jean-Jacques Auf der Maur
Carlos Maria Azpiroz Franch

B
Lutz Pablo Bachmann
Rosario Badessa
John Baker
Teodora Balevska
Laura Ball
Gabriela Barbulescu
Meg Barossi
Enis Basartangil
Bettina Baumberger
Rahel Baumgartner
Diego Bazzotti
Harry Bee
Elsa Beniada
Julia Berger
Stefan Berle
Kārlis Bērziņš
Olga Bialczak
Henrique Bivar
Juliette Blatter
Laura Blaufuss
Lorents-Kristian Blomseth
Thomas Bögel
Daniela Bolli
Corinne Bolliger
Marina Borchert
Szabolcs-László Bordas
Margherita Borroni
Jennifer Bottlang
Amelie Braun
Brigit Brewe
Duarte Brito
Patrick Britt
David Brodbeck
Martin Broder
Mateusz Broniarek
Pia Brückner
Laura Bruder
Kathleen Bruhn
Béatrice Bruneaux
Melanie Buettikofer
Benjamin Bühs
Hannes Bürge
Dorian Bürgy
Dorothee Burkert
Jonathan Burkhard

C
Peter Canisius
Santiago Catanzano
Carolina Catarino Gomes
Alessia Catellani
Carolina Cerchiai
Vanessa Chacón
Laurent Chasson
Kaihong Chen
Pierre Chèvremont
Soufiane Chibani
Mirela-Maria Chrysovergi
Alessandro Citterio
Benoît Clément
Nadine Coetzee
Victoria Collar Ocampo
Chloé Constantini
Justyna Czubaszek

D
Rubén Daluz
Ileana Dan
Nicolas de Courtin
Gino de Giorgi
Robert Dehn
Christian Deis
Vitória de Mendonça
Lucius Delsing
Pascal Deschenaux,
Plamena Dimitrova
Manuela Dinkel
Hoi Ming Du
Yann Dubied
David Duca
Nikolai Dunkel
Jennifer Durand
Liselotte Düsterhus

E
Georgios Eftaxiopoulos
Vera Egli
Stephan Eicher
Gabi Eisenreich
Ramona Elmiger
Markus Emde
Niklas Erlenwein
Marina Esguerra Laudo
Gustavo Espinoza Campos

F
Nina Fedier
Lluís Fernández Vila
Francisco Ferrandiz
Andrea Guido Ferrarini
João Paulo Ferreira Torres
Rodolfo Ferro
Amélie Fibicher
Kai Figge
Jérôme Fischer
Margarida Fonseca
Barbara Frei
Jacob Frei
Jan-Philipp Frenking
Jonas Fritschi
Henrik Frölich
Arnaud Thomas Froment
Christian Furrer

G
Mariantonietta Irene Gadaleta
Christian Gammeter
Marta García de Domingo
María García Orille
Sofia Gaspar
Sarah Gatto
Tanja Gatzen
Marita Gelze de Montiel
Cristina Génova
Salomé Genzoni
Giulia Giardini
Dirk Giessmann
Jesús E. Gijón Carretero
Georgia Gkotsopoulou
Lenka Gmucová
Gregor Goldinger
Isabel Gomes
Jose Gómez Mora
Elói Gonçalves
Sandra Gonon
Erik Gonzalez
Camilla Gormsen
Friso Gouvetor
Antoni Grau Llinàs
Lea Graziani
Miruna Grec
Johannes Greubel
Sarah Greuter
Hannah Griesmann
Rouven Grom
Malte Grünke
Miguel Guimarães
Frank Gysi

H
Mira Hebermann
Elodie Habert
Nadine Hagen
Florian Hägi
Lynn Hamell
Tim Hanke
Dirk Harmdorf
Sarah Haubner
Oke Hauser
Carol Hayman Kan
Matthias Heberle
Fabienne Heinrich
Kevin Helms
Benedikt Hengartner
Guillaume Henry
Frank Herzog
Kevin Hinz
Marc Holle
Julien Honegger
Rahel Horisberger
Fabian Hörmann
Gabriele Hornung
Sven Hummerich

I
Ekaterina Ikonomova
Sven Ilmer
Özgür Irban
Ryoko Iwase
Takumi Iyoda
Laura Izzo

J
Bianca Jacobsen
Benoit Jacques
Peter Jenni
David Jenny
Leonardo Jochim
Frederik Johansson
Philipp Jorisch
Mira Jung
Yann Junod

K
Sabrina Kählert
Sophie Kaiffer
Florian Kaiser
Karolina Kajda
Cornelia Kalmlage
Constantin Kaltenbrunner
Ayça Kapicioğlu
Anne Käppeli
Orkun Kasap
Birgit Kaufmann
Berta Keerl Ferrer
Leon-Pascal Keller
Mia Kepenek
Elke Kirst
Adam Kiryk
Eleni Kitani
Ioannis Kitanis
Nik Klahre
Tim Klauser
Leo Kleine
Fabian Kleiner
Katharina Kleiner
Sebastian Knorr
Roman Koch
Pavel Koláček
Karolina Konecka
Jonathan Konrad
Olivia Kossak
Alioša Kotnjek
Thilo Kroeschell
Morten Krog
Sidsel Kroman
Lucas Krupp
Karolina Krzyżanowska
Robert Kuijper
Sarah Kullak

Former Staff

Roger Küng
Jörn Küsters
Albena Kyuchukova

L
Götz Lachenmann
Bartek Lamperski
Andrea Landell
 de Moura Stähelin
Andreas Lathi
Yorgos Lavantsiotis
Sven Lechner
Sebastian Lenders
Beat Lengen
Joanna Lewańska
Benjamin Li
João Lima Bragança
Konstantin Lohmann
David Lopez
Christina Lucas
Loïc Lugrin
Maria Luisa
 León Palacios
Kinga Łukasińska
Sebastian Lundelius
Anca-Teodora Lungu
Loan Ly

M
Philipp Maaß
Janusz Maczewski
Lisa Mäder
Carlo Magnaguagno
Tina Maier
Ilja Maksimov
Anna Maragkoudaki
Krzysztof Marciszewski
Satu Marjanen
Bartłomiej Markowski
Julia Martignoni
Michael Martin
Alessandro Mattle
Maria Megina
Claudia Meier
Jean-Pierre Meier
Martina Melegari
Raoúl Mera
António Mesquita
Arne Meyer
Natalia Michailidou
Danica Mijonić
Natalia Milerska
Kate Milligan-Mutzke
Benjamin Minder
Francesca Mirone
Daria Mironenko
Marine Miroux
Matteo Missaglia
Alisa Moisei
Stéphanie Morel
Stefano Mori
Simon Mühlebach
Masaaki Murakami

N
Marta Nadal Garcí
Yoshihiro Nagamine
François Nantermod
Noémi Necker
Verena Nelles
Nele Nettelbeck
Anna Nguyen
Benjamin Nordmann
Inês Nunes

O
Ana Olalquiaga
 Cubillo
Ian Omumbwa
Sandra Oppermann
Yurika Orita
Klaudija Oroshi
Fabien Oulvay
Safak Özgen

P
Bojana Papić
Niklas James Parker
Katharina Paulweber
Jeremias Pellaton
Luc Pestalozzi
Francesca Petrarca
Katrin Petzold
Felix Piel
Jakub Grzegorz
 Pieńkowski
Klaus Platzgummer
Johannes Albert
 Pojtinger
Gabriela Popa
Justyna Porowska
Tessa Poth
Paritteepan Premraj
Laura Probst
Julia Przybyszewska
Wojciech Purski

R
Bernhard
 Räder-Grossmann
Bernard Radi
Philipp Reichelt
Yves Reichenbach
Adriano Reis
Sebastian Reumert
Garrett Reynolds
Tony Rhiem
Maude Richner
Sabine Ricken
Florian Rickenbacher
Walter Rigueti
Sina Ringeisen
Miriam Rollwa
Oscar Rosello
Maike Roth
Christoph
 Rothenhöfer
Miguel Ruano Gullón
Patrick Rüegg
Gabriela Rutz

S
Shingo Saito
Sofya Samokhvalova
Vanessa Sanchez
Theodoros Sandros
Indra Santosa
Andrea Sassi
Lukas Schädler
Katie Schakat
Konrad Scheffer
David Schildberger
Ines Schmid
Tanja Schmid
Annette Schmidt
Andreas Schmitz
Frank Schneider
Winfried Schneider
Julia Schöni
Ladina Schöni
Vanessa Schöttes
Martin Schriener
Nicolas Schulz
Kim Schürmann
Cornelia Schwaller
Elena Schwarz
Marcellus Schwarz
Salvatore Maria
 Sebastiano
Berit Seidel
Lorenzo Semeraro
Caroline Senn
Mário Serrano
Asahi Shinoda
Maryia Sidorenko
Daniela Sigg
Sandra Šimić
Christiane Singer
Christopher Sitzler
Simon Sjökvist
Maria Skjerbaek
Anastasia Skorik
Timothy Smith
Sebastian Sokol
Nino Soppelsa
Claudia Soppelsa-Peter
Stanislaw Sosak
Dominic Spalt
Basil Spiess
Lisa Stango
Michaela Štolcová
Nina Störk
Lingkun Su
Xin Su
Wei Sun
Matthias Sutter
Moe Suzuki
Tomoko Suzuki

T
Gustavo Takata
Andrew Tam
Atsushi Tarutani
Sandra ten Dam
Eva-Noemi Thiele
Patricia Tintoré Vilar
Walter Secondo
 Toccaceli
Pauline Toenz
Hugo Torre
Heike Toussaint
Vincent Traber
Carolina Triches
Paul Tschritter
Monica Tusinean
Agata Tyszecka

U
Kana Ueda Thoma
Leena Charlotte
 Unger
Danessa Urquiola

V
Mario Vahos
José Javier
 Vázquez García
Cristina Vega García
Jorrit Verduin
Cristina Vergara
 Lacuey
Michele Versaci
Philipp Vogeley
Jonas von Wartburg

W
Tess Walraven
Weijie Walraven
Carmen Weglorz
Frank Wei-Yang Chen
Balthasar Weiss
Boris Weix
Sascha Welsch
Leonard Wertgen
Adrian Wetherell
Jann Wiegand
Stephanie
 Wiesendanger
Jonas Wolf
Kyung Ho Won
Kenneth Woods

Y
Sizhou Yang

Z
Jan Zachmann
Norbert Zambelli
Andrea Zandalasini
Simon Zemp
Ameng Zhang
Ruiqi Zhang
Anastasia Zharova
Sven Ziegler
Philipp Zindel
Martin Zisterer
Alex Zollinger
Michael Zürcher
Tieme Zwartbol

List of Works

014 QZA
Community Center Aussersihl
 Location
Zurich, Switzerland
 Procedure
Competition, 1st prize
 Client
City of Zurich, as represented by the Municipal Building Department
 Dates
Competition: 1999; planning: 1999–2000 (phase 1) and 2002–2004 (phase 2); construction: 2003–2004
 Size
866 m^2
 Costs
CHF 3 m
 EM2N Team
Partners: Mathias Müller, Daniel Niggli; project heads: Barbara Frei, Christof Zollinger; project team: Luc Pestalozzi, Christoph Rothenhöfer, Cornelia Schwaller, Vincent Traber
 Specialist Contractors/ Technical Planners
Construction management/project delivery: Jaeger Baumanagement GmbH, Zurich; construction consulting/economics: ct Bauberatung + Bauökonomie AG, Zurich; construction engineering: Tragwerk Bauingenieure GmbH, Affoltern a. A.; timber engineering: PIRMIN JUNG Schweiz AG, Rain; building physics/acoustics: Amstein + Walthert, Zurich; HVAC and plumbing design: Amstein+ Walthert, Zurich; electrical design: Amstein + Walthert, Zurich; art: Stefan Altenburger, Zurich

041 LEU
Leutschenbach Schools
 Location
Zurich, Switzerland
 Procedure
Competition, 5th prize
 Client
City of Zurich
 Dates
Competition: 2002
 EM2N Team
Partners: Mathias Müller, Daniel Niggli; project team: Barbara Frei, Luc Pestalozzi, Cornelia Waller
 Specialist Contractors/ Technical Planners
Landscape architects: Kuhn Landschaftsarchitekten GmbH, Zurich (formerly Kuhn + Truninger Landschaftsarchitekten GmbH)

058 VIA
Refurbishment Viaduct Arches
 Location
Zurich, Switzerland
 Procedure
Competition, 1st prize
 Client
Stiftung PWG
 Dates
Competition: 2004; planning: 2005–2009; construction: 2008–2010
 Size
9,008 m^2
 Costs
CHF 35.3 m
 EM2N Team
Partners: Mathias Müller, Daniel Niggli; associates: Marc Holle, Christof Zollinger; project head: Claudia Soppelsa-Peter; project team: Harry Bee, Barbara Frei, Jonas Fritschi, Jose Gómez Mora, Fabienne Heinrich, Peter Jenni, Fredrik Johansson, Jörn Küsters, Claudia Meier, Lene Nettelbeck, Philipp Reichelt, Tanja Schmid, Frank Schneider, Cornelia Schwaller, Marcellus Schwarz, Basil Spiess, Michael Zürcher
 Specialist Contractors/ Technical Planners
Construction management/project delivery: b + p baurealisation AG, Zurich; civil engineering: Schnetzer Puskas Ingenieure AG, Zurich (formerly WGG Schnetzer Puskas Ingenieure AG); landscape architects: Studio Vulkan Landschaftsarchitektur AG, Zurich (formerly Schweingruber Zulauf GmbH); building physics/acoustics: BAKUS Bauphysik & Akustik GmbH, Zurich; HVAC: Consultair AG, Wädenswil; plumbing design: sertis engineering GmbH, Zurich; electrical design: IBG Engineering AG, Winterthur (formerly IBG B. Graf AG Engineering); geology/geotechnics: Gysi Leoni Mader AG, Zurich; vibration engineering: ZC Ziegler Consultants AG, Zurich (formerly Ziegler Consultants); lighting design: Priska Meier Lichtkonzepte, Turgi

064 BHB
Hardbrücke Railway Station Upgrading
 Location
Zurich, Switzerland
 Procedure
Competition, 1st prize
 Client
City of Zurich, as represented by the Civil Engineering Department
 Dates
Competition: 2004; start of construction: 2005 (phase 1); completion: 2007 (phase 2)
 Size
5,650 m^2
 Costs
CHF 3.4 m
 EM2N Team
Partners: Mathias Müller, Daniel Niggli; project heads: Marc Holle, Claudia Meier; project team: Frank Wei-Yang Chen, Jörn Küsters, Marcellus Schwarz, Basil Spiess, Nina Störck, Jonas von Wartburg
 Specialist Contractors/ Technical Planners
Construction management/project delivery: Jaeger Baumanagement GmbH, Zurich; civil engineering: Schnetzer Puskas Ingenieure AG, Zurich (formerly WGG Schnetzer; Puskas Ingenieure AG); HVAC and plumbing design: PGMM Schweiz AG, Worblaufen; electrical design: IBG Engineering AG, Winterthur (formerly IBG B. Graf AG Engineering); lighting technology: vogtpartner, Winterthur

066 HÜR
Aqui Park Hürlimann Site
 Location
Zurich, Switzerland
 Procedure
Commissioned study
 Client
Migros Genossenschaftsbund
 Dates
Study: 2004
 EM2N Team
Partners: Mathias Müller, Daniel Niggli; project team: Jonas Fritschi, Matthias Heberle, Sidsel Kromann, Jörn Küsters, Tina Maier, Claudia Meier, Atsushi Tarutani; model-making: Joey Frei, Jonas Rindlisbacher
 Specialist Contractors/ Technical Planners
Civil engineering: Aerni + Aerni

List of Works

Bauingenieure AG, Zurich; building physics: BAKUS Bauphysik & Akustik GmbH, Zurich; building services: Luginbühl & Partner AG, Zurich

083 ZWL
Zellweger Luwa Site
  Location
Uster, Zurich
  Procedure
Commissioned study, 1st prize
  Client
Firmenpark Uster AG
  Dates
Study: 2005
  Size
117,000 m²
  EM2N Team
Partners: Mathias Müller, Daniel Niggli; associate: Marc Holle; project team: Bettina Baumberger, Rubén Daluz, Gregor Goldinger, Fabienne Heinrich, Fabian Hörmann, Cornelia Kalmlage, Jörn Küsters, Verena Lindenmayer, Maria Megina, Lene Nettelbeck, Philipp Reichelt
  Specialist Contractors/Technical Planners
Construction consulting/economics: Wüest Partner AG, Zurich/Immopoly Holding AG, Zurich; landscape architecture: Studio Vulkan Landschaftsarchitektur AG, Zurich (formerly Schweingruber Zulauf GmbH); traffic planning: Ing. Büro für Verkehrsplanung W. Hüsler AG, Zurich; utilities: Basler & Hofmann AG, Zurich; waterways engineering: Staubli, Kurath & Partner AG, Zurich; environmental impact assessment: SC + P Sieber, Cassina + Partner AG, Zurich

088 TON
Toni Campus
  Location
Zurich, Switzerland
  Procedure
Commissioned study, 1st prize
  Client (general contractor, owner, landlord)
Allreal Toni AG, as represented by Allreal Generalunternehmung AG
  Dates
Study: 2005; planning: 2005–2011; start of construction: 2008; completion: 2014
  Size
125,000 m²
  Costs
CHF 547 m (investment costs)
  EM2N Team
Partners: Mathias Müller, Daniel Niggli; associates: Fabian Hörmann (project head, competition phase), Björn Rimner (implementation phase), Christof Zollinger (implementation phase); project heads: Enis Basartangil, Nils Heffungs, Jochen Kremer; project team: Marius Annen, John Baker, Stefan Berle, Benoît Clément, Rubén Daluz, Melih Dilsiz, David Duca, Vera Egli, Markus Emde, Jerome Fischer, Christian Furrer, Marita Gelze de Montiel, Frank Gysi, Nadine Hagen, Sabrina Kählert, Sophie Kaiffer, Orkun Kasap, Roman Koch, Jörn Küsters, Andrea Landell de Moura Stähelin (sub-project head, specialized spaces), Verena Lindenmayer, Loan Ly, Raúl Mera, Yoshihiro Nagamine, Klaudija Oroshi, Claudia Peter, Paritteepan Premraj, Yves Reichenbach, Gabriela Rutz, Katie Schakat, Ines Schmid, Martin Schriener, Caroline Senn, Christiane Singer, Tomoko Suzuki, Norbert Zambelli; model-making: Jonathan Konrad, Jonas Rindlisbacher
  Specialist Contractors/Technical Planners
Cost and project management: b + p baurealisation AG, Zurich; civil engineering: WaltGalmarini AG, Zurich; landscape architecture: Studio Vulkan Landschaftsarchitektur AG, Zurich; building physics/acoustics: Wichser Akustik + Bauphysik AG, Zurich; façade planning: gkp fassadentechnik ag, Aadorf; BMS planning: ISP und Partner AG, Sursee; HVAC design and heating systems coordination: Portman Planung with Büro 349 GmbH, Zurich; plumbing design and sprinkler planning: GRP Ingenieure AG, Rotkreuz; electrical design: Bürgin & Keller Management & Engineering AG, Adliswil; specialist acoustics: applied acoustics GmbH, Gelterkinden; light design engineers: vogtpartner, Winterthur; fire safety: Gruner AG, Basel; food outlet planning: Creative Gastro Concept & Design AG, Hergiswil; hybrid art installation illuminating main circulation routes: realities:united, studio for art and architecture, Berlin; signage: Bivgrafik GmbH, Zurich (formerly Biv & Hi GmbH, Visuelle Gestaltung c/o Bringolf Irion Vögeli GmbH); quality control and PQM: Conarenco AG, Zurich

106 MON
Alpine Bath Montafon
  Location
Schruns-Tschagguns, Austria
  Procedure
Competition
  Client
Schruns-Tschagguns Tourismus GmbH
  Dates
Competition: 2006
  EM2N Team
Partners: Mathias Müller, Daniel Niggli; project team: Birgit Brewe, Benjamin Bühs, Frank Wei-Yang Chen, Yoshihiro Nagamine, Gerry Schwyter; model-making: Joey Frei, Jonas Rindlisbacher
  Specialist Contractors/Technical Planners
Architecture: weberbrunner architekten ag, Zurich; landscape architecture: Studio Vulkan Landschaftsarchitektur AG, Zurich (formerly Schweingruber Zulauf GmbH)

121 CSP
Cinémathèque suisse
  Location
Penthaz, Switzerland
  Procedure
Competition, 1st prize
  Client
Federal Office for Buildings and Logistics
  Dates
Competition: 2007; planning: 2008–2017; construction 2010–2013 (phase 1); 2013–2015 (phase 2); 2017–2019 (phase 3)
  Size
13,110 m²
  EM2N Team
Partners: Mathias Müller, Daniel Niggli; associates: Marc Holle, Christof Zollinger; project heads: Bettina Baumberger, Jean-Baptiste Joye, Roger Küng; project team (competition phase): Rubén Daluz, Phillippe Jorisch, Yoshihiro Nagamine, Noémi Necker, Miriam Rollwa; project team (implementation phase): Julia Berger, Stefan Berle, Laurent Chassot, Nadine Coetzee, Nicolas de Courten, Pascal Deschenaux, Melih Dilsiz, Yann Dubied, Ramona Elmiger, Amélie Fibicher, Marita Gelze de Montiel, Gregor Goldinger, Sebastian Knorr, Robert Kuijper, Andreas Lahti, Andrea Landell de Moura Stähelin, Minka Ludwig, Raúl Mera, Stéphanie Morel, Klaudija Oroshi, Fabien Oulevay, Jeremias Pellaton, Bernard Radi, Adriano Reis, Tanja Schmid, Daniela Sigg, Eva-Noemi Thiele, Agata Tyszecka, Danessa Urquiola, Jonas von Wartburg, Sven Ziegler, Michael Zürcher
  Specialist Contractors/Technical Planners
Construction management/project delivery: Tekhne SA, Lausanne/a. planir sàrl, Echallens; construction consulting: Brandenberg + Ruosch AG, Bern; civil engineering: Schnetzer Puskas Ingenieure AG, Zurich/Boss & Associés Ingénieurs Conseils SA, Ecublens; landscape architecture: Studio Vulkan Landschaftsarchitektur AG, Zurich; building physics: Kopitsis Bauphysik AG, Wohlen; acoustics: applied acoustics GmbH, Gelterkinden; façade planning: Basler & Hofmann AG, Zurich; HVAC and plumbing design/building services coordination: Gruenberg + Partner AG, Zurich; electrical design: IBG Engineering AG, St. Gallen (formerly IBG B. Graf AG)/Josef Piller SA, Givisiez/Betelec SA, Villars-Sainte-Croix; fire safety: CR Conseils Sàrl, Oron-la-Ville; security: Holliger Consult GmbH, Epsach; geology/geotechnics: De Cérenville Géotechnique SA, Ecublens; traffic planning: IBV Hüsler AG, Zurich; hazardous substance control: hpb consulting AG, Zurich; signage: Jannuzzi Smith Sagl, Lamone; motion design: La Boite Visual Art, Locarno/ L'Immagine Ritrovata, Bologna

126 ROS
Conversion Rosenberg
  Location
Winterthur, Switzerland
  Procedure
Direct commission
  Client
DN2M Projektentwicklung AG
  Dates
Commission: 2008; planning: 2008–2009; construction: 2009–2010
  Size
1,280 m²
  Costs
CHF 6 m
  EM2N Team
Partners: Mathias Müller, Daniel Niggli; associates: Marc Holle, Gerry Schwyter; project head: Fabienne Heinrich; project team: Harry Bee, Jacob Frei, Philippe Jorisch, Sebastian Knorr, Minka Ludwig
  Specialist Contractors/Technical Planners
Construction management/project delivery: Jaeger Baumanagement AG, Zurich; civil engineering: Schnetzer Puskas Ingenieure AG, Zurich (formerly WGG Schnetzer Puskas Ingenieure AG); landscape architecture: Balliana Schubert Landschaftsarchitekten AG, Zurich; building physics/acoustics: BAKUS Bauphysik & Akustik GmbH, Zurich; HVAC design: Consultair AG, Wädenswil; plumbing design: sertis engineering GmbH, Zurich; electrical design: IBG Engineering AG, St. Gallen (formerly IBG B. Graf AG Engineering)

134 ORS
Mongolian School Project
  Location
Ordos, Inner Mongolia, China
  Procedure
Invitation-only competition, 1st prize
  Client
Ordos Mongolian School
  Dates
Competition: 2008; planning: 2008–2010; construction: 2010–2012
  Size
99,000 m²
  Costs
CHF 60 m
  EM2N Team
Partners: Mathias Müller, Daniel Niggli; associate: Fabian Hörmann; project head: Mathias Kampmann; project team: Duarte Brito, David Brodbeck, Francisco Ferrandiz, Lenka Gmucová, Ryoko Iwase, Ioannis Kitanis, Tim Klauser, Andrea Landell de Moura Stähelin, Minka Ludwig
  Specialist Contractors/Technical Planners
Construction management/project delivery: UA Design Architects & Engineers; civil engineering: Schnetzer Puskas Ingenieure AG, Zurich; landscape architecture: Studio Vulkan Landschaftsarchitektur AG, Zurich

147 HER
Extension Herdern Railway Service Facility
  Location
Zurich, Switzerland
  Procedure
Fee quotation with sketch-based selection process
  Client
SBB Immobilien
  Dates
Commission: 2009; planning: 2009–2010; construction: 2012–2013
  Size
13,000 m²
  Costs
CHF 70 m
  EM2N Team
Partners: Mathias Müller, Daniel Niggli; associates: Fabian Hörmann (competition phase), Christof Zollinger (implementation phase); project head: Stefan Berle; project team: Duarte Brito, Mathias Kampmann, Benjamin Nordmann
  Specialist Contractors/Technical Planners
Civil engineering: EBP Schweiz AG, Zurich (formerly Ernst Basler + Partner AG); building physics: mühlebach partner ag, Winterthur; façade planning: H. Wetter AG Hallen Stahl- + Metallbau, Stetten; HVAC design: EBP Schweiz AG, Zurich (formerly Ernst Basler + Partner AG); electrical design: EBP Schweiz AG, Zurich (formerly Ernst Basler + Partner AG)

152 GLT
Glattal Study
  Location
Zurich, Switzerland
  Procedure
Unsolicited proposal
  Dates
2008–2011 (first study phase), 2011–2012 (second study phase)
  Size
40,000,000 m²
  Architektengruppe Krokodil

List of Works

Boltshauser Architekten: Roger Boltshauser; EM2N: Mathias Müller, Daniel Niggli, Fabian Hörmann; Frank Zierau: architect Frank Zierau; pool Architekten: Raphael Frei, Andreas Sonderegger, Mischa Spoerri; Schweingruber Zulauf Landschaftsarchitekten: Lukas Schweingruber
    EM2N Team
Partners: Mathias Müller, Daniel Niggli; associate/project head: Fabian Hörmann; project team: Onur Akin, Laura Blaufuss, Marina Borchert, Duarte Brito, Pascal Deschenaux, Gabi Eisenreich, Natalia Milerska, Winfried Schneider, Heike Toussaint, Caroline Vogel; model-making: Jonas Rindlisbacher
    Specialist Contractors/
    Technical Planners
Traffic planning: ewp AG, Effretikon; landscape architecture: Studio Vulkan Landschaftsarchitektur AG, Zurich (formerly Schweingruber Zulauf GmbH)

165 BLU
School Complex Blumenfeld
    Location
Zurich, Switzerland
    Procedure
Competition, 3rd prize
    Client
City of Zurich
    Dates
Competition: 2010–2011
    Size
14,000 m²
    Costs
CHF 68.7 m
    EM2N Team
Partners: Mathias Müller, Daniel Niggli; associate/project head: Fabian Hörmann; project team: David Brodbeck, Duarte Brito, Sven Ilmer, Mathias Kampmann; model-making: Jonathan Konrad, Jonas Rindlisbacher
    Specialist Contractors/
    Technical Planners
Construction management/project delivery: b + p baurealisation AG, Zurich; construction consulting/economics: b + p baurealisation AG, Zurich; civil engineering: WMM Ingenieure AG, Münchenstein (formerly Walther Mory Maier Bauingenieure AG); landscape architecture: Westpol Landschaftsarchitekten GmbH, Basel; building services: BSP-Energie GmbH, Zurich; electrical design: gutknecht elektroplanung ag, Au, Zurich

175 MEM
Monosuisse Campus Master Plan
    Location
Emmenbrücke, Switzerland
    Procedure
Commissioned study, 1st prize
    Client
Viscosistadt AG (previously Monosuisse AG)
    Dates
Commission: 2011; master plan and development plan: 2012
    Size
150,000 m²
    EM2N Team
Partners: Mathias Müller, Daniel Niggli; associate/project head: Fabian Hörmann; project team: Martin Broder, Kathleen Bruhn, David Jenny, Jean-Baptiste Joye, Mathias Kampmann, Leo Kleine, Natalia Milerska, Fabien Oulevay, Oscar Rosello, Shingo Saito, Konrad Scheffer, Hugo Torre, Monica Tusinean, Jorrit Verduin, Caroline Vogel;
    Specialist Contractors/
    Technical Planners
Building phsyics/acoustics: Kopitsis Bauphysik AG, Wohlen; landscape architecture: Studio Vulkan Landschaftsarchitektur AG (formerly Schweingruber Zulauf GmbH), Zurich; traffic planning: ewp AG, Effretikon; real estate strategy: Immopoly Holding AG, Zurich; spatial planning: Planteam S AG, Lucerne; environmental impact assessment: EBP Schweiz AG, Zurich

178 SED
Headquarters Brunner AG Furniture Solution
    Location
Schönbühl, Switzerland
    Procedure
Direct commission
    Client
Sedorama-Immobilien AG
    Dates
Commission: 2011; planning: 2011–2012; construction: 2012–2013
    Size
1,980 m²
    Costs
CHF 5.2 m
    EM2N Team
Partners: Mathias Müller, Daniel Niggli; associate: Bernd Druffel; project head: Roger Küng; project team: Dorothee Burkert, Lucius Delsing, Sofia Gaspar, Martin Schriener, Tanja Schmid, Balthasar Weiss; model-making: Jonas Rindlisbacher
    Specialist Contractors/
    Technical Planners
Construction management/project delivery: Wenger Architekten AG, Ostermundigen; civil engineering/structural planning: Weber + Brönnimann AG, Bern; landscape architecture: Balliana Schubert Landschaftsarchitekten AG, Zurich; building physics/acoustics: MBJ Bauphysik + Akustik AG, Kirchberg; façade planning: Ediltecnica AG, Schönbühl, Bern; HVAC and plumbing design: Roschi + Partner AG, Bern; electrical design: CSP Meier AG, Bern; lighting concept: Lichtkompetenz AG, Zurich; interior design: Ippolito Fleitz Group GmbH, Stuttgart

183 HEU
Heuried Sports Center
    Location
Zurich, Switzerland
    Procedure
Competition, 1st prize
    Client
City of Zurich
    Dates
Competition: 2011–2012; planning: 2012–2016; construction: 2015–2017
    Size
9,187 m²
    Costs
CHF 77.7 m
    EM2N Team
Partners: Mathias Müller, Daniel Niggli; associates: Bernd Druffel (implementation phase), Fabian Hörmann (competition phase); project head: Jochen Kremer; project team: Andri Andrésson, Laura Blaufuss, Martin Broder, Peter Canisius, Maria Garcia, Miguel Guimarães, Mathias Kampmann, Leo Kleine, Minka Ludwig, Wojciech Mateusz-Purski, Inês Nunes, Gabriela Popa, Shingo Saito, Tanja Schmid, Julia Schöni, Susan Singer, Tomoko Suzuki, Agata Tyszecka, Cristina Vergara Lacuey, Caroline Vogel, Balthasar Weiss; model-making: Gustavo Espinoza Campos, Jonathan Konrad, Jonas Rindlisbacher
    Specialist Contractors/
    Technical Planners
Landscape architecture: Balliana Schubert Landschaftsarchitekten AG, Zurich; construction management: b + p baurealisation AG, Zurich; civil engineering: Schnetzer Puskas Ingenieure AG, Zurich; timber engineering: PIRMIN JUNG Schweiz AG, Rain; façade planning: gkp fassadentechnik ag, Aadorf; HVAC design: Balzer Ingenieure AG, Winterthur; cooling design/ice engineering: BBP Ingenieurbüro AG, Lucerne/Leplan AG, Winterthur; electrical design: Enerpeak AG, Dübendorf; building physics/acoustics: Bakus GmbH, Zurich; signage: Bivgrafik GmbH, Zurich; security design: Sictech GmbH, Bergdietikon; food outlet planning: Axet GmbH, Embrach; aquatic design: Probading, Zumikon/Kannewischer Ingenieurbüro AG, Cham; geology/geotechnics: Gysi Leoni Mader AG, Zurich; tree preservation: Baumbüro, Dipl.-Ing. Antje Lichtenauer, Zurich; art: Wiedemann Mettler, Zurich

187 KIV
Headquarters Roshen Confectionery Corporation
    Location
Kyiv, Ukraine
    Procedure
Direct commission
    Client
Architectural Bureau ZOTOV&CO, Kyiv
    Developer
Private
    Dates
Study: summer 2012; planning: 2012–2014;
    Size
5,100 m²
    EM2N Team
Partners: Mathias Müller, Daniel Niggli; associates: Fabian Hörmann, Gerry Schwyter; project heads: Florian Kaiser, Roger Küng; project team: Dorian Bürgy, Pierre Chèvremont, Lucius Delsing, Jennifer Durand, Jesús E. Gijón Carretero, Isabel Gomes, Benoit Jacques, Mathias Kampmann, Natalia Milerska, Alisa Moisei, Fabien Oulevay, Oscar Rosello, Mário Serrano, Caroline Vogel; model-making: Gustavo Espinoza Campos, Jonas Rindlisbacher
    Specialist Contractors/
    Technical Planners
Construction management/project delivery: Architectural Bureau ZOTOV&CO, Kyiv; civil engineering: WaltGalmarini AG, Zurich; HVAC and plumbing design, electrical design, building physics/acoustics: Kiwi Beratende Ingenieure, Dübendorf

195 HSL
Lucerne School of Art and Design
    Location
Emmenbrücke, Switzerland
    Procedure
"Monosuisse Campus" study, 1st prize
    Client
Viscosistadt AG
    Dates
Study: 2012; planning: 2013–2016; construction: 2014–2016
    Size
13,000 m²
    Costs
CHF 24 m
    EM2N Team
Partners: Mathias Müller, Daniel Niggli; associates: Fabian Hörmann (competition phase), Bernd Druffel, Marc Holle (implementation phase); project heads: Christoph Abächerli, Claudia Soppelsa-Peter; project team: Dorothee Burkert, Niklas Erlewein, Margarida Fonseca, Giulia Giardini, Olivia Kossak, Ana Olalquiaga Cubillo, Gabriela Popa, Tomoko Suzuki; model-making: Jonathan Konrad, Jonas Rindlisbacher
    Specialist Contractors/
    Technical Planners
Construction management: Architektur & Baumanagement AG, Lucerne; construction economics: TGS Bauökonomen AG, Lucerne; civil engineering: Schnetzer Puskas Ingenieure AG, Zurich; landscape architecture: Studio Vulkan Landschaftsarchitektur AG, Zurich; building physics/acoustics: RSP Bauphysik AG, Lucerne; HVAC and plumbing design: Josef Ottiger + Partner AG, Emmenbrücke; electrical design: Jules Häfliger AG, Lucerne; geomatics: Emch + Berger WSB AG, Emmenbrücke; signage: Velvet Creative Office GmbH, Lucerne

197 ZVB
Main Base Zugerland Verkehrsbetriebe
    Location
Zug, Zurich
    Procedure
Competition
    Client
Zugerland Verkehrsbetriebe AG
    Dates
Competition: 2013
    Size
21,000 m²
    EM2N Team
Partners: Mathias Müller, Daniel Niggli; associate: Fabian Hörmann; project head: Mathias Kampmann; project team: Martin Broder, Justyna Czubaszek, Salomé Genzoni, Bernhard Räder-Grossmann, Dominic Spalt, Michele Versaci, Caroline Vogel, Sizhou Yang; model-making: Jonas Rindlisbacher
    Specialist Contractors/
    Technical Planners
Construction management/project delivery: WR Architekten AG, Zurich (formerly webereinhardt Generalplaner AG); construction consulting/construction economics: WR Architekten AG, Zurich (formerly webereinhardt Generalplaner AG); civil engineering: dsp Ingenieure + Planer AG, Zurich; landscape architects: Balliana Schubert Landschaftsarchitekten AG, Zurich; building physics/acoustics: Gartenmann Engineering AG, Lucerne; façade planning: FACHWERK F+K Engineering AG, Muri bei Bern; HVAC and plumbing design: Gruenberg + Partner AG, Zurich; electrical design: HKG Consulting AG, Rotkreuz; fire safety: Gruner AG, Zurich

206 SLE
Haus der Gegenwart, Stapferhaus Lenzburg
    Location
Lenzburg, Switzerland
    Procedure
Competition, 2nd prize

List of Works

Client
Stiftung Stapferhaus Lenzburg
Dates
Competition: 2014–2015
Size
4.600 m²
EM2N Team
Partners: Mathias Müller, Daniel Niggli; associate: Fabian Hörmann; project head: Andri Andrésson; project team: Moe Suzuki, Caroline Vogel, Sizhou Yang; model-making: Gustavo Espinoza Campos, Jonas Rindlisbacher
Specialist Contractors/Technical Planners
Construction management/project delivery: b + p baurealisation AG, Zurich; civil engineering: Walt-Galmarini AG, Zurich; landscape architecture: Balliana Schubert Landschaftsarchitekten AG; HVAC and plumbing design: Abicht Zürich AG, Zurich (formerly Hans Abicht AG)

208 RTS
Campus Radio Télévision Suisse
Location
Lausanne, Switzerland
Procedure
Competition, finalist
Client
RTS Radio Télévision Suisse
Dates
Competition: 2014
Size
18,000 m²
EM2N Team
Partners: Mathias Müller, Daniel Niggli; associate: Fabian Hörmann; project head: Konrad Scheffer; project team: Georgios Eftaxiopoulos, Aljoša Kotnjek, Andrea Landell de Moura Stähelin, Konrad Scheffer, Lingkun Su, Moe Suzuki, Caroline Vogel, Sizhou Yang; model-making: Gustavo Espinoza Campos, Jonas Rindlisbacher
Specialist Contractors/Technical Planners
Construction management/project delivery: Pragma Partenaires SA, Lausanne; civil engineering: WMM Ingenieure AG, Münchenstein; building physics/acoustics: Gartenmann Engineering AG, Zurich; HVAC and plumbing design: Amstein + Walthert AG, Lausanne; fire safety: Gruner AG, Zurich; traffic planning: ewp AG, Effretikon; media concept and lighting design: realities:united, Berlin

210 BAS
New Museum of Natural History Basel and State Archives Basel-City
Location
Basel, Switzerland
Procedure
Competition, 1st prize
Client
Basel-Stadt canton
Dates
Competition: 2014; planning: 2015–2026; construction: 2021–2026
Size
35,500 m²
Costs
CHF 214 m
EM2N Team
Partners: Mathias Müller, Daniel Niggli; associates: Fabian Hörmann, Christof Zollinger; project heads: Kerstin Rienecker, Claudia Soppelsa-Peter; project team (competition phase): Christian Deis, Georgios Eftaxiopoulos, Mathias Kampmann, Aljoša Kotnjek, Andrea Landell de Moura Stähelin, Krzysztof Marciszewski, Kim Schürmann, Lingkun Su, Hugo Torre, Caroline Vogel; project team (implementation phase): Isabel Ammann, Enis Basartangil, Diego Bazzotti, Kārlis Bērziņš, Szabolcs-László Bordas, Dario Bruhin, Béatrice Bruneaux, Tomasz Bulczak, Santiago Catanzano, Plamena Dimitrova, Lluís Fernández Vila, Rodolfo Ferro, Jana Galovic, Marta García de Domingo, Jesús E. Gijón Carretero, Carol Hayman Kann, Anne Käppeli, Berta Keerl Ferrer, Raphaël Klucker, Yorgos Lavantsiotis, Loïc Lugrin, Anca-Teodora Lungu, Krysztof Piotr Marciszewski, Kamile Medolago, Danica Mijonić, Silvia Miralles Pérez, Francesca Mirone, Miguel Ruano Gullón, Theodoros Sandros, Lorenzo Semeraro, Domenico Spagnolo, Tomoko Suzuki, Gustavo Takata, Sandra ten Dam, Pauline Toenz; model-making: Jelena Bottani, Jennifer Bottlang, Gustavo Espinoza Campos, Joey Frei, Jonas Rindlisbacher
Specialist Contractors/Technical Planners
Competition phase: general management/project management: b + p baurealisation ag, Zürich; civil engineering: Schnetzer Puskas Ingenieure AG, Zurich; building services/energy (HVAC, plumbing, cooling, electrics, BMS): ahochn AG, Dübendorf; façade planning: gkp fassadentechnik ag, Aadorf; acoustics, building physics/energy, sustainability: Gartenmann Engineering AG, Zurich; fire safety: AFC Air Flow Consulting AG, Zurich; scenography consultants: südstudio Hannes Bierkämper, Stuttgart
Implementation phase: general management/project management: Akeret Baumanagement AG, Bern; civil engineering: Schnetzer Puskas Ingenieure AG, Zurich; building services/energy (HVAC, plumbing, cooling, electrics, BMS): ahochn AG, Dübendorf; electrical design/building automation: Pro Engineering AG, Basel; façade planning: gkp fassadentechnik ag, Aadorf; façade engineering: ZPF Ingenieure AG, Zurich; building physics/energy, sustainability: Gartenmann Engineering AG, Zurich; acoustics: applied acoustics GmbH, Gelterkinden; fire safety: AFC Air Flow Consulting AG, Zurich; lab design: Laborplaner Tonelli AG, Gelterkinden; scenography, public displays: EMYL GmbH, Basel

224 WIN
WIN4 Sports Center
Location
Winterthur, Switzerland
Procedure
Competition, 1st prize; follow-up project
Client
WIN4 AG
Dates
Commission: 2015; planning phase: 2015–ongoing; construction phase: 2016–ongoing
Size
30'300 m²;
Multi-sport arena: 13,600 m²; campus building: 6,100 m²; multi-functional training space: 2,200 m²; additional sports facilities: 8,400 m²
EM2N Team
Partners: Mathias Müller, Daniel Niggli; associate: Bernd Druffel; project heads: Dorothee Burkert, Melih Dilsiz, Roger Küng, Philipp Maaß, Susan Singer, Sandra ten Dam, Martin Zisterer; project team: Jan Francisco Anduaga, Margherita Borroni, Jelena Bottani, Patrick Britt, Dario Bruhin, Béatrice Bruneaux, Santiago Catanzano, Robert Dehn, Vitória de Mendonça, Yann Junod, Marina Esguerra, Ian Omumbwa, Laura Probst, Sandra Quiros Navas, Sandra Šimić, Tomoko Suzuki, Leena Unger, Kenneth Woods; model-making: Jennifer Bottlang, Gustavo Espinoza Campos, Jonas Rindlisbacher
Specialist Contractors/Technical Planners
Construction management/project delivery: BW Generalbau AG, Winterthur; civil engineering: Dr. Deuring + Oehninger AG, Winterthur; landscape architecture: Balliana Schubert Landschaftsarchitekten AG, Zurich; building physics/acoustics: Zehnder & Kälin AG, Winterthur; HVAC and plumbing design: 3-Plan Haustechnik AG, Winterthur/Brandwerk GmbH, Arch; electrical design: Marquart Elektroplanung + Beratung, Buchs/St. Gallen; fire safety: 3-Plan Haustechnik AG, Winterthur; geology/geotechnics: Dr. Heinrich Jäckli AG, Zurich; traffic planning: ewp AG, Effretikon; signage: Pikka GmbH, Zurich

227 BRI
New Housing on Briesestrasse
Location
Berlin-Neukölln, Germany
Procedure
Competition, 1st prize
Client
STADT UND LAND Wohnbauten-Gesellschaft mbH
Dates
Competition: 2015; planning: 2016–2019; construction: 2016–2020
Size
13,343 m²
EM2N Team
Partners: Mathias Müller, Daniel Niggli; associates: Fabian Hörmann (competition phase), Verena Lindenmayer (implementation phase); project head: Henrike Kortemeyer; project team (competition phase): Mathias Kampmann, António Mesquita, Inês Nunes, Caroline Vogel, Leonard Wertgen; project team (implementation phase): Laura Ball, Pia Brückner, Felix Dechert, Götz Lachenman; model-making: Jonas Rindlisbacher
Specialist Contractors/Technical Planners
General planning: Implenia Hochbau GmbH, Leipzig; tendering/quality control: HW-Ingenieure GmbH, Berlin; civil engineering (competition phase): Schnetzer Puskas Ingenieure AG, Zurich; demolition plan and structural planning: Ingenieurbüro Rüdiger Jockwer GmbH, Berlin; underground parking garage ventilation: Ingenieur- und Sachverständigenbüro Karl-Heinz Quenzel, Berlin; building services: GNEISE Planungs- und Beratungsgesellschaft mbH, Berlin; cost and timeline planning: GNEISE Planungs- und Beratungsgesellschaft mbH, Berlin; noise control: Bauphysik Ritter, Potsdam; thermal insulation and energy audit: Andreas Wilke Ingenieurbüro für Bauphysik und Baukonstruktion GmbH, Potsdam; fire safety planning: Andreas Wilke Ingenieurbüro für Bauphysik und Baukonstruktion GmbH, Berlin; fire safety testing: KLW Ingenieure GmbH, Berlin; traffic planning: R + T Verkehrsplanung GmbH, Darmstadt; landscape architecture: MAN MADE LAND Bohne Lundqvist Mellier GbR, Berlin; surveying: Ingenieursozietät Rek & Wieck, Berlin; signage: EM2N, Caroline Vogel, Zurich

229 VDM
Together! The New Architecture of the Collective
Location
Weil am Rhein, Germany
Procedure
Direct commission
Client
Vitra Design Museum
Dates
Commission: 2016; exhibition: June–September 2017; displays at coproduction partners: fall 2017–spring 2018; tour: 2018–2021
Exhibition area:
600–1,000 m²
Exhibits
1:100 urban model, 1:1 mock-ups, film footage, drawings, photographs, and more
Catalog
2017, Ruby Press, 352 pages, approx. 443 images, 230 × 302 mm, published in German and in English
Curators
Mathias Müller, Daniel Niggli, Andreas and Ilka Ruby, in conjunction with Vitra Design Museum
EM2N Team
Partners: Mathias Müller, Daniel Niggli; associate: Fabian Hörmann; project head: Michaela Štolcová; project team: Sebastian Andersson, Juliette Blatter, Elói Gonçalves, Benjamin Li, Ilja Maksimov, António Mesquita, Justyna Porowska, Sebastian Reumert, Kim Schürmann, Walter Secondo Toccaceli, Carmen Weglorz; model-making: Jonas Rindlisbacher

244 HEI
Quartier Heidestrasse, QH Track
Location
Berlin, Germany
Procedure
Competition, 1st prize
Client
Quartier Heidestrasse GmbH
Dates
Competition: 2016–2017; planning: 2017–2023; construction: 2018–2023
Size
165,793 m²
EM2N Team
Partners: Mathias Müller, Daniel Niggli; associates: Fabian Hörmann (competition phase), Verena Lindenmayer, Björn Rimner (implementation phase); project head (competition phase): Mathias Kampmann; project heads (implementation phase): Henrike Kortemeyer, Tony Rhiem; sub-project heads (implementation phase): Kevin Helms, Tessa Poth, Marcin Szczodry, Jonathan Zimmermann; project team (competition phase): Baptiste Blot, Henrike Kortemeyer, Götz Lachenmann, António Mesquita, Justyna Porowska, Laura Probst, Walter Toccaceli, Caroline Vogel, Carmen Weglorz; project team (implementation phase): Güley Alagöz, Thomas Bögel, Björn Böök, Margherita Borroni, Christof Braun, Jonathan Burkhard, Mirela-Maria Chrysovergi, Robert Dehn, Lieselotte

List of Works

Düsterhus, Henriette von Flocken, Cristina Génova, Miruna Grec, Johannes Greubel, Eleni Kitani, Olga Konovalova, Albena Kyuchukova, Joanna Lewańska, Maike Roth, Annette Schmidt, Vanessa Schöttes, Nicolas Schulz, Susan Singer, Marina Stoynova, Cristina Vergara Lacuey, Jann Wiegand, Jonas Wolf, Kyung Ho Won; model-making: Jennifer Bottlang, Joey Frei, Jonas Rindlisbacher
  Specialist Contractors/
  Technical Planners
  (Competition Phase)
Civil engineering: wh-p Ingenieure AG, Basel; landscape architecture: MAN MADE LAND Bohne Lundqvist Mellier GbR, Berlin; façade planning: KD Fassadenplanung, Düsseldorf; HVAC and plumbing design: HTW, Hetzel, Tor-Westen + Partner Ingenieurgesellschaft mbH & Co. KG, Düsseldorf; fire safety: Müller-BBM Industry Solutions GmbH, Planegg
  Specialist Contractors/
  Technical Planners
  (Implementation Phase)
Construction management/project delivery: Drees & Sommer, Stuttgart; civil engineering: WSK Ingenieure Berlin GmbH, Berlin; landscape architecture: relais Landschaftsarchitekten Heck Mommsen PartGmbB, Berlin; façade planning: Drees & Sommer, Stuttgart; HVAC and plumbing design: Drees & Sommer, Berlin; building physics/acoustics: Drees & Sommer, Berlin; fire safety: HHP® West Beratende Ingenieure GmbH, Bielefeld; vibration control: GuD Geotechnik und Dynamik Consult GmbH, Berlin

250 BIN
Office and Commercial Building Binzstrasse
  Location
Zurich, Switzerland
  Procedure
Direct commission
  Client
Swiss Life Asset Management AG
  Dates
Commission: 2017; planning: 2018–2022; construction: 2021–2023
  Size
5,500 m²
  EM2N Team
Partners: Mathias Müller, Daniel Niggli; associate: Gerry Schwyter; project heads: Kristina Strecker, Hugo Torre; project team: Carlos Maria Azpiroz Franch, Lorents-Kristian Blomseth, Mariantonietta Irene Gadaleta, Kevin Hinz, Sebastian Lenders, Martina Melegari, Kseniia Ponomar, Julia Przybyszewska, Maria Remma, Theodoros Sandros, Lukas Schädler, Sandra ten Dam, Kenneth Woods; model-making: Joey Frei, Jonas Rindlisbacher
  Specialist Contractors/
  Technical Planners
Landscape architecture: Balliana Schubert Landschaftsarchitekten AG, Zurich; project development: Fischer Immobilien AG, Zurich; construction management/project delivery: b+p baurealisation ag, Zurich; civil engineering: WaltGalmarini AG, Zurich; HVAC and plumbing design: Aicher, De Martin, Zweng AG, Zurich; electrical design: Inelplan AG, Rapperswil; building physics/acoustics: Kopitsis Bauphysik AG, Wohlen; fire safety: Conti Swiss AG, Zurich; geology/geotechnics: Jäckli Geologie AG, Zurich; signage: EM2N, Caroline Vogel, Zurich

257 BRX
KANAL – Centre Pompidou
  Location
Brussels, Belgium
  Procedure
Competition, 1st prize, collaboration with noAarchitecten, Brussels, and Sergison Bates architects, London
  Clients
Gouvernement de la Région de Bruxelles-Capitale, city of Brussels as represented by Fondation KANAL
  Dates
Competition: 2017–2018 (phases 1 and 2); planning: 2018–2024; construction (projected): 2020–2024
  Size
40,000 m²; Museum of Modern and Contemporary Art: 12,000 m²; CIVA architecture center (archive and museum): 7,000 m²; public areas: 12,000 m²; shared-used areas: 9,000 m²
  Costs
CHF 125 m
  Atelier Kanal/EM2N Team
Competition team: Francesco Apostoli, Stephen Bates, Baptiste Blot, Béatrice Bruneaux, Jasper Caenepeel, Serafina Eipert, Damiano Finetti, An Fonteyn, Kirsten Gabriëls Webb, Fabian Hörmann, Sunayana Jain, Estelle Jakubowski, Mathias Müller, Daniel Niggli, Evelien Pletinckx, Marije van Diemen, Konrad Scheffer, Elke Schoonen, Jonathan Teuns, Mark Tuff, Jitse van den Berg, Philippe Viérin, Andrea Zandalasini; planning team: Francesco Apostoli, Dennis Baganz, Stephen Bates, Kristoffel Boghaert, Job Borgonjon, Jasper Caenepeel, Zacharie Cabaud, Arnaud De Francesco, Arabella El Ginawy, Emmanuelle Farine, An Fonteyne, Nicole Fröhlich, Ludovic Gaffarel, Nils Köpfer, Louis Lories, Francesca Martellono, Mathias Müller, Daniel Niggli, Cristina Pérez Guillén, Sebastian Pfammatter, Ellen Piot, Kerstin Rienecker, Andrea Sassi, Edmund Savory, Miguel Steel Lebre, Daniel Trimmel, Mark Tuff, Jitse van den Berg, Konstantijn Verbrugge, Philippe Viérin; model-making: Jennifer Bottlang, Jonas Rindlisbacher
  Specialist Contractors/
  Technical Planners
Competition phase: civil engineering/building services: Buro Happold Ltd, London/Bureau d'études greisch sa, Liège; building physics: Egeon Ingenieurs, Melle/Bureau d'études greisch sa, Liège; acoustics: Kahle Acoustics srl, Brussels; façade planning: Gevelinzicht ingenieur-architecten, Antwerp; fire safety: FESG, Ghent/Bureau d'études greisch sa, Liège; HVAC and plumbing design: Buro Happold Ltd, London/Bureau d'études greisch sa, Liège; electrical design: Buro Happold Ltd, London/Bureau d'études greisch sa, Liège; cost planning: eld architects bv, Antwerp; health and safety: Buro Happold Ltd, London/Bureau d'études greisch sa, Liège; lighting design: Buro Happold Ltd, London/Bureau d'études greisch sa, Liège; media architecture: iart ag, Basel; art: Benoît van Innis, Brussels
Implementation phase: building physics: Egeon Ingenieurs, Melle/Bureau d'études greisch sa, Liège; acoustics: Kahle Acoustics srl, Brussels; HVAC, cooling, and plumbing design: Bureau d'études greisch sa, Liège; electrical design: Bureau d'études greisch sa, Liège; fire safety: FESG, Ghent/Bureau d'études greisch sa, Liège; cost planning: eld architects bv, Antwerp; façade planning: Gevelinzicht ingenieur-architecten, Antwerp; health and safety: Arvico, Herent; lighting design: Bureau d'études greisch sa, Liège; media architecture: iart ag, Basel; signage: Cartlidge Levene, London; art: Benoît van Innis, Brussels + Sarah Smolders, Brussels

258 LCS
HSG Learning Center
St. Gallen
  Location
St. Gallen, Switzerland
  Procedure
Competition
  Client
HSG Stiftung
  Dates
Competition: 2017
  Size
7,000 m²
  EM2N Team
Partners: Mathias Müller, Daniel Niggli; associate: Fabian Hörmann; project head: António Mesquita; project team: Emmanuel Álvarez Sánchez, Jesús E. Gijón Carretero, Santiago Catanzano, Elói Gonçalves, Mathias Kampmann, Judith Kimmeyer, Konrad Scheffer, Anastasia Zharova; model-making: Jennifer Bottlang, Jonas Rindlisbacher
  Specialist Contractors/
  Technical Planners
Civil engineering: Schnetzer Puskas Ingenieure AG, Zurich; landscape architecture: Balliana Schubert Landschaftsarchitekten AG, Zurich; HVAC and plumbing design: ahochn AG, Dübendorf; model-making (1:500): Modellbau Zaborowsky GmbH, Zurich

268 KOC
Koch-Areal, Plot A
  Location
Zurich, Switzerland
  Procedure
Competition, 2nd prize
  Client
Municipal Building Department, City of Zurich
  Dates
Competition: 2018
  Size
12,000 m²
  EM2N Team
Partners: Mathias Müller, Daniel Niggli; associate: Fabian Hörmann; project head: Mathias Kampmann; project team: Kārlis Bērziņš, Béatrice Bruneaux, Eleni Kitani; model-making: Jennifer Bottlang, Andrea Ferrarini, Jesús E. Gijón Carretero, Jonas Rindlisbacher
  Specialist Contractors/
  Technical Planners
Construction management/project delivery: Güntensperger Baumanagement AG, Zurich; construction consulting/construction economics: Güntensperger Baumanagement AG, Zurich; civil engineering: Schnetzer Puskas Ingenieure AG, Zurich; timber engineering: PIRMIN JUNG Schweiz AG, Rain (formerly Pirmin Jung Ingenieure AG); landscape architecture: Balliana Schubert Landschaftsarchitekten AG, Zurich; HVAC and plumbing design: Anex Ingenieure AG, Zurich; building physics/acoustics: PIRMIN JUNG Schweiz AG, Rain (formerly Pirmin Jung Ingenieure AG); fire safety: PIRMIN JUNG Schweiz AG, Rain (formerly Pirmin Jung Ingenieure AG)

273 AKE
Aker BP Headquarters | Paradis Midt/Nord Masterplan
  Location
Stavanger, Norway
  Procedure
Competition, 1st prize, in collaboration with Ghilardi + Hellsten Arkitekter AS, Oslo
  Client
Aker BP ASA
  Dates
Competition: 2018–2019; planning: 2019
  Size
110,000 m²
  EM2N Team
Partners: Mathias Müller, Daniel Niggli; associate: Fabian Hörmann; project team: Gabriela Barbulescu; model-making: Joey Frei, Jonas Rindlisbacher

276 KUZ
Uster Culture Center
  Location
Uster, Switzerland
  Procedure
Competition, 1st prize
  Client
Municipality of Uster
  Dates
Competition: 2019; planning: 2019–ongoing
  Size
7,000 m²
  EM2N Team
Partners: Mathias Müller, Daniel Niggli; associates: Fabian Hörmann, Bernd Druffel, Gerry Schwyter; project head: Mathias Kampmann; project team (competition phase): Béatrice Bruneaux, Georgia Gkotsopoulou, Carolina Gomes, Elói Gonçalves, Jean-Baptiste Joye, Mathias Kampmann, Jochen Kremer, Kinga Łukasińska, Philipp Maaß, Paul Tschritter, Kenneth Woods; model-making: Jennifer Bottlang, Andrea Guido Ferrarini, Joey Frei, Jonas Rindlisbacher, Theodoros Sandros
  Specialist Contractors/
  Technical Planners
Civil engineering: Dr. Deuring + Oehninger AG, Winterthur; building physics/acoustics: applied acoustics GmbH, Gelterkinden; landscape architecture: Balliana Schubert Landschaftsarchitekten AG, Zurich; HVAC and plumbing design: Abicht Zug AG, Zug; noise control: applied acoustics GmbH, Gelterkinden

279 HFC
Hammerbrooklyn Digital Campus
  Location
Hamburg, Germany
  Procedure
Ideas competition, 1st prize
  Client
Hammerbrooklyn Immobilien GmbH
  Dates
Competition: 2019–2020; planning: 2020–ongoing
  Size
50,000 m²
  EM2N Team
Partners: Mathias Müller, Daniel Niggli; associates: Fabian Hörmann, Björn Rimner, Henrike Kortemeyer;

Image Credits 493

project heads: Emmanuel Laux, Maike Roth, Marcin Szczodry, Jonathan Zimmermann; project team (competition phase): Alessandro Citterio, Hoi Ming Du, Antoni Grau, Guido Greco, Karolina Kajda, Ayça Kapicioğlu, António Mesquita, Walter Rigueti, Olivia Rudolph; project team (implementation phase): Kārlis Bērziņš, Max Blake, Katja Gockel, Olga Konovalova, Andrea Malagnino, Anna Stevenson, Wei Sun, Adrian Wetherell, Jonas Wolf; model-making: Gabriela Barbulescu, Jennifer Bottlang, Joey Frei, Viviane Kägi, Titus Keller, Jonas Rindlisbacher
  Specialist Contractors/ Technical Planners
Civil engineering: sbp ag, Stuttgart; landscape architecture: Henning Larsen GmbH, Hamburg (formerly Ramboll Studio Dreiseitl, Hamburg); building services design: ZWP Ingenieur-AG, Bochum/Hamburg; climate-responsive design: Transsolar Energietechnik GmbH, Stuttgart; façade planning: Schellhorn & Heese Ingenieure für Fassaden GmbH, Potsdam; traffic planning: ARGUS Stadt und Verkehr Partnerschaft mbB, Hamburg

283 OER
Oerlikon Sports Center
  Location
Zurich, Switzerland
  Procedure
Competition, 3rd prize
  Client
City of Zurich
  Dates
Competition: 2020
  Size
35,000 m²
  EM2N Team
Partners: Mathias Müller, Daniel Niggli; associate: Fabian Hörmann; project head: Mathias Kampmann; project team: Laura Bruder, Matteo Donghi, Guido Greco, Ayça Kapicioğlu, Emmanuel Laux, Anna Maragkoudaki, Vitória de Mendonça, António Mesquita, Maryia Sidorenko, Adrian Wetherell; model-making: Joey Frei, Jonas Rindlisbacher
  Specialist Contractors/ Technical Planners
Civil engineering: Dr. Deuring + Oehninger AG, Winterthur; landscape architecture: Balliana Schubert Landschaftsarchitekten AG, Zurich; building physics/acoustics: Lemon Consult AG, Zurich; HVAC and plumbing design: Leplan AG, Winterthur; pool engineering: Kannewischer Ingenieurbüro AG, Cham; ice engineering: BBP Ingenieurbüro AG, Lucerne; Leplan AG, Winterthur; electrical design: Elektro-Ingenieure Meyer + Partner AG, Stäfa; sustainability: Lemon Consult AG, Zurich; photovoltaics: Basler & Hofmann AG, Zurich; fire safety: Gruner AG, Basel

Front cover: Damian Poffet
Front flap: Joël Tettamanti
Front flap, inside: ETH Library Zurich, Image Archive/ Photographer: Baumann, Heinz
Back cover: Daniel Niggli
Back flap: Simon Menges
Back flap, inside: ETH Library Zurich, Image Archive/ Photographer: Krebs, Hans

Pp. 1–5, 13, 14–20, 24, 32–33, 108, 114–115, 423 (2,3): Joël Tettamanti
6–7, 45 (20–23), 146 (26), 148–153, 196 (13), 197 (16–18), 197 (20,21), 198 (23), 199–201, 291 (12,13), 294–295, 306 (4), 307 (6), 308–309, 318 (4), 323 (15), 326 (21,22), 327 (24), 331 (33), 367, 372, 377 (2), 387 (19), 415, 416 (2,3), 418 (6,7), 422, 433, 435, 481–486, 495–500: Damian Poffet
22, 423 (1): Alexa Wright, 1997
26–27, 28 (4), 30 (10–12): Media Archive, Zurich University of the Arts
29 (5), 68 (2–6), 234 (9), 288 (2): swisstopo
29 (6,7): Construction History and City Archive Zurich
30 (9): Verband Nordostschweizer Käserei- und Milchgenossenschaften
35 (1), 96–97, 98 (2–5): Construction History and City Archive Zurich and Friedrich Ruef-Hirt
36–37: Eduard Spelterini
39: Tina Fassbind, June 30, 2011, tagesanzeiger.ch
39 (6): Gertrud Vogler, 1982; Swiss Social Archives / F 5107-Na-05-211-015
39 (7): Gertrud Vogler, 1987; Swiss Social Archives / F 5107-Na-12-014-010
42–43, 44 (16), 112 (21,23), 113, 272–273, 276 (13,16), 277 (17–20), 290 (10), 296, 298–300, 315–317, 318 (3,6), 319 (7,9), 320–321, 322 (12–14), 323 (16), 324–325, 327 (25), 328–329, 330 (28,30,31), 331 (32,34), 332 (36,37,38), 333 (41,42), 381 (9), 382–383, 384 (12), 388: Filip Dujardin, 2023, ProLitteris, Zurich
45 (19), 213–216, 235 (14–18), 241, 242 (6), 251 (12), 269, 282 (8–11), 293 (17,18), 302 (3), 342–343, 344 (3), 345–346, 348 (10), 375–376, 465 (3), 466–467, 472–473 (11–13), 474: Hannes Henz
46, 50–53, 117–124, 389–396, 475: Ingo Giezendanner, GRRRR.net, 2023, ProLitteris, Zurich
54: IMAGO/China Foto Press
55 (top left): UAA Ungers Archiv für Architekturwissenschaften, Köln
55 (bottom left): Rem Koolhaas, Delirious New York. A retroactive manifesto for Manhattan, Monacelli Press, 1994
56 (bottom right): ETH Library Zurich, Image Archive/Luftbild Schweiz Archive/Photographer: Walter Mittelholzer
69: *Neue Zürcher Zeitung*, November 2, 2000, p. 49
71–72, 85, 112 (22), 132 (11,12), 133 (13,14), 154–155, 188–189, 190 (3,5), 196 (14,15), 202 (1), 203 (5), 220 (2,3), 234 (13), 242 (7), 251 (9–11), 258 (2,4,5), 271 (4,6,7), 280–281, 284 (1), 326 (23), 333 (40), 341, 355 (30,31), 356–357, 364, 417 (4,5), 425 (3), 432, 436–438, 449 (5,6), 450 (7,8), 452 (2,3), 453 (3), 459 (14,15,17), 460–462: EM2N
73 (4): Archizoom Associati
77–84, 126 (1), 205–212, 221–223, 226–230, 233, 261 (2), 264–268, 305 (2), 306 (3), 307 (5), 308–309, 310–312, 318 (5), 337 (47,48), 381 (10): Simon Menges
88 (6): Colourlight-Center, Zurich University of the Arts
88 (7): *Tages-Anzeiger*, December 8, 2001, p. 54: Thomas Kramer, "Der Club mit dem Vegi Mehrwert," Media Concept and Realisation: Ruf Lanz Werbeagentur AG, Zurich
88 (9–11), 99 (7,9): Photo: Museum für Gestaltung Zürich, Plakatsammlung, ZHdK
88 (9): Swissandfamous, Zurich
88 (11): mva gst28
89 (12), 90 (20): Betty Fleck
89 (13): Van Nutt
89 (14, 15): Walter Hügli
90 (17): Alessandro Della Bella
90 (18, 19): Zurich University of the Arts, Regula Bearth
90 (21), 91 (23): Matthias Auer
91 (24): Barbara Staib
99 (7): Alain C. Kupper (top left, middle left and right, bottom left and right), Patrick Hollenstein (top right)
99 (8), 110 (15,16), 111 (18,19): Ralph Hut
99 (9): Marco Walser, Elektrosmog, Zurich, Print: Urs Jost, Druckwerkstatt
101, 111 (17), 112 (20): Antje Quiram
136, 144–146, 147 (27), 156–157, 158 (4,5), 191, 194–195, 197 (19), 198 (22), 202 (2,3), 203 (6–10), 217–218, 224–225, 248–249, 253 (18,19), 254–257, 258 (6,7), 290 (11), 297, 330 (29), 332 (35), 334–335, 336 (45), 370–371, 377 (1), 378 (3,4), 379 (5,6), 380 (7,8), 385 (14): Roger Frei
137 (8): GIS-ZH, Canton of Zurich, 10.08.2018
138 (9): Stadtarchiv & Kläui Bibliothek Uster
182, 184 (4–7): Google Inc. All rights reserved
190 (4): André Locher, www.swisscastles.ch
219 (3): The Architectural Archives, University of Pennsylvania by the gift of Robert Venturi and Denise Scott Brown
231 (1–5): State Archives of Lucerne: Archive Viscosuisse
232 (7): ETH Library Zurich, Image Archive/Luftbild Schweiz Archive/Photographer: Swissair Photo AG
240 (2,3): Roshen Confectionary Corporation
250: Martin Bissig
258 (3): Ewelina Guzik
259 (2): *Life* magazine
260 (3,4): Meili, Peter & Partner Architekten AG
261 (1), 399, 401 (9), 444–445: Kim Zwarts
271 (5), 276 (15): Daniela Burkart
276 (14), 278: Roland Bernath
279 (1–3): Stapferhaus
284 (2), 285 (4): Gerd Pinsker, Dokumentationsstelle Gemeinde Riehen
286–287: Swiss Social Archives/ F 5146-Da-B005-1246
288 (5): Keystone/Aubrey Diem
288 (3): ETH Library Zurich, Image Archive/Luftbild Schweiz Archive/Photographer: Mittelholzer,Walter/LBS_MH03-1670/Public Domain Mark
289 (7): City of Zurich
289 (8): Amt für Hochbauten Stadt Zürich, Photo: Iris Stutz
302 (1,2), 351 (5): EM2N, Rendering: Luxigon
313 (1): Graphic Collection of the Academy of Fine Arts Vienna
314 (5): F.L.C./2023, ProLitteris, Zurich
319 (8), 327 (26): Zurich University of the Arts, Johannes Dietschi
319 (10), 323 (17), 326 (20), 333 (39), 338, 386 (16–18): Roland Tännler
336 (44, 46): Daniela Valentini
344 (1): City Archive St. Gallen, PA Foto Gross
344 (2): Phillip Harrington/Alamy Stock Foto
348 (11), 441, 442 (3–6): EM2N, Photo: Diego Bazzotti
351 (2): Staatsarchiv Basel-Stadt, AL 45, 1-79-2
S. 351 (3): Staatsarchiv Basel-Stadt, Hö D 28725 (Fotoarchiv Höflinger)
354: EM2N, Rendering: Ponnie Images
373 (1): EPA / J.L.Cereijido
384 (13), 385 (15): Photo: Pierre Kellenberger © ZHdK
400 (2): Archives d'Architecture Moderne (AAM), Brussels
400 (3), 401 (7,8): Brussels City Archive
402 (12, 15), 403 (19, 22, 24): Axo: Atelier Kanal
402 (13, 14, 16, 17), 403 (18, 20, 21, 23): Rendering: Secchi Smith
424, 425 (4), 426–430, 439 (19, 20), 440: Andrew Alberts
431 (1): HENN
431 (2): Courtesy of Ricardo Bofill – Taller de Arquitectura
439 (18): EM2N, Rendering: LMNB
446 (2): André Verstraeten, KANAL Brut, Privatized Event, 2019 © KANAL Foundation
446 (4): Stephan Glagla | stage-photographie.de
446 (5): Mathieu Golinvaux
446 (6): for the work of Jean Tinguely: 2023, ProLitteris, Zurich; Localisation: Paris, Centre Pompidou – Musée national d'art moderen – Centre de création industrielle. Photo © Centre Pompidou, MNAM-CCI, Dist. RMN-Grand Palais / Philippe Migeat
446 (7): STOP KANAL, 2019 © Veerle Vecauteren © KANAL Foundation
447 (8, 9): Jörn Schiemann
447 (10): Nicolas Lobet
447 (11): Ross Lovegrove For Lasvit, Lasvit Liquidkristal Pavilion, 2012 © Veerle Vecauteren © KANAL Foundation
447 (12): Maxime Delvaux
454 (5): bildarchiv-hamburg.com
456–457: EM2N, Rendering: ALMA
464 (1): Kazuo Shinohara
475: Ingo Giezendanner, GRRRR.net, 2023, ProLitteris, Zurich

Despite best efforts, we have not been able to identify the holders of copyright and printing rights for all the illustrations. Copyright holders not mentioned in the credits are asked to substantiate their claims, and recompense will be made according to standard practice.

Caption sources:
p. 22/1: Alexa Wright, *After Image – RD2*, 1997, https://www.alexawright.com/after-image (last accessed Mar. 7, 2022).
p. 24/2+3: Marc Kocher Architekten, "Müller-Martini-Areal," https://www.kocher-architekten.com/mueller-martini-areal (last accessed Feb. 25, 2022).
p. 137/7: *The Unbroken Attraction of Water*, https://www.zellwegerpark.ch/en/zellwegerpark/history.php (last accessed Mar. 1, 2022).

Imprint

Edited by
Mathias Müller
Daniel Niggli
Caspar Schärer
Medine Altiok

With contributions by
Marc Angélil
Max Küng
Marcel Meili
Peter Swinnen

Design
Bonbon—Diego Bontognali,
Valeria Bonin

Book concept
Mathias Müller
Daniel Niggli
Caspar Schärer
Medine Altiok
Fabian Hörmann

Coordination
Fabian Hörmann
Kārlis Bērziņš

Photography
Filip Dujardin
Roger Frei
Simon Menges
Damian Poffet
Joël Tettamanti

Illustrations
GRRRR, Ingo Giezendanner

Translations
Iain Reynolds

Proofreading
Colette Forder, Lisa Schons

Image processing
Marjeta Morinc

Printing and binding
DZA Druckerei zu Altenburg
GmbH, Thuringia

Staff contributors:
Kārlis Bērziņš
Fabian Hörmann
Eirini Afentouli
Sebastian Andersson
Andri Andrésson
Jan Francisco Anduaga
Rahel Baumgartner
Jelena Bottani
Patrick Britt
Béatrice Bruneaux
Melanie Buettikofer
Santiago Catanzano
Hoi Ming Du
Georgios Eftaxiopoulus
Gabi Eisenreich
Rodolfo Ferro
Salomé Genzoni
Ayça Kapicioğlu
Karolina Krzyżanowska
Carlo Magnaguagno
Ilja Maksimov
Anna Maragkoudaki
António Mesquita
Kate Milligan-Mutzke
Walter Rigueti
Oscar Rosello
Konrad Scheffer
David Schildberger
Ines Schmid
Maryia Sidorenko
Anastasia Skorik
Walter Secondo Toccaceli
Hugo Torre
Caroline Vogel
Balthasar Weiss
Leonard Wertgen
Sizhou Yang
Anastasia Zharova

© 2023 EM2N Zurich/Berlin and
Park Books AG, Zurich
© for the texts: the authors
© for the images: the artists

Park Books
Niederdorfstrasse 54
8001 Zurich
Switzerland
www.park-books.com

Park Books is being supported
by the Federal Office of Culture
with a general subsidy for the years
2021–2024.

Despite extensive research we
have not been able to determine
copyright and printing right holders
of some illustrations. Copyright
holders not mentioned in the credits
are asked to substantiate claims, and
recompense will be made according
to standard practice.

All rights reserved; no part of this
publication may be reproduced,
stored in a retrieval system or
transmitted in any form or by any
means, electronic, mechanical, photocopying, recording, or otherwise,
without the prior written consent of
the publisher.

ISBN 978-3-03860-086-2

ISBN 978-3-03860-085-5
(German edition)